More HOMEBREW FAVORITES

260 New Brews!

Karl Lutzen & Mark Stevens

A Storey Publishing Book

STOREY

Storey Communications, Inc.
Schoolhouse Road
Pownal, Vermont 05261

The mission of Storey Communications is to serve our customers by publishing practical information that encourages personal independence in harmony with the environment.

Edited by Deborah Thornton Pendleton and Elizabeth McHale
Cover design by Susan Bernier
Cover photograph by Nicholas Whitman
Text design by Cindy McFarland and Allison Hayes
Production by Nat Stout; Design & Format, Erin Lincourt and Sarah Crone
Indexed by Northwind Editorial Services

The information in this book is true and complete to the best of our knowledge. All recommendations are made without guarantee on the part of the authors or Storey Communications, Inc. The authors and publisher disclaim any liability in connection with the use of this information. For additional information please contact Storey Communications, Inc., Schoolhouse Road, Pownal, Vermont 05261.

Storey Publishing books are available for special premium and promotional uses and for customized editions. For further information, please call the Custom Publishing Department at 1-800-793-9396.

Printed in the United States by R.R. Donnelley
10 9 8 7 6 5 4 3 2 1

Library of Congress Cataloging-in-Publication Data

More homebrew favorites : 260 new brews! / [compiled by] Karl Lutzen
and Mark Stevens.
        p.   cm.
      "A Storey Publishing Book"
      Includes bibliographical references and index.
      ISBN 0-88266-968-0 (pb : alk. paper)
      1. Brewing—Amateur's manuals.   I. Lutzen, Karl F., 1961–
      II. Stevens, Mark, 1960–
TP570.M59   1997
641.8'73—dc21   97-6490
                                                  CIP

Contents

Preface 1

1   Brewing to Style 3
     What Are Styles? • How Do Styles Originate?
     Why Do We Need Style Names? • Ingredients Make The Style
     The Brewing Process • Beer Styles and Competitions

2   Pale Ales 15
     English Pale Ales • American Pale Ales
     India Pale Ales • Adelaide Sparkling Ale

3   Brown Ales 47
     Mild Ales • English Brown Ales
     American Brown Ales • Specialty Brown Ale

4   Porters 63
     Robust and Brown Porters • Specialty Porters

5   Stouts 85
     Classic Irish Dry Stouts • Sweet Stouts • Foreign Stouts
     Oatmeal Stouts • Russian Imperial Stouts • Specialty Stouts

6   Belgian Ales 106
     Belgian Pale Ales • Belgian Strong Ales • Oud Bruin
     Trappist Ales: Dubbel and Tripel • Wit Beers • Lambics

7   German, Scottish, Strong & Specialty Ales 130
        German Ales: Kölsch and Alt • Scottish Ales
    Strong Ales: Barleywine and Old Ale • Specialty Ale

8   European Light Lagers 158
        Pilsners • Bavarian Light Lager: Helles
     Dortmunder • Vienna: Märzen, Oktoberfest

9   European Dark Lagers 180
        Bavarian Dark Lagers • Schwarzbiers
          Bocks: Maibock, Doppelbock

10 American Lagers 202
    American Light Lagers • Pre-Prohibition-Style American Lagers
          American Dark Lagers • Cream Ale

11 Wheat Beers 215
        Weizen: Bavarian Wheats • Dunkelweizens
          Weizenbocks • American Wheats

12 Fruit Beers 234
        Blueberry Beers • Raspberry Beers • Blackberry Beers
        Cranberry Beer • Pumpkin Beers • Squash Beer
      Apple Beer • Peach Beers • Prune Beer • Cherry Beers
          Lemon Beer • Orange Beer • Banana Beer

13 Herb & Spice Beers 263
        Gruit • Winter Mulling Spice Beers • Ginger Beers
              Herb Beers • Pepper Beers

14 Hybrid Styles 284
        California Commons • Smoked Beers • Specialty Beers

15 Meads 294
        Traditional Mead • Metheglin: Spiced Meads
          Melomel: Fruit Meads • Cyser • Braggots

Bibliography 308

Index 310

Preface

Since the introduction in 1994 of *Homebrew Favorites*, the homebrewing community continues to change, with more homebrewers, and a growing sophistication and understanding of techniques, ingredients, and beer styles. Manufacturers and suppliers are making available ingredients of higher quality as well as specialty products that make it possible to brew more challenging styles with better results.

This recipe collection reflects the brewing efforts of hundreds of homebrewers who enthusiastically offered to share their recipes with us. The recipes in most cases represent award-winning beers at the regional and national level. Others represent solid, workable recipes, in a wide range of styles using a variety of brewing methods. As you work with the recipes, you may find ways to modify or personalize them using your own techniques or favorite ingredients.

More Homebrew Favorites is organized by loosely defined styles. We begin each chapter with an overview of a style, its history and lore, and the ingredients and processes that characterize the style. Each chapter concludes with a collection of recipes for that style.

When brewing these recipes, keep in mind that your results may vary somewhat based on differences in brewing skill, ingredient substitution, and individual technique. Regional water variation, too, will affect the mashing performance in all-grain beers, and the flavor characteristics of all beers. A few ingredients may be difficult to locate in some parts of the country, but if you can't find a particular ingredient, ask your local homebrew-supply store. Knowledgeable suppliers can suggest good substitutions. Or check with your local brewclub for suggestions on mail-order options.

We would like to thank our friends in the homebrewing community who shared these recipes with us, especially our friends in the Missouri Association of Serious Homebrewers (MASH) and Brewers United for Real Potables (BURP), our two local clubs.

See you at the pub!

To submit recipes for consideration for future volumes of *Homebrew Favorites*, write to:

Homebrew Favorites
P.O. Box 1966
Rolla, MO 65402

I n the world of brewing, beer styles are broad descriptive categories that tell us — the brewers and beer drinkers — what qualities and characteristics to expect in a beer: how dark it should be, what kind of body it should have, and what flavors to anticipate. *More Homebrew Favorites* is a collection of beer recipes, organized by style.

WHAT ARE STYLES?

Style defines characteristics, such as color, flavor, and aroma, that we expect to find in each category of beer. Style also implies production methods and ingredients — the type of yeast used (ale or lager) and the fermentation temperature range, for example. In some ways, styles are to a brewer what colors are to an artist. The term *red* is understood by an artist without looking at a painting, just as the term *porter* is understood by a knowledgeable beer drinker without having to taste it.

Room for creativity and individual interpretation is as important in brewing as it is in painting. The painter may choose to make his red a brownish brick red, a fire-engine red, or perhaps the purplish red of a setting sun. Likewise, the brewer can make a porter a bit drier on the palate, or perhaps a bit sweeter, maybe heavier in body, perhaps lighter; the possibilities are endless. Working within the framework of a beer style, the individual brewer can express creativity while at the same time retaining the essential qualities that a knowledgeable beer drinker or beer judge would understand as the crux of the style.

Beer substyles are brewed as variations on the broader style category. Sometimes a style will have several significant variations.

HOW DO STYLES ORIGINATE?

Throughout history, cultural and social factors, technological development, and the variations in the ingredients contributed to the emergence of individual style. Regional differences in the character of an ingredient, such as a high protein malt, led to specific brewing processes developed to compensate for and exploit the malt's properties. Over time, the flavors, aroma, and taste imparted by the ingredients and brewing processes result in a defined style.

Qualities of water contribute to the development of beer style. The hard water of Burton and the soft water of Plzen are crucial to pale ale and pilsner. Fortunately, with today's filtration technology and understanding of water chemistry, local water supplies can usually be altered to suit a brewer's needs.

Styles change when technology changes. Among other "advances," the development of refrigeration, filtration, pasteurization, distribution methods, and yeast cultivation have all affected the character of the drink we call beer.

External forces such as political or cultural changes can contribute to the evolution of an accepted beer style. Countries that impose taxes based on beer density or strength often find their brewing heritage altered along with the tax code as brewers water down robust beers in an effort to control prices. Scarcity of ingredients during wartime can also affect beer styles as brewers substitute ingredients that eventually become accepted by beer drinkers and incorporated into style. Market demographics and fashionable trends can cause beer styles to emerge or evolve, such as the introduction of low-calorie beers in the mid-1970s.

Usually, these factors team up to force changes in brewing and drinking habits. Keep in mind that beer styles are not rigidly defined. Guidelines reflect a consensus as to what brewers and beer connoisseurs understand a style to represent at a particular time. What most competition style guidelines today call "India pale ale" bears little resemblance to the style that was brewed a century ago. Similarly, brewers can and do, misuse style descriptors in an effort to gain market share. Eventually, some elements of an interloper's style become incorporated into the style guidelines.

WHY DO WE NEED STYLE NAMES?

Style is an important tool that enables brewers and drinkers to discuss beers in meaningful ways. A simple style name can tell us about beers we've never tried before. Occasionally, a novice brewer will say, "It's beer, it's good, who cares what the style is?" If that brewer is happy with the beer, and he's the only person who will ever taste it, then there's nothing wrong with that attitude. But imagine sharing a bottle of homebrew with a fellow brewer and saying, "This is beer." You're likely to be asked, "What kind of beer?" If you don't know styles, you might say, "Wet," or maybe, "Cold." On the other hand, if you want to say something that will communicate its characteristics, such as aroma, color, body, and flavor, then you could answer, "Porter." That one-word style label tells a fellow brewer that this beer is intended to be a dark brew made with an ale yeast, probably having some chocolate-like flavors and an average body. Styles are guidelines, not commandments, but an understanding of beer styles is necessary to communicate the characteristics of your beer.

INGREDIENTS MAKE THE STYLE

Ingredients and processes act in concert to make a beer style. The four major ingredients that are used to brew most beer styles are malted barley, hops, water, and yeast. Some styles may also use other ingredients to impart particular flavors or characteristics to the beer.

Malt

Malt, which provides the fermentable sugars for beers, is a cereal grain that has been allowed to germinate and then had its growth curtailed by heating in a kiln. It may then be further roasted to achieve certain color and flavor characteristics that it will impart to the beer. Brewers use barley as the cereal, although other grains, such as wheat and rye, are also malted occasionally.

Most beginning homebrewers use packaged syrups or powders known as *malt extract* to provide the fermentable sugars for their beers. Advanced homebrewers, who usually want complete control over the brewing process, prefer to select and mash their grains themselves.

Extract brewers can usually choose the form of extract (dry or liquid syrup), and the color (usually light, amber or gold, or dark). They can also choose whether they want hopped or unhopped extract. Many extracts are sold as "can kits." These kits are simply hopped extracts (balanced in terms of color and flavor to approximate a certain beer style). Be aware that there are variations in these kits among manufacturers. A can labeled "bitter" by one manufacturer may produce quite a different beer from a bitter sold by another manufacturer. If you substitute a kit from another manufacturer for the one listed in a brewing recipe from this book, the brewer's results may not match yours — although you could very well come out a winner if you made the better choice.

Understanding malt types can be difficult because of the way brewers refer to malt. Usually, malts are described in terms of type, color, number of rows, variety of barley used to make the malt, country of origin, or perhaps the company that made the malt. Color of malt is gauged on a scale called *Lovibond*, in which the lower the number, the lighter the color. The color of the malt determines the color of the beer.

Virtually all beers start with a light-colored malt. The base malt, referred to as *pale malt*, usually accounts for 50 to 100 percent of a grain mix. Because there are differences among the base malts used in the United States, England, and Europe, brewers choose the type of pale malt they want by considering style. In addition to pale malt, smaller amounts of specialty malts (often called *kilned malts*), such as chocolate or black patent, are used to contribute colors and roast flavors to a beer. Caramel or crystal malts (sometimes called *stewed malts*) contribute sweetness and body. Colored and caramel malts usually account for 20 percent or less of a grain mix.

Here are some of the major types of malt used in the recipes in this book. The first three are pale malts that can be used as the base malt:

Pale malts

pale ale malt: Good enzyme levels; can convert 15% adjunct content. Light color (2° Lovibond). Best for infusion-mash. Good choice for pale ales and any English or American ale style.

6-row lager malt: High protein levels and tannin content. High enzyme levels. Can convert 25 – 50% adjunct content. Best used with step mash. Often used in light lagers. Fully modified.

2-row lager malt: Often called pils or pilsner malt. Somewhat lower in enzymes and tannin than 6-row. High in proteins. Often used with step mash or decoction mash. Good choice for European lagers.

Munich malt: Darker than pale malts (about 6° – 8° Lovibond). Contributes dark, full malt flavor, usually in lagers. Typically blended at 10 – 60% with a lighter pale malt for the remaining 90 – 40%.

Vienna malt: Lightly kilned (3° – 4° Lovibond) with good enzyme levels. Can be used at up to 100% of grain mix. Used for märzen, Oktoberfest, and similar amber Vienna-style lagers.

Kilned malts (colored)

biscuit malt: Lends malty, biscuit flavor to beer. Light color (23° Lovibond). Used in small amounts (less than 5%).

black patent malt: Very black, highly roasted malt (500° Lovibond). No enzymes. Imparts deep-roasted, burnt flavor. Used cautiously at 1 – 4% of grain in very black beers, such as stout.

chocolate malt: Dark brown color (350° – 400° Lovibond). Adds smooth, roast flavor with chocolate or coffee notes. Often used in porters, milds, and brown ales. Used at 1 – 10% of grain.

roast barley: Unmalted barley roasted to black color. Used at about 10% in stouts, seldom in any other styles.

victory malt: Lightly roasted (25° Lovibond). Used to impart flavor and aroma without residual sweetness. Used at 5 – 15%, usually in dark ales and dark lagers.

Caramel malts (crystal)

cara-Munich: Medium colored (about 70° Lovibond). Contributes deep
    color, usually in lagers.

cara-pils: Also known as dextrin. Gives malty character to beer. Used at
    rates of 5 – 20%, but yields excessive sweetness above 10%.

caramel malt: 40° Lovibond crystal malt.

crystal malt: Available in various colors from about 10° – 120° Lovibond.
    Provides unfermentable sugars and residual body. Typically used
    at rates of 5 – 20%, but most commonly 10% or less.

Adjunct grains

malted wheat: No husk; use with pale malt at 40 – 60% for a German weizen.
    High enzyme levels. High protein levels can cause haze. Light color
    (2° Lovibond). (Unmalted wheat may be used in some Belgian styles
    at 30 – 50%.)

corn: Used in conjunction with pale malt, usually 6-row at levels up to 50% in
    American pale lagers. Used at lower percentages in other styles.
    Gelatinize before mashing by cooking, unless used in flaked form.

Hops

Hops give beer its characteristic bitter flavors and aromas that
balance the sweetness from the malt. Hops are the flowers (or cones)
of a climbing vine *Humulus lupulus*. Many forms and varieties of
hops are used in homebrewing. They can be purchased as whole
cones in sealed plastic bags, as ground-up pressed pellets, or as com-
pressed plugs that expand into whole hops in the kettle. Extracts of
hop oil are also available.

There are many varieties of hops. One category of European hops,
known as *noble hops*, are prized for their aromas and flavors. These
varieties are Hallertauer Mittelfrüh, Czech Saaz, Spalt Spalter, and
Tettnang Tettnanger.

Hops are broadly categorized as either bittering or aromatic,
based on their predominant use in brewing. The potential bitterness
of any given hop variety is determined from its *alpha acid content*
which is expressed as a percentage of the total weight. The higher
the number, the more bitter the hop will be. Hops with low alpha
ratings, often used for aroma, will have 3 to 6 percent alpha acid.

Bittering hops have 7 to 14 percent.

Hops are added at various stages in the brewing process. When added at the beginning of a boil, *bittering hops* lend beer its bitter character. Hops added in the middle of a boil impart flavor. *Finishing hops* or *aromatic hops*, added at the end of the boil, contribute hop aromas to the beer.

The following table suggests some pairings for hop varieties and beer styles:

Brewers Gold	English ales, heavier German lagers
Bullion	English ales, heavier German lagers
Cascade	American pale ales, American wheat beers
Centennial	American pale ales, American wheat beers
Chinook	American pale ales, India pale ales
Cluster	Any style
East Kent Goldings	English milds, bitters, porters, stouts, Belgian ales
Fuggles	English milds, bitters, porters, stouts
Hallertauer	German lagers, German ales, Belgian ales, wheat beers
Hersbrucker	German lagers, German ales, Belgian ales
Lublin	Pilsners
Mt. Hood	American lagers, German lagers, German ales, wheat beers
Northern Brewer	California common, German lagers, English and Belgian ales
Nugget	American ales, India pale ales
Perle	American pale ales, porters, German ales
Pride of Ringwood	Australian ales
Saaz	Pilsners
Spalt	German lagers
Styrian Goldings	English milds, bitters, porters, stouts, Belgian ales
Tettnang	American lagers, German lagers, wheat beers
Wye Target	English ales

These pairings are common matches of hop type to style. Many brewers deviate substantially from these recommendations and make excellent beer in the process. If you see recipes in this book that call for a particular hop type that you can't locate, these pairings may help you choose an appropriate substitute if your local homebrew shop doesn't offer recommendations.

Water

Water is a concern to brewers because it may contain unwanted elements, (such as the chlorine added to most municipal water supplies), or various minerals that affect mash performance. Some homebrewers filter their water before brewing, some use bottled water, and others carefully analyze and balance their water. For most brewers, tap water is fine. But, you may want to filter it, let it sit overnight, or boil it before brewing to drive off the chlorine.

Minerals in the water are interesting to all-grain brewers. Ions change the acidity of the mash. An ideal mash has an acidity of about 5.3 to 5.5 pH. Brewers often adjust their water's mineral content by adding gypsum, chalk, or Epsom salts. This complex subject is explained in *Dave Miller's Homebrewing Guide*.

Many of the world's famous brewing cities achieve a reputation for their styles based on characteristics imparted by the water. In England, Burton is the best example. The city's water is very hard, lending a sharp flavor that enhances the perception of bitterness in its ales.

Many brewing recipes list ingredients such as salt and gypsum. These change the character of the water and should generally not be added without consideration of your own water's characteristics.

Yeast

There are generally two types of yeast used by brewers: ale yeast (*Saccharomyces cerevia*) and lager yeast (*S. uvarum*). Ale yeasts ferment best at temperatures from 58° to 68°F (14° to 21°C); lager yeasts, from 45° to 50°F (7° to 10°C). An enormous number of strains of these two basic yeasts are available through most homebrew-supply shops. Different strains will produce different flavors in otherwise identical beers. Some brewers list yeasts that they have cultured from bottles. This technique is described in most general homebrewing texts, such as Charlie Papazian's *New Complete Joy of Homebrewing*. If you're not sure how to culture yeasts, substitute a similar commercial strain.

THE BREWING PROCESS

While ingredients form the crux of a beer recipe, the choices made during the brewing process — the mashing method, yeast pitching practice, and fermentation regimen — have a considerable influence on the character of a beer.

Extract Brewing

Because extract brewers use prepackaged malt extracts, they have less control over many of their processes than do all-grain brewers. But there are still some decisions to be made by the brewer that can influence the finished beer's character. One of these is the size of the boil. Most extract recipes call for boiling only a small portion of the total wort, and then diluting it in the fermenter with cold water to bring the batch up to its full volume. This is a good strategy for beginners and works well with many styles; however, homebrewers using such methods to make light beers, like American lagers, have trouble getting the beer light enough in color without imparting too much caramel flavor. This comes about in part because extracts are often not light enough, but also because the denser wort of a small boil tends to brown much more quickly than would a large batch. Moving up to a full boil requires a bigger brewpot and a wort chiller, but it can help you brew lighter beers.

Mashing

Mashing is the process of soaking the grains in water at a controlled temperature in order to accelerate enzyme activity. The most important enzyme activity is the conversion of starch to sugar, accomplished by the enzymes *alpha amylase* and *beta amylase*. Alpha amylase produces more unfermentable sugars (dextrins) and works best at temperatures of 152° to 158°F (67° to 70°C). Beta amylase produces more fermentable sugars and is most active at temperatures of about 144° to 148°F (62° to 64°C).

A *single-step infusion mash* is one of the most popular mashing schedules among homebrewers. All that it requires is bringing the mash up to a temperature of about 150°F (66°C) and holding it for 60 to 90 minutes. This mashing method is best suited to most ale styles, especially those using English pale ale malt.

The *step mash* is a strategy that employs multiple temperature levels, in an increasing order, to allow other enzymes to do their work. The step mash may begin with an acid rest, although normally it's done with two steps: a *protein rest* and a *saccharification rest*. The rests are simply the temperatures and time intervals at which the mash is left alone for the enzymes to break down complex molecules. The protein rest begins at about 120° to 125°F (49° to 52°C) for about 30 minutes; this maximizes activity of the proteolytic enzymes, which break down long protein chains. This is especially useful for high-protein malts.

Another mashing process that is used in homebrewing is the *decoction mash*. In this method, the thick part of the mash is removed from the mashing vessel and brought to a boil for about 15 to 30 minutes, and then returned to the mashing vessel. Boiling breaks down starches and proteins. Decoction mashes produce a more rounded, malty character and are used for most European lager beers and German wheat beers.

Fermentation

One of the most critical aspects of the fermentation process is ensuring a healthy, vigorous start by the yeast. Yeast starters are often grown up to ever-increasing quantities to ensure that a large amount of yeast is available for pitching. You can encourage yeast activity by aerating the chilled wort, that is, by shaking it to introduce air, or sometimes by pumping air or oxygen into the fermenter before pitching.

Temperature control and, more importantly, temperature stability are critical in ensuring the quality of a beer. High-temperature fermentations produce myriad off flavors in beer. The optimal temperature for most yeasts is lower than most homebrewers keep their fermenters. When available, we list the optimal fermentation temperatures for various yeast strains in the chapter descriptions.

In addition to mashing and fermentation, many other process decisions can affect the characteristics of your beer. Filtration can help clear up clarity problems; careful bottling procedures can reduce possible oxidation problems. Most of these factors are not very important when you first start brewing, but as you become more aware of them and more aware of the subtle flavors in your beer, you may find that changes anywhere in your brewing process can affect the character of your beers.

BEER STYLES AND COMPETITIONS

Not everybody wants to enter competitions, but they can be great fun and an excellent way to hone brewing skills. Many homebrewers enjoy trying to brew the best possible versions of a particular style. For them, the challenge of brewing a beer that comes closest to an established style target is part of the hobby of homebrewing.

Remember, beers are not evaluated by how well they might slake your thirst on a hot summer day (even though that may be your own measure of a great beer). Competitions are judged according to style guidelines. Even a well-crafted, solid beer, free of any flavor or aroma defects, will do poorly if entered in an inappropriate style category. Style (and an understanding of the style guidelines) is the language by which a beer's qualities are communicated. A brewer knows what judges (and beer drinkers) look for in a certain style, and judges know the brewer's goals for his beer when he enters it in that style category. It's communication, and it works.

Finding Competitions

Competitions are held throughout the U.S. and Canada. A list of upcoming competitions is published in each issue of *zymurgy* magazine. Local homebrew-supply shops will often know of upcoming competitions.

Look for competitions that use judges from the Beer Judge Certification Program (BJCP). These are usually the most experienced, most knowledgeable judges, and you are likely to get better feedback on your beers from them.

Winning Strategies

If winning a competition is important to you, there are several strategies you can employ to improve your odds: brew to style; enter several beers in each competition; and look for the less popular categories that attract fewer entries. Brewing a good, solid beer that adheres to style guidelines is the most important element in winning.

Some brewers try the shotgun approach to winning ribbons — they enter a lot of beers. This strategy is generally ineffective if the beers are not themselves solid.

A better strategy is to lessen your competition by brewing a style that doesn't usually get a large number of entries. American pale ales, stouts, fruit beers, and porters are very popular categories, often with numerous strong entries. Although a bit more challenging to brew, mild ales, Scottish ales, and American light lagers may offer greater opportunities for new competitors. As always, though, a good solid beer brewed to style is what counts.

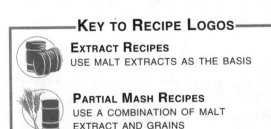

KEY TO RECIPE LOGOS

EXTRACT RECIPES
USE MALT EXTRACTS AS THE BASIS

PARTIAL MASH RECIPES
USE A COMBINATION OF MALT
EXTRACT AND GRAINS

ALL-GRAIN RECIPES
USE ONLY MASHED GRAINS

More HOMEBREW FAVORITES 2

Pale Ales

We often think of pale ale as the quintessential English beer, but outstanding pale ales are also brewed in Belgium, Australia, Canada, and the United States. The family of styles called *pale ale* is large and varied, including substyles that show only subtle differences. Pale ale styles include the various types of bitter (bitter, best bitter, and extra special bitter), India pale ale (IPA), American pale ale, Belgian pale ale, blond ale, golden ale, amber ale, Irish red ale, and Adelaide sparkling ale.

Pale ale, as a distinct style, evolved in England during the 17th century. In his writings on beer style, style guru Fred Eckhardt has speculated that the original pale ale was a Burton ale dating from the 1630s or even earlier. Traditionally, the English called a pale ale served on draft a "bitter" but labeled it as "pale ale" when bottled. Today, either label may be applied to a bottled or draft product. The term *bitter* is not often used in the United States, although quite a few brewpubs use the name for their English-style pale ales.

Description. Pale ales are a deep golden to deep amber color, typically a color of about 5 to 15 SRM. The beer is a normal-gravity brew (typically about 12° Plato—that's an original gravity of about 1.048). The hops

KEY TO RECIPE LOGOS

 EXTRACT RECIPES   PARTIAL MASH RECIPES   ALL-GRAIN RECIPES

are usually about 20 to 40 IBU, although this will vary by substyle. Alcoholic content on pale ales can be fairly low (3.2 to 4.0 %) for an ordinary bitter, fairly high for an IPA (7 %), but will generally be moderate at about 5 %. A range of flavors is possible in these beers. A pale ale intended to mimic those of Burton will be dry with a nice bitter hop character enhanced by the salts in the water. A beer brewed as a bitter will have a softer character. An India pale ale might be aggressively hoppy.

When brewing a pale ale from extract, light or amber extracts are generally used with an adjunct grain—usually a little bit of crystal malt to add a touch of color and a little caramel flavor. Use English-style hops, such as Fuggles or East Kent Goldings, for an English-style pale ale, or U.S. hops of average alpha acid content (like Cascade or Willamette) for an American pale ale.

There are quite a number of yeasts that will do well for brewing pale ales. Brewers making English-style pale ales often prefer the Wyeast London Ale or English Ale liquid strains, or their equivalent. Good dry yeasts include the Whitbread or Edme ale yeasts. Brewers making American pale ales often like the Wyeast Chico ale yeast, or dry yeasts like the Nottingham and Windsor strains made by Lallemand.

Many pale ale recipes call for gypsum or similar minerals to be added to the water. Such additives should never be considered "ingredients," but rather they are used to change the character of a local water source to match more closely the water profile of a specific geographic region. In the case of pale ales, water is often *burtonized*, which means that it is made harder, in an attempt to match the characteristics of the water of Burton-on-Trent in England—historically one of the world's great brewing capitals. In many cases, adding gypsum will help your water more closely match Burton's, but if you live in an area that already has very hard, high-carbonate-content water, adding more gypsum may give your beer an unpleasant harshness with a mineral bite. We have left gypsum and similar additives in the recipes when the original brewers listed them as ingredients; however, we recommend that you use them judiciously if you suspect that your water may already be hard. On the other hand, if you are brewing with store-bought distilled water or reverse-osmosis-filtered water, then by all means add the gypsum.

For those brewers who understand water chemistry and know the profile of their local water source, here is a typical water profile for Burton-on-Trent from *A Textbook of Brewing* by Jean DeClerck:

TOTAL DISSOLVED SOLIDS (MG/L): 1,790
CALCIUM (Ca): 520
MAGNESIUM: 145
SULPHATE (SO$_3$): 756
CHLORIDE: 34
NITRATES (N$_2$O$_5$): 22

Other sources, such as Charlie Papazian's *Home Brewers Companion*, show dissolved solid contents for Burton at about 1,200 parts per million (ppm), so the profile given above should be considered an upper limit.

All-grain brewers usually use English 2-row pale ale malt for their base grist. An American 2-row pale malt will work well for American pale ales. The mash is usually a single-step infusion mash at about 152°F (67°C). Variations are always possible, of course.

Fermentation typically takes place at cellar or cool room temperatures below 70°F (21°C). While novice homebrewers may do only one fermentation step — a process that works fine — racking to a secondary fermenter can help improve clarity and deliver cleaner tasting beers. Some commercial breweries and homebrewers ferment the beers using open fermenters during the period of high yeast activity. In England, bitters are generally *cask conditioned*, which means that they are allowed to mature naturally in the barrel, are unfiltered, and are generally served by means of a hand pump rather than under CO$_2$ pressure. Some advanced homebrewers have had enormous success using these methods to create authentic bitters that are much like those produced by England's small independent breweries.

The English pale ales are often referred to as "ordinary bitter," "special bitter," and "extra special bitter." The ingredients for these beers are the same, as are the basic brewing processes. The difference is largely one of degree. If a brewery offers different bitters, then ordinary will be its lightest, and extra special bitter — or ESB — its heavier, or more assertive, beer. It is possible, however, that one brewery's special or ESB could be lighter than a competitor's ordinary. Typical differences might be an ordinary at 1.035 OG with 25 IBUs, a special at 1.040 OG with 35 IBUs, and an ESB at 1.055 OG and 45 IBUs.

An American pale ale is similar to those made in England, but will be more vigorously carbonated and it will often use American hops like Cascade, which give it a more citric or floral character in the hops. An India pale ale will be aggressively hopped because the style originated in the practice of exploiting the natural preservative qualities of hops so that the beer could withstand long sea voyages from England to India. An Adelaide ale will be fermented warm and have a fruity aroma and flavor, as well as a robust carbonation.

In homebrew competitions, some fruity esters, diacetyl, and other traditional yeast-produced flavors are technically acceptable parts of the flavor profile, and certainly these flavors can be found in commercial examples of English pale ales. However, many judges are not accustomed to, or tolerant of, these flavors, and may penalize entrants whose beers are actually not flawed. If winning a competition is important to you, then you might want to try cooler fermentation temperatures and experiment with yeasts that are less likely to produce by-products. Traditionally, these beers are fermented at cellar temperatures, which are cooler than a typical kitchen in the United States.

With the English-style pale ales, stick to English-style malts and hops — do not hop your beer with obviously American hop types, such as Cascade, and expect it to do well. Similarly, use yeast strains intended for English ales, like the popular Wyeast British Ale and London Ale yeasts (number 1098 and number 1028). In the American pale ale style, use American malts and hops and don't be shy about hops. Sierra Nevada is considered an outstanding example of the American pale ale style. Judges generally look for India pale ales that are hoppier and heavier than described in most style guidelines.

ENGLISH PALE ALES: BITTER, SPECIAL BITTER, AND ESB

Big Murphy Special Red

YIELD: .... 5 GAL. (18.9 L)
TOTAL BOILING TIME: .... 60 MIN.
STARTING GRAVITY: 1.042
ENDING GRAVITY: 1.013
PRIMARY FERMENT: .... 8 DAYS
SECONDARY FERMENT: .... 5 DAYS

This beer is a beautiful deep reddish amber. Well balanced with noticeable hops and subtle malt.

- ¼ lb. (113 g) crystal malt, 80° Lovibond
- ½ c. (138 ml) roasted barley
- 6 ⁶⁄₁₀ lb. (3 kg) Munton & Fison unhopped amber malt extract
- 2 oz. (57 g) English Kent Goldings hops, 5.0% alpha, in boil 60 min.
- 2 tsp. (9.9 ml) gypsum
- 1 tbsp. (14.8 ml) Irish moss
- ½ oz. (14 g) Fuggles hops, 4.0% alpha, in boil 20 min.
- ½ oz. (14 g) Fuggles hops, 4.0% alpha, in boil 2 min.
- Wyeast #1028 London Ale yeast
- 1 tsp. (4.9 ml) ascorbic acid
- 1 tbsp. (14.8 ml) polyclar
- ¾ c. (206 ml) corn sugar

Crush grains and add to a nylon grain bag. Place grain bag in 1½ gal. (5.7 L) cold water and bring to a boil. Remove grains when water begins to boil. Add malt extract, gypsum, and the Kent Goldings hops. Boil 40 min., then add Irish moss and ½ oz. (14 g) of Fuggles hops. Boil 18 min., then add last ½ oz. (14 g) of Fuggles hops. Boil a final 2 min. and turn off heat. Pour wort through a strainer and into a fermenter containing 3½ gal. (13.2 L) of cold water. Pitch yeast when wort is below 80°F (27°C). Ferment for 8 days at 64° – 68°F (18° – 20°C). Rack to a secondary fermenter and continue fermenting for 5 days at 64° – 68°F (18° – 20°C). Add ascorbic acid, polycar and corn sugar to 1 pt. (0.5 L) of water, boil 5 min. Prime and bottle.

— *Mike Poynton, Chicago, Illinois*

Indy Racing Ale

YIELD: .... 5 GAL. (18.9 L)
TOTAL BOILING TIME: .... 35 MIN.
STARTING GRAVITY: 1.040–45
ENDING GRAVITY: 1.012–14
PRIMARY FERMENT: .... 4–5 DAYS
SECONDARY FERMENT: .... 1–2 WEEKS

1 lb. (454 g) crystal malt
4 lb. (1.81 kg) Muntons Bitter Kit
1 lb. (454 g) light dry malt extract
1 lb. (454 g) brown sugar
1 oz. (28 g) Hallertauer hops, in boil 35 min.
1 oz. (28 g) Goldings hops, in boil 15 min.
1 oz. (28 g) Goldings hops, 10-min. steep
   ale yeast
1 c. (275 ml) corn sugar, for priming

In a brewpot, add 2 gal. (7.6 L) of cold water and crushed grains. Bring almost to a boil and steep the grain for 30 min. Strain out grain and add malt extracts, brown sugar, and Hallertauer hops. Boil 20 min. Add 1 oz. (28 g) of Goldings hops and boil 15 min. Remove from heat, add final oz. (28 g) of Goldings hops, and steep 10 min. Pour wort into primary fermenter with 3 gal. (11.4 L) of very cold water. When temperature reaches 80°F (27°C), add yeast and stir vigorously. Ferment 4 to 5 days. When specific gravity falls below 1.020, rack beer to a glass secondary fermenter and continue fermenting 1 – 2 weeks. Prime with the corn sugar and bottle. Store in warm area for 7 days. Age 4 weeks.

— *Ivan Crash, Indianapolis, Indiana, Wine-Art*

Black Whisker Bitter

YIELD: .... 5 GAL. (18.9 L)
TOTAL BOILING TIME: .... 60 MIN.
STARTING GRAVITY: 1.062
ENDING GRAVITY: 1.013
PRIMARY FERMENT: .... 5 DAYS
SECONDARY FERMENT: .... 14 DAYS

   1 lb. (454 g) crystal malt, 40° Lovibond
¼ lb. (113 g) torrified wheat
   8 lb. (3.63 kg) Alexander's pale malt extract
   1 lb. (454 g) dry malt extract
   2 oz. (57 g) East Kent Goldings hops, in boil 60 min.
   1 oz. (28 g) East Kent Goldings hops, in boil 15 min.
   1 oz. (28 g) East Kent Goldings hops, in boil 1 min.
   Wyeast #1098 British Ale yeast
¾ c. (206 ml) corn sugar, for priming

Crush grains and add to 2 gal. (7.6 L) of cold water in a large pot. Heat until the temperature reaches 175°F (79°C). Strain out grains and add all malt extracts. Bring to a boil and add 2 oz. (57 g) East Kent Goldings hops. Boil 45 min., then add 1 oz. (28 g) East Kent Goldings hops. Boil 14 min., then add 1 oz. (28 g) East Kent Goldings hops. Boil 1 min. Turn off heat, cool, and strain wort into a fermenter containing 3 gal. (14.4 L) of cold water. Pitch yeast when wort is at 70°F (21°C), aerate well, and let ferment 5 days. Rack to a secondary fermenter and continue fermenting for 14 days. Keg, carbonate with CO_2, condition, and serve. Alternatively, prime with the corn sugar and bottle.

    — *Scott Dittenber, Grand Rapids, Michigan, Prime Time Brewers*

Ed's Red

YIELD:	5 GAL. (18.9 L)
TOTAL BOILING TIME:	60 MIN.
STARTING GRAVITY:	1.045
ENDING GRAVITY:	1.011
PRIMARY FERMENT:	6 DAYS
SECONDARY FERMENT:	11 DAYS

Copper colored with medium body, sweetness, and bitterness.

   8 lb. (3.63 kg) pale ale malt
1½ lb. (680 g) roasted barley
   1 lb. (454 g) caramel malt
   2 oz. (57 g) Mt. Hood hops, 4.3% alpha, in boil 60 min.
½ oz. (¼ g) Cascade hops, 5.5% alpha, in boil 3 min.
   Munton & Fison ale yeast
¾ c. (206 ml) corn sugar, for priming

Mash all grains in 3½ gal. (13.2 L) of water at 154°F (68°C) for 60 min. Sparge with 170°F (77°C) water and collect 5½ – 6 gal. (20.7 – 22.7 L) of wort. Bring to a boil and add Mt. Hood hops. Boil 57 min., then add the Cascade hops. Boil 3 min. and turn off heat. Chill the wort, transfer to a fermenter, and pitch yeast. Ferment at 65°F (18°C) for 6 days. Rack to secondary and ferment 11 days at 66°F (19°C). Prime with corn sugar and bottle.

— Ed Cosgrove, Woodbridge, Virginia
Brewers Association of Northern Virginia (BANOVA)

Holiday Ale

YIELD: .... 5 GAL. (18.9 L)
TOTAL BOILING TIME: .... 45 MIN.
PRIMARY FERMENT: .... 7 DAYS
SECONDARY FERMENT: .... 7 DAYS

Second place in the American light lager category at the 1995 Green Mountain Homebrew Competition.

  ½ lb. (227 g) 2-row pale English malt
5–6 lbs. (2.27–2.72 kg) Alexander's Sun Country pale malt extract
1½ oz. (43 g) Hallertauer hops, in boil 45 min.
  1 tsp. (4.9 ml) Irish Moss
  ½ oz. (14 g) Tettnanger hops, in boil 15 min.
  ½ oz. (14 g) Tettnanger hops, in boil 5 min.
  ¼ oz. (7 g) package Cooper's ale yeast
  ¾ c. (206 ml) corn sugar, for priming

In a large pot, add 1½ gal. (5.7 L) water and pale malt. Heat until boil is about to begin. Strain out grains and add malt extract and Hallertauer hops. Boil 15 min. Add Irish moss and boil 15 min. Add ½ oz. (14 g) of Tettnanger hops and boil 10 min. Add last ½ oz. (14 g) of Tettnanger hops and boil 5 more min. Turn off heat, cool, and strain into fermenter containing 3½ gal. (13.2 L) cold water. Pitch yeast when temperature is below 75°F (24°C). Ferment for 1 week, then rack to a secondary fermenter. Ferment 1 more week, prime with the corn sugar, and bottle.

— Peter Cammann, Waitsfield, Vermont

Mitch's Best Bitter

YIELD: .... 5 GAL. (18.9 L)
TOTAL BOILING TIME: .... 60 MIN.
STARTING GRAVITY: 1.054
ENDING GRAVITY: 1.012
PRIMARY FERMENT: .... 3 DAYS
SECONDARY FERMENT: .... 14 DAYS

This beer has a good mouthfeel with classic bitterness and a beautiful Styrian hops nose.

- 1 tsp. (4.9 ml) gypsum, for mash water
- 6.6 lb. (3 kg) 2-row malt
- 4 oz. (113 g) crystal malt
- 2 oz. (57 g) roasted barley
- 2 tsp. (9.9 ml) gypsum, for sparge water
- ¼ tsp. (1.2 ml) salt
- 1 lb. (454 g) brown sugar
- 2 oz. (57 g) Fuggles hops, 4.2% alpha, in boil 60 min.
- 1 oz. (28 g) East Kent Goldings hops, 5.2% alpha, in boil 30 min.
- ¼ oz. (7 g) Styrian hops, 2.9% alpha, 15-min. steep
  Wyeast #1028 London Ale yeast
- ¾ c. (206 ml) corn sugar, for priming

Treat 2½ gal. (9.5 L) of water with 1 tsp. (4.9 ml) gypsum. Add crushed grains, heat to 122°F (50°C), and let rest 20 min. Heat mash to 144°F (62°C) and let rest 30 min. Heat mash to 158°F (70°C) and let rest 20 min. Mash-out at 168°F (76°C) for 10 min. Sparge with 4 gal. (15.1 L) of 170°F (77°C) water, treated with 2 tsp. (9.9 ml) gypsum. Bring to a boil and add salt, brown sugar, and the Fuggles hops. Boil 30 min., then add the East Kent Goldings hops. Boil 30 min., then turn off heat. Add the Styrian hops and steep 15 min. Chill wort, transfer to fermenter, and pitch yeast. Ferment 3 days and rack to a secondary fermenter. Continue fermenting another 14 days, then prime with the corn sugar and bottle.

— *Mitch Hamilton, Dorval, Quebec, Canada, Technovin*

Trolleyman ESB

YIELD: .... 5 GAL. (18.9 L)
TOTAL BOILING TIME: .... 60 MIN.
STARTING GRAVITY: 1.050
ENDING GRAVITY: 1.013
PRIMARY FERMENT: .... 7 DAYS
SECONDARY FERMENT: .... 14 DAYS

A very close rendition of Redhook ESB.

```
   2   tsp. (9.9 ml) gypsum
  10   oz. (284 g) crystal malt, 60° Lovibond
 6.6   lb. (3 kg) Alexander's ultra-light malt extract
   4   oz. (113 g) malto-dextrin
2.10   oz. (60 g) Willamette hop pellets, 4.8% alpha, in boil 60 min.
   1   tsp. (4.9 ml) Irish moss
   1   oz. (28 g) Tettnanger hop pellets, 4.8% alpha, in boil 2 min.
   1   oz. (28 g) Tettnanger leaf hops, 5.2% alpha, dry hop
       Wyeast #1098 British Ale yeast
   1   tbsp. (14.8 ml) polyclar
  ¾    c. (206 ml) corn sugar, for priming
```

Heat 4 gal. (15.1 L) of water, treated with gypsum, to 160°F (71°C). Add crushed crystal malt and steep 30 min. Strain out grain. Bring to a boil and add malt extract, malto-dextrin, and Willamette hops. Boil 30 min. and add Irish moss. Boil 28 min., then add 1 oz. (28 g) of Tettnanger hop pellets. Boil a final 2 min. and turn off heat. Chill the wort and transfer to a primary fermenter. Top off to 5 gal. (18.9 L) with cold water and pitch yeast. Ferment 7 days at 65°F (18°C), then rack to a secondary fermenter and add 1 oz. (28 g) Tettnanger hops. Continue fermenting for 10 days at 65°F (18°C), then add the polyclar to fermenter. Ferment 4 more days, then prime with the corn sugar and bottle.

— *Michael G. Lloyd, Mukilteo, Washington*

O'Brien Pale Ale

YIELD: .... 5 GAL. (18.9 L)
TOTAL BOILING TIME: .... 60 MIN.
STARTING GRAVITY: 1.052
ENDING GRAVITY: 1.014
PRIMARY FERMENT: .... 5 DAYS
SECONDARY FERMENT: .... 7–14 DAYS

4.4 lb. (2 kg) pale ale malt
9 oz. (250 g) crystal malt, 40° Lovibond
9 oz. (250 g) torrified wheat
3 ¾ lb. (1.7 kg) Cooper's light malt extract syrup
3 oz. (87.5 g) Fuggles hops, 4.5% alpha, in boil 60 min.
½ oz. (12.5 g) Fuggles hops, 4.5% alpha, in boil 10 min.
2 tsp. (10 ml) Irish moss
Yeast Lab A09 English Ale yeast
⅝ c. (175 ml) corn sugar, for priming

Mash the grain in 1.3 gal. (5.0 L) of 155°F (68°C) water. Let rest 30 min. Add 0.53 gal. (2 L) of 212°F (100°C) water and let rest for 45 min. Sparge the grains into the brewpot. Add the malt extract and bring to a boil. Skim the foam as it is produced. Add 3 oz. (87.5 g) of Fuggles hops and boil 50 min. Add ½ oz. (12.5 g) of Fuggles hops and the Irish moss. Boil 10 min. Cool and transfer to fermenter. Pitch yeast. Ferment 5 days at 65°–68°F (18°–20°C). Rack to secondary for 7–14 days. Prime and bottle.

— *Douglas O'Brien, Ottawa, Ontario, Canada*

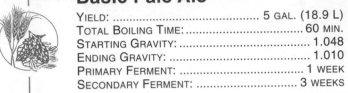

Basic Pale Ale

YIELD:	5 GAL. (18.9 L)
TOTAL BOILING TIME:	60 MIN.
STARTING GRAVITY:	1.048
ENDING GRAVITY:	1.010
PRIMARY FERMENT:	1 WEEK
SECONDARY FERMENT:	3 WEEKS

A beautiful red beer with a spicy finish that comes into balance with aging.

8 lb. (3.63 kg) 2-row pale malt
1 lb. (454 g) crystal malt, 53° Lovibond
½ lb. (227 g) Victory malt, toasted
1 oz. (28 g) Eroica hops, 12% alpha, in boil 60 min.
1 oz. (28 g) Fuggles hops, 4% alpha, in boil 10 min.
1 oz. (28 g) Kent Goldings hops, 5% alpha, steep
½ oz. (14 g) Tettnanger hops, 4.4% alpha, dry hop in secondary fermenter
     Wyeast #1338 European Ale yeast
¾ c. (206 ml) corn sugar, for priming

Mash-in grains in 3 gal. (11.4 L) of 100°F (38°C) water. Let rest 30 min., then raise mash temperature to 148°F (64°C) and hold until starch conversion is complete. Mash-out at 170°F (77°C) for 5 min. Sparge with 170°F (77°C) water and collect 6 gal. (22.7 L). Bring wort to a boil and add Eroica hops. Boil 50 min., then add Fuggles hops. Boil 10 min. then turn off heat. Add the Kent Goldings hops and steep 5 min. Chill the wort, transfer to a primary fermenter, and pitch yeast. Ferment 1 week, rack to a secondary fermenter. Ferment another 3 weeks, adding ½ oz. (14 g) Tettnanger hops 2 – 3 days before bottling. Prime and bottle.

— *Julianne Targan, Morristown, New Jersey, Hop & Vine*

Whales Ales Ya

YIELD: .... 5 GAL. (18.9 L)
TOTAL BOILING TIME: .... 70 MIN.
STARTING GRAVITY: 1.040
ENDING GRAVITY: 1.009
PRIMARY FERMENT: .... 7 DAYS
SECONDARY FERMENT: .... 7 DAYS

A smooth beer that compares favorably to Double Diamond.

- 7 lb. (3.18 kg) pale malt
- 1 lb. (454 g) crystal malt, 40° Lovibond
- 1 lb. (454 g) cara-pils malt
- 1 lb. (454 g) Munich malt
- 1 oz. (28 g) Kent Goldings hops, 4.7% alpha, in boil 60 min.
- 1 oz. (28 g) Fuggles hops, 3.6% alpha, in boil 30 min.
- ½ oz. (14 g) Fuggles hops, 3.6% alpha, in boil 15 min.
- 1 tsp. (4.9 g) Irish moss
- ½ oz. (14 g) Fuggles hops, 3.6% alpha, in boil 1 min.
- Wyeast #1028 London Ale yeast
- ¾ c. (206 ml) corn sugar, for priming

Add crushed grains to 3⅓ gal. (12.5 L) of 166°F (74°C) water. Mash at 155°F (68°C) for 90 min. Sparge with 170°F (77°C) water until 6½ gal (24.6 L) of wort are collected in brew kettle. Bring wort to a boil and let boil 10 min. before adding Kent Goldings hops. Boil 30 min., then add 1 oz. (28 g) of Fuggles hops. Boil 15 min., then add ½ oz. (14 g) of Fuggles hops and Irish moss. Boil 14 min., then add last ½ oz. (14 g) of Fuggles hops. Boil 1 more min. and turn off heat. Chill the wort, transfer to the fermenter, and pitch yeast. Ferment 7 days, then rack to secondary. Continue fermenting 7 more days, then prime with corn sugar and bottle.

— *Ronald J. Sup, Morrow, Ohio, Bloatarian Brewing League*

Old Familiar

YIELD:	5 GAL. (18.9 L)
TOTAL BOILING TIME:	75 MIN.
STARTING GRAVITY:	1.060
ENDING GRAVITY:	1.016
PRIMARY FERMENT:	3 WEEKS

- 8 lb. (3.63 kg) pale ale malt
- 1 lb. (454 g) 2-row malt
- 1 lb. (454 g) crystal malt, 120° Lovibond
- ½ lb. (227 g) flaked barley
- 1 oz. (28 g) Kent Goldings hops, 4.9% alpha, in boil 45 min.
- 1 oz. (28 g) Fuggles hops, 2.6% alpha, in boil 20 min.
- ½ c. (118 ml) Lyle's treacle
  Wyeast #1084 Irish Ale yeast
- ½ c. (118 ml) treacle, for priming

Add crushed grains to 10 qt. (9.5 L) of 170°F (77°C) water. Mash for 60 min., or until starch conversion is complete. Sparge with 170°F (77°C) water and collect 6½ gal. (24.6 L) of wort. Bring to a boil and boil 30 min. before adding the Kent Goldings hops. Boil 25 min., then add Fuggles. Boil 19 min., then add ½ c. (118 ml) of treacle. Boil 1 min., then turn off heat. Chill the wort, transfer to primary fermenter, and pitch yeast. Ferment 3 weeks at 60°F (16°C), then prime with ½ c. (118 ml) of treacle and bottle.

— *Keith Schwols, Ft. Collins, Colorado*

Nothook ESB

YIELD:	10 GAL. (37.9 L)
TOTAL BOILING TIME:	60 MIN.
STARTING GRAVITY:	1.050
ENDING GRAVITY:	1.013
PRIMARY FERMENT:	2 WEEKS
SECONDARY FERMENT:	2 WEEKS

Smooth, but bitter and complex with an underlying dryness.

- 16 lb. (7 kg) 2-row malt
- 2 lb. (907 g) crystal malt, 60° Lovibond

¼ lb. (113 g) Belgian biscuit malt
6 oz. (170 g) German Tettnanger hops, 2.8% alpha, in boil 60 min.
2 oz. (57 g) German Tettnanger hops, 2.8% alpha, in boil 15 min.
1 oz. (28 g) German Tettnanger hops, 2.8% alpha, in boil 1–2 min.
   Wyeast #1725 Thames Valley Ale yeast
1½ c. (413 ml) corn sugar, for priming

Mash grains in 6 gal. (22.7 L) water at 152°F (67°C) for 1 hour. Mash-out at 170°F (77°C) for 10 min. Sparge with 170°F (77°C) water and collect 12 gal. (45.4 L) of wort. Bring to a boil and add 6 oz. (170 g) of Tettnanger hops. Boil 45 min., then add 2 oz. (57 g) of Tettnanger hops. Boil 8–9 min., then add final 1 oz. (28 g) of Tettnanger hops. Boil 1–2 min. and turn off heat. Chill the wort, transfer to a fermenter, and pitch yeast. Ferment 2 weeks at 62°–64°F (17°–18°C). Rack to secondary for 2 weeks at 62°–64°F (17°–18°C). Prime with the corn sugar and bottle.

— Steve Zabarnick, Dayton, Ohio
Dayton Regional Amateur Fermentation Technologists (DRAFT)

Hoppy Hoppy, Joy Joy

YIELD: .... 5 GAL. (18.9 L)
TOTAL BOILING TIME: .... 60 MIN.
STARTING GRAVITY: 1.046
PRIMARY FERMENT: .... 10 DAYS
SECONDARY FERMENT: .... 2 WEEKS

First place at the 16th annual AugustFest Competition. A traditional ESB.

6½ lb. (2.95 kg) British pale ale malt
1 lb. (454 g) domestic Munich malt
4 oz. (113 g) torrified wheat
2 oz. (57 g) Special-B Belgian malt
1½ oz. (43 g) Styrian Goldings hops, 5.2% alpha, in boil 45 min.
1 oz. (28 g) Styrian Goldings hops, 5.2% alpha, in boil 10 min.
   Wyeast #1028 London Ale yeast
2 oz. (57 g) Styrian Goldings hops, 5.2% alpha, dry hop
¾ c. (206 ml) corn sugar, for priming (if bottling), or force carbonate

Crush grains, add to 11 qt. (10.4 L) of 170°F (77°C) water, and stabilize temperature to 152°F (67°C). Mash for 60 min., then sparge with 168°F (76°C) water until 6½ gal. (24.6 L) of wort is collected. Boil 15 min. Add 1½ oz. (43 g) of Styrian Goldings hops. Boil 35 min., then add 1 oz. (28 g) of Styrian Goldings hops. Boil a final 10 min., then turn off heat. Chill the wort, transfer to primary fermenter, and pitch yeast. Ferment 10 days at 64°F (18°C), then rack to a secondary fermenter, adding 2 oz. (57 g) of Styrian Goldings hops to the fermenter. Continue fermenting for 2 weeks at 55°F (13°C), then keg or bottle.

— *Keith Schwols, Ft. Collins, Colorado*

AMERICAN PALE ALES

Hoppy Pale Ale

YIELD:	5 GAL. (18.9 L)
TOTAL BOILING TIME:	60 MIN.
PRIMARY FERMENT:	1–2 WEEKS
SECONDARY FERMENT:	NONE

Clone of Sierra Nevada Pale Ale.

　　1　lb. (454 g) crystal malt, 13°–17° Lovibond
　7½　lb. (3.4 kg) Alexander's pale malt extract
　　1　tbsp. (14.8 ml) Irish moss
　2½　oz. (71 g) Cascade hops, 5% alpha, in boil 60 min.
　1½　oz. (43 g) Cascade hops, 5% alpha, in boil 5 min.
　1½　oz. (43 g) Cascade hops, 5% alpha, 20–30 min. steep
　　　　Wyeast #1056 American Ale yeast
　¾　c. (206 ml) corn sugar, for priming

Steep crystal malt in 2½ gal. (9.5 L) of water until the water reaches 180°F (82°C). Strain out grains and add malt extract. Bring to a boil and add Irish moss and 2½ oz. (71 g) of Cascade hops. Boil 55 min., then add 1½ oz. (43 g) of Cascade hops. Boil a final 5 min., then turn off heat and add the last 1½ oz. (43 g) of Cascade hops. Cover and let steep for 20 – 30 min. Chill the wort, transfer to a primary fermenter, and pitch yeast. When fermentation is complete, prime with the corn sugar and bottle.

— *Mark Garetz, Pleasanton, California, HopTech*

American "CRAB" Ale

YIELD:	5 GAL. (18.9 L)
TOTAL BOILING TIME:	45 MIN.
STARTING GRAVITY:	1.052
ENDING GRAVITY:	1.002
PRIMARY FERMENT:	14 DAYS

3.3 lb. (1.5 kg) Premier Reserve American rice extract
1 lb. (454 g) Muntons light dried malt extract
5 c. (1.38 L) corn sugar
1 oz. (28 g) Bullion hop pellets, 7.5% alpha, in boil 45 min.
½ oz. (14 g) Tettnanger hop pellets, 4.5% alpha, in boil 10 min.
1 oz. (28 g) Fuggles leaf hops, 3.2% alpha, dry hop
1 3.5 oz. (10 g) package dry ale yeast
¾ c. (206 ml) corn sugar, for priming
1 tbsp. (14.8 ml) beverage settler, for priming

Boil extracts, corn sugar, and the Bullion hop pellets in 1½ gal. (5.7 L) of water for 35 min. Add Tettnanger hops and boil another 10 min. Pour wort into primary fermenter containing 3 gal. (11.4 L) of cold water. Top off to 5 gal. (18.9 L) and pitch yeast when temperature is below 80°F (27°C) . Add Fuggles leaf hops after kraeusen begins to fall (usually 3 – 4 days). Ferment another 10 days, prime with the corn sugar, add beverage settler, and bottle.

— *Marc Battreall, Plantation Key, Florida*

Alleycat Stock Ale

YIELD: .... 5 GAL. (18.9 L)
TOTAL BOILING TIME: .... 60 MIN.
STARTING GRAVITY: 1.056
ENDING GRAVITY: 1.018
PRIMARY FERMENT: .... 4 DAYS
SECONDARY FERMENT: .... 3–7 DAYS

This brew is a good rendition of Samuel Adams Stock Ale.

- 1 lb. (454 g) crystal malt, 80° Lovibond
- 3 ¾ lb. (1.7 kg) Cooper's Real Ale Kit
- 3 lb. (136 kg) Munton & Fison amber dry malt extract
- ½ oz. (14 g) Cascade hop pellets, 4.6% alpha, in boil 60 min.
- ½ oz. (14 g) Cascade hop pellets, 4.6% alpha, in boil 10 min.
  Cooper's ale yeast or Wyeast #1007 German Ale yeast
- ¾ c. (206 ml) corn sugar, for priming

Steep crushed crystal malt for 30 min. at 150°F (66°C) in 1½ gal. (5.7 L) of water. Remove grains and add the Cooper's Real Ale Kit, dry malt extract, and ½ oz. (14 g) of Cascade hop pellets. Boil 50 min. Add ½ oz. (14 g) of Cascade hop pellets, boil 10 min., and turn off heat. Transfer wort to a primary fermenter and top off to 5 gal. (18.9 L) with cold water. Pitch yeast when wort is below 70°F (21°C). Ferment 4 days, then rack to a secondary fermenter. Ferment another 3 – 7 days, then prime with corn sugar and bottle.

— *Steve Rogers, Dover, New Hampshire, Let's Brew*

Craig's Pale Ale (CPA)

YIELD: .... 5 GAL. (18.9 L)
TOTAL BOILING TIME: .... 60 MIN.
STARTING GRAVITY: 1.052
ENDING GRAVITY: 1.010
PRIMARY FERMENT: .... 10 DAYS
SECONDARY FERMENT: .... 7 DAYS

A Sierra Nevada or Red Nectar imitator with my own touches.

    6 oz. (170 g) crystal malt, 60° Lovibond
    ¼ oz. (7 g) wheat malt
    ¼ oz. (7 g) cara-pils malt
    6½ lb. (2.95 kg) light malt extract syrup
    1½ oz. (43 g) Cascade hops, 4.4% alpha, in boil 60 min.
    ½ oz. (14 g) Cascade hops, 4.4% alpha, in boil 45 min.
    ¼ tsp. (1.2 ml) Irish moss
    ½ oz. (14 g) Willamette hops, 4.9% alpha, in boil 30 min.
    ½ oz. (14 g) Willamette hops, 4.9% alpha, in boil 10 min.
       Wyeast #1056 American Ale yeast
    1 oz. (28 g) Willamette hops, 4.9% alpha, dry hop in secondary
    ¾ c. (206 ml) corn sugar, for priming

Add grains to 2½ gal. (9.5 L) of water and steep at 150°F (66°C) for 45 min.
Strain out grains and add malt extract. Bring to a boil and add 1½ oz. (43
g) of Cascade hops. Boil 15 min., then add ½ oz. (14 g) of Cascade. Boil
15 min., then add Irish moss and ½ oz. (14 g) of Willamette hops. Boil 20
min., then add ½ oz. (14 g) of Willamette hops. Boil a final 10 min., then
turn off heat. Chill wort, transfer to fermenter, and bring up to 5 gal.
(18.9 L) with cold water. Pitch yeast and let ferment for 10 days. Rack to
a secondary fermenter, add 1 oz. (28 g) of Willamette hops, and ferment
another 7 days. Prime with corn sugar and bottle.

— *Craig M. Jan, Sacramento, California*

Smilin' Red

YIELD:	5 GAL. (18.9 L)
TOTAL BOILING TIME:	60 MIN.
STARTING GRAVITY:	1.054
ENDING GRAVITY:	1.018
PRIMARY FERMENT:	5 DAYS
SECONDARY FERMENT:	6 DAYS

  1 lb. (454 g) crystal malt, 80° Lovibond
  ½ lb. (227 g) German Munich malt
3.3 lb. (1.5 kg) Munton & Fison extra light malt extract
  3 lb. (1.36 kg) Briess light dry malt extract
1½ oz. (43 g) Styrian Goldings hops, in boil 60 min.
  ½ oz. (14 g) Styrian Goldings hops, in boil 15 min.
  1 tsp. (4.9 ml) Irish moss
      Wyeast #1084 Irish Ale yeast, 2-qt. (1.9 L) starter
  ½ oz. (14 g) Cascade hops, dry hopped
  ¾ c. (206 ml) corn sugar, for priming

Add crushed grains to 2 gal. (7.6 L) of water and steep for 45 min. at 160°F (71°C). Strain out grains and add to 2½ gal. (9.5 L) of boiling water in brew kettle. Add malt extracts and resume boiling. Add 1½ oz. (43 g) of Styrian Goldings hops when boil commences. Boil 45 min., then add ½ oz. (14 g) of Styrian Goldings hops and Irish moss. Boil 15 min. and turn off heat. Chill the wort, transfer to fermenter, and top off to 5 gal. (18.9 L) with cold water. Pitch yeast and ferment 5 days at 63°F (17°C). Rack to secondary fermenter and add Cascade hops. Ferment 6 days at 63°F (17°C), then prime with corn sugar and bottle.

— *Peter T. Sabin, Stow, Ohio*

American Pale Ale

YIELD: .... 15 GAL. (56.8 L)
TOTAL BOILING TIME: .... 90 MIN.
STARTING GRAVITY: 1.045
PRIMARY FERMENT: .... 7 DAYS
SECONDARY FERMENT: .... 7–14 DAYS

Pale and crisp with an underlying maltiness.

   Wyeast #1056 American Ale yeast, in ⅔-gal. (2.5 L) starter
28 lb. (12.7 kg) 2-row malt
 1 lb. (454 g) cara-pils malt
 1 lb. (454 g) caramel malt, 90° Lovibond
 1 lb. (454 g) malted wheat
 1 tsp. (4.9 ml) 30% phosphoric acid
 1 tsp. (4.9 ml) non-iodized salt
 1 tsp. (4.9 ml) water salts
 1 oz. (28 g) Chinook hops, 10.4% alpha, in boil 60 min.
 1 oz. (28 g) Liberty hops, 5.4% alpha, in boil 60 min.
 1 oz. (28 g) Liberty hops, 5.4% alpha, in boil 40 min.
 1 oz. (28 g) Chinook hops, 10.4% alpha, in boil 30 min.
 1 oz. (28 g) Liberty hops, 5.4% alpha, in boil 30 min.
 1 tbsp. (14.8 ml) Irish moss
 3 oz. (85 g) Cascade hops, 4.4% alpha, in boil 5 min.
1¼ oz. (7 g) packet gelatin, for fining

Four days in advance, make yeast starter.
   Mash-in all grains with 168°F (76°C) water. Treat mash with phosphoric acid, salts. Let rest for 1 hour at 150° – 157°F (66° – 69°C). Mash-out at 165°F (74°C) for 10 – 15 min. Sparge with 175°F (79°C) water to collect 15 gal. (56.8 L) of wort. Boil 30 min. before adding 1 oz. (28 g) each of Chinook and Liberty hops. Boil 20 min.; add 1 oz. (28 g) of Liberty hops. Boil 10 min., then add 1 oz. (28 g) each of Chinook and Liberty hops. Boil 10 min., then add Irish moss. Boil 15 min., then add Cascade hops. Boil 5 min., then turn off heat. Chill the wort, transfer to a primary fermenter, and pitch yeast. Ferment 7 days at 68°F (20°C). Rack to a secondary fermenter and ferment 7–14 days. Keg or bottle.

— Kurt Johnson, Schaumburg, Illinois

Sinner's Ale

YIELD:	9½ GAL. (36 L)
TOTAL BOILING TIME:	60 MIN.
STARTING GRAVITY:	1.053
ENDING GRAVITY:	1.011
PRIMARY FERMENT:	10–14 DAYS

10 lb. (4.54 kg) 2-row malt
5½ lb. (2.49 kg) Durst pilsner malt
1 lb. (454 g) Durst Munich malt
½ lb. (227 g) crystal malt, 120° Lovibond
2 ¾ oz. (78 g) Cascade leaf hops, 6.4% alpha, in boil 60 min.
1 tsp. (4.9 ml) Irish moss
½ oz. (14 g) Cascade leaf hops, 6.4% alpha, in boil 15 min.
    Yeast Lab A02 American Ale yeast, 2-quart (1.9 L) starter
2 c. (551 ml) malt extract, for priming

Mash in at 122° – 124°F (50° – 51°C). Let rest for 30 min. Heat mash to 152°F (67°C) and hold for 60 min. Mash-out at 170°F (77°C) for 10 min. Sparge with 8 gal. (30.3 L) of 170°F (77°C) water adjusted to pH 5.6 with lactic acid. Collect 12 gal. (45.4 L) of wort in brew kettle. Heat brew kettle to boiling and add 2¾ oz. (78 g) of Cascade leaf hops. Boil 40 min., then add Irish moss. Boil 5 min., then add ½ oz. (14 g) of Cascade hops. Boil 15 min., then turn off heat. Chill the wort, transfer to fermenter, and pitch yeast. Ferment 10–14 days, then prime with the malt extract and bottle.

— Mike Mueller and Steve Stacy, Rolla, Missouri
Missouri Association of Serious Homebrewers (MASH)

Three Roys Agree Ale

YIELD:	5 GAL. (18.9 L)
TOTAL BOILING TIME:	60 MIN.
STARTING GRAVITY:	1.050
ENDING GRAVITY:	1.011
PRIMARY FERMENT:	7 DAYS
SECONDARY FERMENT:	9 DAYS

9 lb. (4.08 kg) 2-row malt
1 lb. (454 g) 6-row malt
½ lb. (227 g) wheat malt

½ lb. (227 g) crystal malt, 80° Lovibond
½ lb. (227 g) crystal malt, 60° Lovibond
½ lb. (227 g) crystal malt, 40° Lovibond
2 oz. (57 g) Cluster whole hops, 7.4% alpha, in boil 60 min.
2 oz. (57 g) Cascade whole hops, 5.9% alpha, in boil 30 min.
1 oz. (28 g) Centennial hops, 11.3% alpha, in boil 2 min.
    Wyeast #1056 American Ale yeast
1 oz. (28 g) Centennial hops, 11.3% alpha, dry hop in keg

Add crushed grains to 3 gal. (11.4 L) of water and mash at 155°F (68°C) for 90 min. Mash-out at 170°F (77°C) for 10 min. Sparge with 4½ gal. (17 L) of 170°F (77°C) water. Bring to a boil and add the Cluster hops. Boil 30 min., then add the Cascade hops. Boil 28 min., then add 1 oz. (28 g) of Centennial hops. Boil 2 min. and turn off heat. Chill the wort, transfer to fermenter, and pitch yeast. Ferment 7 days, then rack to secondary. Ferment 9 days, then keg and add 1 oz. (28 g) of Centennial hops placed in a tea ball. Force carbonate and let age a week or two.

— Robert Erwin, Port Orchard, Washington

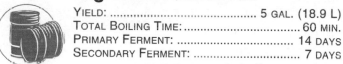

Big Chief Amber Ale

YIELD:	5 GAL. (18.9 L)
TOTAL BOILING TIME:	60 MIN.
PRIMARY FERMENT:	14 DAYS
SECONDARY FERMENT:	7 DAYS

Very smooth with a creamy head and nice hops aroma and flavor.

½ lb. (227 g) crystal malt, 40° Lovibond
6.6 lb. (3 kg) light unhopped malt extract
1½ oz. (43 g) Northern Brewer hops, 6.8% alpha, in boil 60 min.
1 oz. (28 g) Northern Brewer hops, 6.8% alpha, in boil 15 min.
2 tsp. (9.9 ml) Irish moss
    Wyeast #1028 London Ale yeast, 2-qt. (1.9 L) starter
1¼ c. (344 ml) dry malt extract, for priming

Crush grain, place in a grain bag, and steep in 2 gal. (7.6 L) of water until it reaches 170°F (77°C). Remove grain. Add malt extract and stir. Bring to a boil and add 1½ oz. (43 g) of Northern Brewer hops. Boil 45 min. Add 1 oz. (28 g) Northern Brewer hops and Irish moss. Boil 15 min. and turn off heat. Chill the wort, transfer to fermenter, and top off to 5 gal. (18.9 L) with cold water. Pitch yeast and ferment 14 days at 65°F (18°C). Rack to secondary fermenter and ferment 7 days at 62°F (17°C). Prime with the dry malt extract and bottle.

— *Gabrielle Palmer, Livonia, Michigan*

Fermental Order of Renaissance Draughtsmen (FORD)

Load King

YIELD:	12 GAL. (45.4 L)
TOTAL BOILING TIME:	60 MIN.
STARTING GRAVITY:	1.056
ENDING GRAVITY:	1.012
PRIMARY FERMENT:	5 DAYS
SECONDARY FERMENT:	10 DAYS

Hoppy with a hint of roast flavor.

22½ lb. (10.21 kg) 2-row pale malt
2 lb. (907 g) crystal malt, 40° Lovibond
1½ lb. (680 g) Victory malt
½ lb. (227 g) cara-pils malt
¼ lb. (113 g) roasted barley
1 tbsp. (14.8 ml) gypsum
2½ oz. (71 g) Chinook hops, 11.8% alpha, in boil 60 min.
1 oz. (28 g) Willamette hops, 4.7% alpha, in boil 30 min.
1 tbsp. (14.8 ml) Irish moss
1 oz. (28 g) Willamette hops, 4.7% alpha, in boil 15 min.
1 oz. (28 g) Cascade hops, 4.2% alpha, steep
Wyeast #1056 American Ale yeast
¼ oz. (7 g) Cascade hops, 4.2% alpha, dry hop in secondary

Add crushed grains to 10 gal. (37.9 L) of 165°F (69°C) water, treated with gypsum. Mash at 156°F (69°C), slowly dropping to 152°F (67°C) over 90 min. Sparge with 170°F (77°C) water and collect 13 gal. (49.2 L) of wort. Bring to a boil and add the Chinook hops. Boil 30 min., then add 1 oz. (28 g) of Willamette hops and Irish moss. Boil 15 min., then add 1 oz. (28 g) of Willamette hops. Boil 15 min., then turn off heat. Add 1 oz. (28 g) of Cascade hops and steep a few min. Chill the wort, transfer to fermenter, and pitch yeast. Ferment 5 days at 62°F (17°C). Rack to a secondary fermenter adding ¼ oz. (7 g) Cascade hops and ferment 10 days at 62°F (17°C). Keg and force carbonate.

— *John Nicholas Varady, Lafayette Hill, Pennsylvania*

Canadian Ale

YIELD:	5 GAL. (18.9 L)
TOTAL BOILING TIME:	60 MIN.
STARTING GRAVITY:	1.052
ENDING GRAVITY:	1.012
PRIMARY FERMENT:	1 WEEK
SECONDARY FERMENT:	1 WEEK

2 lb. (907 g) domestic 6-row lager malt
½ lb. (227 g) Belgian cara-pils malt
5 lb. (2.27 kg) light malt extract
1 package Burton water salts
1 lb. (454 g) brewery-grade corn syrup
⅔ oz. (19 g) Cluster hop pellets, in boil 55 min.
½ oz. (14 g) Cascade hops, in boil 15 min.
½ oz. (14 g) Cascade hops, steep
   Wyeast #1056 American Ale yeast or Wyeast #1007
1 package Bru-Vigor yeast food
⅞ c. (241 ml) brown sugar, for priming

Add crushed grains to 1 gal. (3.8 L) of 160°F (71°C) water and steep 30 min. Sparge grains with 1 gal. (3.8 L) of 168°F (76°C) water into brew kettle. Bring wort to a boil and add malt extract and corn syrup. Boil 5 min. before adding the Cluster hop pellets. Boil 40 min., then add ½ oz. (14 g) of Cascade hops. Boil 15 min., add last ½ oz. (14 g) of Cascade hops, and turn off heat. Steep a few min., then chill the wort, transfer to primary fermenter, and top off to 5 gal. (18.9 L) with cold water. Pitch yeast along with Bru-Vigor yeast food. Ferment 1 week. Rack to secondary fermenter and continue fermenting for 1 week. Prime with the brown sugar and bottle.

— DeFalco's Home Wine & Beer Supplies, Houston, Texas

Parachute Pale Ale

YIELD: .... 5 GAL. (18.9 L)
TOTAL BOILING TIME: .... 90 MIN.
PRIMARY FERMENT: .... 4 DAYS
SECONDARY FERMENT: .... 7 DAYS

7¼ lb. (3.24 kg) pale ale malt
1⅛ lb. (510 g) Munich malt
½ lb. (227 g) Belgian aromatic malt
½ lb. (227 g) Belgian biscuit malt
½ lb. (227 g) Belgian wheat malt
¼ lb. (113 g) Belgian Special-B malt
⅘ oz. (23 g) Centennial hops, 11.3% alpha, in boil 60 min.
1½ oz. (43 g) Cascade hops, 4.9% alpha, in boil 15 min.
1 oz. (28 g) Cascade hops, 4.9%, steep
Wyeast #1028 London Ale yeast
¾ c. (206 ml) corn sugar, for priming

Crush grains and add to 3½ gal. (13.1 L) of 163°F (73°C) water. Mash temperature should stabilize at 152°F (67°C). Mash for 100 min. Sparge with 170°F (77°C) water, collecting 6½–7 gal. (24.6–26.5 L) of wort. Boil 30 min. before adding the Centennial hops. Boil 45 min., then add 1½ oz. (43 g) of Cascade hops. Boil 15 min. Remove from heat and add 1 oz. (28 g) of Cascade hops. Chill the wort, transfer to a fermenter, and pitch yeast. Ferment 4 days at about 67°F (19°C). Rack to secondary fermenter and let sit another week. Prime with the corn sugar and bottle.

— Keith Chamberlin, Riverdale, Maryland
Brewers United for Real Potables (BURP)

Democratic Sunrise Pale Ale

YIELD: .... 5 GAL. (18.9 L)
TOTAL BOILING TIME: .... 90 MIN.
STARTING GRAVITY: 1.052–1.055
PRIMARY FERMENT: .... 5–7 DAYS
SECONDARY FERMENT: .... 7 DAYS

An award-winning pale ale with an unmistakable Cascade character.

    Wyeast #1098 British Ale yeast
9 ¾ lb. (4.42 kg) English pale ale malt
  ¼ lb. (113 g) crystal malt, 35° Lovibond
  ¼ lb. (113 g) malted wheat
1½ oz. (43 g) Cascade hops, 6.5% alpha, in boil 90 min.
  1 tsp. (4.9 ml) Irish moss
1½ oz. (43 g) Cascade hops, 6.5% alpha, in boil 15 min.
  1 oz. (28 g) Cascade hops, steep
  ¼ oz. (7 g) Cascade hops, dry hop in keg
  ¾ c. (206 ml) corn sugar, for priming, or force carbonate

Several days before brewing, begin growing up yeast starter.
    Crush grains and add to 3½ gal. (13.2 L) of 162°F (72°C) water. Mash for 60 min. at 151°F (66°C). Sparge with 170°F (77°C) water and collect 6½ gal. (24.6 L) of wort in brew kettle. Bring wort to a boil and add 1½ oz. (43 g) of Cascade hops. Boil 60 min., then add Irish moss. Boil 15 min., then add 1½ oz. (43 g) of Cascade hops. Boil 15 min. Remove from heat and add 1 oz. (28 g) of Cascade hops. Chill the wort, transfer to primary fermenter. Pitch yeast and ferment 5 – 7 days at 60° – 65°F (16° – 18°C). Transfer to secondary fermenter and ferment another week. Prime with the corn sugar and bottle, or keg and force carbonated.

— *David Brockington, Seattle, Washington*
Seattle Secret Skinny Brewers Society

INDIA PALE ALES

Skipjack IPA

YIELD:	5 GAL. (18.9 L)
TOTAL BOILING TIME:	90 MIN.
STARTING GRAVITY:	1.070
ENDING GRAVITY:	1.018
PRIMARY FERMENT:	7 DAYS
SECONDARY FERMENT:	7 DAYS

1½ tsp. (7.4 ml) calcium sulfate
1 lb. (454 g) 2-row pale malt
½ lb. (227 g) crystal malt, 64° Lovibond
6.6 lb. (3 kg) Northwestern Gold malt extract
1 lb. (454 g) dry malt extract
1½ oz. (43 g) Nugget hops, 12% alpha, in boil 75 min.
2 oz. (57 g) Kent Goldings hops, 5.5% alpha, in boil 30 min.
1 oz. (28 g) Kent Goldings hops, 5-min. steep
Wyeast #1028 London Ale yeast, 1-qt. (946 ml) starter

Add calcium sulfate to 6 gal. (22.7 L) of water in brew kettle; bring to a boil. Remove from heat. Place pale and crystal malts in a grain bag and add to water. Steep 10 min. Remove malt from water and discard. Add malt extracts and Nugget hops and bring to boil. Boil 45 min., then add 2 oz. (57 g) of Kent Goldings hops. Boil 30 min. Remove from heat and add 1 oz. (28 g) of Kent Goldings hops. Steep 5 min., then force chill the wort and transfer to primary fermenter. Pitch yeast and ferment 1 week at 60° – 65°F (16° – 18°C). Rack to a secondary fermenter and ferment an additional week. Keg and force carbonate.

— *Keith Hooker, Upper Marlboro, Maryland*
Brewers United for Real Potables (BURP)

Sister Star of the Sun

YIELD: .... 5 GAL. (18.9 L)
TOTAL BOILING TIME: .... 90 MIN.
STARTING GRAVITY: 1.060–1.065
ENDING GRAVITY: 1.010–1.012
PRIMARY FERMENT: .... 5–7 DAYS
SECONDARY FERMENT: .... 1–2 WEEKS

I consider this to be the perfect IPA. Don't be afraid of the large amount of hops in the kettle.

Wyeast #1028 London Ale yeast, 1-pt. (473 ml) starter
13 lb. (5.9 kg) Hugh Baird pale ale 2-row malt
¼ lb. (113 g) Hugh Baird crystal malt, 130° Lovibond
¼ lb. (113 g) wheat malt
3 oz. (85 g) Chinook hops, 10.9% alpha, in boil 90 min.
1 tsp. (4.9 ml) Irish moss
2 oz. (57 g) Kent Goldings hops, 5.1% alpha, in boil 15 min.
2 oz. (57 g) U.K. Fuggles hops, 4.4% alpha, steep
¼ oz. (7 g) U.K. Fuggles, dry hop in keg

Several days before brewing, start growing a fresh yeast starter.
Crush grains and add to 4½ gal. (17 L) of 162°F (72°C) water. Mash at 151°F (66°C) for 60 min. Sparge with 170°F (77°C) water and collect 6½ gal. (24.6 L) of wort. Bring wort to a boil and add the Chinook hops. Boil 60 min., then add Irish moss. Boil 15 min., then add Kent Goldings hops. Boil 15 min. Remove from heat and add 2 oz. (57 g) of U.K. Fuggles hops. Chill the wort and transfer to fermenter. Ferment 5 – 7 days at 60° – 65°F (16° – 18°C), transfer to secondary and ferment 1 – 2 weeks. Keg beer and add ¼ oz. (7 g) U.K. Fuggles in a hop bag.

— *David and Melinda Brockington, Seattle, Washington*
Seattle Secret Skinny Brewers Society

Yellow Aster IPA

YIELD: .... 5 GAL. (18.9 L)
TOTAL BOILING TIME: .... 60 MIN.
STARTING GRAVITY: 1.062
ENDING GRAVITY: 1.015
PRIMARY FERMENT: .... 10 DAYS
SECONDARY FERMENT: .... 11 DAYS

Full-bodied dark amber brew with intense hop bitterness and citric Cascade finish.

Sierra Nevada Pale Ale yeast culture
1 tsp. (4.9 ml) gypsum
10 lb. (4.54 kg) 2-row pale malt
1 lb. (454 g) cara-pils malt
1 lb. (454 g) crystal malt, 40° Lovibond
¾ oz. (21 g) Centennial hops, 11.3% alpha, in boil 60 min.
¾ oz. (21 g) Chinook hops, 12.7% alpha, in boil 60 min.
¼ oz. (7 g) Cascade hops, 5.6% alpha, in boil 60 min.
1 tsp. (4.9 ml) Irish moss
½ oz. (14 g) Centennial hops, in boil 15 min.
½ oz. (14 g) Cascade hops, in boil 15 min.
½ oz. (14 g) Centennial hops, in boil 2 min.
½ oz. (14 g) Cascade hops, in boil 2 min.
½ oz. (14 g) Cascade hops, dry hop in secondary fermenter
¾ c. (206 ml) corn sugar, for priming

Begin a yeast starter several days in advance.

Mash in at 122° F for 30 min. Raise to 155° F for 60 min. Sparge to collect 6 gal. Bring wort to a boil and add ¾ oz. (21 g) each of Centennial hops and Chinook hops and ¼ oz. (7 g) of Cascade hops. Boil 45 min.; add the Irish moss and ½ oz. (14 g) each of Centennial hops and Cascade hops. Boil 13 min.; add ½ oz. (14 g) each of Centennial hops and Cascade hops. Boil 2 min. Turn off heat, chill wort, and transfer to fermenter. Pitch yeast. Ferment 10 days at 62°F (17°C). Rack to secondary, dry hop with ½ oz. (14 g) of Cascade and ferment 11 days at 62°F (17°C). Prime with corn sugar and bottle.

— *Scott Graham, Bellingham, Washington*

Columbian Gold IPA

YIELD: .... 5 GAL. (18.9 L)
TOTAL BOILING TIME:.................................. 90 MIN.
STARTING GRAVITY: 1.064
ENDING GRAVITY: 1.016
PRIMARY FERMENT: .... 1 WEEK
SECONDARY FERMENT: .... 1–2 WEEKS

American Type Culture Collection #1187 yeast, 1.6-qt.
   (1½-L)starter
12 lb. (5.4 kg) Briess 2-row pale malt
½ lb. (227 g) DeWolf-Cosyns biscuit malt
½ lb. (227 g) Gambrinus honey malt
1 lb. (454 g) DeWolf-Cosyns cara-Vienne malt
1 lb. (454 g) DeWolf-Cosyns Munich malt
2 oz. (57 g) Columbus hops, 9.5% alpha, in boil 60 min.
½ oz. (14 g) Columbus hops, 9.5% alpha, in boil 15 min.
½ oz. (14 g) Cascade hops 5.5% alpha, in boil 15 min.
½ oz. (14 g) Columbus hops, steep
1 oz. (28 g) Cascade hops, steep
¾ c. (206 ml) corn sugar for priming (if bottling)

Several days before brewing, start growing up a yeast starter.

    Add crushed grains to 5 gal. (18.9 L) of 169°F (76°C) water. Mash at 158°F (70°C) for 60 min. Raise temperature to 168°F (76°C) for a 10 min. mash-out. Sparge with 170°F (77°C) water, collecting 7 gal. (26.5 L) of wort. Boil 30 min. before adding 2 oz. (57 g) of Columbus hops. Boil 45 min., then add ½ oz. (14 g) each of Columbus and Cascade. Boil 15 min., then turn off heat. Add another ½ oz. (14 g) of Columbus and 1 oz. (28 g) of Cascade and steep a few min. Chill the wort and transfer to primary fermenter. Pitch yeast starter and ferment at 65° – 70°F (18° – 21°C) for several days, then rack to secondary fermenter for another 1–2 weeks. Keg or bottle.

— Delano Dugarm, Arlington, Virginia
Brewers United for Real Potables (BURP)

ADELAIDE SPARKLING ALE

A2 Sparkling Ale

YIELD: .... 5 GAL. (18.9 L)
TOTAL BOILING TIME: .... 120 MIN.
STARTING GRAVITY: 1.058
ENDING GRAVITY: 1.016
PRIMARY FERMENT: .... 5 WEEKS

A good approximation of Cooper's Sparkling Ale.

- 10 lb. (4.54 kg) 2-row pale malt
- 1 lb. (454 g) crystal malt, 40° Lovibond
- ½ oz. (14 g) Pride of Ringwood hop pellets, 11% alpha, added during sparge
- 1½ oz. (43 g) Pride of Ringwood hop pellets, 11% alpha, in boil 120 min.
- 1 lb. (454 g) table sugar
- Yeast Lab A01 Australian Ale yeast
- 1 c. (275 ml) corn sugar, for priming

Crush malt and add to 7½ qt. (7.1 L) of 140°F (60°C) water. Let sit for 40 min. Add 3½ qt. (3.3 L) of boiling water to the mash and stir until the temperature settles at 156°F (69°C). Rest for 1½ hours. Heat to 170°F (77°C) and hold for 10 min. Sparge with 5 gal. (18.9 L) of 170°F (77°C) water and collect wort in brew kettle. Add ½ oz. (14 g) of Pride of Ringwood hop pellets as soon as the bottom of the brew kettle is covered with the wort. Bring wort to a boil and add remaining hop pellets and the table sugar. Boil 2 hours, then turn off heat. Chill the wort, transfer to fermenter, pitch yeast, and aerate well. Ferment 5 weeks at 60°F (16°C), then prime with the corn sugar and bottle.

— *Craig D. Amundsen, St. Paul, Minnesota*

More
HOMEBREW FAVORITES
3
Brown Ales

Brown ale is known as a drink of the working man (or woman): a light-bodied, but malty beer. Darker in color with less hops than pale ales, it is lighter in color than porter, with more golden hues in its brownness than the red hues in a porter's blackness. Brown ales are not heavy beers nor excessively sweet, although they often have some toasty caramel or nut-like flavors. The three main subcategories of brown ale that are typically recognized in homebrew competitions are: mild, English brown, and American brown.

Mild ale is a light-bodied, malty-tasting brown ale with fairly low hopping rates. According to Roger Protz, in his book *The Ultimate Encyclopedia of Beer*, in England, mild ales and brown ales are the same beer, but a mild ale is served on draft and a brown ale is bottled. In America, however, homebrewers tend to view an English brown ale as being a bit more full bodied than the mild. A mild should be a soft, gentle ale that can be consumed in good quantities. Milds are usually quite low in alcohol, about 3.5 percent by volume, and are brewed to low original gravities (1.030 to 1.038). The color should be a light amber to dark brown, about 8 to 35 SRM.

KEY TO RECIPE LOGOS

 EXTRACT RECIPES

 PARTIAL MASH RECIPES

 ALL-GRAIN RECIPES

The grain bill for a mild ale can vary. A popular combination is a base malt such as Maris Otter with caramel malt for color, although other brewers may use a touch of brown, black, or chocolate malt. Exercise a restrained touch if using darker grains. A single ounce of chocolate malt might be too much for a 5-gal. (18.9 L) batch of mild. Use typical English varieties of hops, such as East Kent Goldings. Milds should be hopped at between 10 and 25 IBUs. The key to a successful mild is to make the beer as malty as possible.

English browns and milds are brewed using typical English methods: a single-step infusion mash and typical ale fermentation. Yeasts used for a brown ale are the same as you would use for a pale ale. Some reasonable choices might be the Wyeast #1028 London Ale or #1098 British Ale yeasts, or the Yeast Lab British Ale (A04). An American brown ale might use an American ale yeast.

English brown ale is a malty beer with a light body. It's very much like a mild ale, lending credence to Protz's view that they're the same beer. The hops should be fairly subdued, with low bitterness. The classic example of an English brown ale is Newcastle. The beer is not by any means dark, but rather a deep golden brown. The flavor can be nutty. Southern brown ales may be darker and sweeter. As is the case with virtually all beer styles, historically accurate recipes would be substantially heavier in body and color (probably 1.050 or higher for a 19th-century mild). Mild ales are the inverse of bitter ales in terms of their flavors. Whereas bitter emphasizes hop flavor, mild emphasizes malt flavor.

American brown ales tend to be normal-gravity beers (1.045 to 1.055) with a lot of maltiness but an assertive hop character. The hops are two to three times the amount used for an English brown; otherwise the grain bills and processes would be similar. American varieties of hops are generally preferred. Pete's Wicked Ale, often regarded as the quintessential American brown ale, is made using Brewers Gold and Cascade hops at 29 IBU.

Some brewers enjoy experimenting with variations on a classic style, perhaps adding an ingredient or changing a process. Some of the specialty variations on brown ale include the popular honey-brown, incorporating a bit of fresh honey, or sometimes more unusual things, like a touch of smoked malt.

In competitions, the key to successful milds and English browns is subtlety. The beers should be clear, malty, and refreshingly light.

The color should not be too light or dark, but a variant of brown. If the beer is black, or hard to see through, it would probably do better competing as a porter. If the mild ale you brewed has a gravity over 1.040, it should do better competing as an English or American brown. If the beer is noticeably hoppy, try the American brown category.

MILD ALES

Halloween Mild

YIELD: .... 5 GAL. (18.9 L)
TOTAL BOILING TIME: .... 60 MIN.
STARTING GRAVITY: 1.036
ENDING GRAVITY: 1.010
PRIMARY FERMENT: .... 5 DAYS
SECONDARY FERMENT: .... 7 DAYS

1¼ lb. (567 g) 2-row palo malt
¼ lb. (113 g) crystal malt
¼ lb. (113 g) chocolate malt
¼ lb. (113 g) black patent malt
3.3 lb. (1.5 kg) Northwestern Gold malt extract
1 oz. (28 g.) East Kent Goldings hops, 5.2% alpha, in boil 60 min.
2 oz. (59 ml) Brer Rabbit mild molasses
1 tsp. (4.9 ml) Irish moss
Wyeast #1098 British Ale yeast
⅓ c. (92 ml) corn sugar, for priming

Mash grains in ¾ gal. (2.8 L) of water at 151°F (66°C), until starch conversion is complete. Sparge with 2 gal. (7.6 L) or so of 170°F (77°C) water. Bring wort to a boil and add malt extract. Add hops, and boil 15 min., then add molasses. Boil 15 min., then add the Irish moss. Boil 30 min., then turn off heat. Chill the wort, transfer to fermenter, and bring up to 5 gal. (18.9 L) with cold water. Pitch yeast and ferment 5 days at 65°F (18°C). Rack to secondary fermenter and ferment 7 days at 65°F (18°C). Prime with corn sugar and bottle.

— Lisa Hudock, West Chester, Pennsylvania
Beer Unlimited Zany Zymurgists (BUZZ)

Special Session

YIELD: .... 5 GAL. (18.9 L)
TOTAL BOILING TIME: .... 90 MIN.
STARTING GRAVITY: 1.036
PRIMARY FERMENT: .... 5–7 DAYS
SECONDARY FERMENT: .... 1–2 WEEKS

Wyeast #1318 London Ale III yeast

gypsum and Burton salts, to bring waters to Burton profile

6 lb. (2.72 kg) English pale ale malt

½ lb. (227 g) Hugh Baird crystal malt (80° Lovibond)

½ lb. (227 g) Hugh Baird brown malt

¼ lb. (113 g) chocolate malt

¼ lb. (113 g) wheat malt

¾ oz. (21 g) East Kent Goldings hops, 7.3% alpha, in boil 60 min.

1 tsp. (4.9 ml) Irish moss

1 oz. (28 g) U.K. Fuggles hops, 4.6% alpha, in boil 15 min.

1 oz. (28 g) Willamette hops, steep

¼ oz. (7 g) U.K. Fuggles, dry hop in keg

¾ c. (206 ml) corn sugar, for priming (if bottling) or force
carbonate

Several days before brewing, begin growing up yeast starter.

Treat water to Burton profile. Add crushed grains to 2½ gal. (9.5 L) of 167°F (75°C) water. Mash at 156°F (69°C) for 60 min. Raise temperature to 170°F (77°C) for a 10-min. mash-out. Sparge with 170°F (77°C) water and collect 7 gal. (26.5 L) of wort. Boil 30 min. Add the East Kent Goldings hops. Boil 30 min.; add Irish moss. Boil 15 min.; add 1 oz. (28 g) of U.K. Fuggles hops. Boil 15 min. and turn off heat. Add Willamette hops; steep for a couple minutes. Chill the wort and transfer to fermenter. Pitch yeast starter and ferment 5 – 7 days at 60° – 65°F (16° – 18°C). Transfer to secondary, ferment another 1 – 2 weeks. Keg and put ¼ oz. U.K. Fuggles in hop bag, adding to keg.

— *David Brockington, Seattle, Washington*
Seattle Secret Skinny Brewers Society

American Mild

YIELD: .... 10 GAL. (37.9 L)
TOTAL BOILING TIME: .... 90 MIN.
STARTING GRAVITY: 1.034
ENDING GRAVITY: 1.005
PRIMARY FERMENT: .... 3–4 DAYS
SECONDARY FERMENT: .... 7 DAYS

Yeast Culture Kit Company ale yeast, 67.6-oz. (2-L) slurry
11 lb. (4.99 kg) Briess 2-row pale malt
¾ lb. (340 g) cara-Vienne malt
¼ lb. (113 g) black patent malt
½ lb. (227 g) Special-B malt
½ lb. (227 g) chocolate malt
1 lb. (454 g) Munich malt
¼ lb. (113 g) brown malt
¼ lb. (113 g) aromatic malt
¼ lb. (113 g) biscuit malt
1⅔ oz. (47 g) Centennial hops, 8.8% alpha, in boil 60 min.
1 oz. (28 g) Cascade hops, 5.5% alpha, in boil 15 min.
1 oz. (28 g) Cascade hops, 5.5% alpha, in boil 5 min.
1½ oz. (43 g) Cascade hops (cask hopped)

Several days before brewing, begin growing up a starter of the ale yeast.
    Add crushed grains to 5 gal. (18.9 L) of 161°F (72°C) water. Mash at
150°F (66°C) for 90 min. Sparge with 170°F (77°C) water, collecting 12
gal. (45.4 L) of wort. Boil 30 min. before adding the Centennial hops. Boil
45 min.; add 1 oz. (28 g) of Cascade hops. Boil 10 min.; add 1 oz. (28 g) of
Cascade hops. Boil 5 min.; turn off heat. Chill the wort, transfer to
fermenter, and pitch yeast slurry. Ferment 3 – 4 days; transfer to a
secondary fermenter. Let ferment for another week. Prepare two hop
bags with ¾ oz. (21 g) of Cascade hops in each. Keg beer, adding one hop
bag to each keg.

— Delano Dugarm, Arlington, Virginia
Brewers United for Real Potables (BURP)

Domestic Bliss Mild

YIELD: .... 5 GAL. (18.9 L)
TOTAL BOILING TIME: .... 90 MIN.
STARTING GRAVITY: 1.038
ENDING GRAVITY: 1.008
PRIMARY FERMENT: .... 7 DAYS
SECONDARY FERMENT: .... 7 DAYS

6 lb. (2.72 kg) pale ale malt

1 lb. (454 g) Munich malt

½ lb. (227 g) cara-Munich malt

2 oz. (57 g) black patent malt

¼ lb. (113 g) crystal malt, 80° Lovibond

¼ lb. (113 g) cara-Vienne malt

1 oz. (28 g) East Kent Goldings hops, in boil 60 min.

Wyeast #1056 American Ale yeast

¾ c. (206 ml) corn sugar, for priming

Add crushed grains to 2⅔ gal. (10.1 L) of 164°F (73°C) water. Mash at 153°F (67°C) for 60 min. Sparge with 170°F (77°C) water, collecting 7 gal. (26.5 L) of wort. Boil 30 min. before adding the East Kent Goldings hops. Boil 1 hour, then turn off heat. Chill the wort, transfer to a primary fermenter, and pitch yeast. Ferment 7 days at 65°F (18°C). Rack to a secondary fermenter and ferment 7 more days. Prime with the corn sugar and bottle.

— Polly Goldman, Alexandria, Virginia
Brewers United for Real Potables (BURP)

English Mild

YIELD: .... 12 GAL. (45.4 L)
TOTAL BOILING TIME: .... 60 MIN.
STARTING GRAVITY: 1.036
PRIMARY FERMENT; .... 7 DAYS
SECONDARY FERMENT: .... 12 DAYS

10 lb. (4.54 kg) DeWolf-Cosyns pale ale malt
 1 lb. (454 g) DeWolf-Cosyns cara-Munich malt
 ½ lb. (227 g) chocolate malt
 ¼ lb. (113 g) black patent malt
 30 g gypsum
 1 lb. (454 g) brown sugar
   lactic acid, for water pH
 2 oz. (57 g) Kent Goldings leaf hops, 5.0% alpha, in boil 60 min.
 7/10 oz. (20 g) Irish moss
 ½ oz. (14 g) Kent Goldings leaf hops, 5.0% alpha, in boil 2 min.
 3.2 c. (1.5-L) BrewTek CL-160 British Draft Ale yeast starter
 1½ c. (413 ml) corn sugar, for priming

Crush grains and add to 4 gal. (15.1 L) of 165°F (74°C) water, treated with gypsum. Mash at 155°F (68°C) for 60 min. Mash-out at 170°F (77°C) for 10 min. Sparge with 12 gal. (45.4 L) of 170°F (77°C) water, adjusted to pH 5.4 with lactic acid. Collect 12½ gal. (47.3 L) of wort in brew kettle. Boil and add 2 oz. (57 g) of Kent Goldings hops. Boil 40 min., then add Irish moss. Boil 18 min., then add ½ oz. (14 g) of Kent Goldings hops. Boil 2 min., then turn off heat. Chill the wort, transfer to a primary fermenter, and pitch yeast starter. Ferment 7 days at 64°F (18°C). Rack to a secondary fermenter and ferment at 49°F (9°C) for 12 days. Prime with the corn sugar and bottle.

— *Steve Stacy and Mike Mueller, Rolla, Missouri*
Missouri Association of Serious Homebrewers (MASH)

ENGLISH BROWN ALES

Nekkid Druids Nut Brown Ale

YIELD: .... 5 GAL. (18.9 L)
TOTAL BOILING TIME: .... 75 MIN.
PRIMARY FERMENT: .... 8 DAYS
SECONDARY FERMENT: .... 2–3 WEEKS

A sweet brown ale, perfectly balanced by hops, with a unique nuttiness.

  1 lb. (454 g) chocolate malt, cracked
  ¼ lb. (113 g) crystal malt, 60° Lovibond, cracked
6.6 lb. (3 kg) light unhopped malt extract
  ½ oz. (14 g) Fuggles hops, 4.4% alpha, in boil 75 min.
  ½ oz. (14 g) Fuggles hops, 4.4% alpha, in boil 60 min.
  ½ oz. (14 g) Fuggles hops, 4.4% alpha, in boil 45 min.
  ½ oz. (14 g) Fuggles hops, 4.4% alpha, in boil 30 min.
  2 tsp. (10 ml) Irish moss
  ½ oz. (14 g) Fuggles hops, 4.4% alpha, in boil 15 min.
  ½ oz. (14 g) Fuggles hops, 4.4% alpha, in boil 5 min.
      Wyeast #1028 London Ale yeast, 2-qt. (1.9-L) starter
1¼ c. (344 ml) dry malt extract, for priming
  1 tbsp. (14.8 ml) vanilla extract, for priming

Place cracked grains in a grain bag. Steep bag in 2 gal. (7.6 L) of water; heat until it reaches 165°F (74°C). Remove from heat, cover, and let sit for 45 – 60 min. Remove grain bag (and grains); add malt extract. Return to heat; bring to a boil. Add ½ oz. (14 g) of Fuggles hops; boil 15 min. Add ½ oz. (14 g) of Fuggles hops; boil 15 min. Add another ½ oz. (14 g) of Fuggles hops; boil 15 min. Add ½ oz. (14 g) of Fuggles hops; boil 15 min. Add Irish moss and ½ oz. (14 g) of Fuggles hops; boil 10 min. Add last ½ oz. (14 g) of Fuggles hops; boil 5 min. Chill the wort, transfer to a fermenter, and top off to 5 gal. (18.9 L) with cold water. Pitch yeast and ferment 8 days at 65°F (18°C). Rack to a secondary fermenter; continue fermenting 2–3 weeks at 65°F (18°C). Prime with dry malt and vanilla extracts, then bottle.

— Gabrielle Palmer, Livonia, Michigan
Fermental Order of Renaissance Draughtsmen (FORD)

Beagle Boys Brown Ale

YIELD: .... 5 GAL. (18.9 L)
TOTAL BOILING TIME: .... 80 MIN.
STARTING GRAVITY: 1.048
ENDING GRAVITY: 1.013

This is a very rich-tasting, English-type brown ale, inspired by Deschutes Bond Street Brown.

    8 oz. (227 g) cara-Munich malt
    8 oz. (227 g) Belgian special-B malt
    2 oz. (57 g) black patent malt
  3.3 lb. (1.5 kg) John Bull light unhopped malt extract
  2½   lb. (1.13 kg) Briess amber dry malt extract
    1 oz. (28 g) Northern Brewer hops, 7.5% alpha, in boil 60 min.
  ½   oz. (14 g) Fuggles hops, 4.4% alpha, in boil 30 min.
  ³⁄₁₆ oz. (5.3 g) East Kent Goldings hops, 5.0% alpha, in boil
        10–15 min.
       Yeast Lab A07 Canadian Ale yeast
  ⅝   c. (172 ml) corn sugar, for priming

Steep crushed grains in 3 gal. (11.4 L) of water at 150° – 160°F (66° – 71°C) for 30 min. Sparge with 3 gal. (11.4 L) of water. Add malt extracts and bring to a boil. Boil 20 min. Add the Northern Brewer hops and boil 30 min. Add the Fuggles hops and boil 15 – 20 min. Add the East Kent Goldings hops and boil 10 – 15 min. Turn off heat and chill the wort. Transfer to a primary fermenter and pitch yeast. Rack to a secondary fermenter after primary fermentation subsides. Prime with the corn sugar and bottle.

— *Douglas Faynor, Salem, Oregon, Homebrew Heaven*
Capitol Brewers of Salem

Dark Ale

YIELD: .... 5 GAL. (18.9 L)
TOTAL BOILING TIME: .... 25 MIN.
STARTING GRAVITY: 1.040–1.045
ENDING GRAVITY: 1.012
PRIMARY FERMENT: .... 4–5 DAYS
SECONDARY FERMENT: .... 7–14 DAYS

½ lb. (227 g) crystal malt
¼ lb. (113 g) chocolate malt
6.6 cans (3 kg) Muntons amber hopped extract
1 oz. (28 g) Goldings hops, 4.5% alpha, in boil 20 min.
½ lb. (227 g) Brewbody malto-dextrins
1 oz. (28 g) Goldings hops, 4.5% alpha, steep 10 min.
ale yeast
1 c. (275 ml) corn sugar, for priming

In a large pot, add 1 gal. (3.8 L) of cold water and crushed grains. Bring near to a boil, then turn off heat and steep grains 30 min. Remove grains from the water. Add 1 oz. (28 g) of Goldings hops and boil 20 min. Turn off heat and dissolve cans of malt extract and Brewbody. Boil 5 min. Turn off heat, add 1 oz. (28 g) of Goldings hops, and steep 10 min. Strain out hops and add hot wort to the primary fermenter. Add very cold water until you reach 5 gal. (18.9 L) in the primary fermenter. When the wort temperature is below 80°F (27°C), add yeast and stir vigorously. Ferment 4–5 days, then rack to 5-gal. (18.9-L) secondary fermenter. Ferment 1–2 weeks. Prime with the corn sugar and bottle.

— Ivan Crash, Indianapolis, Indiana, Wine-Art

Brown Ale

YIELD: .... 5 GAL. (18.9 L)
TOTAL BOILING TIME: .... 60 MIN.
STARTING GRAVITY: 1.046
ENDING GRAVITY: 1.012
PRIMARY FERMENT: .... 7 DAYS
SECONDARY FERMENT: .... OPTIONAL

Wyeast #1098 British Ale yeast (or #1338)
1 lb. (454 g) mild ale malt

 1 lb. (454 g) medium crystal malt
½ lb. (227 g) Special-B malt
 1 package Burton water salts
 6 lb. (2.72 kg) amber unhopped malt extract
⅔ oz. (19 g) British Blend hop pellets, in boil 55 min.
½ oz. (14 g) Fuggles or Willamette hops, in boil 15 min.
½ oz. (14 g) Fuggles or Willamette hops, steep
 1 package Bru-Vigor yeast food
½ c. (138 ml) dark brown sugar, for priming

Prepare yeast starter prior to brewing day.

Add crushed grains and water salts to 1 gal. (3.8 L) of 160°F (71°C) water and steep 30 min. Remove grains, rinsing with 1 gal. hot water. Bring wort to a boil, then turn off heat and add malt extract. Boil 5 min., add ⅔ oz. (19 g) of British Blend hop pellets, boil another 40 min., then add ½ oz. (14 g) of Fuggles or Willamette hops. Boil 15 min., then add last ½ oz. (14 g) of Fuggles or Willamette hops and turn off heat. Steep a few min., then chill the wort, transfer to fermenter, and top off to 5 gal. (18.9 L) with cold water. Pitch yeast along with Bru-Vigor yeast food. Ferment for 1 week. Prime with the dark brown sugar and bottle.

— *DeFalco's Home Wine & Beer Supplies, Houston, Texas*

Buffalo-Buttocks Brown Ale

YIELD: .... 5 GAL. (18.9 L)
TOTAL BOILING TIME: .... 60 MIN.
PRIMARY FERMENT: .... 7 DAYS
SECONDARY FERMENT: .... 7 DAYS

  2 lb. (908 g) 2-row pale malt
 ½ lb. (227 g) crystal malt, 40° Lovibond
 ¼ oz. (7 g) chocolate malt
3.3 lb. (1.5 kg) light malt extract
  1 lb. (454 g) brown sugar
1½ oz. (43 g) Fuggles hop pellets, 3.8% alpha, in boil 60 min.
    Wyeast #1028 London Ale yeast
 ¾ c. (206 ml) corn sugar, for priming

Mash all grains in 1½ gal. (5.7 L) of water at 150°F (66°C) for 60 min. Sparge with 5 gal. (18.9 L) of 170°F (77°C) water. Add malt extract and brown sugar, then bring to a boil. Add Fuggles hop pellets and boil 60 min. Chill the wort, transfer to fermenter, and pitch yeast. Ferment 7 days at 65°F (18°C). Rack to a secondary fermenter and ferment 7 days. Prime with corn sugar and bottle, or keg.

— *Tom Sallese, Baltimore, Maryland, Cross Street Irregulars*

AMERICAN BROWN ALES

Beaver Brown Ale

YIELD: .... 5 GAL. (18.9 L)
TOTAL BOILING TIME: .... 60 MIN.
STARTING GRAVITY: 1.054
ENDING GRAVITY: 1.015
PRIMARY FERMENT: .... 9 DAYS
SECONDARY FERMENT: .... 10 DAYS

First place at the 1995 Oregon Homebrew Festival.

    ½ lb. (227 g) crystal malt, 40° Lovibond
    ½ lb. (227 g) chocolate malt
    7 lb. (3.18 kg) amber malt extract
    2½ oz. (71 g) Kent Goldings hops, 5.0% alpha, in boil 60 min.
    ½ oz. (14 g) Kent Goldings hops, 5.0% alpha, in boil 5 min.
    2 packs Edme ale yeast
    ¾ c. (206 ml) corn sugar, for priming

Add crushed grains to 2 gal. (7.6 L) of cold water and bring to a boil. Strain out grains as boil begins. Add malt extract and 2½ oz. (71 g) of Kent Goldings hops and boil 55 min. Add ½ oz. (14 g) of Kent Goldings hops and boil 5 min. Chill the wort and transfer to fermenter, topping off to 5 gal. (18.9 L) with cold water. Pitch yeast and ferment 9 days at 68°F (20°C). Rack to secondary and ferment 10 days at 68°F (20°C). Prime with corn sugar and bottle.

— *Herky Gottfried, Corvallis, Oregon*

Tyrant Ale

YIELD: .... 5 GAL. (18.9 L)
TOTAL BOILING TIME: .... 60 MIN.
STARTING GRAVITY: 1.063
ENDING GRAVITY: 1.020
PRIMARY FERMENT: .... 1 WEEK
SECONDARY FERMENT: .... 3 WEEKS

  1 lb. (454 g) amber crystal malt
6.6 lb. (3 kg) Northwestern amber malt extract
  1 lb. (454 g) Laaglander extra light dry malt extract
1¼ oz. (35 g) Brewers Gold hops, 7.8% alpha, in boil 60 min.
  1 tsp. (4.9 ml) Irish moss
  1 oz. (28 g) Willamette hops, 4.0% alpha, steep
     Wyeast #1028 London Ale yeast
  ½ oz. (14 g) Willamette hops, 4.0% alpha, dry hop
  1 tsp. (4.9 ml) gypsum
  ¾ c. (206 ml) corn sugar, for priming

Crush grain and add to 2 gal. (7.6 L) of water. Steep at 150°F (66°C) for 30 min. Strain out grain and heat to boiling. Add malt extracts and the Brewers Gold hops. Boil 45 min., then add Irish moss. Boil 15 min., then turn off heat. Add 1 oz. (28 g) of Willamette hops and steep for a few min. Chill the wort; transfer to primary fermenter while straining out hops. Top off to 5 gal. (18.9 L) with cold water and pitch yeast. Ferment 1 week, then rack to secondary and add ½ oz. (14 g) of Willamette hops. Ferment 3 weeks, then prime.

— *Jeff Hewit, Midlothian, Virginia, James River Homebrewers*

Best Brown This Side o' the Pecos

YIELD:	5 GAL. (18.9 L)
TOTAL BOILING TIME:	60 MIN.
STARTING GRAVITY:	1.060
ENDING GRAVITY:	1.023
PRIMARY FERMENT:	1 WEEK
SECONDARY FERMENT:	2 WEEKS

12 oz. (340 g) crystal malt, 60° Lovibond

3.3 lb. (1.5 kg) Stone Brewery dark malt extract

2½ lb. (1.13 kg) Premier light dry malt extract

1½ lb. (680 g) Premier amber dry malt extract

1 oz. (28 g) Cascade hops, 5.5% alpha, in boil 60 min.

½ oz. (14 g) Cascade hops, 5.5% alpha, in boil 30 min.

3 oz. (85 g) malto-dextrin

½ oz. (14 g) Cascade hops, 5.5% alpha, in boil 15 min.

2 tsp. (9.9 ml) Irish moss

1 oz. (28 g) Cascade hops, 5.5% alpha, in boil 2 min.

Yeast Lab A06 Dusseldorf Ale yeast

¾ c. (206 ml) corn sugar, for priming

Bring 2½ gal. (9.5 L) of water to 170°F (77°C) and add the crystal malt. Steep 30 min. Strain out and sparge grains. Bring to a boil. Remove from heat and add malt extracts. Resume boiling and add 1 oz. (28 g) of Cascade hops. Boil 30 min. Add ½ oz. (14 g) of Cascade hops and malto-dextrin. Boil 15 min., then add ½ oz. (14 g) of Cascade hops and Irish moss. Boil 13 min., then add 1 oz. (28 g) of Cascade hops. Boil 2 min., then turn off heat. Chill the wort, transfer to fermenter, and pitch yeast. Ferment 1 week, then rack to secondary. Ferment 2 more weeks, then prime and bottle.

— *Craig Seiffert, Billings, Montana, Billings Homebrewers' Supply*

American Brown Ale

YIELD: .... 5 GAL. (18.9 L)
TOTAL BOILING TIME: .... 60 MIN.
STARTING GRAVITY: 1.050
ENDING GRAVITY: 1.012
PRIMARY FERMENT: .... 1 WEEK
SECONDARY FERMENT: .... 1 WEEK

    Wyeast #1056 American Ale yeast, in a starter
1½ lb. (680 g) 2-row malt
 ½ lb. (227 g) British medium crystal malt
 ½ lb. (227 g) British cara-pils malt
 ¼ lb. (113 g) chocolate malt
 6 lb. (2.7 kg) amber malt extract
 1 oz. (28 g) Cascade hop pellets, in boil 55 min.
⅔ oz. (19 g) Willamette hops, in boil 15 min.
⅓ oz. (9 g) Willamette hops, steep
 1 package Bru-Vigor yeast food
¾ c. (206 ml) corn sugar, for priming

Prepare yeast starter prior to brewing day.

Add crushed grains to 1 gal. (3.8 L) of 160°F (71°C) water and steep 30 min. Sparge grains with 1 gal. (3.8 L) of 168°F (76°C) water into brew kettle. Bring to a boil, then turn off heat and add malt extract. Return wort to a boil and add the Cascade hops. Boil 45 min., then add ⅔ oz. (19 g) of Willamette hops. Boil 15 min., add last ⅓ oz. (9 g) of Willamette hops, and turn off heat. Steep a few min., then chill the wort, transfer to fermenter, and top off to 5 gal. (18.9 L) with cold water. Pitch yeast along with Bru-Vigor yeast food. Ferment 1 week. Rack to secondary and ferment 1 week. Prime with corn sugar and bottle.

— *DeFalco's Home Wine & Beer Supplies, Houston, Texas*

SPECIALTY BROWN ALE

"Two P's in the Pot"
Honey Nut Brown Ale

YIELD: .... 5 GAL. (18.9 L)
TOTAL BOILING TIME: .... 35 MIN.
STARTING GRAVITY: 1.046
ENDING GRAVITY: 1.009
PRIMARY FERMENT: .... 10 DAYS

Pistachios and pecans enhance the nut flavor of this beer.

- ½ lb. (227 g) crystal malt, 40° Lovibond
- 4 oz. (680 g) pistachios, shelled
- 4 oz. (680 g) pecans, shelled
- 4 lb. (1.8 kg) Munton & Fison Nut Brown Ale extract
- 2 lb. (907 g) clover honey
- 1 c. (275 ml) corn sugar
- ½ c. (138 ml) raw cane sugar
- 1 oz. (28 g) Northern Brewers hops plug, 8.7% alpha, in boil 35 min.
- ½ oz. (14 g) Saaz hops plug, 4.5% alpha, in boil 10 min.
- 1 pack (6 g) dry ale yeast
- ¾ c. (206 ml) corn sugar, for priming
- 1 tbsp. (14.8 ml) beverage settler, for priming

Crush the nuts and grain and add to a pot with ½ gal. (1.9 L) of hot water. Steep 30 min. Strain into brewpot and add 1 gal. (3.8 L) of water, malt extract, honey, 1 c. (275 ml) of corn sugar, ½ c. (138 ml) cane sugar, and Northern Brewer hops. Boil 25 min., then add the Saaz hops. Boil 10 min., then turn off heat. Pour into a fermenter containing 3 gal. (11.4 L) of cold water. Bring up volume to 5 gal. (18.9 L) with cold water. Pitch yeast when wort has cooled to below 80°F (67°C). When fermentation stops in about 10 days, prime with ¾ c. (206 ml) corn sugar and beverage settler, then bottle. Age at least 1 month.

— *Marc Battreall, Plantation Key, Florida*

More HOMEBREW FAVORITES
4
Porters

Darker and more assertive than a brown ale but lighter than a stout, *porter* is a favorite among homebrewers and was, in its day, every bit as popular as thin, light lagers are today. According to some accounts, porter got its start in the early 18th century when publicans would mix different kinds of beer to make an "entire" — much as today's pubs often mix stout and pale ale to make a "black and tan." There is some uncertainty as to exactly which beer styles were blended, probably a couple of ales of different densities and perhaps an Old Ale as well. In the Summer, 1996 issue of *zymurgy*, writer Keith Thomas stated that one source described the blend as being ale, beer, and two-penny: hardly a description that clarifies the uncertainty. One story has it that, in 1722, a brewer named Ralph Harwood brewed porter as a single beer that combined the tastes of these different beers, thus saving time for overworked bartenders.

Another theory of how porter came to be a style focuses on the brewers themselves, who found that the water in London was well suited to brewing with darker malts. A darker, more robust beer also masked some flaws.

KEY TO RECIPE LOGOS

 EXTRACT RECIPES

 PARTIAL MASH RECIPES

 ALL-GRAIN RECIPES

Historically, porters were made from a base of brown malt — a type of malt that is, today, generally unavailable, though some homebrewers make it themselves. Modern commercial porters — and certainly most porters made by homebrewers — use a base of pale malt (and occasionally crystal malt), with most of the color and roast malt bitterness coming from chocolate malt. Sometimes a darker, black malt is used, or even roasted unmalted barley, but these generally have a sharper bite than most brewers want in their porters.

In today's craft-brewing marketplace, most small ale breweries produce porters. English craft brewers tend to produce a somewhat lighter-bodied, less hearty beer than do American craft brewers. While an English microbrewery is likely to start with an original gravity of 11° Plato (1.044), American microbreweries generally start at 12 to 13° Plato (1.049 to 1.052). John Harrison, of the Durden Park Beer Circle, includes several recipes for porter in his book *Old British Beers and How to Make Them.* These recipes have starting gravities of 1.060, so the American craft brewers are closer than the English to the style as it existed in its heyday. Homebrewers today tend to produce porters ranging in gravity from 11 to 16° Plato (1.044 to 1.064) — sometimes even a bit higher.

Description. Terry Foster, author of *Porter*, suggests that the color of porter should not be an opaque black, like a stout, but rather should show tinges of red. Most porters do exhibit such color, which comes from the addition of crystal malt. Hop bitterness should be apparent, he says, though not overwhelming. Porters should always be ales, that is, fermented with ale yeasts, even though it is true that Yuengling Porter, America's oldest commercial porter, has been brewed as a lager since 1933 (prior to that, it was brewed as an ale). Yeast by-product flavors in the form of fruity esters and low diacetyl are to be expected in a porter. Although judges are often critical of these flavors, they should probably be considered a necessary component of a historical porter. While there is evidence that sourness and some smokiness from the malting processes used in the 18th and 19th century were present in porter, they are not regarded as part of the style in today's craft-brewing community. However, a number of outstanding smoked porters have been produced as specialty beers, notably the smoked porter at Greg Noonan's Vermont Pub Brewery in Burlington and the Alaskan Smoked Porter available in the Pacific Northwest.

Methods. Most porters are made using English brewing methods, namely, a single-step infusion mash at about 148° to 156°F (64° to 69°C). The grain bill for an all-grain version is primarily English pale ale malt, or an American 2-row pale malt. A grain bill composed primarily of brown malt could be an interesting venture into historical brewing, and would likely result in a nuttier taste than you get with pale malt. Extract brewers could use any light, gold, or pale extract. Those labeled "gold" or "amber" might be expected to deliver a bit more sweetness from caramel malts. All grain brewers will probably want to use up to 1 lb (454 g) of caramel or crystal malt to add sweetness, body, and a reddish hue. The color and the chocolatey or roasted-coffee flavors come from chocolate malt, which should be used in fairly light proportions — usually ¼ to ½ lb. (113 to 227 g) but never more than 1 lb. (454 g) in a 5-gal. (18.9-L) batch. Quite a number of homebrewers prefer the more acrid, coffeelike flavors of black patent malt. If used in porter, the amount should be very small, perhaps ¼ lb. (113 g) as an upper limit.

In porters, hops can be either English or American. The key is to keep the hopping level fairly subdued, even though some authors cite examples of American porters brewed in the late 19th century with hopping rates of 60 IBU. Half that, or about 30 IBU, would be appropriate today.

Any number of English or American yeast strains are suitable for porters. Dry yeasts like Edme, Whitbread, Nottingham, and Windsor have been used with success. Among the liquid yeasts, the Wyeast London Ale (#1028), British Ale (#1098), and British II (#1335) are often used. Yeast Lab London Ale (A03) and American Ale (A02) are also good choices. Many other ale yeasts would also work well.

A winning porter in competition will be a malty beer with a good hops balance and fairly soft without the sharp, acrid bite of black patent malts. Chocolate notes are fine. If you have noticeable hops in your porter, or if you taste coffee flavors, the robust category may be more appropriate for you (if available). Porter should not be cloudy or totally black — some red is preferred. Porters are normal-gravity beers, that is, 11 to 12° Plato or about 1.045 to 1.050 original gravity, so if your beer is very heavy in body, judges may tell you that it should have been entered as a stout.

ROBUST AND BROWN PORTERS

Pegleg Porter

YIELD: .... 5 GAL. (18.9 L)
TOTAL BOILING TIME: .... 60 MIN.
STARTING GRAVITY: 1.050
PRIMARY FERMENT: .... 1 WEEK
SECONDARY FERMENT: .... 2 WEEKS

First place in the porter category at the November 1994 Ale About Ales competition in Toronto, Canada.

```
 1  lb. (454 g) crystal malt
 ½  lb. (227 g) Munich malt
 ½  lb. (227 g) chocolate malt
 ¼  lb. (113 g) roasted malt
 ¼  lb. (113 g) black patent malt
2½  lb. (1.1 kg) John Bull dark malt extract
2.2 lb. (1 kg) dark dried malt extract
 1  lb. (454 g) dark malt extract
 2  c. (551 ml) brown sugar
 ½  c. (118 ml) molasses
 2  oz. (57 g) Willamette hop pellets, in boil 60 min.
 2  packs Red Star ale yeast
 ¾  c. (206 ml) corn sugar, for priming
```

Steep grains for 30 min. in 2 gal. (7.6 L) of 150°F (66°C) water. Strain out grains and add malt extracts, brown sugar, and molasses. Bring to a boil and add the Willamette hops. Boil 60 min. Remove from heat, chill wort, and transfer to fermenter. Top off to 5 gal. (18.9 L) and pitch yeast. Ferment 1 week at 65°F (18°C). Rack to secondary and ferment 2 weeks at 65°F (18°C). Prime and bottle.

— Rick Bedor, Merrickville, Ontario, The Boilover Boys

Irish Porter

YIELD:	5 GAL. (18.9 L)
TOTAL BOILING TIME:	45 MIN.
STARTING GRAVITY:	1.044
ENDING GRAVITY:	1.010
PRIMARY FERMENT:	5–7 DAYS

¼ lb. (113 g) black patent malt
¼ lb. (113 g) crystal malt, 60° Lovibond
½ tsp. (2.5 ml) gypsum (if using soft water)
6.6 lb. (3 kg) Briess dark malt extract
2 oz. (57 g) Nugget hops, 11.1% alpha, in boil 45 min.
½ tsp. (2.5 ml) Irish moss
1 oz. (28 g) Fuggles hops, 3.2% alpha, in boil 2 min.
Yeast Lab A05 Irish Ale yeast
¾ c. (206 ml) corn sugar, for priming

Crush grains and add to 2 gal. (7.6 L) of cold water in a kettle. If water is soft, add ½ tsp. (2.5 ml) gypsum. Heat to near boil and strain out grains. Add malt extract and the Nugget hops. Boil 30 min. Add Irish moss and boil 13 min. Add Fuggles and boil 2 min. Turn off heat. Chill wort, and transfer to fermenter. Top off to 5 gal. (18.9 L) and pitch yeast. After primary fermentation has completed, prime and bottle.

— Daniel Pals, Grafton, Wisconsin

Cole Porter

YIELD:	5 GAL. (18.9 L)
TOTAL BOILING TIME:	60 MIN.
STARTING GRAVITY:	1.045
ENDING GRAVITY:	1.010
PRIMARY FERMENT:	7 DAYS
SECONDARY FERMENT:	14 DAYS

Ribbon winner at the 1995 California State Fair. It has a nice roasty flavor and aroma.

- 8 oz. (227 g) roasted barley
- 4 oz. (113 g) chocolate malt
- 6 lb. (2.72 kg) light dry malt extract
- 1 oz. (28 g) Northern Brewer hops, 7.0% alpha, in boil 60 min.
  Wyeast #1028 London Ale yeast
- ¾ c. (206 ml) corn sugar, for priming

Add grains to ½ gal. (1.9 L) water. Bring to boil, then turn off heat. Steep for 30 min. (1.9 L) of water Heat. Strain into brew kettle. Add malt extract and bring to a boil. Add Northern Brewer hops and boil 60 min. Chill the wort, transfer to a primary fermenter, and bring the total volume up to 5 gal. (18.9 L) with cold water. Pitch yeast when below 80°F (27°C). Ferment 7 days, then rack to a secondary fermenter. Ferment for 14 days. Prime and bottle.

— Patrick Thalken, Sacramento, California

Palmer's Perfect Porter

YIELD: .... 5 GAL. (18.9 L)
TOTAL BOILING TIME: .... 60 MIN.
STARTING GRAVITY: 1.054
ENDING GRAVITY: 1.016
PRIMARY FERMENT: .... 8 DAYS
SECONDARY FERMENT: .... 6 DAYS

A Sierra Nevada clone that could perhaps use a bit more hops.

      2 lb. (907 g) 2-row malt
    ½ lb. (227 g) cara-Vienne malt
    ½ lb. (227 g) chocolate malt
    ¼ lb. (113 g) crystal malt, 40° Lovibond
    ¼ lb. (113 g) crystal malt, 80° Lovibond
    ⅕ lb. (91 g) chocolate malt
   6.6 lb. (3 kg) light unhopped malt extract
    ¾ oz. (21 g) Perle hops, in boil 60 min.
    ½ oz. (14 g) Willamette hops, in boil 30 min.
    ¼ oz. (7 g) Perle hops, in boil 15 min.
    ½ oz. (14 g) Willamette hops, in boil 15 min.
      2 tsp. (9.9 ml) Irish moss
         Wyeast #1056 American Ale yeast, 2-qt. starter
   1¼ c. (344 ml) dry malt extract, for priming

Crush grains and mash in 5 qt. (4.7 L) of 155°F (68°C) water for 1 hour. Sparge with 5 qt. (4.7 L) of 170°F (77°C) water. Collect wort in brew kettle and bring to a boil. Turn off heat and add malt extract. Return to a boil and add ¾ oz. (21 g) of Perle hops. Boil 30 min., then add ½ oz. (14 g) of Willamette hops. Boil 15 min., then add ¼ oz. (7 g) of Perle hops, ½ oz. (14 g) of Willamette hops, and Irish moss. Boil 15 min., then turn off heat. Chill the wort, transfer to fermenter, and top off to 5 gal. (18.9 L) with cold water. Ferment 8 days at 66°F (19°C), then rack to a secondary fermenter. Ferment 6 days at 68°F (20°C), then prime with the dry malt extract and bottle.

— *Gabrielle Palmer, Livonia, Michigan*
Fermental Order of Renaissance Draughtsmen (FORD)

Sierra Nevada Porter Clone

YIELD: .... 5 GAL. (18.9 L)
TOTAL BOILING TIME: .... 90 MIN.
STARTING GRAVITY: 1.060
ENDING GRAVITY: 1.016
PRIMARY FERMENT: .... 5 DAYS
SECONDARY FERMENT: .... 7 DAYS

*First-place porter winner in the 1995 Spirit of Free Beer
competition.*

9¼ lb. (4.2 kg) pale ale malt
¾ lb. (340 g) chocolate malt
⅜ lb. (170 g) cara-pils malt
¼ lb. (113 g) black patent malt
¼ lb. (113 g) crystal malt, 80° Lovibond
¼ lb. (113 g) wheat malt
⅘ oz. (23 g) Nugget hops, 13.3% alpha, in boil 60 min.
⅖ oz. (11 g) Nugget hops, 13.3% alpha, in boil 30 min.
1 oz. (28 g) Willamette hops, 5% alpha, steep
Wyeast #1056 American Ale yeast
¾ c. (206 ml) corn sugar, for priming

Add crushed grains to 3¾ gal. (14.2 L) of 163°F (73°C) water. Mash at
152°F (67°C) for 60 min. Raise temperature to 170°F (77°C) for a 10 min.
mash-out. Sparge with 170°F (77°C) water, collecting 6½ – 7 gal.
(24.6 – 26.5 L) of wort. Boil 30 min. before adding ⅘ oz. (23 g) of Nugget
hops. Boil 30 min., then add ⅖ oz. (11 g) of Nugget hops. Boil 30 min.,
then turn off heat and add 1 oz. (28 g) of Willamette hops. Chill the wort,
transfer to fermenter, and pitch yeast. Ferment 5 days at 65°F (18°C),
then rack to secondary. After 1 week, prime and bottle.

— *Keith Chamberlin, Riverdale, Maryland*
Brewers United for Real Potables (BURP)

Dog Day Dark

YIELD: .... 5 GAL. (18.9 L)
TOTAL BOILING TIME: .... 90 MIN.
STARTING GRAVITY: 1.053–1.055
PRIMARY FERMENT: .... 5–7 DAYS
SECONDARY FERMENT: .... 1–2 WEEKS

This beer took a first place in the 1995 Dixie Cup competition.

    King and Barnes ale yeast
9 lb. (2.72 kg) pale ale malt
½ lb. (227 g) crystal malt, 30° Lovibond
½ lb. (227 g) crystal malt, 135° Lovibond
½ lb. (227 g) chocolate malt
¼ lb. (113 g) brown malt
¼ lb. (113 g) malted wheat
1 oz. (28 g) Tettnanger hops, 6.2% alpha, in boil 60 min.
½ oz. (14 g) Cascade hops, 6.5% alpha, in boil 60 min.
1 tsp. (4.9 ml) Irish moss
½ oz. (14 g) East Kent Goldings hops, 5.1% alpha, in boil 15 min.
½ oz. (14 g) Cascade hops, in boil 15 min.
½ oz. (14 g) East Kent Goldings hops, steep
½ oz. (14 g) U.K. Fuggles hops, steep
¼ oz. (7 g) Fuggles hops (dry hop in keg)

Several days before brewing, begin growing up yeast starter.
    Crush grains and add to 3 ⅔ gal. (13.9 L) of 162°F (72°C) water. Mash at 151°F (66°C) for 60 min. Raise temperature to 170°F (77°C) and mash-out for 10 min. Sparge with 170°F (77°C) water and collect 6½ gal. 24.6 L) of wort in brew kettle. Boil 30 min. Add Tettnanger hops and ½ oz. (14 g) of Cascade hops. Boil 30 min., then add Irish moss. Boil 15 min., then add ½ oz. (14 g) each of East Kent Goldings and Cascade hops. Boil 15 min. Remove from heat and add remaining ½ oz. (14 g) each of East Kent Goldings and U.K. Fuggles. Chill wort and transfer to fermenter. Pitch yeast and ferment 5–7 days at 60° – 65°F (16° – 18°C). Transfer to secondary for 1–2 weeks. To dry hop, put ¼ oz. (7 g) Fuggles hops in a hop bag and drop it in the keg before sealing.

— David Brockington, Seattle, Washington
Seattle Secret Skinny Brewers Society

Special-B Porter

YIELD: .... 5 GAL. (18.9 L)
TOTAL BOILING TIME: .... 60 MIN.
STARTING GRAVITY: 1.053
ENDING GRAVITY: 1.017
PRIMARY FERMENT: .... 7 DAYS
SECONDARY FERMENT: .... 7 DAYS

Second place in the porter category at the 1995 TRASH Competition. Chocolate and coffee flavor and aroma.

    8 lb. (3.63 kg) 2-row pale malt
    1 lb. (454 g) crystal malt, 60° Lovibond
    ½ lb. (227 g) chocolate malt
    ¼ lb. (113 g) Special-B malt
    2 oz. (57 g) East Kent Goldings hops, 5.1% alpha, in boil 60 min.
    1 oz. (28 g) East Kent Goldings hops, 5.1% alpha, in boil 10 min.
    1 oz. (28 g) East Kent Goldings hops, 5.1% alpha, in boil 1–2 min.
       Wyeast #1968 London ESB yeast
    ¾ c. (206 ml) corn sugar, for priming

Mash grains in 3¼ gal. (12.3 L) water at 152°F (67°C) for 60 min. Mash-out at 170°F (77°C) for 10 min. Sparge with 170°F (77°C) water and collect 6 to 6½ gal. (22.7 to 24.6 L) of wort in brew kettle. Bring to a boil and add 2 oz. (57 g) of East Kent Goldings hops. Boil 50 min., then add 1 oz. (28 g) of East Kent Goldings hops. Boil 8 – 9 min., then add last oz. (28 g) of East Kent Goldings hops. Boil 1 – 2 min. and turn off heat. Chill the wort, transfer to a fermenter, and pitch yeast. Ferment 7 days at 65°F (18°C), then rack to secondary for 7 days at 65°F (18°C). Prime with corn sugar, and bottle.

— *Steven Zabarnick, Dayton, Ohio*
Dayton Regional Amateur Fermentation Technologists (DRAFT)

Sandy Porter

YIELD: .... 5 GAL. (18.9 L)
TOTAL BOILING TIME: .... 60 MIN.
STARTING GRAVITY: 1.049
ENDING GRAVITY: 1.012
PRIMARY FERMENT: .... 6 DAYS
SECONDARY FERMENT: .... 30 DAYS

8 lb. (3.63 kg) pale malt
½ lb. (227 g) black patent malt
½ lb. (227 g) chocolate malt
½ lb. (227 g) crystal malt, 40° Lovibond
1 c. (275 ml) roasted barley
½ lb. (227 g) Quaker Quick Oats
1 tbsp. (14.8 ml) gypsum
2 oz. (57 g) Brewers Gold hops, 8.8% alpha, in boil 60 min.
1 oz. (28 g) Cascade hops, 4.9% alpha, in boil 20 min.
1 tsp. (4.9 ml) Irish moss
Wyeast #1028 London Ale yeast
¾ c. (206 ml) corn sugar, for priming

Mash in at 130°F. Heat 3 gal. (11.4 L) of water treated with gypsum to 180°F (82°C). Stir heated water into mash, to reach 152°F for 45 min. Sparge with 170°F (77°C) water. Collect about 6 gal. of wort. Add Brewers Gold hops and boil 40 min. Add Cascade hops and boil 5 min. Add Irish moss and boil 15 min. Turn off heat, chill the wort, and transfer to fermenter. Pitch yeast and ferment 6 days at 78°F (26°C). Rack to secondary for 30 days. Prime with the corn sugar and bottle.

— *Aaron Dionne, Clinton Township, Michigan*
Fermental Order of Renaissance Draughtsmen (FORD)

Tume Olu

YIELD: .... 5 GAL. (18.9 L)
TOTAL BOILING TIME: .... 60 MIN.
STARTING GRAVITY: 1.072
ENDING GRAVITY: 1.028
PRIMARY FERMENT: .... 3 WEEKS
SECONDARY FERMENT: .... 6 WEEKS

10 lb. (4.54 kg) Belgian pilsner malt
1 lb. (454 g) crystal malt, 80° Lovibond
½ lb. (227 g) crystal malt, 120° Lovibond
¼ lb. (113 g) Belgian special-B malt
1 oz. (28 g) Styrian Goldings hops, 5.2% alpha, in boil 60 min.
½ oz. (227 g) Styrian Goldings hops, 5.2% alpha, in boil 30 min.
1 tsp. (4.9 ml) Irish moss
Wyeast #2308 Munich Lager yeast
¾ c. (206 ml) corn sugar, for priming

Add crushed grains to 4 gal. (15.1 L) of water and heat to 122°F (50°C). Rest for 30 min., then remove a portion of the mash and bring it to a boil. Return the decoction portion to the mash and let rest at 154°F (68°C) for 60 min., or until starch conversion is complete. Sparge with 168°F (76°C) water and collect 6½ gal. (24.6 L) of wort. Bring to a boil and add 1 oz. (28 g) of Styrian Goldings hops. Boil 30 min., then add ½ oz. (14 g) of Styrian Goldings hops. Boil 10 min., then add the Irish moss. Boil 20 min., then turn off heat. Chill the wort, transfer to fermenter, and pitch yeast. Ferment 3 weeks, then rack to secondary. Ferment 6 weeks at lager temperatures (50°F [10°C] or less), then prime with corn sugar and bottle.

— *Keith Schwols, Ft. Collins, Colorado*

Bodacious Bellhop

YIELD: .... 5 GAL. (18.9 L)
TOTAL BOILING TIME: .... 60 MIN.
STARTING GRAVITY: 1.050
ENDING GRAVITY: 1.012
PRIMARY FERMENT: .... 1 WEEK
SECONDARY FERMENT: .... 1 WEEK

First place in the porter category at the 1995 HOPS-BOPS.

7½ lb. (3.4 kg) Briess or English 2-row malt
12 oz. (340 g) Munton & Fison crystal malt
5 oz. (142 g) English chocolate malt
4 oz. (113 g) wheat malt
3 oz. (85 g) black patent malt
1 oz. (28 g) Kent Goldings hop pellets, 5% alpha, in boil 60 min.
¾ oz. (21 g) Kent Goldings hops plug, 5% alpha, in boil 60 min.
1 tsp. (5 ml) Irish moss, powdered
¼ oz. (7 g) Tettnanger hop pellets, 4.8% alpha, in boil 10 min.
½ oz. (14 g) Kent Goldings hops plug, 5% alpha, 5 min. steep
    BrewTek CL-170 British Ale yeast
¾ c. (206 ml) corn sugar, for priming

Mash grains in 3 gal. (11.4 L) of water at 152°F (67°C) for 90 min. Raise temperature to 165°F (74°C) and mash-out for 10 min. Sparge with 170°F (77°C) water and collect 6½ – 7 gal. (24.6 – 26.5 L) of wort in brew kettle. Bring wort to a boil and add 1 oz. (28 g) of Kent Goldings hop pellets and ¾ oz. (21 g) of Kent Goldings hops plug. Boil 45 min. Add rehydrated Irish moss. Boil 5 min. Add ¼ oz. (7 g) of Tettnanger hop pellets and boil 10 min. Add ½ oz. (14 g) Kent Goldings hops plug. Turn off heat and steep 5 min. Chill the wort, transfer to fermenter, and pitch yeast. Ferment 1 week, then rack to secondary. Ferment 1 more week, then prime with the corn sugar and bottle.

— *Alan L. Folsom, Jr., Warrington, Pennsylvania, Keystone Hops*

Holistic Porter II

YIELD: .... 5 GAL. (18.9 L)
TOTAL BOILING TIME: .... 90 MIN.
STARTING GRAVITY: 1.050
ENDING GRAVITY: 1.018
PRIMARY FERMENT: .... 1 WEEK
SECONDARY FERMENT: .... 3 WEEKS

7½ lb. (3.4 kg) English pale ale malt
 1 lb. (454 g) crystal malt, 60° Lovibond
½ lb. (227 g) chocolate malt
½ lb. (227 g) black patent malt
 1 oz. (28 g) Bullion hop pellets, 8.5% alpha, in boil 60 min.
¼ oz. (7 g) Tettnanger hop pellets, 4.4% alpha, in boil 10 min.
½ oz. (14 g) Kent Goldings hop pellets, steep
    Wyeast #1084 Irish Ale yeast
¾ c. (206 ml) corn sugar, for priming

Add crushed grains to 12½ qt. (11.8 L) of 162°F (72°C) water. Rest at 151°F (66°C) until starch conversion is complete. Sparge with 170°F (77°C) water and collect 6½ gal. (24.6 L) of wort. Boil 30 min. before adding the Bullion pellets. Boil 50 min., then add the Tettnanger pellets. Boil 10 min., then turn off heat and add the Kent Goldings. Steep a few min. and then chill the wort. Transfer to fermenter and pitch yeast. Ferment 1 week at 60°F (16°C). Rack to secondary for 3 weeks at 60°F (16°C). Prime with the corn sugar and bottle.

— *Bill Pemberton, Charlottesville, Virginia, Back Door Brewers*

Delano's Entire Butt

YIELD:	5 GAL. (18.9 L)
TOTAL BOILING TIME:	90 MIN.
STARTING GRAVITY:	1.061
ENDING GRAVITY:	1.012
PRIMARY FERMENT:	7 DAYS
SECONDARY FERMENT:	10–14 DAYS

Yeast Culture Kit Company Pale Ale yeast
8½ lb. (3.86 kg) pale ale malt
¾ lb. (340 g) cara-Munich malt
1 lb. (454 g) brown malt
1 lb. (454 g) Munich malt
¼ lb. (113 g) black patent malt
¼ lb. (113 g) chocolate malt
1 oz. (28 g) Perle hops, 9.5% alpha, in boil 60 min.
½ oz. (14 g) East Kent Goldings hops, 6.0% alpha, in boil 30 min.
½ oz. (14 g) East Kent Goldings hops, 6.0% alpha, in boil 15 min.
½ oz. (14 g) East Kent Goldings hops, steep
¾ c. (206 ml) corn sugar, for priming

Several days before brewing, start growing up a yeast starter.
Add crushed grains to 4 gal. (15.1 L) of 153°F (67°C) water. Mash at 142°F (61°C) for 30 min. Raise temperature to 158°F (70°C) for 60 min. Raise temperature to 168°F (76°C) for a 10-min. mash-out. Sparge with 170°F (77°C) water, collecting 7 gal. (26.5 L) of wort. Boil 30 min. before adding the Perle hops. Boil 30 min., then add ½ oz. (14 g) of East Kent Goldings hops. Boil 15 min., then add ½ oz. (14 g) of East Kent Goldings. Boil 15 min. Remove wort from heat and add another ½ oz. (14 g) of East Kent Goldings. Chill the wort, transfer to fermenter, and pitch yeast. Ferment at 65° – 70°F (18° – 21°C) for 1 week. Rack to secondary for 10 – 14 days. Prime and bottle or keg.

— *Delano Dugarm, Arlington, Virginia*
Brewers United for Real Potables (BURP)

English Porter

YIELD: .... 5 GAL. (18.9 L)
TOTAL BOILING TIME: .... 90 MIN.
PRIMARY FERMENT: .... 7 DAYS
SECONDARY FERMENT: .... 2–3 WEEKS

9½ lb. (4.31 kg) pale ale malt
1 lb. (454 g) Hugh Baird brown malt
½ lb. (227 g) chocolate malt
½ lb. (227 g) crystal malt, 80° Lovibond
½ lb. (227 g) wheat malt
¼ lb. (113 g) Special-B malt
1 oz. (28 g) Nugget hops, 13.3% alpha, in boil 60 min.
1 oz. (28 g) East Kent Goldings hops, 6.6% alpha, in boil 15 min.
Wyeast #1028 London Ale yeast (skimmed from previous batch)
1 oz. (28 g) East Kent Goldings hops, dry hop in secondary
¾ c. (206 ml) corn sugar, for priming

Add crushed grains to 4 gal. (15.1 L) of 163°F (73°C) water. Mash at 152°F (67°C) for about 1 – 1½ hours. Heat mash to 170°F (77°C) for 10 min. Sparge with 170°F (77°C) water, collecting 7 gal. (26.5 L) of wort. Boil 30 min. before adding the Nugget hops. Boil 45 min., then add 1 oz. (28 g) of East Kent Goldings. Boil 15 min. and turn off heat. Chill the wort, transfer to fermenter, and add yeast. Ferment 1 week (fermentation could finish in only a couple of days if you harvest a large amount of yeast from a previous batch). Rack to secondary, add East Kent Goldings hops, and let fermentation continue another 2 – 3 weeks. Prime with the corn sugar and bottle.

— *Keith Chamberlin, Riverdale, Maryland*
Brewers United for Real Potables (BURP)

SPECIALTY PORTERS

Cocoa & Cream Porter

YIELD: .... 5 GAL. (18.9 L)
TOTAL BOILING TIME: .... 60 MIN.
STARTING GRAVITY: 1.070
ENDING GRAVITY: 1.018
PRIMARY FERMENT: .... 7 DAYS
SECONDARY FERMENT: .... 14 DAYS

A scrumptious chocolate porter with some residual sweetness. To brew this as an all grain beer, replace the malt extract with 8 lb. of pale malt and 1 lb. of crystal.

  1 lb. (454 g) crystal malt, 80° Lovibond
  ½ lb. (227 g) pale malt
  ½ lb. (227 g) chocolate malt
  ½ lb. (227 g) flaked oats
  4 oz. (113 g) black patent malt
  4 oz. (113 g) Belgian malted wheat
8½ lb. (3.86 kg) light malt extract or 7½ lb. (3.4 kg) dark malt extract
1¼ oz. (35 g) Willamette hops, 2.5% alpha, in boil 60 min.
  1 oz. (28 g) Perle hops, 8.0% alpha, in boil 60 min.
  1 tsp. (4.9 ml) Irish moss
  6 oz. (170 g) unsweetened cocoa powder
2¼ oz. (64 g) Willamette hops, 2.5% alpha, in boil 15 min.
  ¾ oz. (21 g) Perle hops, 8.0% alpha, in boil 15 min.
    Wyeast #1098 British Ale yeast
  ¾ c. (206 ml) dry malt extract

Add crushed grains to 1 gal. (3.8 L) of water and heat to 158°F (70°C). Steep 60 min. Heat to 170°F (77°C). Strain into kettle. Rinse grains with 1 gal. of 170°F (77°C) water. Bring to a boil. Turn off heat; add malt extract. Bring to a boil, and add 1¼ oz. (35 g) of Willamette hops and 1 oz. (28 g) of Perle hops; boil 45 min. Add Irish moss, cocoa powder, 2¼ oz. (64 g) of Willamette hops, and ¾ oz. (21 g) of Perle hops; boil 15 min. Turn off heat, chill the wort, transfer to a fermenter, and pitch yeast. Ferment 1 week; then rack to secondary for 2 weeks. Prime and bottle.

— Pat Babcock, Canton Township, Michigan
The Fermental Order of Renaissance Draughtsmen (FORD)
Cooperative Homebrew Avocation and Obsession Society (CHAOS)

Vermont Porter

YIELD: .... 5 GAL. (18.9 L)
TOTAL BOILING TIME: .... 52 MIN.
PRIMARY FERMENT: .... 4 DAYS
SECONDARY FERMENT: .... 4 DAYS

Very malty with just a taste of maple.

- ½ lb. (227 g) chocolate malt, cracked
- ½ lb. (227 g) crystal malt, cracked
- ¼ lb. (113 g) wheat malt
- 3.3 lb. (1.5 kg) John Bull dark liquid extract
- 2 lb. (907 g) Munton & Fison dark dry extract
- 1½ lb. (680 g) maple syrup
- 1½ oz. (43 g) Saaz leaf hops, in boil 50 min.
- 1 oz. (28 g) Hallertauer leaf hops, in boil 2 min.
- ½ oz. (14 g) Whitbread Ale yeast
- ¾ c. (206 ml) molasses, for priming

Steep grains in 1 gal. (3.8 L) of water at 150°F (66°C) for 30 min. Strain out grains, add malt extracts, and bring to a boil. Add maple syrup and the Saaz hops. Boil 50 min., then add the Hallertauer hops. Boil 2 more min. Cool wort, add to 4½ gal. (17 L) of cold water, and pitch yeast. Ferment 4 days at 65°F (18°C). Rack to secondary for 4 days at 55°F (13°C). Prime with molasses and bottle.

— Carl Meier, Darien, Connecticut

Black Honey Porter

YIELD: .... 5 GAL. (18.9 L)
TOTAL BOILING TIME: .... 60 MIN.
STARTING GRAVITY: 1.068
ENDING GRAVITY: 1.018
PRIMARY FERMENT: .... 16 DAYS

Licorice and honey balance the bitterness of black porter malt.

Wyeast #1028 London Ale yeast, 1-qt. (600-ml) starter
1 lb. (454 g) Munich malt
1 lb. (454 g) crystal malt
½ lb. (227 g) chocolate malt
¼ lb. (113 g) black patent malt
¼ lb. (113 g) cara-pils malt
1 tsp. (4.9 ml) gypsum
6.6 lb. (3 kg) Northwestern Gold malt extract syrup
1½ oz. (43 g) Northern Brewer hops, 8.0% alpha in boil 55 min.
1 brewer's licorice stick, cut into 3 or 4 pieces
1 lb. (454 g) unfiltered orange blossom honey
1 tsp. (4.9 ml) Irish moss
½ oz. (14 g) Fuggles hops, 5.0% alpha, in boil 10 min.
½ oz. (14 g) Fuggles hops, 5.0% alpha, steep for 2 min.
¾ c. (206 ml) corn sugar, for priming

Prepare yeast starter a day before brewing.

Steep grains in 1 gal. (3.8 L) of 160°F (71°C) water with gypsum for 60 min. Sparge grains with 5 qt. (4.7 L) of 170°F (77°C) water into brewpot. Bring to a boil and add malt extract. Boil 5 min. Add Northern Brewer hops. Boil 25 min., then add licorice and honey. Boil 10 min., then add Irish moss. Boil 10 more min., then add ½ oz. (14 g) of Fuggles hops. Boil 10 min., then remove from heat. Add ½ oz. (14 g) of Fuggles and steep 2 min. Chill the wort and transfer to fermenter. Add 2½ gal. (9.5 L) of very cold, preboiled water (top off to 5 gal. [18.9 L]). Pitch yeast. Attach blow-off tube. After fermentation subsides 2–3 days later, attach air lock. Ferment another 13 – 14 days at 66°F (19°C). Prime with corn sugar and bottle.

— *Dr. Michael B. McNeil, Orlando, Florida, Central Florida Homebrewers*

Mission Mountain
Mocha Porter

YIELD: .... 5 GAL. (18.9 L)
TOTAL BOILING TIME: .... 60 MIN.
STARTING GRAVITY: 1.050
ENDING GRAVITY: 1.022
PRIMARY FERMENT: .... 3 DAYS
SECONDARY FERMENT: .... 9 DAYS

½ lb. (227 g) crystal malt, 40° Lovibond

½ lb. (227 g) chocolate malt

½ lb. (227 g) black patent malt

7 lb. (3.18 kg) dark malt extract

2 oz. (57 g) Cascade hops, 5.8% alpha, in boil 60 min.

4 oz. (113 g) Baker's unsweetened chocolate

¾ oz. (21 g) Saaz hops, 4.8% alpha, in boil 10 min.

8 c. (1.9 L) fresh-brewed Kenya coffee

2 packs Muntons ale yeast

¾ c. (206 ml) corn sugar, for priming

Add crushed grains to 1½ gal. (5.7 L) of cold water. Bring to a boil, straining out grains before boil begins. Add malt extract and Cascade hops. Boil 30 min., then add chopped chocolate. Boil 20 min., then add the Saaz hops. Boil 10 min., then turn off heat. Chill wort, transfer to fermenter, and add coffee. Top off to 5 gal. (18.9 L) with cold water. Pitch yeast and ferment 3 days at 64°F (18°C). Rack to secondary for 9 days at 64°F (18°C). Prime and bottle.

— *Herky Gottfried, Corvallis, Oregon*

Honey Porter

YIELD:	5 GAL. (18.9 L)
TOTAL BOILING TIME:	60 MIN.
STARTING GRAVITY:	1.064
PRIMARY FERMENT:	7 DAYS
SECONDARY FERMENT:	8 DAYS

Third place in the specialty beer category at the 1995 Santa Rosa Brewfest, Fort Walton Beach, Florida.

   1 tbsp. (14.8 ml) gypsum
   5 lb. (2.27 kg) English pale ale malt
   5 lb. (2.27 kg) Vienna malt
   2 lb. (90 g) aromatic malt
   2 c. (551 ml) cara-pils, 40° Lovibond
1⅔ c. (459 ml) chocolate malt
   ½ oz. (14 g) Hallertauer hops, 3.9% alpha, in boil 60 min.
   8 oz. (227 g) malto-dextrin
   ½ oz. (14 g) Hallertauer hops, 3.9% alpha, in boil 45 min.
   ½ oz. (14 g) Hallertauer hops, 3.9% alpha, in boil 30 min.
   ½ oz. (14 g) Hallertauer hops, 3.9% alpha, in boil 15 min.
   2 oz. (57 g) Brewers Gold hops, 8.9% alpha, in boil 15 min.
   6 lb. (2.7 kg) honey
      Wyeast #1056 American Ale yeast
   ¾ c. (206 ml) corn sugar, for priming

Treat 5 gal. (18.9 L) of mash water with gypsum and heat until water is at 165°F (74°C). Add crushed grains. Mash at 150°F (66°C) for 1 hour. Mash-out for 10 min. at 168°F (76°C). Sparge slowly and collect 6 gal. (22.7 L) of wort. Bring wort to a boil; add ½ oz. (14 g) of Hallertauer hops and malto-dextrin. Boil 15 min. Add ½ oz. (14 g) of Hallertauer hops; boil 15 min. Add ½ oz. (14 g) of Hallertauer hops; boil 15 min. Add last ½ oz. (14 g) of Hallertauer hops, Brewers Gold hops, and honey. Boil 15 min.; turn off heat. Chill wort, transfer to fermenter, and pitch yeast. Ferment 7 days, then rack to a secondary fermenter for another 8 days. Prime and bottle.

— *Bryan E. Schwab, Panama City, Florida*

Cafe Mocha Porter

YIELD: .... 5 GAL. (18.9 L)
TOTAL BOILING TIME: .... 60 MIN.
STARTING GRAVITY: 1.075
ENDING GRAVITY: 1.015
PRIMARY FERMENT: .... 1 WEEK
SECONDARY FERMENT: .... 1 WEEK

Third place in the BOSS Homebrew Competition in the specialty category.

- ½ lb. (227 g) roasted barley
- ¾ lb. (340 g) crystal malt
- ½ lb. (227 g) chocolate malt
- 3.3 lb. (1.5 kg) Glenbrew dark hopped malt extract
- 3 lb. (1.36 kg) dark dry malt extract
- 1 lb. (454 g) extra dark, dry malt extract
- 2 oz. (57 g) Northern Brewer hops, 8.9% alpha, in boil 60 min.
- 4 oz. (113 g) Baker's bittersweet baking chocolate
- ½ lb. (227 g) fresh ground espresso beans
- Wyeast #1084 Irish Ale yeast
- ¾ c. (206 ml) corn sugar, for priming

Add roasted barley, and the crystal and chocolate malts to 1½ gal. (5.7 L) of water and steep at 165°F (74°C) for 30 min. Remove grains, add malt extracts, and bring to a boil. Add Northern Brewer hops and boil 45 min. Add bittersweet chocolate and boil 15 min. Remove from heat, add espresso, and steep 30 min. Strain wort and fill fermenter. Top off to 5 gal. (18.9 L) and pitch yeast when wort is below 80°F (27°C). Ferment 1 week at 68°F (20°C), then rack to a secondary fermenter. Ferment 1 more week at 68°F (20°C), prime with the corn sugar, and bottle. Age 6 months.

— *Matt Gilmartin, Oak Forest, Illinois*

Historically, stout probably developed from variations on the porter style where denser, more robust varieties were called "stout porter," and eventually just "stout." *Stouts* are always black ales with a firm, full body, low hops aroma, and usually roasty flavors from the use of roasted unmalted barley.

A number of variations on the stout style exist, and the family spans a very broad range of starting gravities — from about 1.038 to 1.100. Members of the stout family include the classic dry stouts of Ireland, sweeter English-style stouts, silky-smooth oatmeal stouts, higher-gravity foreign-style stout, and the enormously rich and complex Russian Imperial stouts.

Description. Stout is thought of as a big, black, robust beer, yet its gravity is often fairly low. Guinness, for example, is actually lower in gravity and alcohol than most craft-brewed porters; it is generally regarded, however, as the best model for the classic Irish dry stout.

Irish-style dry stouts are full-bodied beers with a sharp, dry bitterness from roasted barley. This dryness may be likened to the flavor of roast coffee. (Some homebrewers and U.S. craft brewers

KEY TO RECIPE LOGOS

 EXTRACT RECIPES

 PARTIAL MASH RECIPES

 ALL-GRAIN RECIPES

add coffee to their stouts.) The beer should always be completely black and opaque. Hop bitterness is generally fairly high.

The grain bill for an Irish dry stout will start with English pale ale malt, or U.S. 2-row malt. Dark caramel malt may be added to provide additional body and some sweetness; however, a lot of residual sweetness is not appropriate for the style. Flaked barley can be added to contribute smoothness. Although chocolate and black malts are sometimes used, they are not the best choice for adding color and roast flavors to a stout: the color and flavor should really come from roasted unmalted barley, at about 10 to 15 percent of the grain bill. The mash will usually be a single-step infusion mash. Some sourness may be perceptible in a dry stout. It has been said that Guinness, in fact, adds a small amount of soured stout to each batch. As the gravity increases over 1.050, it becomes more difficult to achieve a good dry character, as more residual sweetness will be likely.

Hopping is fairly assertive in an Irish dry stout, but it should be done entirely in the boil. A pronounced hop nose from aroma additions is inappropriate. Use typical English hops, at a rate of about 25 to 40 IBU.

While good stouts can be made from any number of ale yeasts, there are several yeasts available to the homebrewer that are ideally suited to stout. Wyeast #1084 Irish Ale yeast is used by countless scores of homebrewers with good results. Yeast Lab Irish Ale (A05) might also be a good choice; it gives beers a soft character with a hint of butterscotch.

An English sweet stout, as embodied by Mackeson XXX, is not really heavier than a dry stout — it may just seem that way due to residual sweetness and the lower hopping rate combined with a lack of roast bitterness. The flavor of a sweet stout is one of sweet maltiness, with perhaps some caramel, and subdued hops. The grain bill on a sweet stout will be mostly pale ale malt, but the color comes from chocolate malt, not roasted unmalted barley. Additional crystal malt may be added to the grain bill to enhance the sweetness. Lactose, which is an unfermentable sugar, is often added to the wort, giving rise to the names *milk stout* and *cream stout*, which denote sweet, English-style stouts. The original gravity of a sweet stout will generally be 1.040 to 1.060 and the bitterness about 15 to 25 IBUs.

Oatmeal stout. An interesting variation of sweet stout is oatmeal stout. This style of stout had all but disappeared until it was revived by the Samuel Smith brewery in Yorkshire. Today, several craft brewers make oatmeal stouts, and the style has won many converts in the homebrewing community. Oatmeal stouts are some of the smoothest, creamiest-tasting beers in the brewing world. They have original gravities of about 1.050 to 1.060. Oats are added to the mash, but they are high in protein and glucans, so they have a tendency to create stuck mashes. If a single-step infusion mash is used, 5 percent oats in the mash will be about all that is practical, although if a step mash is used that incorporates a protein rest, you may be able to boost this to 10 percent. Some homebrewers have good success with steel-cut oats, but these must be cooked before using. Roger Bergen in the Nov/Dec 1993 issue of *Brewing Techniques* magazine suggests substituting processed oats, such as quick or instant oats, because these are more gelatinized. Oatmeal stouts should be lightly hopped — no more than 25 IBUs. Their flavor profile should be one of complex maltiness, with traces of caramel and occasionally nuttiness. Chocolate tones are acceptable.

Foreign stouts. Stouts that are a bit heavier in body and more assertively hopped than classic dry Irish-style stouts may be referred to as "foreign stouts." These can have gravities up to 1.075 and hopping rates up to 60 IBU. Foreign stouts are probably closer in flavor profile to an Irish dry stout than to a sweet, English-style stout. Guinness reportedly brews a high-gravity version of their stout for export to tropical markets.

Russian Imperial stouts can be thought of as a cross between a stout and a barleywine. They have enormous amounts of malt sweetness and lots of chocolate, coffee, caramel, and other malt flavors. The original gravity will be somewhere between about 1.075 and 1.100. The beer may sometimes taste slightly burnt, or have other very complex flavors such as sherry. They have high hopping rates to balance this sweetness, often at levels of anywhere from 50 to 100 IBUs. As in barleywines, alcoholic character may be evident in these big beers, as will other yeast by-products, such as fruity esters.

As with all styles, homebrewers make variations on their recipes. Specialty stouts often include non-traditional ingredients, the most popular being coffee and chocolate. Stouts are sometimes also used as a basis for fruit beers.

Stouts are one of the most popular beers in homebrew competitions, which means that they really need to be good, solid examples of the style to do well in competitions. Stouts entered as dry stouts should not be excessively heavy. Similarly, excessive yeast flavor or alcoholic flavors are inappropriate to most stouts and can be a symptom of fermenting at high temperatures. Good stouts, though, are always winners!

CLASSIC IRISH DRY STOUTS

Carpe Diem

YIELD:	5 GAL. (18.9 L)
TOTAL BOILING TIME:	50 MIN.
STARTING GRAVITY:	1.052
ENDING GRAVITY:	1.022
PRIMARY FERMENT:	6 DAYS
SECONDARY FERMENT:	10 DAYS

Best of show at the 1994 Nebraska State Fair.

   1 lb. (454 g) crystal malt
  ½ lb. (227 g) black patent malt
  ½ lb. (227 g) chocolate malt
   4 lb. (113 g) Edme Superbrew Irish Stout extract syrup
   3 lb. (1.36 kg) Laaglander dry, dark malt extract
  ⅘ oz. (23 g) Chinook hops, 12.5% alpha, in boil 40 min.
     Edme dry ale yeast
   1 qt. (946 ml) of wort (gyle) saved prior to pitching yeast

Steep grain 20 min. in 1 gal. (3.8 L) hot water. Strain out grains rinsing with 1 gal. (3.8 L) of hot water. Add malt extracts and bring to a boil. Boil 10 min., then add Chinook hops. Boil 40 min., then turn off heat. Transfer wort to a fermenter containing 3 gal. (11.4 L) of cold water. Reserve 1 qt. (946 ml) of wort in a sanitized container, seal, and refrigerate. Pitch yeast when wort is at 70°F (21°C). Ferment 6 days at 68°F (20°C). Rack to secondary for 10 days at 68°F (20°C). Prime with the reserved wort and bottle.

— Steve Zahn, Bellevue, Nebraska, OMAHOPS

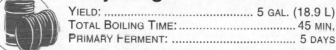

Judy's Light Irish Stout

YIELD: .... 5 GAL. (18.9 L)
TOTAL BOILING TIME: .... 45 MIN.
PRIMARY FERMENT: .... 5 DAYS

½ lb. (227 g) roasted barley
⅖ lb. (181 g) black patent malt
⅖ lb. (181 g) chocolate malt
3.3 lb. (1.5 kg) Mountmellick Stout malt extract
1 oz. (28 g) Perle hops, 8.4% alpha, in boil 45 min.
1 oz. (28 g) Perle hops, 8.4% alpha, in boil 15 min.
1 tsp. (4.9 ml) Irish moss
   Wyeast #1084 Irish Ale yeast
¾ c. (206 ml) corn sugar, for priming

Add crushed grains to 1 gal. (3.8 L) hot water and heat until boiling. Turn off heat. Strain out grains, and add malt extract and 1 oz. (28 g) of Perle hops. Boil 30 min., then add 1 oz. (28 g) of Perle hops and Irish moss. Boil 15 min. Chill the wort, transfer to fermenter, and pitch yeast. Ferment 5 days, then prime and bottle, or keg.

— Judith Charland, Jacksonville, Florida, River City Brewers

Lucky Day Stout

YIELD: .... 5 GAL. (18.9 L)
TOTAL BOILING TIME: .... 60 MIN.
STARTING GRAVITY: 1.060
ENDING GRAVITY: 1.015
PRIMARY FERMENT: .... 2 WEEKS

Wyeast #1084 Irish Ale yeast
10 lb. (4.54 kg) pale 2-row malt
1 lb. (454 g) crystal malt, 60° Lovibond
½ lb. (227 g) chocolate malt
¼ lb. (113 g) roasted barley
1½ oz. (43 g) Cascade hop pellets, 5.8% alpha, in boil 60 min.
1 tbsp. (14.8 ml) Irish moss
½ oz. (14 g) Goldings whole hops, 4.4% alpha, in boil 10 min.

Several days prior to brewing, make up a 1-qt. (946-ml) yeast starter.
Mash-in all grain with 4 gal. (15.1 L) of 170°F (77°C) water. Temperature should settle at 154°F (68°C). Mash for 1 hour at 154°F (68°C). Mash-out for 10 min. at 170°F (77°C). Sparge with 5 gal. (18.9 L) of 170°F (77°C) water. Collect 7 gal. (26.5 L) of wort. Bring to a boil and add the Cascade hops. Boil 40 min., then add the Irish moss. Boil 10 min., then add the Goldings. Boil 10 min. Turn off heat and chill the wort. Siphon into a 6-gal. (22.7 L) fermenter. Pitch the yeast starter. Ferment for 2 weeks at 62°F (17°C). Keg or bottle.

— *Shannon Burgess, Apex, North Carolina*
Cary Apex Raleigh Brewers of Yore (CARBOY)

Overnight Stout Lite

YIELD: .... 5 GAL. (18.9 L)
TOTAL BOILING TIME: .... 60 MIN.
STARTING GRAVITY: 1.044
ENDING GRAVITY: 1.010
PRIMARY FERMENT: .... 4 DAYS
SECONDARY FERMENT: .... 2 WEEKS

6½ lb. (2.95 kg) pale ale malt
2½ lb. (1.13 kg) flaked barley
    lactic acid, for pH
  1 lb. (454 g) roasted barley
1½ oz. (43 g) East Kent Goldings whole hops, in boil 60 min.
1½ oz. (43 g) Fuggles whole hops, in boil 60 min.
  1 tsp. (4.9 ml) calcium carbonate
    Wyeast #1084 Irish Ale yeast, 1-qt. (946-ml) starter
 ¾ c. (206 ml) corn sugar, for priming

Starting at 7 AM, add crushed pale ale malt and flaked barley to 13 qt.
(12.3 L) of 150°F (66°C) water in an uninsulated mash tun. Adjust pH to
just under pH 5.5 with lactic acid. Cover and let rest throughout work-
day. At 5 PM, heat 4 gal. (15.1 L) of water to 170°F (77°C). Remove 1 qt.
of the 170°F (77°C) water and steep the roasted barley in it for 15 min.
Add the steeped barley and water to the main mash. Heat mash tun to
170°F (77°C) and hold for 10 min. Stir mash, then drain out all liquid from
the mash tun after recirculating a quart (946 ml) or two of the runnings.
Add all sparge water and stir for 2 – 3 min. Cover and let rest for 15 min.
Recirculate the runnings, then slowly drain the mash tun into the kettle.
Bring to a boil and add all of the whole hops. Add the calcium carbonate
and boil 60 min. Turn off heat. Chill wort, transfer to fermenter, top off
to 5 gal. (18.9 L) with preboiled water if necessary, and pitch yeast.
Ferment 4 days, then rack to a secondary fermenter for 2 weeks. Prime
with corn sugar and bottle.

— *Mark Thompson, Campbell, California, Worts of Wisdom*

Irish Ambush

YIELD:	5 GAL. (18.9 L)
TOTAL BOILING TIME:	60 MIN.
STARTING GRAVITY:	1.050
ENDING GRAVITY:	1.016
PRIMARY FERMENT:	2 WEEKS
SECONDARY FERMENT:	2 WEEKS

First place at the 4th Annual March Mashfest, and third place at the 5th Annual March Mashfest.

     6 lb. (2.72 kg) pale ale malt
     1 lb. (454 g) roasted barley
    ½ lb. (227 g) Belgian special-B malt
     1 tsp. (4.9 ml) gypsum
     1 oz. (28 g) Kent Goldings hops, 6.0% alpha, in boil 60 min.
     1 tsp. (4.9 ml) Irish moss
        Wyeast #1084 Irish Ale yeast
    ¾ c. (206 ml) corn sugar, for priming

Add crushed grains to 9½ qt. (9 L) of 168°F (76°C) water treated with gypsum. Mash for 60 min. Sparge with 5 gal. (18.9 L) of 170°F (77°C) water. Collect wort in brew kettle and bring to a boil. Add the Kent Goldings hops and boil 45 min. Add Irish moss and boil 15 min. Turn off heat, chill the wort, transfer to the primary fermenter, and pitch yeast. Ferment 2 weeks at 60°F (16°C). Rack to a secondary for 2 more weeks. Prime and bottle.

— Keith Schwols, Ft. Collins, Colorado

SWEET STOUTS

Sweet Stout

YIELD:	5 GAL. (18.9 L)
TOTAL BOILING TIME:	60 MIN.
PRIMARY FERMENT:	6–9 DAYS
SECONDARY FERMENT:	7 DAYS

Second place in the stout division at the Boston Home Brew Competition in 1996.

¾ lb. (340 g) roasted barley
¾ lb. (340 g) chocolate malt
¾ lb. (340 g) black patent malt
10 lb. (4.5 kg) Munton & Fison dark malt extract
2½ oz. (71 g) Willamette hops, in boil 55 min.
¾ tsp. (3.7 ml) Irish moss
½ oz. (14 g) Cascade hops, in boil 5 min.
1 6-g package (0.2 oz.) Muntons ale yeast
1 c. (275 ml) corn sugar, for priming

Add grains to 1½ gal. (5.7 L) water and turn heat on high. Strain out grains just before boil begins and add malt extract and Willamette hops. Boil 30 min. Add Irish moss and boil 25 min. Add Cascade hops and boil 5 min. Turn off heat, chill the wort, and strain into fermenter containing 3½ gal. (13.2 L) cold water. Pitch yeast when the temperature of the wort is below 75°F (24°C). Ferment 7 days. Rack to secondary for another 7 days. Prime and bottle. Age 8 weeks.

— *Peter Cammann, Waitsfield, Vermont*

Sweet Chocolate Stout

YIELD:	5 GAL. (18.9 L)
TOTAL BOILING TIME:	60 MIN.
STARTING GRAVITY:	1.051
ENDING GRAVITY:	1.020
PRIMARY FERMENT:	1 WEEK
SECONDARY FERMENT:	4 WEEKS

1 lb. (454 g) chocolate malt
½ lb. (227 g) crystal malt, 20° Lovibond
½ lb. (227 g) roasted barley
½ lb. (227 g) oats
8 lb. (3.63 kg) Tru-Malt dark malt extract
½ lb. (227 g) light dry malt extract
1½ oz. (43 g) Bullion hop pellets, 8.8% alpha, in boil 60 min.
 Wyeast #1084 Irish Ale yeast
¾ c. (206 ml) corn sugar, for priming

Crush grains and add to 2 gals. (7.6 L) water. Steep at 150° – 155°F (66° – 68°C) for 60 min. Strain out grains and add malt extracts. Bring to a boil and add the Bullion hops. Boil 60 min., then turn off heat. Chill the wort, transfer to fermenter, and pitch yeast. Ferment 1 week at 70°F (21°C). Rack to secondary for 4 weeks at 70°F (21°C). Prime and bottle.

— *Bill Watt, Clarence Center, New York, Watt's Brewing*

Irish Oreo Stout

YIELD: .... 5 GAL. (18.9 L)
TOTAL BOILING TIME: .... 60 MIN.
STARTING GRAVITY: 1.048
ENDING GRAVITY: 1.015
PRIMARY FERMENT: .... 7 DAYS

- 4 oz. (113 g) chocolate malt
- 4 oz. (113 g) black patent malt
- 4 lb. (113 g) Ironmaster Irish stout extract
- 1.4 lb. (635 g) Alexander's Kicker dark malt extract
- 1 lb. (454 g) corn sugar
- 4 oz. (113 g) Baker's unsweetened chocolate
- 1 oz. (28 g) Bullion hop pellets, 7.5% alpha, in boil 60 min.
- ½ oz. (14 g) Fuggles hop pellets, 4.5% alpha, in boil 15 min.
- 1 11.5-g package (0.4 oz.) Edme dry ale yeast
- ½ oz. (14 g) Fuggles hop pellets, 4.5% alpha, dry hop
- ¾ c. (206 ml) corn sugar, for priming
- 6 oz. (170 g) dry lactose, for priming
- 1 tbsp. (14.8 ml) beverage settler, for priming

Steep grains in ½ gal. (1.9 L) hot water. Strain out grains and rinse with another ½ gal. (1.9 L) of water. Add malt extracts, corn sugar, chocolate, and Bullion hop pellets, and boil 45 min. Add ½ oz. (14 g) Fuggles hop pellets and boil 15 min. Turn off heat, and pour wort into fermenter containing 3 gal. (11.4 L) of cold water. Top off to 5 gal. (18.9 L) with cold water. Pitch yeast when wort has cooled to below 80°F (27°C). Ferment 4 days and dry hop with ½ oz. (14 g) Fuggles hop pellets. Ferment another 3 days; prime with the corn sugar, dry lactose, and beverage settler; and bottle. Age for at least 2 weeks.

— *Marc Battreall, Plantation Key, Florida*

FOREIGN STOUTS

Crankcase Stout

YIELD: .... 5 GAL. (18.9 L)
TOTAL BOILING TIME: .... 60 MIN.
PRIMARY FERMENT: .... 3 DAYS
SECONDARY FERMENT: .... 6 DAYS

  1 c. (275 ml) amber dry malt extract for yeast starter
     Wyeast #1084 Irish Ale yeast, 1-qt. (946-ml) starter
  ¾ lb. (340 g) roasted, nonmalted barley
  ¾ lb. (340 g) black patent malt
  ½ lb. (227 g) crystal malt
  4 lb. (1.81 kg) unhopped dark malt extract
3.3 lb. (1.5 kg) Mountmellick Irish Stout kit
  3 lb. (1.36 kg) unhopped amber dry malt extract
1¾ oz. (50 g) Kent Goldings whole leaf hops, in boil 60 min.
  ¼ oz. (7 g) Kent Goldings whole leaf hops, in boil 15 min.
  1 tsp. (4.9 ml) Irish moss
  1 c. (275 ml) corn sugar, for priming

The day before brew day, boil 1 c. (275 ml) amber dry malt extract in 1 qt. (946 ml) of water for 5 min. Cool and pitch contents of swelled yeast package into starter wort.

Steep grains in 3 gal. (11.4 L) hot water. Remove grains. Add malt extracts. Bring to a boil. Add 1¾ oz. (50 g) of Kent Goldings hops. Boil 45 min., add ¼ oz. (7 g) of Kent Goldings and the Irish moss. Boil 15 min., turn off heat. Chill the wort, transfer to fermenter, and top off to 5½ gal. (21 L). Pitch yeast and ferment 3 days at 68°F (20°C). Rack to secondary for 6 days at 68°F (20°C). Prime and bottle. Age at least 3 weeks.

— *Kent Eagle, Newark, Delaware*

No-Name Stout

YIELD: .... 5 GAL. (18.9 L)
TOTAL BOILING TIME: .... 60 MIN.
STARTING GRAVITY: 1.060
ENDING GRAVITY: 1.020
PRIMARY FERMENT: .... 7 DAYS
SECONDARY FERMENT: .... 6 DAYS

  1 lb. (454 g) crystal malt, 120° Lovibond

  ½ lb. (227 g) chocolate malt

  ¼ lb. (113 g) roasted barley

  4 lb. (1.8 kg) British light dry malt extract

3.3 lb. (1.5 kg) Munton & Fison hopped stout kit

  1 oz. (28 g) Willamette hops, 4.0% alpha, in boil 60 min.

  2 packets Muntons ale yeast

  ¾ c. (206 ml) corn sugar, for priming

Steep grain in 2 gal. (7.6 L) hot water. Strain out grains and add malt extracts and hops. Boil 60 min., then turn off heat. Chill the wort, transfer to primary fermenter, and top off to 5 gal. (18.9 L) with cold water. Pitch yeast and ferment 7 days at 65°F (18°C). Rack to secondary fermenter for 6 days at 65°F (18°C). Prime and bottle.

— Bill Muller, Sicklerville, New Jersey

Chocolate Stout

YIELD: .... 5 GAL. (18.9 L)
TOTAL BOILING TIME: .... 60 MIN.
STARTING GRAVITY: 1.050
ENDING GRAVITY: 1.032
PRIMARY FERMENT: .... 10 DAYS

Strong chocolate flavor with roasty finish.

- ¾ lb. (340 g) crystal malt
- ½ lb. (227 g) roasted barley
- ⅓ lb. (151 g) black patent malt
- 4 lb. (1.81 kg) dark dry malt extract
- 3.3 lb. (1.5 kg) Munton & Fison hopped dark malt extract syrup
- 6 tsp. (29.6 ml) gypsum
- 1 oz. (28 g) Northern Brewer hops, 14% alpha, in boil 60 min.
- 8 tbsp. (118 ml) Hershey's unsweetened cocoa
- ¾ oz. (21 g) Fuggles hops, 5% alpha, in boil 10 min.
- Cooper's dry ale yeast
- ½ c. (138 ml) corn sugar, for priming

Steep grains in 1½ gal. (5.7 L) hot water for 15 min. Strain out grains and add malt extracts, gypsum, and Northern Brewer hops. Boil 50 min., then add cocoa and Fuggles. Boil 10 min. Turn off heat, chill the wort, and strain into primary fermenter. Bring volume up to 5 gal. (18.9 L) and pitch yeast. Ferment 10 days, then prime with corn sugar and bottle.

— *Mark D. Sullivan, Laurel, Maryland*
Chesapeake Real Ale Brewers (CRAB)

Lights Out Stout

YIELD: .... 5 GAL. (18.9 L)
TOTAL BOILING TIME: .... 45 MINUTES
STARTING GRAVITY: 1.068
ENDING GRAVITY: 1.018
PRIMARY FERMENT: .... 7 DAYS
SECONDARY FERMENT: .... 7–14 DAYS

*As this brew ages, the grain bitterness turns to a silky chocolate. It
has been favorably compared to Guinness Stout.*

½ lb. (227 g) crystal malt, 80° Lovibond
½ lb. (227 g) malted wheat
¼ lb. (113 g) roasted barley
¼ lb. (113 g) chocolate malt
¼ lb. (113 g) black patent malt
1 lb. (454 g) pale malt
4 lb. (1.81 kg) dark dry malt extract
3.3 lb. (1.5 kg) dark malt extract
3 oz. (85 g) East Kent Goldings hops, 4.75% alpha, in boil
   30 min.
½ oz. (14 grams) Fuggles hops, in boil 5 min.
   Wyeast #1098 British Ale yeast
¾ c. (206 ml) corn sugar, for priming

Crush all grains and place in a grain bag. Add grain bag to brewpot
containing 1 gal. (3.8 L) of 108°F (42°C) water. Let rest for 15 minutes.
Heat to 155° – 158°F (68° – 70°C) and let rest for 30 minutes. Remove
grain bag and add malt extracts. Add 1 gal. (3.8 L) of water and bring to
a boil. Boil 15 minutes, then add the East Kent Goldings. Boil 25 minutes,
then add the Fuggles. Boil for 5 minutes and turn off heat. Chill the wort,
transfer to fermenter, and top off to 5 gal. (18.9 L) with cold water. Pitch
yeast and ferment 7 days at 65°F (18°C). Rack to secondary for 7 – 14
days. Prime and bottle. Age 1½ months.

— Pat Babcock, Canton Township, Michigan
Cooperative Homebrew Avocation and Obsession Society (CHAOS)
Fermental Order of Renaissance Draughtsmen (FORD)

Northwest Stout

YIELD: .... 5 GAL. (18.9 L)
TOTAL BOILING TIME: .... 90 MIN.
PRIMARY FERMENT: .... 5–7 DAYS
SECONDARY FERMENT: .... 1–2 WEEKS

This is an improved version of the recipe that won the gold medal at the 1993 AHA National Homebrew Competition. This is a big stout with assertive American hopping.

    Wyeast #1084 Irish Ale yeast
9 lb. (4.08 kg) English 2-row pale malt
3 lb. (1.36 kg) roasted unmalted barley, 500° Lovibond
¼ lb. (113 g) crystal malt, 130° Lovibond
½ lb. (227 g) black patent malt
½ lb. (227 g) flaked barley
1½ oz. (43 g) Chinook hops, 13.1% alpha, in boil 60 min.
1 tsp. (4.9 ml) Irish moss
1½ oz. (43 g) Cascade hops, in boil 15 min.
½ oz. (14 g) Cascade hops, steep
¾ c. (206 ml) corn sugar, for priming

Several days before brewing, begin growing up yeast starter.

    Crush grains and add to 4½ gal. (17 L) of 167°F (75°C) water. Mash at 156°F (69°C) for 60 min. Raise mash temperature to 170°F (77°C) for a 10-min. mash-out. Sparge with 170°F (77°C) water and collect 6½ gal. (24.6 L). Boil 30 min. before adding Chinook hops. Boil 30 min., then add Irish moss. Boil 15 min., then add 1½ oz. (43 g) of Cascade hops. Boil 15 min. and remove from heat. Add remaining ½ oz. (14 g) of Cascade. Chill wort and transfer to fermenter. Pitch yeast and ferment for 5 – 7 days at 60° – 65°F (16° – 18°C). Transfer to secondary for another 1 – 2 weeks. Prime with corn sugar and bottle, or keg.

— *David and Melinda Brockington, Seattle, Washington*
Seattle Secret Skinny Brewers Society

OATMEAL STOUTS

Eugenehead Oatmeal Stout

YIELD: .... 5 GAL. (18.9 L)
TOTAL BOILING TIME: .... 90 MIN.
PRIMARY FERMENT: .... 5–7 DAYS
SECONDARY FERMENT: .... 1 WEEK

First place at the Dixie Cup in 1994.

      Wyeast #1028 London Ale yeast
  8 lb. (3.63 kg) English pale ale malt
  3 lb. (1.36 kg) flaked oats
  1 lb. (454 g) crystal malt, 35° Lovibond
  1 lb. (454 g) roasted barley
  ½ lb. (227 g) crystal malt, 120° Lovibond
  ½ lb. (227 g) black patent malt
  ½ lb. (227 g) chocolate malt
  ¼ lb. (113 g) wheat malt
  2½ oz. (71 g) Mt. Hood hops, 5.9% alpha, in boil 60 min.
  1 tsp. (4.9 ml) Irish moss
  1 oz. (28 g) Liberty hops, 5.9% alpha, in boil 15 min.
  1½ oz. (43 g) Liberty hops, 5.9% alpha, steep
  ¾ c. (206 ml) corn sugar, for priming

Several days before brewing, begin growing up yeast starter.

Crush grains and add to 5 gal. (18.9 L) of 166°F (74°C) water. Mash at 155°F (68°C) for 60 min. Sparge with 170°F (77°C) water and collect 6½ gal. (24.6 L) of wort in brew kettle. Boil 30 min. before adding Mt. Hood hops. Boil 30 min., then add Irish moss. Boil 15 min. Add 1 oz. (28 g) of Liberty hops. Boil 15 min. and remove from heat, adding 1½ oz. (43 g) of Liberty hops. Chill wort and transfer to fermenter. Pitch yeast and ferment 5 – 7 days at 60° – 65°F (16° – 18°C). Transfer to secondary for 1 week. Prime and bottle, or keg.

— *David and Melinda Brockington, Seattle, Washington,*
Seattle Secret Skinny Brewers Society

Lights Out Oatmeal Stout

YIELD: .... 5 GAL. (18.9 L)
TOTAL BOILING TIME: .... 60 MIN.
ENDING GRAVITY: 1.024
PRIMARY FERMENT: .... 3 DAYS
SECONDARY FERMENT: .... 15 DAYS

8 lb. (3.63 kg) pale ale malt

1 lb. (454 g) Munich malt

1 lb. (454 g) crystal malt

¾ lb. (340 g) roast barley

½ lb. (227 g) chocolate malt

1 lb. (454 g) flaked oats

10 oz. (284 g) flaked barley

5 oz. (142 g) malto-dextrin powder

2 oz. (57 g) Northern Brewer hops, 7.0% alpha, in boil 60 min.

½ oz. (14 g) Willamette hops, 4.5% alpha, in boil 2 min.

Wyeast #1084 Irish Ale yeast

¾ c. (206 ml) corn sugar, for priming

Add all grains, flaked oats, and flaked barley to 3¾ gal. (14.2 L) of 175°F (79°C) water. Let rest until starch conversion is complete. Sparge with 170°F (77°C) water and collect wort in brew kettle. Bring to a boil and add malto-dextrin and Northern Brewer hops. Boil 58 min., then add ½ oz. (14 g) of Willamette hops. Boil a final 2 min. Turn off heat, chill the wort, transfer to the primary fermenter, and pitch yeast. Ferment 3 days at 72°F (21°C). Rack to secondary for 15 days at 72°F (21°C). Prime with corn sugar and bottle.

— *Matt Zaccheo, Phillipsburg, New Jersey*

RUSSIAN IMPERIAL STOUTS

Hammer of the Dogs
Imperial Stout

YIELD: .... 5 GAL. (18.9 L)
TOTAL BOILING TIME: .... 90 MIN.
STARTING GRAVITY: 1.103
ENDING GRAVITY: 1.028
PRIMARY FERMENT: .... 1 WEEK
SECONDARY FERMENT: .... 30 DAYS

1¼ lb. (567 g) roasted barley
1 lb. (454 g) crystal malt, 80° Lovibond
1 lb. (454 g) chocolate malt
1 lb. (454 g) black patent malt
13½ lb. (6.12 kg) dark malt extract
2 oz. (57 g) Galena hops, 13.2% alpha, in boil 60 min.
3 oz. (85 g) Willamette hops, 4.2% alpha, in boil 60 min.
¾ oz. (21 g) East Kent Goldings hops, 5.6% alpha, in boil 10 min.
   ale yeast, highly attenuative
1½ oz. (43 g) Fuggles hops, dry hop in secondary
½ c. (138 ml) corn sugar, for priming

Steep grains in 4 gal. (15.1 L) of water for 30 – 45 min. at 150° – 160°F
(66° – 71°C). Strain out grains and sparge with 2 gal. (7.6 L) of water.
Add malt extract and boil 30 min. Add Galena and Willamette hops.
Boil 50 min. Add the East Kent Goldings and boil 10 min., then turn off
heat. Chill the wort, transfer to fermenter, and pitch yeast. Ferment
1 week, then rack to secondary, add Fuggles hops, and ferment 30
days. Prime with corn sugar and bottle.

— *Douglas Faynor, Salem, Oregon, Homebrew Heaven*
7 Capitol Brewers of Salem

Imperial Stout

YIELD:	5 GAL. (18.9 L)
TOTAL BOILING TIME:	90 MIN.
STARTING GRAVITY:	1.087
ENDING GRAVITY:	1.030
PRIMARY FERMENT:	10 DAYS
SECONDARY FERMENT:	2 WEEKS

Second place in the BURP Stout competition and second place in the 1996 Spirit of Free Beer.

9 lb. (4.08 kg) pale ale malt
3 lb. (1.36 kg) roasted barley
½ lb. (227 g) black patent malt
½ lb. (227 g) wheat malt
½ lb. (227 g) crystal malt, 40° Lovibond
3.3 lb. (1.5 kg) light malt extract
1 oz. (28 g) Chinook hops, 12.7% alpha, in boil 60 min.
1 oz. (28 g) Nugget hops, 13.3% alpha, in boil 60 min.
1 oz. (28 g) Fuggles hops, 5% alpha, in boil 15 min.
1 oz. (28 g) East Kent Goldings hops, 5% alpha, in boil 15 min.
Wyeast #1056 American Ale yeast
¾ c. (206 ml) corn sugar, for priming

Crush grains and add to 4½ gal. (17 L) of 166°F (74°C) water. Mash at 155°F (68°C) for 60 min. Sparge with 170°F (77°C) water, collecting 6 ½ to 7 gal. (24.6 – 26.5 L) of wort. Bring wort to a boil adding the malt extract and boil 30 min. before adding Chinook and Nugget hops. Boil 45 min., then add the Fuggles and East Kent Goldings. Boil 15 min., then turn off heat. Chill wort, transfer to fermenter, and pitch yeast. Ferment at 60° – 67°F (16° – 19°C) for 10 days, then rack to secondary for another 2 weeks. Prime with corn sugar and bottle.

— *Keith Chamberlin, Riverdale, Maryland*
Brewers United for Real Potables (BURP)

SPECIALTY STOUTS

─Kitchen Sink─

YIELD: .... 5 GAL. (18.9 L)
TOTAL BOILING TIME: .... 75 MIN.
STARTING GRAVITY: 1.087
ENDING GRAVITY: 1.023
PRIMARY FERMENT: .... 7 DAYS
SECONDARY FERMENT: .... 7 DAYS

½ lb. (227 g) crystal malt, 60° Lovibond

¼ lb. (113 g) chocolate malt

³⁄₁₀ lb. (136 g) black patent malt

¾ oz. (20 g) espresso coffee

5.2 lb. (2.36 kg) Munton & Fison light dry malt extract

3.3 lb. (1.5 kg) Munton & Fison dark malt extract

¾ lb. (340 g) brown sugar

¾ lb. (340 g) corn sugar

¼ c. (59 ml) molasses

3 oz. (85 g) Northern Brewer hops plug, 7.5% alpha, in boil 75 min.

1 tbsp. (4.9 ml) Irish moss

1½ oz. (143 g) Kent Goldings hop pellets, 5.9% alpha, in boil 30 min.

2 oz. (57 g) Hershey's unsweetened chocolate

¾ oz. (21 g) Kent Goldings hop pellets, 5.9% alpha, in boil 3 min.

Wyeast #1028 London English Ale yeast

¾ c. (206 ml) corn sugar, for priming

Steep grains and espresso in 1 gal. (3.8 L) of hot water. Strain out grains, add malt extracts, ¾ lb. (340 g) each of brown sugar and corn sugar, and ¼ c. (59 ml) molasses. Bring to a rolling boil and add 3 oz. (85 g) of Northern Brewer hops plug and Irish moss. Boil 45 min., then add 1½ oz. (43 g) of Kent Goldings. Boil 27 min., then add chocolate and ¾ oz. (43 g) of Kent Goldings hop pellets. Boil 3 min. and turn off heat. Transfer to fermenter and top off to 5 gal. (18.9 L) with cold water. Pitch yeast when wort is below 80°F (27°C). Ferment 7 days, then rack to a secondary fermenter for 7 days. Prime and bottle.

— *Roger Savoy, Troy, New York*

Chocoberry Stout

YIELD: .... 5 GAL. (18.9 L)
TOTAL BOILING TIME: .... 70 MIN.
STARTING GRAVITY: 1.058
ENDING GRAVITY· 1.024
PRIMARY FERMENT: .... 7 DAYS
SECONDARY FERMENT: .... 4 WEEKS

7 lb. (3.2 kg) pale ale malt
1 lb. (454 g) wheat
½ lb. (227 g) Belgian special-B malt
½ lb. (227 g) chocolate malt
½ lb. (227 g) flaked barley
¼ lb. (113 g) roasted barley
½ oz. (14 g) Perle hops, 8.9% alpha, in boil 60 min.
1 oz. (28 g) Cascade hops, 6.9% alpha, in boil 40 min.
¼ lb. (113 g) cocoa powder
    Wyeast #1084 Irish Ale yeast
24 oz. (710 ml) Chambord liqueur
¾ c. (206 ml) corn sugar, for priming

Heat 12 qt. (11.4 L) of water to 175°F (79°C) and add crushed grains. Mash for 60 min. at 152°F (67°C). Sparge with 18 qt. of 168°F (76°C) water. Boil 10 min. before adding the Perle hops. Boil 20 min., then add the Cascade hops. Boil 10 min., then add cocoa powder. Boil 30 min. and turn off heat. Chill the wort, transfer to fermenter, and pitch yeast. Ferment for 7 days at 65°F (18°C), then rack to a secondary fermenter for 4 weeks at 60°F (16°C). Prime with Chambord liqueur and corn sugar, then bottle.

— *Keith Schwols, Ft. Collins, Colorado*

6

More HOMEBREW FAVORITES

Belgian Ales

N o one else celebrates beer the way the Belgians do. They understand that while technology and science are part of brewing, those elements are no more important than artistry. Belgian brewers are respectful of brewing traditions, and they use that knowledge and respect to craft a wider diversity of tongue-dancing tastes and styles than any other brewing nation. From the unorthodox methods of producing lambic ales to the use of fruits, spices, and processed sugar in many beers, the Belgians exhibit craftsmanship and inventiveness in every bottle.

The real magic of Belgian brewers is highlighted in their unique styles — those unlike beers produced in any other brewing nation. These styles include the famous Trappist ales, such as the malty, sweet, dark dubbel and the lighter colored, but more alcoholic tripel. Belgian wit beers are wheat beers made with unmalted wheat. The oud bruin style is a sweet-and-sour-flavored brown ale. The lambics are always a treasure chest of complex flavors and aromas produced by wild yeasts. Belgian Strong Ales are famous for their ability to hide their alcohol in a pale-colored, light-bodied brew; these beers deserve their association with mischief and devilry!

KEY TO RECIPE LOGOS

EXTRACT RECIPES

PARTIAL MASH RECIPES

ALL-GRAIN RECIPES

Description. For their base malt, most Belgian brewers use pilsner malt, although occasionally an English pale ale malt is used. Munich or caramel malts may be added for color or residual sweetness. Candi sugar, (crystallized sucrose) increases gravities in some Belgian beers while retaining a light body.

Belgian beers are often low in hops. German noble hops, or English varieties such as Kent Goldings, are commonly used. Lambic brewers age their hops for several years before brewing with them.

Yeast is probably the most important ingredient in Belgian beers. Many of the yeasts create unusual fermentation by-products that would be frowned on in any other brewing country, but they combine in Belgian beers to create brews of incredible complexity. In addition to standard yeasts, brewers working on Belgian styles will occasionally use other cultures, such as *Brettanomyces* or *Pediococcus* — bacteria that are known for producing off flavors, like sourness, or off aroma likes those described as "horsey" or "barnyard" — any of which might make a brewer from any other country throw the beer away. While many homebrewers prefer to seek out bottles of beer from specific brewers and culture yeast from those, there is now a wide range of Belgian beer yeasts as well as *Pediococcus* and *Brettanomyces* cultures available from sources, such as Wyeast and the Yeast Culture Kit Company.

Belgian pale ale is much like English pale ale, but may have more yeast character and softer, caramel-like, toffee flavors from the addition of dark candi sugar. These are normal-gravity beers of about 1.045 to 1.055 that are hopped to about 20 to 40 IBUs.

Belgian strong ales are of substantial alcoholic strength, but often have light body and an abundance of yeast character. They have gravities ranging from 1.060 to 1.120, with the strength evident but with little or no alcohol flavor. Some of the paler versions traditionally bear the "mark of the devil" for their reputation as a sly beer that seems innocuous but packs a punch. Darker versions may have full bodies and taste rich and malty with toffee or caramel flavor, but again, yeast character should be prevalent.

Trappist beers are the brews made famous by the six monasteries brewing beer. These are often classified by their relative

strengths, normally either dubbel, or tripel. A dubbel will have a
starting gravity of about 1.050 to 1.070; a tripel will be 1.080 to 1.095.
Dubbels are malty-tasting beers, deep amber or brown in color, with
light hopping rates of about 18 to 25 IBUs. Unique yeast strains are
often used and are key to producing good examples of these beers.
The tripel is quite complex and includes light candi sugar to boost
the gravity. Trappist beers will be full-bodied beers with a lot of complexity, and sometimes some spiciness. Although these are strong
beers, the alcoholic flavors should be evident but not excessive.

Lambic beers. The most famous of the Belgian beers are un-
doubtedly the lambic beers, which are noted for their sour character and complexity — a complexity that is achieved by dozens of
different, naturally occurring yeasts and other bacteria acting in concert on the cooling wort. Yeast is not pitched as it is with other
styles; rather, nature is allowed to take its course, making for highly
variable beers from batch to batch. Lambics are usually brewed using at least 30 percent unmalted wheat, with pilsner malt making
up the bulk of the grist. A lambic wort is often boiled for 3 hours or
more. Hops are aged and are used mostly for their preservative properties, not for aroma or flavor. Hopping rates are low — about 3 to
20 IBUs. The original gravity is about 1.040 to 1.055.

The art of blending is an indispensable craft to the successful
lambic brewer. There are several substyles of lambic. *Gueuze* is a
blend of old and young lambic. It is often quite acidic and tart. Fruity
esters are common. *Faro* is a lambic with sugars added. The beer is
generally pasteurized to prevent the sugars from fermenting in the
bottle. Several lambics have fruit added to them in the fermenter.
Kriek uses cherries, *framboise* is flavored with raspberries, and
pêche with peaches.

The oud bruin style is a distinctive sweet-and-sour tasting
brown ale with a soft caramel maltiness and a lactic acid sourness.
Sometimes old and young batches are blended. The style is exemplified by Liefmans Goudenband.

Wit (white) beer is a wheat beer made with up to 50 percent
unmalted wheat. The beer is sharply flavored and often includes
blends of spices, including, coriander and bitter curaçao orange peel.

Mild acidity from a lactic fermentation or the addition of lactic acid is essential. These beers may be quite cloudy. They are fairly light bodied, despite being brewed to normal gravity. Wit beers are often quite effervescent and undergo a second bottle fermentation, sometimes using different yeast strains than those used for fermentation.

In the past, judges gave wide latitude to homebrewed Belgian beers, but competitions are becoming increasingly challenging as more homebrewers and judges gain experience with the nuances of the myriad styles. Judges will now often look for complexity in these beers with a lot of characteristic yeast by-product flavors, including esters, phenols, and higher alcohols.

BELGIAN PALE ALES

Belgian Ale #1

YIELD: .... 5 GAL. (18.9 L)
TOTAL BOILING TIME: .... 20 MIN.
STARTING GRAVITY: 1.042
ENDING GRAVITY: 1.005
PRIMARY FERMENT: .... 14 DAYS

3.3 lb. (1.5 kg) Brewferm "Diablo" malt extract
2 lb. (907 g) extra light, dry malt extract
1 oz. (28 g) Saaz hops, 2.5% alpha, in boil 20 min.
½ oz. (14 g) Willamette hops, 4.5% alpha, in boil 20 min.
Wyeast #1214 Belgian Abbey yeast
⅔ c. (184 ml) corn sugar, for priming

Combine malt extracts with 2½ gal. (9.5 L) of water and bring to a boil. Add all hops and boil 20 min. Turn off heat, chill the wort, and transfer to fermenter. Bring volume up to 5 gal. (18.9 L) with cold water, pitch yeast, and ferment 14 days. Prime and bottle.

— *Jim White, Southgate, Michigan, Down River Brewers Guild*

Belgian Spice

YIELD:	5 GAL. (18.9 L)
TOTAL BOILING TIME:	60 MIN.
STARTING GRAVITY:	1.047
ENDING GRAVITY:	1.012
PRIMARY FERMENT:	7 DAYS
SECONDARY FERMENT:	2 WEEKS

½ lb. (227 g) Belgian pale ale malt
½ lb. (227 g) Belgian wheat malt
3 oz. (85 g) cara-Vienne malt
⅓ oz. (9 g) Belgian chocolate malt
3.3 lb. (1.5 kg) light malt extract
3 lb. (1.36 kg) light dry malt extract
2 oz. (57 g) Hallertauer hops, 3.2% alpha, in boil 60 min.
1 tsp. (4.9 ml) Irish moss
1 oz. (28 g) coriander seed, crushed
2 tsp. (9.9 ml) ground cinnamon
1 tsp. (4.9 ml) ground nutmeg
1 oz. (28 g) orange peel
⅓ oz. (9 g) Saaz hops, 2.5% alpha, in boil 1–2 min.
½ oz. (14 g) coriander seed, in secondary
     Wyeast #3944 Belgian White Beer yeast
¾ c. (206 ml) corn sugar, for priming

Steep grains in 2 gal. (7.6 L) water at about 160°F (71°C) for 60 min. Strain out grains. Bring to a boil. Add malt extract and Hallertauer hops in a hops bag. Boil 45 min., then add Irish moss. Boil 5 min., then add 1 oz. (28 g) coriander seed, cinnamon, nutmeg, and orange peel in another hops bag. Boil 7 – 8 min., then add Saaz hops. Boil 1 – 2 min. and turn off heat. Chill wort, transfer to fermenter, and pitch yeast. Ferment 7 days. Rack to secondary, add ½ oz. (14 g) of coriander seed, and ferment 7 days. Prime and bottle.

— *Jay Mastri, Malt-N-Hop Stop, Northbrook, Illinois*
Suburban Brew Crew

Belgian Ale #2

YIELD: .... 5 GAL. (18.9 L)
TOTAL BOILING TIME: .... 90 MIN.
STARTING GRAVITY: 1.057
ENDING GRAVITY: 1.014
PRIMARY FERMENT: .... 1 WEEK
SECONDARY FERMENT: .... 1 WEEK

DeKoninck or similar Belgian yeast, in starter
9½ lb. (4.31 kg) Belgian pilsner malt
½ lb. (227 g) cara-Munich malt
½ lb. (227 g) biscuit malt
½ lb. (227 g) wheat malt
¼ lb. (113 g) cara-Vienne malt
1 oz. (28 g) Perle hops, 8.0% alpha, in boil 60 min.
½ oz. (14 g) Saaz hops, 3.57% alpha, in boil 15 min.
1 oz. (28 g) Saaz hops, steep
¾ c. (206 ml) corn sugar, for priming

Several days ahead of time, begin making a starter of a Belgian yeast.
Crush grains and add to 3¾ gal. (14.2 L) of 163°F (73°C) water.
Mash at 152°F (67°C) for 1 hour. Raise temperature to 170°F (77°C)
for 10 min. Sparge with 170°F (77°C) water, collecting 7 gal. (26.5 L)
of wort. Boil 30 min. before adding Perle hops. Boil 45 min., then add
½ oz. (14 g) of Saaz hops. Boil 15 min. and turn off heat. Add last 1 oz.
(28 g) of Saaz hops and steep a few min. Chill the wort, transfer to
fermenter, and pitch yeast. Ferment 1 week at 67°F (19°C). Rack to
secondary fermenter for an additional week. Prime and bottle.

— *Keith Chamberlin, Riverdale, Maryland*
Brewers United for Real Potables (BURP)

Brain Wipe Tripel

YIELD: .... 5 GAL. (18.9 L)
TOTAL BOILING TIME: .... 90 MIN.
STARTING GRAVITY: 1.072
ENDING GRAVITY: 1.017
PRIMARY FERMENT: .... 7 DAYS
SECONDARY FERMENT: .... 3 WEEKS

*First place in the Belgian category at the TRASH competition and
third place in the Belgian category in the Spirit of Free Beer
competition.*

    12 lb. (5.44 kg) DeWolf-Cosyns pilsner malt
     1 lb. (454 g) DeWolf-Cosyns cara-pils malt
     1 lb. (454 g) flaked maize
     2 lb. (907 g) sugar
    1½ oz. (43 g) Hallertau hops, 4.0% alpha, in boil 60 min.
     ½ oz. (14 g) Saaz hops, 2.0% alpha, in boil 5 min.
        La Chouffe yeast, 1-pt. (473-ml) slurry
     ¾ c. (206 ml) corn sugar, for priming

Crush grains and add with flaked maize to 4 ⅔ gal. (17.7 L) of 164°F
(73°C) water. Mash at 153°F (67°C) for 60 min. Sparge with 170°F (77°C)
water, collecting 7 gal. (26.5 L) of wort. Bring wort to a boil, add sugar,
and boil 30 min. Add Hallertauer hops and boil 55 min. Add the Saaz hops,
boil 5 min., and turn off heat. Chill the wort to 65°F (18°C), transfer to
fermenter, and pitch yeast. Ferment for 7 days. Rack to secondary for
another 3 weeks. Prime and bottle.

— Delano Dugarm, Arlington, Virginia
Brewers United for Real Potables (BURP)

BELGIAN STRONG ALES

Kris Krumple

YIELD: .... 12½ GAL. (4.73 L)
TOTAL BOILING TIME: .... 90 MIN.
STARTING GRAVITY: 1.068
ENDING GRAVITY: 1.012
PRIMARY FERMENT: .... 7 DAYS
SECONDARY FERMENT: .... 3 WEEKS

15 lb. (6.8 kg) DeWolf-Cosyns pilsner malt
5 lb. (2.27 kg) DeWolf-Cosyns Munich malt
1 lb. (454 g) DeWolf-Cosyns cara-Munich malt
1 lb. (454 g) DeWolf-Cosyns aromatic malt
½ lb. (227 g) DeWolf-Cosyns special-B malt
2 oz. (57 g) DeWolf-Cosyns roast malt
9.2 oz. (260 g) light candi sugar
13.4 oz. (380 g) dark candi sugar
0.65 lb. (295 g) raw sugar
3 oz. (85 g) Perle hops, 7.8% alpha, in boil 60 min.
1 oz. (28 g) Tettnanger hops, 5.5% alpha, steep
0.18 oz. (5 g) star anise, steep
La Chouffe ale yeast slurry
1½ c. (413 ml) sugar, for priming

Mash all grains in 7½ gal. (28.4 L) of water at 150°F (66°C) for 90 min. Raise temperature to 170°F (77°C) for a mash-out of 10 min. and then sparge to collect 15 gal. (56.4 L). Bring wort to a boil, add the adjunct sugars, and boil 30 min. Add the Perle hops. Boil 60 min., then turn off heat. Add the Tettnanger hops and star anise and steep several min. Force-chill the wort to 60°F (16°C) and pitch La Chouffe yeast. Ferment in primary for 7 days at 60°F (16°C), then rack to secondary for 21 days. Prime with ¾ c. (206 ml) sugar per 6¼ gal. (23.7 L).

— *Tim Artz, Lorton, Virginia*
Brewers United for Real Potables (BURP)

Belgian Strong Ale

YIELD: .... 5 GAL. (18.9 L)
TOTAL BOILING TIME: .... 90 MIN.
PRIMARY FERMENT: .... 6 WEEKS
SECONDARY FERMENT: .... 3 DAYS

Third place in the strong ale category at the 1996 Spirit of Belgium competition.

     Westmalle yeast
 15 lb. (6.8 kg) Belgian pilsner malt
  1 lb. (454 g) wheat malt
1½ lb. (680 g) dextrose
1½ oz. (43 g) Styrian Goldings hops, 5.0% alpha, in boil 60 min.
 ½ oz. (14 g) Saaz hops, 3.57% alpha, steep
 ¾ c. (206 ml) corn sugar, for priming

Several days before brewing, culture yeast from a bottle of Westmalle and grow a starter.

       Crush grains and add to 5 ⅓ gal. (20.2 L) of 164°F (73°C) water. Mash at 153°F (67°C) for 1 hour, then heat mash for a 10-min. mash-out at 170°F (77°C). Sparge with 170°F (77°C) water, collecting 7 gal. (26.5 L) of wort in brew kettle. Bring wort to a boil and add dextrose. Boil 30 min. before adding the Styrian Goldings hops. Boil 60 min., then remove from heat and add the Saaz hops. Steep a few min. Chill the wort, transfer to fermenter, and pitch yeast. Ferment at 65°F (18°C) for 6 weeks, with several yeast additions. Rack to secondary for about 3 days. Prime and bottle.

— Keith Chamberlin, Riverdale, Maryland
Brewers United for Real Potables (BURP)

OUD BRUIN

Divine Wind Oud Bruin

YIELD: .... 10 GAL. (37.9 L)
TOTAL BOILING TIME: .... 90 MIN
STARTING GRAVITY: 1.055
ENDING GRAVITY: 1.008

16 lb. (7.26 kg) DeWolf-Cosyns pilsner malt
 2 lb. (907 g) DeWolf-Cosyns Munich malt
 2 lb. (907 g) DeWolf-Cosyns wheat malt
 1 lb. (454 g) DeWolf-Cosyns aromatic malt
 ½ lb. (227 g) DeWolf-Cosyns special-B malt
 1 oz. (28 g) East Kent Goldings hops, 5% alpha, in boil 60 min.
 1 oz. (28 g) Saaz hops, 3.3% alpha, in boil 60 min.
   Liefman's ale yeast
   Head Start *Lactobacillus* culture
   Head Start oud bruin culture (premixed yeast and lacto culture)
 1½ c. (512 ml) corn sugar, for priming

Mash at 150°F (66°C) for 90 min. Raise temperature to 170°F (77°C) for mash-out and then sparge to collect 12½ gal. (47.3 L). Boil 30 min. before adding all hops. Boil 60 min., then turn off heat. Force-chill to 60°F (16°C). Split batch into two carboys. In one carboy, pitch the Liefman's yeast and the Head Start *Lactobacillus* culture. In the other carboy, pitch the Head Start oud bruin culture. Ferment using the BrewCo Brewcap setup to allow yeast collection and sampling for monitoring flavor development. Ambient fermentation temperature was about 70°F (21°C). Ferment until flavor is as desired. The batch fermented with the Head Start oud bruin mix took about 2 months to achieve the desired flavor. The batch fermented with the Liefman's and *Lactobacillus* culture took almost a year to develop a similar flavor. When ready, prime with corn sugar and bottle.

— *Tim Artz, Lorton, Virginia*
Brewers United for Real Potables (BURP)

TRAPPIST ALES: DUBBEL AND TRIPEL

—Phil's Sippin' Abbey Bier—

YIELD: .... 6 GAL. (22.7 L)
TOTAL BOILING TIME: .... 45 MIN.

1 lb. (454 g) pale ale malt
½ lb. (227 g) wheat grain
¼ lb. (113 g) roasted barley
1 oz. (28 g) Northern Brewer hops, 7.5% alpha, in boil 45 min.
1 oz. (28 g) Hallertauer hops, 3.2% alpha, in boil 45 min.
3 lb. (1.36 kg) light dry malt extract
1 can Brewferm Belgian Abbey malt extract
1 oz. (28 g) Hallertauer hops, 3.2% alpha, in boil 15 min.
1 tsp. (4.9 ml) Irish moss
   Wyeast #1214 Belgian Abbey yeast
   Judy's Primer Pack (malt extract, corn sugar, and gelatin)

Steep grains in hot water. Strain out grain. Add Northern Brewer hops
and 1 oz. (28 g) of Hallertauer hops and heat to a boil for 30 min., then add
malt extracts, 1 oz. (28 g) of Hallertauer hops, and Irish moss. Boil 15
min., then turn off heat. Chill wort, strain into fermenter, and top off to
6 gal. (22.7 L). Pitch yeast and ferment until fermentation has completed
(10 – 14 days). Prime with Judy's Primer pack and bottle.

— *Judith Charland, Judy's Homebrew Shoppe, Jacksonville, Florida*
River City Brewers

A Kick in the Abbey

YIELD: .... 5 GAL. (18.9 L)
TOTAL BOILING TIME: .... 60 MIN.
STARTING GRAVITY: 1.071
ENDING GRAVITY: 1.020
PRIMARY FERMENT: .... 14 DAYS

   1 lb. (454 g) crystal malt
   1 lb. (454 g) wheat malt
   ½ lb. (227 g) chocolate malt
   6 lb. (2.72 kg) Northwestern weizen malt extract
 3.3 lb. (1.5 kg) Brewferm Abbey malt extract
   1 lb. (454 g) brown sugar
   ½ oz. (14 g) Czech Saaz hops, 2.5% alpha, in boil 60 min.
   ½ oz. (14 g) Hallertauer hops, 2% alpha, in boil 60 min.
   ½ oz. (14 g) Czech Saaz hops, 2.5% alpha, in boil 10 min.
   ½ oz. (14 g) Hallertauer hops, 2% alpha, in boil 10 min.
      Wyeast #1214 Belgian Abbey yeast
   ⅔ c. (184 ml) corn sugar, for priming

Steep grains in 2 gal. (7.6 L) of water at 160° to 170°F (71° – 77°C) for 30 min. Strain out grains; add malt extracts and brown sugar. Bring to a boil; add ½ oz. (14 g) each of Czech Saaz hops and Hallertauer hops. Boil 50 min. Add ½ oz. (14 g) each of Czech Saaz hops and Hallertauer hops. Boil 10 min.; turn off heat. Chill the wort, transfer to fermenter, bring volume up to 5 gal. (18.9 L) with cold water; pitch yeast. Ferment 14 days; prime with corn sugar and bottle. Age at least 6 weeks.

— *Jim White, Southgate, Michigan, Down River Brewers Guild*

Trappist-style Ale

YIELD: .... 5 GAL. (18.9 L)
TOTAL BOILING TIME: .... 60 MIN.
STARTING GRAVITY: 1.064
ENDING GRAVITY: 1.014
PRIMARY FERMENT: .... 1 WEEK
SECONDARY FERMENT: .... 1 WEEK

Wyeast #1214 Belgian Abbey yeast or Wyeast #3944
Belgian White Beer yeast
1 lb. (454 g) Belgian cara-Vienne malt
1 lb. (454 g) Belgian cara-Munich malt
6 lb. (2.72 kg) Old Bavarian Munich Blend malt extract
2 lb. (907 g) wheat malt extract
1 lb. (454 g) dark brown sugar
½ oz. (14 g) Northern Brewer hops, in boil 55 min.
1 oz. (28 g) Hallertauer Hersbrucker hops, in boil 15 min.
1 package Bru-Vigor yeast food
½ c. (138 ml) brown sugar, for priming

Prepare yeast starter prior to brewing day.

Crush grains and add to 1 gal. (3.8 L) of 160°F (71°C) water and steep for 30 min. Sparge the grains with 1 gal. (3.8 L) or more of 168°F (76°C) water into brew kettle. Bring wort to a boil, then turn off heat and add malt extracts and 1 lb. (454 g) dark brown sugar. Boil 5 min. before adding Northern Brewer hops. Boil 40 min., then add Hallertauer Hersbrucker hops. Boil 15 min., then turn off heat. Chill wort, transfer to fermenter, and top off to 5 gal. (18.9 L) with cold water. Pitch yeast along with Bru-Vigor yeast food. Ferment 1 week. Rack to secondary for 1 week. Prime with brown sugar and bottle.

— *DeFalco's Home Wine & Beer Supplies, Houston, Texas*

Belgian Triple

YIELD:	5 GAL. (18.9 L)
TOTAL BOILING TIME:	60 MIN.
STARTING GRAVITY:	1.074
ENDING GRAVITY:	1.016
PRIMARY FERMENT:	1 WEEK
SECONDARY FERMENT:	1 WEEK

Wyeast #1214 Belgian Abbey yeast (or Wyeast #3944)

2 lb. (907 g) Belgian pilsner malt

½ lb. (227 g) Belgian cara-pils malt

6 lb. (2.72 kg) light malt extract

2 lb. (907 g) Old Bavarian Munich Blend malt extract

1 lb. (454 g) light brown sugar

1½ oz. (43 g) Hallertauer Hersbrucker hops, in boil 55 min.

1 oz. (28 g) Fuggles hops, in boil 15 min.

½ oz. (14 g) Czech Saaz hops, steep

1 package Bru-Vigor yeast food

½ c. (138 ml) light brown sugar, for priming

Prepare yeast starter prior to brewing day.

Crush grains and add to 1 gal. (3.8 L) of 160°F (71°C) water and steep 30 min. Sparge grains with 1 gal. (3.8 L) or more of 168°F (76°C) water into brew kettle. Bring wort to a boil, then turn off heat and add malt extracts and 1 lb. (454 g) of light brown sugar. Boil 5 min. before adding Hallertauer Hersbrucker hops. Boil 40 min., then add Fuggles hops. Boil 15 min., then add Czech Saaz hops and turn off heat. Steep a few min., then chill the wort, transfer to fermenter, and top off to 5 gal. (18.9 L) with cold water. Pitch yeast along with Bru-Vigor yeast food. Ferment 1 week at 60° – 65°F (16° – 18°C). Rack to secondary for 1 week. Prime and bottle.

— *DeFalco's Home Wine & Beer Supplies, Houston, Texas*

Light Dubbel

YIELD: .... 5 GAL. (18.9 L)
TOTAL BOILING TIME: .... 90 MIN.
STARTING GRAVITY: 1.050
ENDING GRAVITY: 1.008
PRIMARY FERMENT: .... 1 WEEK
SECONDARY FERMENT: .... 5 WEEKS

10 lb. (4.54 kg) Belgian 2-row malt

½ lb. (227 g) crystal malt, 20° Lovibond

¾ oz. (43 g) Bullion hops, 8.5% alpha, in boil 60 min.

1 lb. (454 g) Belgian light candi sugar

¼ oz. (7 g) Hallertauer hops, 3.1% alpha, in boil 5 min.

   Wyeast #3787 Trappist Ale yeast

¾ c. (206 ml) corn sugar, for priming

Add crushed grains to 13 qt. (12.3 L) of 164°F (73°C) water. Let rest at
153°F (67°C) until starch conversion is complete. Sparge with 170°F
(77°C) water and collect 6 ½ gal. (24.6 L) of wort. Bring wort to a boil for
30 min. Add ¾ oz. (43 g) of Bullion hops. Boil 30 min., then add candi
sugar. Boil 55 min., then add Hallertauer hops. Boil 5 min. and turn off
heat. Chill the wort, transfer to fermenter, and pitch yeast. Ferment
1 week at 60°F (16°C). Rack to secondary for 5 weeks at 60°F (16°C).
Prime and bottle.

— *Bill Pemberton, Charlottesville, Virginia, Back Door Brewers*

Belgian Nectar

YIELD: .... 5 GAL. (18.9 L)
TOTAL BOILING TIME: .... 2½ HOURS
STARTING GRAVITY: 1.085
ENDING GRAVITY: 1.023
PRIMARY FERMENT: .... 13 DAYS
SECONDARY FERMENT: .... 26 DAYS

First place in the tripel category at the 1994 Spirit of Belgium competition.

Wyeast #3944, Belgian White Beer yeast
15 lb. (6.8 kg) Belgian pilsner malt
 1 lb. (454 g) flaked maize
2.2 lb. (1 kg) Belgian light candi sugar
1¼ oz. (35 g) U.S. Hallertauer whole hops, 5.3% alpha, in boil 90 min.
 ½ oz. (14 g) Saaz hops plug, 5.0% alpha, in boil 60 min.
 2 tsp. (10 ml) Irish moss
 ½ oz. (14 g) Saaz hops plug, 5.0% alpha, in boil 15 min.
1¼ c. (344 ml) corn sugar, for priming

Several days before brewing, start the yeast and grow up to a 2-qt. (1.9-L) slurry.

Crush grains and add to 6 gal. (22.7 L) of 135°F (57°C) water. Allow a protein rest at 124°F (51°C) for 30 min. Raise mash temperature to 136°F (58°C) and hold for 15 min. Raise mash to 144°F (62°C) and hold for 10 min. Raise mash temperature to 156°F (69°C) and hold for 75 min. Raise temperature to 170°F (77°C) for mash-out and hold for 10 min. Sparge with 170°F (77°C) water and collect 8½ – 9 gal. (32.2 – 34.1 L) of wort in brew kettle. Bring wort to a boil, add candi sugar and boil 1 hour. Add the U.S. Hallertauer hops and boil 30 min. Add ½ oz. (14 g) of Saaz hops and boil 45 min. Add Irish moss and ½ oz. (14 g) of Saaz hops plug. Boil 15 min. and turn off heat. Chill, transfer to fermenter, and pitch yeast slurry. Ferment 13 days, then rack to secondary for 26 days. Prime and bottle.

— *Andy Anderson, Bath, England*
Brewers United for Real Potables (BURP)

Belgian Tripel

YIELD:	15 GAL. (56.8 L)
TOTAL BOILING TIME:	60 MIN.
STARTING GRAVITY:	1.084
ENDING GRAVITY:	1.013
PRIMARY FERMENT:	7 DAYS
SECONDARY FERMENT:	14 DAYS
TERTIARY FERMENT:	9 MONTHS

12 lb. (5.44 kg) DeWolf-Cosyns pilsner malt

12 lb. (5.44 kg) Ireks pilsner malt

12 lb. (5.44 kg) Durst pilsner malt

3 lb. (1.36 kg) clear Belgian candi sugar

6.6 oz. (187 g) German Hersbrucker hops, 3.0% alpha, in boil 60 min.

1.2 oz. (34 g) Styrian Goldings hops, 5.7% alpha, in boil 60 min.

1.4 oz. (40 g) Czech Saaz hops, 3.3% alpha, in boil 10 min.

yeast cultured from Hoegaarden Grand Cru (not the Wit beer), ½ gal. (1.9-L) starter

Crush grains and add to 12 gal. (45.4 L) of very soft water. Heat to 138°F (59°C) for 30 min. Heat mash to 150°F (66°C) for 60 min. Heat mash to 157°F (69°C) for 30 min. Heat to 160°F (71°C) for 15 min. Recirculate runoff slowly for 30 min. Sparge with 169°F (76°C) water adjusted to pH 5.3 with lactic acid. Collect 17 gal. (64.4 L) of wort in brew kettle. Bring wort to a boil and add Belgian candi sugar, German Hersbrucker hops, and Styrian Goldings hops. Boil 50 min., then add Czech Saaz hops. Boil 10 min. and turn off heat. Chill wort, transfer to fermenter, and pitch yeast. Ferment 7 days at 65°F (18°C). Rack to secondary for 14 days. Keg and age 9 months.

— *"Beer" Rich Mansfield, San Jose, California*
Washoe Zephyr Zymurgists

Aaron's Abbey Ale

YIELD:	11 GAL. (41.6 L)
TOTAL BOILING TIME:	90 MIN.
STARTING GRAVITY:	1.069
ENDING GRAVITY:	1.022
PRIMARY FERMENT:	12 DAYS
SECONDARY FERMENT:	7 DAYS

First place in the Belgian category at the 1994 Home Wine and Beer Trade Association's National Homebrew Competition. It also took first place in the dubbel category and third place for best of show at the 1994 Spirit of Belgium competition.

  10 lb. (4.54 kg) Belgian pilsner malt
  10 lb. (4.54 kg) German pilsner malt
   4 lb. (1.81 kg) Belgian biscuit malt
   2 lb. (907 g) Belgian aromatic malt
   1 lb. (454 g) Belgian cara-Munich malt
   1 lb. (454 g) wheat malt
  ¾ lb. (340 g) Belgian special-B malt (added at mash-out)
 2.2 lb. (1 kg) Belgian dark candi sugar
   2 oz. (57 g) U.S. Tettnanger whole hops, 6.2% alpha, in boil 60 min.
  ½ oz. (14 g) East Kent Goldings hops plug, 5.0% alpha, in boil 15 min.
   2 tbsp. (29.8 ml) Irish moss
   3 qt. (2.8 L) La Chouffe yeast starter
   1 gal. (3.8 L) gyle, for priming

Crush grains and add to 14 gal. (53 L) of 140°F (60°C) water. Allow a protein rest at 132°F (56°C) for 30 min. Pull off 40% of the mash for a first decoction. Raise temperature on the decoction to 158°F (70°C) and hold for 25 min. Raise decoction to a boil and hold for 15 min. Add the decoction back to the mash and add enough boiling water to raise temperature to 158°F (70°C). Rest for 60 min. Add special-B malt and raise temperature to 170°F (77°C) for mash-out. Sparge with 170°F (77°C) water and collect 13 gal. (49.2 L) of wort in brew kettle. Boil 30 min., and then add the U.S. Tettnanger whole hops. Boil 45 min., then add the East Kent Goldings hops plug and Irish moss. Boil 15 min. and turn off heat. Chill the wort to 50°F (10°C). Save about 1 gal. (3.8 L) of the wort for priming, storing it in a sanitized container in the refrigerator. Add yeast and ferment 12 days. Rack to secondary fermenter for 7 days. When ready to bottle, add gyle at a ratio of 86 oz. per 5 gal. (2.5 L per 18.9 L) of beer, then bottle.

— Andy Anderson, Bath, England
Brewers United for Real Potables (BURP)

WIT BEERS

Texas/Belgian White Beer

YIELD: .... 5 GAL. (18.9 L)
TOTAL BOILING TIME: .... 60 MIN.
STARTING GRAVITY: 1.046
ENDING GRAVITY: 1.011
PRIMARY FERMENT: .... 1 WEEK
SECONDARY FERMENT: .... 1 WEEK

    Wyeast #3944 Belgian White Beer yeast
 1 lb. (454 g) wheat malt
 6 lb. (2.72 kg) wheat malt extract
    zest of two oranges
 ¾ oz. (21 g) coriander
 ⅔ oz. (19 g) Saaz hop pellets, in boil 55 min.
 ½ oz. (14 g) Cascade hops, in boil 15 min.
 1 package Bru-Vigor yeast food
 ¾ c. (206 ml) corn sugar, for priming

Prepare yeast starter prior to brewing day.

　　　　Crush grains and add to 1 gal. (3.8 L) of 160°F (71°C) water and steep 30 min. Sparge the grains with 1 gal. (3.8 L) or more of 168°F (76°C) water into brew kettle. Bring wort to a boil, then turn off heat and add malt extract, orange zest, and coriander. Boil 5 min. before adding Saaz pellets. Boil 40 min., then add Cascades. Boil 15 min. and turn off heat. Chill the wort, transfer to fermenter, and top off to 5 gal. (18.9 L) with cold water. Pitch yeast along with Bru-Vigor yeast food. Ferment 1 week. Prime with corn sugar and bottle.

— DeFalco's Home Wine & Beer Supplies, Houston, Texas

Zoso White

YIELD:	5 GAL. (18.9 L)
TOTAL BOILING TIME:	90 MIN.
STARTING GRAVITY:	1.050
PRIMARY FERMENT:	7 DAYS
SECONDARY FERMENT:	2–3 WEEKS

Second place at the 1993 Dixie Cup.

Wyeast #3944 Belgian White Beer yeast

6 lb. (2.72 kg) DeWolf-Cosyns Belgian pilsner malt

1 lb. (454 g) Great Western malted wheat

5 lb. (2.27 kg) unmalted wheat flakes

1¼ oz. (35 g) Ultra hops, 3.8% alpha, in boil 60 min.

⅓ oz. (9 g) curaçao

½ oz. (14 g) Ultra hops, 3.8% alpha, in boil 15 min.

0.7 oz. (20 g) coriander

¼ oz. (7 g) Ultra hops, steep

0.28 oz. (8 g) curaçao

0.1 oz. (3 g) coriander

¾ c. (206 ml) corn sugar, for priming

Several days before brewing, begin growing up culture.

Crush grains and add with wheat flakes to 4 gal. (15.1 L) of 131°F (55°C) water. Allow a 30-min. protein rest at 120°F (49°C). Heat mash to 152°F (67°C) for 60 min. Sparge and collect 6 ½ gal. (24.6 L) of wort in brew kettle. Boil wort for 30 min., before adding 1¼ oz. (35 g) of Ultra hops. Boil 40 min., then add ⅓ oz. (9 g) curaçao. Boil 5 min., then add ½ oz. (14 g) of Ultra hops. Boil 10 min., then add 0.7 oz. (20 g) of coriander. Boil 5 min. Remove from heat and add ¼ oz. (7 g) Ultra hops, 0.28 oz. (8 g) of curaçao, and 0.1 oz. (3 g) of coriander. Chill to 60°F (16°C), transfer to fermenter, and pitch yeast. Ferment 1 week at 60° – 65°F (16° – 18°C), transfer to secondary for 2 – 3 weeks. Prime and bottle.

— *David and Melinda Brockington, Seattle, Washington*
Seattle Secret Skinny Brewers Society

Wits End

YIELD: .... 10 GAL. (37.9 L)
TOTAL BOILING TIME: .... 90 MIN.
STARTING GRAVITY: 1.054
ENDING GRAVITY: 1.014
PRIMARY FERMENT: .... 1 WEEK
SECONDARY FERMENT: .... 2 WEEKS

    La Chouffe yeast, 1-qt. (946-ml) starter
10 lb. (4.54 kg) hard red wheat berries (unmalted wheat)
 1 lb. (454 g) steel-cut oats
11 lb. (5 kg) pilsner malt
1½ oz. (43 g) Styrian Goldings hops, 5.0% alpha, in boil 60 min.
⅔ oz. (19 g) curaçao orange peel, crushed
 2 oz. (57 g) coriander seed, crushed
1½ c. (413 ml) corn sugar, for priming

Before brew day, make a 1-qt. (946-ml) yeast starter.

Before mashing, crush wheat berries and boil, along with oats, in 4 gal. (15.1 L) of water for 15 min. to gelatinize starches. Cool and add to mash tun. For the mash, add crushed pilsner malt and 4 gal. (15.1 L) of 130°F (54°C) water to reach a stable temperature of 120°F (48°C). Hold for 45 min. Add 2 gal. (7.6 L) of boiling water to bring mash to 140°F (60°C). Hold for 30 min. (alpha amylase rest). Pull off 4 gal. (15.1 L) of thick decoction from the mash, bring to a boil, and add back to the mash to bring temperature to 158°F (70°C). Hold for 30 min. Pull 3-gal. (11.4 L) thin decoction from the mash, bring to a boil, and add back to the mash to reach mash-out temperature of 165°F (74°C). Sparge with 170°F (77°C) water and collect 12 ½ gal. (47.3 L) of wort. Boil 30 min. before adding the Styrian Goldings hops. Boil 40 min., then add curaçao orange peel. Boil 15 min., then add coriander. Boil 5 min., then turn off heat. Chill the wort to 65°F (18°C) and transfer to fermenter. Pitch yeast. Ferment 1 week at 65°F (18°C). Rack to secondary for 2 more weeks. Prime and bottle.

— *Wendy Aaronson and Bill Ridgely, Alexandria, Virginia*
Brewers United for Real Potables (BURP)

—Framboise Wit Ale—

YIELD: .... 5¼ GAL. (19.9 L)
TOTAL BOILING TIME: .... 90 MIN.
ENDING GRAVITY: 1.012
PRIMARY FERMENT: .... 10 DAYS
SECONDARY FERMENT: .... 10 DAYS

5 lb. (2.27 kg) 2-row Belgian pale malt
1 lb. (454 g) 2-row English pale malt
1 lb. (454 g) oats
3 lb. (1.36 kg) flaked wheat
1¼ lb. (567 g) dry light malt extract
    lactic acid, to adjust pH
½ lb. (227 g) basswood honey
3 oz. (85 g) Hallertauer hops plug, 2.6% alpha, in boil 60 min.
1½ oz. (43 g) Hallertauer hops plug, 2.6% alpha, in boil 30 min.
6 lb. (2.72 kg) red raspberries
    Wyeast #3944 Belgian White Beer yeast
1 c. (275 ml) corn sugar, for priming

Mash grains and flaked wheat at 155°F (68°C) in 10 qt. (9.5 L) of water. Sparge with 5 gal. (18.9 L) of 170°F (77°C) water, adjusted to pH 5.0 with lactic acid. Add malt extract and honey and boil 30 min. Add 3 oz. (85 g) of Hallertauer hops and boil 30 min. Add 1½ oz. (43 g) of Hallertauer hops and boil 30 min. Remove from heat and chill the wort. Transfer to fermenter. Prepare raspberries by adding them to 1 qt. (946 ml) of water and heating for 10 min. Do not boil. Add berries to fermenter and pitch yeast. Primary ferment for 10 days at 68°F (20°C). Rack to secondary fermenter for 10 days. Prime and bottle.

— *Matt Gilmartin, Oak Forest, Illinois*

LAMBICS

Black Currant Lambic

YIELD: .... 10 GAL. (37.9 L)
TOTAL BOILING TIME: .... 45 MIN.
PRIMARY FERMENT: .... 10 DAYS
SECONDARY FERMENT: .... 20 DAYS

4.2 qt. (4 L) light malt extract
2.2 lb. (1 kg) light dry malt extract
  1 tsp. (4.9 ml) gypsum
  1 lb. (454 g) pale or crystal malt
  4 oz. (113 g) Hallertauer hops, in boil 45 min.
  1 oz. (28 g) Hallertauer hops, steep for 5 min.
1.1 gal. (4 L) Frutical black currant syrup
    lambicus yeast
    Wyeast #3068 Weihenstephan Wheat yeast
    Wyeast #3278 Brettanomyces bruxellensis
  1 c. (275 ml) dry malt extract

Add 1.1 gal. (4 L) light malt extract and 2.2 lb. (1 kg) light dry malt extract to 3 gal. (11.4 L) of soft water treated with gypsum. Bring to a boil, then let cool to 130° – 135°F (54° – 57°C). Add the crushed pale or crystal malt. Pour all into a sanitized food-grade plastic bucket and cover with aluminum foil. Wrap bucket in a sleeping bag or other heavy insulator and keep warm for 15 – 24 hours. Remove foil and skim anything on the surface, then strain into a brew kettle. Bring to a boil and add 4 oz. (113 g) of Hallertauer hops. Boil 45 min. Turn off heat and add last oz. of Hallertauer hops and black currant syrup. Steep 15 min. Chill the wort to 75°F (24°C), then add Wyeast #3068 wheat yeast. After fermentation is under way, add Wyeast #3278 and lambicus yeast. Ferment 10 days, then rack to secondary fermenter for 20 days. Prime with dry malt extract and bottle.

— *Jim Hanemaayer, Kitchener, Ontario*

Sourpuss

YIELD: .... 10 GAL. (37.9 L)
TOTAL BOILING TIME: .... 45 MIN.
STARTING GRAVITY: 1.054
ENDING GRAVITY: 1.006
PRIMARY FERMENT: .... 10 DAYS
SECONDARY FERMENT: .... 6 MONTHS
TERTIARY FERMENT: .... 3 MONTHS

7½ lb. (3.4 kg) hard red winter wheat berries
17 lb. (6.8 kg) DeWolf-Cosyns pilsner malt
2 oz. (57 g) mixed 3-year-old hops (Perle and Willamette), in boil 90 min.
ale yeast slurry (obtained from Old Dominion brewery; could substitute Chico ale yeast)
20 lb. (9.1 kg) frozen sour cherries, thawed, added to secondary
Orval yeast culture
Yeast Lab 3220 *Brettanomyces lambicus* culture, see procedure
Yeast Lab 3200 *Pediococcus cerevisiae* culture, see procedure
Cantillon yeast culture
Boon yeast culture

Mash-in wheat berries and 2 lb. of the pilsner malt in 3 gal. (11.4 g) of water and let rest for 10 min. at 158°F (70°C), then raise temperature and boil 30 min. Mash-in 15 lb. of pilsner malt, resting at 140°F (60°C) for 15 min., then add the boiled grains and rest for 60 min. at 150°F (66°C). Sparge to collect 12½ gal. (47.3 L). Boil wort 90 min., adding hops for full boil time. At end of boil, chill to 60°F (68°C) and pitch yeast. After 10 days, rack in two batches to two secondary fermenters. Add 10 lb. (4.54 kg) of cherries to each fermenter. To one fermenter, add active Orval yeast culture, Yeast Lab *Brettanomyces* culture, and half Yeast Lab *Pediococcus* culture. To the other fermenter, add active Cantillon and Boon cultures and half Yeast Lab *Pediococcus* culture. After 6 months, rack the beer off the fruit to two tertiary fermenters. After 3 months, blend the two batches and transfer to kegs to develop carbonation. Periodically bleed gas from kegs to avoid overcarbonation. Sample beer at regular intervals. Counterpressure bottle after approximately 2 months in the keg.

— *Tim Artz, Lorton, Virginia*
Brewers United for Real Potables (BURP)

7
More HOMEBREW FAVORITES
German, Scottish, Strong

& Specialty Ales

This chapter is an amalgam of generally unrelated styles, but each is a vital piece of the puzzle that is a well-rounded knowledge of brewing styles. Kölsch and alt have found enormous favor among homebrewers in recent years. Scottish ale styles are quite a bit different from the pale ales and brown ales of England, and in some ways their differences reflect the attitudes and national identity of Scottish brewers. The strong ales included here, such as barleywines and old ales, are perennial favorites among homebrewers and beer lovers. This chapter ends with recipes for specialty ales: those beers that use unusual adjuncts, ingredients, or processes that don't fit in easily with other styles.

Alt **beers.** Associated with the city of Dusseldorf, Germany, *alt* is the German word for "old," referring to older ale-making practices. Although the beer is fermented at a warm temperature with a top-fermenting yeast, the beer is then lagered at cool temperatures, reducing the levels of traditional yeast by-products, such as fruity esters. Alt beers are somewhat dry, with a fairly hoppy bitterness and aftertaste.

KEY TO RECIPE LOGOS

 EXTRACT RECIPES

 PARTIAL MASH RECIPES

 ALL-GRAIN RECIPES

Alt beer has considerable maltiness, but this should not be confused with sweetness. These beers have the smoother maltiness of Munich malts, not unfermented residual sugars, as would be the case if you used caramel malts. The Munich malt may be combined with a German pilsner malt to form the base grist. Some breweries reputedly use wheat in the grist as well. A single-decoction mash would be appropriate; however, Michael Jackson says that some brewers in Dusseldorf use an infusion mash.

In alt beers, hops can be fairly assertive, generally using noble varieties, such as Spalt. Hops will be reflected in both the flavor and the bitterness. Alt beer is typically hopped at a level between 40 and 65 IBUs.

Color for alt beer should be similar to brown ale — a light to deep coppery brown. Style guidelines typically specify 10 to 20 SRM. An obscure variation of alt called *sticke* that is slightly more robust and malty seems to be available only from three brewpubs in the old city of Dusseldorf, and then only on special occasions.

While *altbier* is usually associated with the city of Dusseldorf, it is also brewed — with some variations in flavor — in Münster and Hanover. The Hanover altbier is usually lighter in color, and less aggressively hopped. The Münster alt is even lighter, both in color and hops, than that of Hanover.

Kölsch is a pale, light-bodied beer a bit like an American lager, but with some of the light fruity esters of an ale. It is named for the city of Köln, Germany, where the style originates. The beer is brewed to an original gravity of about 1.040 to 1.048. Hops are usually fairly low. A good Kölsch is a soft, subtle beer without strong flavors. Some Kölschs are described as being slightly drier or more acidic than others, but, according to Michael Jackson, differences among Kölschs are generally slight. With an alcohol level below 4 percent, Kölsch is a beer that can be enjoyed throughout an evening.

A Kölsch is usually mashed using a single decoction. The grain bill includes pale pilsner or Vienna malts, with up to about 15 to 20 percent malted wheat — although wheat is by no means a required part of the grain bill. German or Belgian pilsner malts should work well for most homebrewers. German noble hops, such as Hallertauer and Saaz, are used at restrained levels — about 25 to 30 IBUs. Use an ale yeast, ideally one of those intended for Kölsch, such as the Wyeast German Ale yeast (#1007) or the Yeast Culture Kit Company's German Ale yeast (A04). There are also yeast strains on the market that are a combination or a hybrid of ale and lager yeasts, intended specifically for Kölsch, such as the Wyeast Kölsch Lager (#2565) — this could be an excellent choice if you're formulating your own recipe for Kölsch.

Like altbiers, Kölsch is typically fermented like an ale using a top-fermenting ale yeast, but is then lagered at cool temperatures to achieve a smoother character. This gives Kölsch a less distinct, more subdued, fruity aroma than its American golden ale cousins.

Scottish ales are generally malty, full-bodied, and brown in color. They often are referred to by shilling designations that reflect their relative strength. The four different designations — 60, 70, 80, and 90 shilling — correspond to light, heavy, export, and strong ales, respectively. Above even the strong ale category is yet another substyle called Scottish Wee Heavy — a very dense beer like barleywine or strong ale.

The 60 shilling (light) is brewed to a low starting gravity — generally about what you'd shoot for in an English mild — 1.030 to 1.035. This is a light, quaffable beer. The 70 shilling is just a bit heavier, generally 1.035 to 1.040. Although it is sometimes called "heavy," there is certainly nothing heavy about a 1.035 beer!

The 80 shilling approaches the level of what might be considered a normal gravity beer, ranging from about 1.040 to 1.050. The maltiness is quite good and round in this beer. The 90 shilling, or Scottish strong, is very malty. Some caramel flavors may be evident. The 90 shilling is almost black, with a sweet and robust flavor. McEwans Scotch Ale is a good example of this style.

By English standards, hopping rates for Scottish ales are generally a bit lower than their gravities might suggest. The scent of Scottish ales is dominated by malt, often with no discernible hop aroma. These beers are less likely than English varieties to exhibit esters because Scottish beers are usually fermented at cooler temperatures.

The color of a Scottish ale is brown to almost black. The grain bill is pale malt, with roast barley added for color and flavor. Although colored malts, such as chocolate, are sometimes used by homebrewers, they are not the traditional grain of choice for Scottish brewing. Hugh Baird Malting Company makes authentic Scottish malts that can now be purchased in the United States.

Some very slight smoky flavor is often found in Scottish ales, but the smokiness comes from yeast strains that produce phenols, not from smoked grain. While smoked malts have been used in Scotland in the production of whisky, some homebrewers and craft brewers experiment with peat-smoked malt in their Scottish ales. Samuel Adams Scottish Ale, widely available in the United States, uses smoked malt in very small proportions. The smokiness in the beer is subtle and adds complexity to the flavor profile.

In addition to the phenols that sometimes give Scottish beers a faint smoky character, Scottish ale yeasts produce diacetyl, which is often characterized as a buttery aroma or flavor. Low levels of diacetyl are acceptable for the lighter designations and fairly high levels can be found in the 90 shilling. Wyeast #1728 Scottish Ale yeast has been used by many homebrewers with good results. Wyeast says that the yeast can be used at temperatures up to 70°F (21°C), but better, more authentic results will be produced at temperatures of 55° to 60°F (13° to 16°C). Another yeast that reputedly works well at cooler temperatures is the Yeast Culture Kit Company's Scotch Ale strain (A34).

Strong ales. The term "old ale" is often used synonymously with *strong ale*. English brewers make a wide range of old ales, some of which are not very strong at all, but in this book we will consider the stronger types of old ales and will generically refer to them as "strong ales." Strong ales have gravities of anywhere from 1.060 on up into the realm of barleywines, which might have gravities between 1.080 and 1.110.

Strong ales fill the area in style definitions that lie between the rich, thick, syrupy barleywines and the lighter-bodied pale ales. Strong ales can be quite alcoholic with a noticeable warming effect. With complex fruity aromas and flavors, the beers are usually sweet and are hopped aggressively to balance the high sugar levels.

The grain bill consists mostly of English pale malt, crystal, and sometimes a little chocolate or black malt for color. Even when brewed with only pale malts, the color will likely be quite dark, since browning effects in the boil increase as density increases.

Strong ales are often regarded as laying-down beers, meaning that they will withstand long-term storage. Several brewers suggest that 5 to 20 years is an optimal aging period for their beers, breaking the rule that beer is best consumed young.

Barleywines are the strongest ales made: they are thick, syrupy, powerfully alcoholic brews that have enormously complex flavor, abundant esters, and sherry-like character. The beers are always heavily hopped to balance the very high malt levels.

Typically English pale ale malt, or American 2-row pale malt, is used to brew barleywines. Some adjunct malts may be added for sweetness, complexity, or color. Two to 4 pounds of malt will be used for each gallon of beer produced, depending on the strength of the beer. Molasses, brown sugar, or other types of sucrose may be added to the wort to increase gravity and augment the brew's complexity. English or American hops will be used in abundance. Commonly used hops in barleywine include Kent Goldings, Fuggles, and Willamette. These beers are hopped at 50 to 100 IBUs.

Although some homebrewers use wine yeasts when brewing barleywine, most commercial brewers, especially in England, use ale yeasts and regularly agitate the beer to get the yeast to ferment beyond its normal limits. Sometimes, multiple pitchings will be done. Some yeast strains are available to the homebrewer for use in barleywines and strong ales, such as the Yeast Culture Kit Company's Barleywine Ale (A08), which claims to be derived from Dorchester.

Specialty ales. Brewers have always been an inventive and adaptive group. When we hear of homebrewers experimenting with strange grains or unusual sugars, we can be pretty sure that whatever they're doing has been tried before, even if the concept has long since been forgotten. Beer has been brewed for thousands of years and somewhere, *someone* has brewed beer with anything you could imagine — and some things that you're probably better off not imagining. This chapter includes the novelty recipes, which use specialty adjunct grains or perhaps unusual processes that don't fit neatly into accepted beer styles.

In the competition setting, judges in the alt category look for a clean-tasting beer with a rounded, smooth, malty character and fairly assertive hops. Although many of the books on beer mention "fruitiness" in relation to alt, most judges will score down for noticeable esters, as the lagering process tends to reduce these to very subtle levels. A Münster-style alt may have trouble in alt flights because of its light color and low hopping.

In homebrew competitions, the judges of the Kölsch style look for a pale, eminently drinkable beer. Cloudiness, excessive fruitiness, and hoppiness are all flaws. The beer should be very light in color. If it's much darker than a typical American lager, your beer will probably fare poorly.

In barleywine competitions, judges expect a heavy beer, with a good balance — an evident sweetness, cut by aggressive hopping. Judges call thin, highly attenuated beers with lots of higher alcohol "hot." Fairly high alcohol levels are expected, but the alcohol should be balanced with a malty syrup character. Avoid the alcoholic sensation of higher, fusel alcohols. This may be caused by high fermentation temperatures.

GERMAN ALES: KÖLSCH AND ALT

Kölsch Call III

YIELD: .... 11 GAL. (41.6 L)
TOTAL BOILING TIME: .... 70 MIN.
PRIMARY FERMENT: .... 5 DAYS
SECONDARY FERMENT: .... 7 DAYS
LAGERING: .... 4 WEEKS

7 lb. (3.2 kg) 2-row lager malt

7 lb. (3.2 kg) pilsner malt

6 lb. (2.72 kg) wheat malt

2 lb. (907 g) Vienna malt

1½ lb. (680 g) cara-pils malt

1 oz. (28 g) Liberty whole hops, 2.6 % alpha, in boil 60 min.
1½ oz. (43 g) Tettnanger whole hops, 4.5% alpha, in boil 30 min.
1 oz. (28 g) Crystal whole hops, 4.0% alpha, in boil 1 min.
2 tsp. (99 ml) Irish moss
   Wyeast #2565 Kölsch yeast

Crush and add grains to 7 ⅔ gal. (29 L) of 166°F (74°C) water. Mash for
2 hours at 155°F (68°C). Heat mash to 165°F (74°C) and hold for 15 min.
Sparge with 170°F (77°C) water and collect 12 gal. (45.4 L) of wort in
kettle. Boil 10 min. before adding Liberty hops. Boil 30 min., then add
Tettnanger hops. Boil 15 min., then add Irish moss. Boil 14 min., then add
crystal hops. Boil 1 min., then turn off heat. Chill the wort, transfer to
fermenter, and pitch yeast. Ferment 5 days, then rack to secondary
fermenter for 7 days, then lager for 4 weeks at 40°F (4°C). Keg and force
carbonate.

— *Ronald J. Sup, Morrow, Ohio*
Bloatarian Brewing League

Cream Kölsch

YIELD:	10 GAL. (37.9 L)
TOTAL BOILING TIME:	90 MIN.
STARTING GRAVITY:	1.050
ENDING GRAVITY:	1.012
PRIMARY FERMENT:	1 WEEK
SECONDARY FERMENT:	2 WEEKS
COLD CONDITIONING:	2–3 WEEKS

17 lb. (7.71 kg) pilsner malt
 3 lb. (1.36 kg) wheat malt
 1 lb. (454 g) crystal malt, 20° Lovibond
 1 oz. (28 g) Hersbrucker hops, 3.5% alpha, in boil 60 min.
 1 oz. (28 g) Perle hops, 9.5% alpha, in boil 60 min.
    Wyeast #1056 American Ale yeast
1½ c. (413 ml) corn sugar, for priming, or force carbonate

Combine malts and 7 gal. (26.5 L) of 130°F (54°C) water to reach protein-
rest temperature of 120°F (49°C). Hold for 30 min. Pull 4 gal. (15.1 L) of
thick decoction from mash, bring to a boil, and return to mash to bring

temperature to 158°F (70°C). Hold for 30 min. Pull a 3-gal. (11.4-L) thin decoction from mash, bring to boil, and add back to mash to reach mash-out temperature of 165°F (74°C). Sparge with 170°F (77°C) water and collect 12½ gal. (47.3 L) of wort. Boil 30 min. before adding Hersbrucker and Perle hops. Boil 60 min., then turn off heat. Chill wort to 65°F (18°C) and transfer to primary fermenter. Aerate well and pitch yeast. Ferment 1 week at no more than 60°F (16°C). Transfer to secondary fermenter for 2 more weeks at 55°F (13°C). If possible, cold condition beer at 30° – 35°F (-1° – 2°C) for 2 – 3 weeks. Prime and bottle.

— *Wendy Aaronson and Bill Ridgely, Alexandria, Virginia*
Brewers United for Real Potables (BURP)

Alki Point Sunset Kölschbier

YIELD:	5 GAL. (18.9 L)
TOTAL BOILING TIME:	90 MIN.
STARTING GRAVITY:	1.047
ENDING GRAVITY:	1.007
PRIMARY FERMENT:	9 DAYS
SECONDARY FERMENT:	10 DAYS
LAGERING:	28 DAYS

First place in the German ale category at the 1994 Home Wine and Beer Trade Association National Homebrew Competition. The honey keeps the body light and provides a bit of dryness.

Wyeast #2565 Kölsch yeast

5 lb. (2.27 kg) Belgian pilsner malt

1.625 lb. (737 g) Belgian wheat malt

1 lb. (454 g) German light crystal malt

⅛ lb. (57 g) cara-Vienne malt

½ oz. (14 g) Tettnanger hops, 4.3% alpha, in boil 60 min.

½ oz. (14 g) Mt. Hood hops, 4.5% alpha, in boil 60 min.

½ oz. (14 g) Liberty hops, 4.3% alpha, in boil 60 min.

½ oz. (14 g) Tettnanger hops, 4.3% alpha, in boil 20 min.

¼ oz. (7 g) oz. Liberty hops, 4.3% alpha, in boil 10 min.

1⅛ lb. (510 g) clover honey

1.4 qt. (1300 ml) gyle, for priming

Several days before brewing, begin starter of the Wyeast Kölsch yeast.
        Add grains to 2½ gal. (9.5 L) of 132°F (56°C) water. Mash at 124°F
(51°C) for a 30-min. protein rest. Heat mash to 150°F (66°C) for a
90-min. starch conversion. Mash-out for 5 min. at 168°F (76°C). Sparge to
collect 6 ¾ gal. (25.6 L) of wort. Boil 30 min. Add ½ oz. (14 g) each of
Tettnanger, Mt. Hood, and Liberty hops. Boil 40 min., then add ½ oz.
(14 g) of Tettnanger hops. Boil 10 min., then add ¼ oz. (7 g) oz. of Liberty
hops and honey. Boil 10 min., then turn off heat. Chill, transfer to the primary fermenter, reserving 1.4 qt. (1300 ml) of wort (gyle) and store in a
sanitized container in the refrigerator. Pitch yeast. Ferment 9 days at
60°F (16°C). Rack to secondary for 10 days. Lager for 28 days. Krausen
with 1.4 qt. (1300 ml) of gyle and bottle.

— *Charlie Gow, Santa Rosa, California, Maltose Falcons*
Brewers United for Real Potables (BURP)

Kölsch

YIELD:	8 GAL. (30.3 L)
TOTAL BOILING TIME:	60 MIN.
STARTING GRAVITY:	1.036
ENDING GRAVITY:	1.010
PRIMARY FERMENT:	1 WEEK

First place at the 1996 Spirit of Free Beer competition.

12 lb. (5.44 kg) Briess 2-row pale malt
 2 lb. (907 g) Ireks 2-row wheat malt, crushed fine
 1 lb. (454 g) Briess 2-row caramel malt, 80° Lovibond
½ lb. (227 g) Munich malt, 10° Lovibond
 2 oz. (57 g) Perle hops, 7.0% alpha, in boil 60 min.
 2 oz. (57 g) Hallertauer Mittelfrüh hops, 2.8% alpha, in boil
    60 min.
    Wyeast #1007 German Ale yeast
¾ c. (206 ml) corn sugar, for priming

Add crushed grains to 5 gal. (18.9 L) of 163°F (73°C) water. Mash at
152°F (67°C) for 1 hour. Sparge with 168°F (76°C) water, collecting

6 ½ gal. (24.6 L) of wort. Bring wort to a boil and add all hops. Boil 1 hour, then turn off heat. Chill the wort to 75°F (24°C), transfer to the primary fermenter, and pitch yeast. Ferment 1 week at 65° – 67°F (18° – 19°C). Prime with corn sugar and bottle.

— Steve Marler, Arlington, Virginia
Brewers United for Real Potables (BURP)

Kölsch '96

YIELD: .... 5 GAL. (18.9 L)
TOTAL BOILING TIME: .... 70 MIN.
STARTING GRAVITY: 1.044
ENDING GRAVITY: 1.008
PRIMARY FERMENT: .... 5 DAYS
SECONDARY FERMENT: .... 5 DAYS
LAGERING: .... 10 DAYS

First place in the light ale category at the 1996 Boston Homebrew Competition.

    4 lb. (1.81 kg) Belgian pilsner malt
    3 lb. (1.36 kg) Belgian pale malt
    ½ lb. (227 g) wheat malt
    ¼ lb. (113 g) Vienna malt
    ¼ lb. (113 g) cara-Vienne malt
    1 oz. (28 g) Hallertauer Tradition hop pellets, 5.9% alpha, in boil 60 min.
    ¼ oz. (7 g) oz. Hallertauer Mittelfrüh hop pellets, 2.8% alpha, in boil 15 min.
    ¼ oz. (7 g) oz. Hallertauer Mittelfrüh hop pellets, 2.8% alpha, in boil 5 min.
       Wyeast #1007 German Ale yeast
    ¾ c. (206 ml) corn sugar, for priming

Crush grains and add to 8 qt. (7.6 L) of mash, water stabilizing temperature at 125°F for 30 min. Add 1 gal. (3.8 L) of boiling water to raise mash temperature to 150°F (66°C) and hold for 60 min. Sparge with 4 gal. (15.1 L) of 170°F (77°C) water. Boil 10 min.; add 1 oz. (28 g) of

Hallertauer Tradition hop pellets. Boil 45 min., then add ¼ oz. (7 g) oz. of Hallertauer Mittelfrüh. Boil 10 min., then add last ¼ oz. (7 g) oz. of Hallertauer Mittelfrüh. Boil 5 min. and turn off heat. Chill the wort, transfer to fermenter, and pitch yeast. Ferment 5 days at 64°F (18°C), then rack to secondary for 5 days at 50°F (10°C). Lager at 40°F (4°C) for 10 days. Prime with corn sugar and bottle.

— John McCafferty, Chelmsford, Massachusetts

Demonick Alt

YIELD:	5¼ GAL. (19.9 L)
TOTAL BOILING TIME:	120 MIN.
STARTING GRAVITY:	1.048
ENDING GRAVITY:	1.014
PRIMARY FERMENT:	5 DAYS
SECONDARY FERMENT:	5 DAYS
COLD CONDITIONING:	3 WEEKS

⅓ oz. (9 g) gypsum
   Wyeast #1338 European Ale yeast
 4 lb. (1.81 kg) Munich malt
 3 lb. (1.36 kg) 2-row Pilsner malt
 1 lb. (454 g) aromatic malt
 ½ oz. (14 g) Mt. Hood hops, 6.3% alpha, in boil 60 min.
 ½ oz. (14 g) Mt. Hood hops, 6.3% alpha, in boil 30 min.
 1 oz. (28 g) Mt. Hood hops, 4.2% alpha, in boil 15 min.
 1 oz. (28 g) Tettnanger hops, 3.4% alpha, in boil 15 min.
 1 oz. (28 g) Mt. Hood hops, 4.2% alpha, in boil 5 min.
 1 oz. (28 g) Tettnanger hops, 3.4% alpha, in boil 5 min.
¹⁄₁₂ oz. (2¼ g) non-iodized table salt
 ¾ c. (206 ml) corn sugar, for priming

Treat 9 gal. (34.1 L) of water with gypsum and table salt. Crush grains and add to 2 ⅔ gal. (10.1 L) of 163°F (73°C) water to yield a final mash temperature of 151°F (66°C). Mash for 60 min., then add 1½ gal. (5.7 L) of boiling water to raise temperature to 167°F (75°C) and let stand for 10 min. for the mash-out. Sparge with 5 gal. (18.9 L) of 175°F (79°C) water and collect about 8 gal. (30.3 L) of wort. Boil 60 min. before adding ½ oz. (14 g) of Mt. Hood. Boil 30 min., then add another ½ oz. (14 g) of Mt. Hood. Boil 15 min., then add 1 oz. (28 g) each of Mt. Hood and Tettnanger hops. Boil 10 min., then add 1 oz. each of Mt. Hood and Tettnanger. Boil 5 min., then turn off heat. Chill wort, transfer to fermenter, and pitch yeast. Ferment 5 days at 65° – 68°F (16° – 18°C), then rack to a secondary fermenter for 5 days. Rack to another fermenter and cold condition for 3 weeks at 34°F (1°C). Prime and bottle.

— *Domenick Venezia, Seattle, Washington*

Alt Enough to Drink

YIELD:	5 GAL. (18.9 L)
TOTAL BOILING TIME:	00 MIN.
STARTING GRAVITY:	1.045
ENDING GRAVITY:	1.016
PRIMARY FERMENT:	2 WEEKS
SECONDARY FERMENT:	2 WEEKS

6   lb. (2.72 kg) pilsner malt
2   lb. (907 g) Munich malt
½   lb. (227 g) crystal malt, 80° Lovibond
½   lb. (227 g) torrified wheat
2   oz. (57 g) black patent malt
2   oz. (57 g) Tettnanger hops, 4.5% alpha, in boil 70 min.
1   oz. (28 g) Tettnanger hops, 4.5% alpha, in boil 30 min.
1   tsp. (5 ml) Irish moss
½   oz. (14 g) Tettnanger hops, 4.5% alpha, in boil 5 min.
    Wyeast #1338 European Ale yeast
¾   c. (206 ml) corn sugar, for priming

Crush grains and add to 3 gal. (11.4 L) of 168°F (76°C) water. Mash 60 min., or until starch conversion is complete. Raise mash temperature to 170°F (77°C) and hold for 10 min. Sparge with 5 gal. (18.9 L) of 170°F (77°C) water and collect 6 ½ gal. (24.6 L) of wort in kettle. Boil 20 min. Add 2 oz. (57 g) of Tettnanger hops. Boil 40 min., then add 1 oz. (28 g) of Tettnanger hops. Boil 10 min., then add Irish moss. Boil 15 min., then add last ½ oz. (14 g) of Tettnanger hops. Boil 5 min., then turn off heat. Chill wort, transfer to fermenter, and pitch yeast. Ferment 2 weeks at 60°F (16°C). Rack to secondary and lager for 2 weeks at 40°F (4°C). Prime and bottle.

— *Keith Schwols, Ft. Collins, Colorado*

Altbier

YIELD: .... 5 GAL. (18.9 L)
TOTAL BOILING TIME: .... 90 MIN.
STARTING GRAVITY: 1.056
ENDING GRAVITY: 1.017
PRIMARY FERMENT: .... 1 WEEK
SECONDARY FERMENT: .... 2 WEEKS
LAGERING: .... 1 WEEK

9 lb. (4.08 kg) Belgian pilsner malt
1 lb. (454 g) German Vienna malt
½ lb. (227 g) crystal malt, 40° Lovibond
½ lb. (227 g) wheat malt
1 oz. (28 g) chocolate malt
1½ oz. (43 g) Perle hops, 8.4% alpha, in boil 60 min.
⅔ oz. (19 g) Hallertauer hops, 2.5% alpha, in boil 60 min.
⅓ oz. (9 g) Hallertau hops, 2.5% alpha, steep
   Wyeast #1007 German Ale yeast

Crush grains and add to 3 ⅔ gal. (13.9 L) of 160°F (71°C) water. Mash at 149°F (5°C) for 1½ hours. Remove a small portion of the mash, boil it, and return to main mash to raise the mash temperature to 170°F (77°C). Sparge with 170°F (77°C) water, collecting 7 gal. (26.5 L) of wort. Boil 30 min. Add Perle hops and ⅔ oz. (19 g) of Hallertauer. Boil 60 min. and turn off heat. Add ⅓ oz. (9 g) of Hallertauer and steep a few min. Chill the wort, transfer to fermenter, and pitch yeast. Ferment at 60° – 65°F (16° – 18°C) for 1 week. Rack to secondary for 2 weeks, then put in the refrigerator and lower temperature about 4 – 5 degrees per day until it reaches about 34° – 35°F (1° – 2°C). Lager 1 week, then keg or bottle.

— *Keith Chamberlin, Riverdale, Maryland*
Brewers United for Real Potables (BURP)

Miner Alt

YIELD: .... 5 GAL. (18.9 L)
TOTAL BOILING TIME: .... 60 MIN.
STARTING GRAVITY: 1.038
ENDING GRAVITY: 1.001
PRIMARY FERMENT: .... 17 DAYS

First place in the alt/steam category in the 1993 TRASH competition.

     Wyeast #1007 German Ale yeast
     Wyeast #2038 Munich Lager yeast
  2 lb. (907 g) Munich malt
 ½ lb. (227 g) crystal malt, 40° Lovibond
2.4 oz. (68 g) chocolate malt
 ½ oz. (14 g) Chinook hops, 11.8% alpha, in boil 45 min.
 ½ oz. (14 g) Chinook hops, 11.8% alpha, in boil 30 min.
 ½ oz. (14 g) Tettnanger hops, 4.2% alpha, in boil 30 min.
  1 c. (275 ml) dry malt extract, for priming

Begin yeast starters, growing up to about 1 pt. (250 ml) each.

Crush grain and add to 2 ⅔ gal. (10.1 L) of 165°F (74°C) water. Mash at 154°F for 60 min. Heat to 170°F (77°C) for 10 min. Sparge with 5 gal. (18.9 L) of 170°F (77°C) water and collect 6 ½ gal. (24.6 L) of wort in kettle. Boil 15 min. Add ½ oz. (14 g) of Chinook hops. Boil 15 min., then add ½ oz. (14 g) each of Chinook and Tettnanger. Boil 30 min., then turn off heat. Chill the wort, transfer to fermenter, and pitch both yeast starters. Ferment 17 days, then prime with extract and bottle.

— Mike Mueller, and Steve and Paula Stacy, Rolla, Missouri
Missouri Association of Serious Homebrewers (MASH)

Dusseldorf-Style Alt — The Alternative

YIELD: .... 5 GAL. (18.9 L)
TOTAL BOILING TIME: .... 75 MIN.
STARTING GRAVITY: 1.050
ENDING GRAVITY: 1.012
PRIMARY FERMENT: .... 7 DAYS
SECONDARY FERMENT: .... 5 DAYS
LAGERING: .... 3 WEEKS

Third place in Vermont's 1996 Green Mountain Homebrew Competition.

     Wyeast #1007 German Ale yeast
5.5 lb. (2.5 kg) Belgian pilsner malt
1½ lb. (680 g) German dark Munich malt, 13° Lovibond
1 lb. (454 g) German wheat malt
¾ lb. (340 g) British caramel malt, 38° Lovibond
¼ lb. (113 g) Belgian aromatic malt
½ oz. (14 g) chocolate malt
2¾ oz. (78 g) Hallertauer Mittelfrüh hop pellets, 2.9% alpha, in boil 60 min.
½ oz. (14 g) Czech Saaz hops plug, 3.3% alpha, in boil 30 min.
⅔ c. (184 ml) corn sugar, for priming

Begin yeast starter a day or two in advance, growing up to about 1 qt. (1 L).

     Crush grains and add to 9 qt. (8.5 L) of 148°F (64°C) water. Hold for protein rest at 126°F (52°C) for 30 min. Add 1 gal. (3.8 L) of boiling water to raise mash temperature to 140°F (60°C) and let rest for 30 min. Heat mash to 158°F (70°C) and rest for 30 min. Sparge with 4½ gal. (17 L) of 170°F (77°C) water. Boil 15 min. and add 2 ¾ oz. (78 g) of Hallertauer Mittelfrüh. Boil 30 min., then add ½ oz. (14 g) of Czech Saaz. Boil 15 min. and turn off heat. Chill to 64°F (18°C), transfer to fermenter, and pitch yeast. Ferment 7 days at 64°F (18°C). Rack to secondary for 5 days at 50°F (10°C). Lager at 33°F for 3 weeks. Prime and bottle.

— John McCafferty, Chelmsford, Massachusetts

SCOTTISH ALES

Robb Roy's Scotch Ale

YIELD:	5 GAL. (18.9 L)
TOTAL BOILING TIME:	60 MIN.
STARTING GRAVITY:	1.052
ENDING GRAVITY:	1.017
PRIMARY FERMENT:	15 DAYS
SECONDARY FERMENT:	11 DAYS

Sweet, malty flavor with a slight smokiness from the yeast.

- 2 lb. (907 g) Munich malt
- 8 oz. (227 g) crystal malt, 20° Lovibond
- 4 oz. (113 g) crystal malt, 80° Lovibond
- 4 oz. (113 g) crystal malt, 40° Lovibond
- 4 oz. (113 g) wheat malt
- 3 oz. (85 g) chocolate malt
- 6.6 lb. (3 kg) Ireks Munich light malt extract syrup
- 1 oz. (28 g) East Kent Goldings hops, 4.6% alpha, in boil 60 min.
- 1 oz. (28 g) Fuggles hops, 3.6% alpha, in boil 15 min.
- 2 tsp. (9.9 ml) Irish moss
- Wyeast #1728 Scottish ale yeast, 2-qt. starter
- 1¼ c. (344 ml) dry malt extract, for priming

Crush grains and mash in 1 gal. (3.8 L) water at 156°F (69°C) for 1 hour. Sparge with 4 qt. (3.8 L) of 170°F (77°C) water. Add malt extract syrup and stir. Bring to a boil and add East Kent Goldings hops. Boil 45 min., then add Fuggles hops and Irish moss. Boil 15 min. and turn off heat. Chill wort, transfer fermenter, top off to 5 gal. (18.9 L) with cold water, and pitch yeast. Ferment 15 days at 62°F (17°C). Rack to secondary fermenter for another 11 days. Prime with extract and bottle.

— *Gabrielle Palmer, Livonia, Michigan*
Fermental Order of Renaissance Draughtsmen (FORD)

Fire Island Scotch Ale

YIELD: .... 5 GAL. (18.9 L)
TOTAL BOILING TIME: .... 45 MIN.
STARTING GRAVITY: 1.045–1.050
ENDING GRAVITY: 1.010–1.014
PRIMARY FERMENT: .... 5–7 DAYS
SECONDARY FERMENT: .... 14–18 DAYS

½ lb. (227 g) English crystal malt
½ lb. (227 g) English chocolate malt
8 lb. (3.63 kg) Superbrau plain light malt extract
1 lb. (454 g) brown sugar
2 tsp. (9.9 ml) gypsum
2 oz. (57 g) B.C. Kent Goldings hops, 4.6% alpha, in boil 45 min.
2 tsp. (9.9 ml) yeast nutrient
1 packet Whitbread ale yeast
¾ c. (206 ml) corn sugar, for priming

Crush grains and place in grain bag. Steep grain bag in 1½ gal. (5.7 L) of 160°F (71°C) hot water. Remove grain. Add malt extract, brown sugar, gypsum, and hops. Boil 45 min., then turn off heat. Chill wort, transfer to fermenter, and top off to 5 gal. (18.9 L) with cold water. Add yeast nutrient and pitch yeast. Ferment 5 – 7 days, then rack to a secondary fermenter for 14 – 18 days. Prime with corn sugar and bottle. Age for 2 weeks.

— *James C. Whitely, Arbor Wine & Beermaking Supplies*
East Islip, New York

Scotch Ale

YIELD: .... 5 GAL. (18.9 L)
TOTAL BOILING TIME: .... 60 MIN.
STARTING GRAVITY: 1.070
ENDING GRAVITY: 1.015
PRIMARY FERMENT: .... 1 WEEK
SECONDARY FERMENT: .... 1 WEEK

Wyeast #1728 Scottish Ale yeast
1 lb. (454 g) British pale ale malt
1 lb. (454 g) British cara-pils malt
1 lb. (454 g) British crystal malt, 60° Lovibond
1 package Burton water salts
8 lb. (3.63 kg) amber malt extract
1 lb. (454 g) dark brown sugar
⅔ oz. (19 g) British Blend hop pellets, in boil 55 min.
½ oz. (14 g) Fuggles hops, in boil 15 min.
½ oz. (14 g) Fuggles hops, steep
1 package Bru-Vigor yeast food
½ c. (138 ml) brown sugar, for priming

Prepare yeast starter prior to brewing day.

Add crushed grains and water salts to 1 gal. (3.8 L) of 160°F (71°C) water and steep for 30 min. Sparge grains with 1 gal. (3.8 L) or more of 168°F (76°C) water into brew kettle. Bring wort to a boil, then turn off heat and add malt extract and 1 lb. (454 g) dark brown sugar. Boil 5 min. before adding the British Blend hop pellets. Boil 40 min., then add ½ oz. (14 g) of Fuggles hops. Boil 15 min., add last ½ oz. (14 g) of Fuggles hops and turn off heat. Steep a few min., then chill the wort, transfer to fermenter, and top off to 5 gal. (18.9 L) with cold water. Pitch yeast along with Bru-Vigor yeast food. Ferment 1 week. Rack to a secondary fermenter for 1 week. Prime with brown sugar and bottle.

— *DeFalco's Home Wine & Beer Supplies, Houston, Texas*

Snowflake Strong
Scottish Ale

YIELD:	5 GAL. (18.9 L)
TOTAL BOILING TIME:	90 MIN.
STARTING GRAVITY:	1.080
ENDING GRAVITY:	1.028
PRIMARY FERMENT:	13 DAYS
SECONDARY FERMENT:	3 WEEKS

Second place in the 1996 Spirit of Free Beer competition.

    Belhaven yeast
13½ lb. (6.12 kg) pale ale malt
  1 lb. (454 g) Belgian cara-Munich malt
  1 lb. (454 g) crystal malt, 80° Lovibond
  ½ lb. (227 g) biscuit malt
  ½ lb. (227 g) wheat malt
  1 oz. (28 g) roasted barley
1¾ oz. (50 g) Yakima Goldings hops, 5.5% alpha, in boil 90 min.
  ¾ c. (206 ml) corn sugar, for priming

Several days before brewing, begin starter of cultured Belhaven yeast.
    Crush grains and add to 5 ½ gal. (20.8 L) of 169°F (76°C) water.
Mash at 158°F (70°C) for 60 min. Raise temperature to 170°F (77°C) for
a 10-min. mash-out. Sparge with 170°F (77°C) water and collect 6 ½ – 7
gal. (24.6 – 26.5 L) of wort. Bring wort to a boil and add the Yakima hops.
Boil 90 min., then turn off heat. Chill wort, transfer to fermenter, and
pitch yeast. Ferment at 60°F (16°C) for 13 days, then rack to a secondary
fermenter for another 3 weeks. Prime with corn sugar and bottle.

— Keith Chamberlin, Riveraale, Maryland
Brewers United for Real Potables (BURP)

Auld Rabbie Burns

YIELD:	10 GAL. (L)
TOTAL BOILING TIME:	90 MIN.
STARTING GRAVITY:	1.072
ENDING GRAVITY:	1.021
PRIMARY FERMENT:	1 WEEK
SECONDARY FERMENT:	2 WEEKS

Wyeast #1728 Scottish Ale yeast, 2-qt. (1.9-L) starter

25 lb. (11.34 kg) Belgian pale malt

2 lb. (907 g) aromatic malt

1 lb. (454 g) wheat malt

1 lb. (454 g) crystal malt, 60° Lovibond

¼ lb. (113 g) roast barley

2 oz. (57 g) East Kent Goldings hops, 5.0% alpha, in boil 60 min.

1½ c. (413 ml) of corn sugar, for priming

Prior to brewing day, make up a 2-qt. (1.9-L) yeast starter.

Crush grains and add to 5 gal. (18.9 L) of 130°F (54°C) water in mash tun to reach stable protein-rest temperature of 120°F (49°C). Hold for 30 min. Add 3 gal. (11.4 L) of boiling water to bring mash to 140°F (60°C). Hold for 30 min. Pull a thick, 6-gal. (22.7-L) decoction from the main mash, bring to a boil, and add back to main mash to bring mash temperature to 158°F (70°C). Hold for 30 min. Pull a 3-gal. (11.4-L) thin decoction from the main mash, boil, and add back to main mash to reach mash-out temperature of 165°F (74°C). Sparge with 170°F (77°C) water and collect 12½ gal. (47.3 L) of wort. Boil wort 30 min. before adding East Kent Goldings. Boil 60 min., then turn off heat. Chill to 65°F (18°C) and transfer to a fermenter. Aerate well and pitch yeast. Ferment 1 week at no more than 60°F (16°C). Transfer to secondary for 2 more weeks at 55°F (13°C). If possible, cold condition beer at 30° – 35°F (-1° – 2°C) for 2 – 3 more weeks before packaging. Prime and bottle.

— *Wendy Aaronson and Bill Ridgely, Alexandria, Virginia*
Brewers United for Real Potables (BURP)

STRONG ALES: BARLEYWINE AND OLD ALE

Revenge!

YIELD: .... 5 GAL. (18.9 L)
TOTAL BOILING TIME: .... 90 MIN.
STARTING GRAVITY: 1.110
ENDING GRAVITY: 1.020
PRIMARY FERMENT: .... 7 DAYS
SECONDARY FERMENT: .... 108 DAYS

Best of show at the 1995 Santa Rosa Brewfest in Fort Walton Beach, Florida.

12 oz. (340 g) light crystal malt
 8 oz. (227 g) cara-pils malt
12 lb. (5.44 kg) Alexander's pale malt extract
 7 lb. (3.18 kg) clover honey
 2 oz. (57 g) Pride of Ringwood hops, in boil 60 min.
 2 oz. (57 g) Liberty hops, in boil 15 min.
 1 tsp. (4.9 ml) Irish moss
 1 tbsp. (14.8 ml) gypsum
    Lalvin #1118 dry yeast
¾ c. (206 ml) corn sugar, for priming

Put grain in grain bag and steep in 1½ gal. (5.7 L) of 165°F (71°C) water for 30 min. Remove grain. Bring wort to a boil and add gypsum and malt extract. Boil 30 min., then add Pride of Ringwood hops in a hops bag. Boil 45 min., then add honey, Irish moss, and Liberty hops in a hops bag. Boil 15 min. and turn off heat. Chill the wort and transfer to fermenter, topping off to 5 gal. (18.9 L) with cold water. Pitch yeast and ferment 7 days. Rack to secondary for 3 months. Prime with corn sugar and bottle. Age 6 months.

— *Bryan E. Schwab, Panama City, Florida*

Barleywine

YIELD: .... 5 GAL. (18.9 L)
TOTAL BOILING TIME: .... 60 MIN.
STARTING GRAVITY: 1.090
ENDING GRAVITY: 1.020
PRIMARY FERMENT: .... 1 WEEK
SECONDARY FERMENT: .... 2 WEEKS

Wyeast #1056 American Ale yeast
1 lb. (454 g) Belgian biscuit malt
1 lb. (454 g) medium crystal malt
1 lb. (454 g) cara-pils malt
12 lb. (5.44 kg) light unhopped malt extract
1 c. (275 ml) light brown sugar
1 oz. (28 g) British Blend hop pellets, in boil 55 min.
1 oz. (28 g) Northern Brewer hops, in boil 15 min.
1 oz. (28 g) Willamette hops, steep
1 package Burton water salts
1 package Bru-Vigor yeast food
½ c. (138 ml) corn sugar, for priming

Prepare yeast starter prior to brewing day.

Add crushed grains and water salts to 1 gal. (3.8 L) of 160°F (71°C) water and let steep for 30 min. Sparge the grains with 1 gal. (3.8 L) or more of 168°F (76°C) water into brew kettle. Bring wort to a boil, then turn off heat and add malt extract and brown sugar. Boil 5 min. before adding the British Blend hop pellets. Boil 40 min., then add the Northern Brewer hops. Boil 15 min., add the Willamette hops, and turn off heat. Steep a few min., then chill the wort, transfer to fermenter, and top off to 5 gal. (18.9 L) with cold water. Pitch yeast along with Bru-Vigor yeast food. Ferment 1 week. Rack to secondary for 2 weeks. Prime with corn sugar and bottle.

— *DeFalco's Home Wine & Beer Supplies, Houston, Texas*

Imhoff Triple Bock

YIELD: .... 2½ GAL. (9.5 L)
TOTAL BOILING TIME: .... 30 MIN.
PRIMARY FERMENT: .... 10 DAYS

    1 lb. (454 g) crystal malt
  6.6 lb. (3 kg) Munton & Fison light malt extract
    1 in (2.5 cm) brewer's licorice stick
    2 oz. (57 g) Hallertauer hops, in boil 30 min.
    1 c. (237 ml) maple syrup
    1 packet dry ale yeast
    1 packet dry champagne yeast

Crush crystal malt and place in a grain bag. Steep in 2 gal. (7.6 L) of
170°F (77°C) water. Remove bag. Add malt extract, licorice, hops, and
maple syrup. Boil 30 min., then turn off heat. Chill the wort, transfer
to the fermenter, and pitch both strains of yeast. Ferment 10 days and
bottle without priming sugar.

— *Dan Imhoff, Andover, Minnesota*

Tall, Dark & Strong

YIELD: .... 5 GAL. (18.9 L)
TOTAL BOILING TIME: .... 60 MIN.
STARTING GRAVITY: 1.092
ENDING GRAVITY: 1.036
PRIMARY FERMENT: .... 12 DAYS
SECONDARY FERMENT: .... 20 DAYS

Earned a 1995 AHA silver certificate.

    1 lb. (454 g) crystal malt
   ¼ lb. (113 g) chocolate malt
  6.6 lb. (3 kg) Munton & Fison light malt extract
    1 lb. (454 g) amber dry malt extract
    3 oz. (85 g) Fuggles hops, 4.5% alpha, in boil 60 min.
      Munton & Fison ale yeast
   ¾ c. (206 ml) corn sugar, for priming

Crush grains and steep in 2½ gal. (9.5 L) of 170°F (77°C) water. Strain out grains and add malt extracts. Bring to a boil and add Fuggles. Boil 60 min., then turn off heat. Chill the wort, transfer to fermenter, and bring up to 5 gal. (18.9 L) with cold water. Pitch yeast and ferment 12 days at 67°F (19°C). Rack to secondary for 20 days at 67°F (19°C). Prime with corn sugar and bottle.

— Ed Cosgrove and Rory Schultz, Woodbridge, Virginia
Brewers Association of Northern Virginia (BANOVA)

Old Ale

YIELD:	5 GAL. (18.9 L)
TOTAL BOILING TIME:	60 MIN.
STARTING GRAVITY:	1.056
ENDING GRAVITY:	1.014
PRIMARY FERMENT:	1 WEEK
SECONDARY FERMENT:	1 WEEK

    Wyeast #1028 London Ale yeast
    1 package Burton water salts
1½ lb. (680 g) British mild malt
 ½ lb. (227 g) British cara-pils malt
 ½ lb. (227 g) British dark crystal malt
 ½ lb. (227 g) British medium crystal malt
  4 lb. (1.81 kg) amber malt extract
  2 lb. (907 g) Old Bavarian Munich blend malt extract
  1 lb. (454 g) dark malt extract
1½ oz. (43 g) British Fuggles hops, in boil 55 min.
 ½ oz. (14 g) British Fuggles hops, in boil 15 min.
 ½ oz. (14 g) British Fuggles hops, steep
  1 package Bru-Vigor yeast food
 ⅝ c. (172 ml) brown sugar, for priming

Prepare yeast starter prior to brewing day.

    Crush grains and add water salts to 1 gal. (3.8 L) of 160°F (71°C) water and steep for 30 min. Sparge the grains with 1 gal. (3.8 L) or more of 168°F (76°C) water into brew kettle. Bring wort to a boil, then turn off heat and add malt extracts. Boil 5 min. before adding 1½ oz. (43 g) of Fuggles hops. Boil 40 min., then add ½ oz. (14 g) of Fuggles hops. Boil 15 min., add last ½ oz. (14 g) of Fuggles, and turn off heat. Steep a few min., then chill the wort, transfer to fermenter, and top off to 5 gal. (18.9 L) with cold water. Pitch yeast along with Bru-Vigor yeast food. Ferment 1 week. Rack to secondary for 1 week. Prime with brown sugar and bottle.

— *DeFalco's Home Wine & Beer Supplies, Houston, Texas*

Buck's Brutal Barleywine

YIELD: .... 8 GAL. (30.3 L)
TOTAL BOILING TIME: .... 150 MIN.
STARTING GRAVITY: 1.101
ENDING GRAVITY: 1.022
PRIMARY FERMENT: .... 10 DAYS
SECONDARY FERMENT: .... 32 DAYS

Best of show at the 1996 World Cup of Beer competition.

    22   lb. (9.98 kg) 2-row Klages pale malt
 1.625 lb. (737 g) wheat malt
    1½   lb. (680 g) Belgian cara-Vienne malt
    1¼   lb. (567 g) Belgian aromatic malt
    ¾   lb. (340 g) Belgian cara-Munich malt
    ¾   lb. (340 g) Belgian Munich malt
   6.3   oz. (179 g) Willamette whole hops, 4.7% alpha, in boil 60 min.
   1.9   oz. (54 g) U.S. Tettnanger whole hops, 4.3% alpha, in boil 10 min.
         Wyeast #1056 American Ale yeast

Crush grains and add to 9¼ gal. (35 L) of 168°F (76°C) water. Mash at 158°F (70°C) for 90 min. Boost temperature to 175°F (79°C) for a 10-min. mash-out. Acidify sparge water to 5.7 pH. Sparge with 170°F (77°C) water and collect 13 gal. (49.2 L). Boil 90 min. before adding Willamette hops. Boil 50 min., then add Tettnanger. Boil 10 min., then turn off heat. Force-chill to 68°F (20°C), transfer to fermenter, and pitch yeast slurry. Ferment 10 days at 64°F (18°C). Rack to secondary for 32 days at 60°F (16°C). Keg.

— *Charlie Gow, Santa Rosa, California, Maltose Falcons*
Brewers United for Real Potables (BURP)

1995 Surreal Cap

YIELD: .... 5 GAL. (18.9 L)
TOTAL BOILING TIME: .... 75 MIN.
STARTING GRAVITY: 1.071–1.075
PRIMARY FERMENT: .... 2 WEEKS
SECONDARY FERMENT: .... 1 MONTH

This is a clone of Pyramid's Snow Cap from about 1992.

Wyeast #1056 American Ale yeast
14 lb. (6.35 kg) Hugh Baird 2-row pale ale malt
1½ lb. (680 g) crystal malt, 80° Lovibond
½ lb. (227 g) chocolate malt
¼ lb. (113 g) malted wheat
2½ oz. (71 g) Perle hops, 5.5% alpha, in boil 60 min.
1 tsp. (4.9 ml) Irish moss
½ oz. (14 g) Mt. Hood hops, in boil 15 min.
¼ oz. (7 g) oz. Mt. Hood hops, steep
¾ c. (206 ml) corn sugar, for priming, or force carbonate

Several days before brewing, begin growing up yeast starter.

Add crushed grains to 5 ½ gal. (20.8 L) of 164°F (73°C) water and mash for 60 min. Sparge with 170°F (77°C) water and collect 6½ – 7 gal. (24.6 – 26.5 L) of wort. Boil 15 min. before adding Perle. Boil 30 min., then add Irish moss. Boil 15 min., then add ½ oz. (14 g) of Mt. Hood hops. Boil 15 min. and remove from heat. Add ¼ oz. (7 g) of Mt. Hood hops and steep for a few min. Chill the wort and transfer to fermenter. Pitch yeast and ferment 2 weeks at 65°F (18°C). Transfer to secondary fermenter and lager for 1 month before priming and bottling.

— *David and Melinda Brockington, Seattle, Washington*
Seattle Secret Skinny Brewers Society

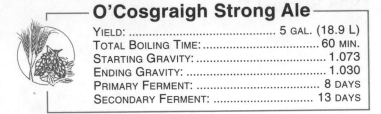

O'Cosgraigh Strong Ale

YIELD: .... 5 GAL. (18.9 L)
TOTAL BOILING TIME: .... 60 MIN.
STARTING GRAVITY: 1.073
ENDING GRAVITY: 1.030
PRIMARY FERMENT: .... 8 DAYS
SECONDARY FERMENT: .... 13 DAYS

Second place in the 1995 Spirit of Free Beer competition in the strong ale category.

 4 oz. (113 g) pale malt, toasted
11 lb. (4.99 kg) pale malt
 3 lb. (1.36 kg) cara-Munich malt
 1 lb. (454 g) crystal malt
 2 oz. (57 g) chocolate malt
 2 oz. (57 g) Willamette hops, 4.8% alpha, in boil 60 min.
 1 oz. (28 g) Fuggles hops, 3.6% alpha, in boil 60 min.
½ oz. (14 g) Cascade hops, in boil 3 min.
    Munton & Fison ale yeast
¾ c. (206 ml) corn sugar, for priming

Toast 4 oz. (113 g) of pale malt in a 350°F (177°C) oven for 10 min. Crush all grains and add to 5 gal. (18.9 L) of water. Raise temperature to 122°F (50°C) for 30 min. Raise temperature to 157°F (69°C) for 90 min. Mash-out at 168°F (76°C) for 10 min. Sparge with 170°F (77°C) water and collect 5½ – 6 gal. (20.8 – 22.7 L). Bring wort to a boil, add Willamette hops and Fuggles hops, and boil 57 min. Add Cascade hops, boil 3 min., then turn off heat. Chill the wort, transfer to fermenter, and pitch yeast. Ferment 8 days at 67°F (19°C), then rack to secondary for 13 days. Prime with corn sugar and bottle.

— Ed Cosgrove and Rory Schultz, Woodbridge, Virginia
Brewers Association of Northern Virginia (BANOVA)

SPECIALTY ALE

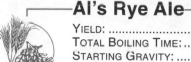

Al's Rye Ale

YIELD: .... 5 GAL. (18.9 L)
TOTAL BOILING TIME: .... 150 MIN.
STARTING GRAVITY: 1.071
PRIMARY FERMENT: .... 3 WEEKS

Rye malt adds a subtle flavor like rye bread (without caraway), but mostly adds mouthfeel.

- 8 lb. (3.63 kg) Munton & Fison pale ale malt
- 6 lb. (2.72 kg) Briess rye malt
- 4 oz. (113 g) Fuggles hop pellets, 3.0% alpha, in boil 60 min.
- 1 tsp. (4.9 ml) Irish moss, rehydrated
  Wyeast #1968 London ESB yeast starter
- ¾ c. (206 ml) corn sugar, for priming

Mash-in grains with 12 qt. (11.4 L) of 163°F (73°C) water. The temperature should settle in at 145°F (63°C). Rest for 30 min. Add 5 qt. (4.7 L) of boiling water to raise the mash temperature to 154°F (68°C). Rest 90 min. Sparge with 170°F (77°C) water and collect 7 ¾ gal. (15.1 L) of runnings. Bring wort to a boil and, with the lid off, boil 1½ hours. Add hop pellets in a hop bag to wort and boil 45 min. Add the rehydrated Irish moss and boil 15 min. Turn off heat and remove hop bag. Chill the wort to 75°F (24°C), transfer to fermenter, and pitch yeast starter. Attach blow-off tube and ferment at 65°F (18°C) for 3 weeks. Replace blow-off tube with an air lock when violent phase of fermentation ceases. Prime with corn sugar and bottle.

Al Korzonas, Palos Hills, Illinois, Chicago Beer Society
Brewers of South Suburbia (BOSS), Urban Knaves of Grain

More Homebrew Favorites

European Light Lagers

Lagers represent some of the world's most popular beers. Technically complex, time consuming, expensive, and less forgiving to brew than most ale styles, *lagers* can be regarded as a test of a homebrewer's skill and knowledge.

Lagers are often described as having "clean" flavor profiles. This means that they are often less complex than the ale styles that we have presented up to this point. Ales are more likely to have fruity esters, the rounded, creamy mouthfeel of low diacetyl levels, and the sherry-like notes of alcoholic warming. However, lagers make up for this, to some degree, by simplifying the flavor components so that the underlying malt flavors become more predominant. Lagers also offer smoothness as a result of their long, cold maturation periods.

Light lager styles include the classic, crisp, hoppy pilsner style, the maltier Munich Helles style, the crisper Dortmunder export style, and the soft, sweet-malt Vienna-style lagers.

Pilsner. Originating in the Czech Republic city of Plzen in the 1840s, pilsner quickly traveled to other European and American brewing capitals. Today, pilsner (in all its variations) is the world's

KEY TO RECIPE LOGOS

 EXTRACT RECIPES   PARTIAL MASH RECIPES   ALL-GRAIN RECIPES

most widely produced beer style by major brewing corporations. The classic pilsner is the Bohemian, or Czech, style, which is known for its assertive Saaz hop aroma and flavor. Pilsner is clean and crisp, very pale in color, sometimes with a slight caramel taste from low diacetyl, but free from esters. Very pale pilsner malt is used to achieve an original gravity of 1.044 to 1.056 (Pilsner Urquell — the classic example of the style from Plzen — is about 1.048). Saaz hops are added at the rate of 25 to 45 IBUs. Soft water contributes to the flavor.

German pilsners differ from their Czech counterparts with a drier, more bitter flavor, although they are not hopped more than the Czech beers. The difference is attributed to Munich's harder water, with its higher sulfate levels.

Pilsner-style beers made in other countries may deviate from the classic — often with lower original gravities and lower hopping rates. In Scandinavia and the Netherlands, adjunct grains — corn and rice, for example — are sometimes used.

Munich Helles beer is known for its malty character, with residual sweetness and a taste of caramel. The malty flavor is achieved using Munich malt and a decoction mash. It is also less attenuated than a pilsner. Hops are fairly low, and noble type hops are used. No flavors from yeast by-products should be present. Original gravity should be 1.045 to 1.055, with hops at 18 to 25 IBUs.

The Dortmunder style (the name is derived from the city of Dortmund, Germany, where it is brewed) is also known as *export*. Similar to a Munich Helles, but sometimes slightly hoppier with a less prominent malt character, Dortmunder is typically well balanced, with neither hops nor malt dominating the beer. The original gravity should be in the range of 1.050 to 1.060 and hopped at 23 to 30 IBUs.

Hard water, with both calcium carbonate and calcium sulfate, is necessary to brew the Dortmunder style. The beer is mashed with a slightly high saccharification temperature that leaves a firm body. This beer should be cleanly brewed with no trace of esters, diacetyl, or other yeast by-products. The hard water also contributes a somewhat dry palate.

Vienna-style lagers. Most beers described as "amber" are, in fact, Vienna-style lagers. Originated in 1841 by Anton Dreher in Austria, the style is now seldom found there. The beer is malty, with a toasty, nut-like flavor that comes from Vienna malt, which also gives the beer its reddish color. The beer is well attenuated with a dry finish. Noble hops are used at fairly low levels (18 to 30 IBUs). Yeast by-product flavors are inappropriate for this style of beer. The original gravity should be about 1.046 to 1.052.

The German Oktoberfest- and Märzen-style beers were adapted from the Vienna style by Gabriel Sedelmayr of the Spaten Brewery in Munich at about the same time the style developed in Austria, but the German variations have a bit more malt with more sweetness than their Austrian cousins. Noble hops are fairly low, being used to balance the sweetness rather than as a dominant component of the flavor profile. The original gravity should be 1.050 to 1.065 and the hops at 20 to 30 IBUs.

Ingredients. European 2-row lager malts or pilsner malts will generally be more suitable for these styles of beer than American lager malts. Many lager styles will use Munich malt, which helps impart a malty character.

Noble-type hops are the best choices for most European lager styles; however, there are other hops, including Northern Brewer and Cluster, that might be used occasionally. Hopping rates are low for most lagers, tending to balance rather than dominate the flavor, with the exception of pilsner, which has an assertive hop character. Dry hopping is not appropriate for these beers.

Yeast selection is an important aspect of lager recipe formulation. There are several dry lager yeasts on the market, as well as a wide range of liquid yeasts and slants. Some of these yeasts are better suited toward certain styles than others. For pilsner-style beers, Yeast Lab L31 (optimal temperature: 50° to 52°F [10° to 11°C]), Wyeast #2007, and Wyeast #2278 yeasts (optimal temperature: 46° to 54°F [8° to 12°C]) are good choices. For a Munich Helles or a Vienna-style beer, try Yeast Lab L32 (optimal temperature: 48° to 52°F [9° to 11°C]) or L33 (optimal temperature: 50° to 52°F [10° to 11°C]), or the Wyeast #2206 (optimal temperature: 48° to 52°F [9° to 11°C]) or #2308 (optimal temperature: 50° to 53°F [10° to 12°C]).

For a Dortmunder, any of the yeasts used for Munich-style beers are acceptable.

Method. Extract brewers often find that brewing light lagers is difficult. The beers come out darker, heavier, and fruitier than they'd like. Most light extracts are darker than needed for light lagers, and boiling a concentrated wort further darkens it as the sugars caramelize.

All-grain versions of most European lager-styles will be brewed using either a step mash or a decoction mash. Depending on the protein levels of your malt, you may want to start your mash with a protein rest at about 120° to 122°F (49° to 50°C), then raise the temperature to 142° to 146°F (61° to 63°C) to allow the beta amylase to produce a more fermentable wort. Decoction mashes generally give a more malty character to the beer than will a step mash. Single-step decoctions are often used, particularly for lighter-colored lagers.

As with most beer styles, pitching a good, healthy yeast in fairly large quantities at the best temperature for that yeast is the best way to get a vigorous fermentation. Liquid yeasts give the greatest flexibility in selecting for various characteristics. These can be grown up to pitching levels over several days before you start brewing. While room temperatures are generally acceptable for growing up ale yeasts, cooler temperatures (about 50°F [10°C]) are more appropriate for lager yeasts. Keep in mind that yeast activity will raise the temperature of your fermenting beer, so try to pitch at about 45°F (7°C).

Temperature control is very important for producing clean lager beers. Most of the lager yeasts work best with a primary fermentation temperature of between 48° to 53°F (9° to 12°C). This range may vary for certain yeasts, so check the optimal range when trying a new strain. It is also important to keep temperatures stable — avoid periodic changes, such as day-night fluctuations. The secondary fermentation will usually be about 10° to 15°F (5° to 8°C) colder and will last much longer than the primary fermentation (some authors recommend lagering temperatures of 31°F [-1°C]). When decreasing the temperature from primary to secondary fermentation, it is best to lower the temperature slowly over several days rather than to simply turn the thermostat down. You may want to try the beer between the primary and secondary fermentations. If you detect buttery flavors, do a diacetyl rest before lowering the temperature for the secondary.

To do a diacetyl rest, increase the temperature to about 60°F (16°C) and hold it for a day or so, then slowly cool it to secondary fermentation temperatures. By raising the temperature slightly, yeast activity increases, breaking down diacetyl.

Whether or not you do a diacetyl rest, you will want to lager your beers at cool temperatures for several weeks or even months. Generally, a light lager will need at least 2 to 3 weeks, while higher-gravity lagers (such as doppelbocks) will require much longer periods — sometimes as much as 6 to 9 months.

PILSNERS

Bill's Pils

YIELD: .... 5 GAL. (18.9 L)
TOTAL BOILING TIME: .... 60 MIN.
PRIMARY FERMENT: .... 1–2 WEEKS
SECONDARY FERMENT: .... 3 WEEKS
BOTTLE CONDITIONED: .... 3 WEEKS

Light-colored rich, full-bodied, and loaded with hops.

½ lb. (227 g) Victory malt, cracked
5 lb. (2.27 kg) extra light dry malt extract
1 lb. (454 g) rice syrup solids
1½ oz. (43 g) Tettnanger hops, 5.3% alpha, in boil 60 min.
½ oz. (14 g) Tettnanger hops, 5.3% alpha, in boil 30 min.
½ oz. (14 g) Tettnanger hops, 5.3% alpha, in boil 15 min.
½ oz. (14 g) Tettnanger hops, 5.3% alpha, in boil 5 min.
1 oz. (28 g) Tettnanger hops, 5.3% alpha, steep 10 min.
   Wyeast #2007 Pilsen Lager yeast
¾ c. (206 ml) corn sugar, for priming

Steep cracked Victory malt 1 2 gal (7 6 L) of 160°F (71°C) water Strain out the grain. Add the malt extract, rice syrup solids, and 1½ oz. (43 g) of Tettnanger hops. Boil 30 min. Add ½ oz. (14 g) of Tettnanger hops and boil 15 min. Add ½ oz. (14 g) of Tettnanger hops and boil another 10 min. Add ½ oz. (14 g) Tettnanger hops and boil 5 min. Remove from heat, add 1 oz. (28 g) of Tettnanger, and steep for 10 min. Cool wort and strain as you fill the fermenter. Top off fermenter to 5 gal. (18.9 L). Pitch yeast when wort is 70°F (21°C) or lower. Drop the fermenter temperature to between 45° and 55°F (7° and 13°C) and ferment for 1 2 weeks. Rack to a secondary fermenter for 3 weeks at 38°F (3°C). Prime with corn sugar and bottle.

— *Bill Sproules, Olympic Brewing Supplies, Bremerton, Washington*

West Sound Brewers and Grain Peace

Czech Pilsner

YIELD: .... 5 GAL. (18.9 L)
TOTAL BOILING TIME: .... 60 MIN.
STARTING GRAVITY: 1.049
ENDING GRAVITY: 1.012
PRIMARY FERMENT: .... 1 WEEK
SECONDARY FERMENT: .... 2 WEEKS

Wyeast #2206 Bavarian Lager yeast
1½ lb. (680 g) German pilsner malt
¼ lb. (113 g) German light crystal malt
4½ lb. (2.04 kg) light malt extract
1½ lb. (680 g) Old Bavarian Munich Blend extract
1 oz. (28 g) Northern Brewer hops, in boil
55 min.
1½ oz. (43 g) Czech Saaz hops, in boil 15 min.
½ oz. (14 g) Czech Saaz hops, steep
#2124 Bohemian Lager yeast
1 package Bru-Vigor yeast food
¾ c. (206 ml) corn sugar, for priming

Prepare yeast starter prior to brewing day.

Crush grains and add to 1 gal. (3.8 L) of 160°F (72°C) water and steep 30 min. Sparge grains with 1 gal. (3.8 L) or more of 168°F (76°C) water. Bring wort to a boil, then turn off heat and add malt extracts. Boil 5 min. before adding German Northern Brewer hops. Boil 40 min., then add 1½ oz. (43 g) of Czech Saaz hops. Boil 15 min., then add the last ½ oz. (14 g) of Saaz. Turn off heat. Steep a few min., then chill the wort, transfer to fermenter, and top off to 5 gal. (18.9 L) with cold water. Pitch yeast along with Bru-Vigor yeast food. Ferment 1 week at 45° – 55°F (7° – 13°C). Rack to secondary for 2 weeks at 45° – 55°F (7° – 13°C). Prime with corn sugar and bottle.

— DeFalco's Home Wine & Beer Supplies, Houston, Texas

Czecherboard Pilsner

YIELD: .... 5 GAL. (18.9 L)
TOTAL BOILING TIME: .... 120 MIN.
STARTING GRAVITY: 1.056
PRIMARY FERMENT: .... 1 MONTH
SECONDARY FERMENT: .... 3 DAYS
BOTTLE CONDITION: .... 2 WEEKS
LAGERED IN BOTTLES: .... 2 MONTHS

Use soft water for this beer. Keep sulfate and carbonate levels below 50 ppm.

    10 lb. (4.54 kg) Ireks pilsner malt
     1 lb. (454 g) DeWolf-Cosysns biscuit malt
  2 ¼ oz. (64 g) Czech Saaz hop pellets, 3.8% alpha, in boil 120 min.
   ⅔ oz. (19 g) Czech Saaz hops, 3.8% alpha, in boil 30 min.
     1 tsp. (4.9 ml) Irish moss
       Wyeast #2278 Czech Pilsner yeast, ⅔-gal. (2½-L) starter
  2 ¾ oz. (78 g) corn sugar, for priming

Mash-in the 11 lb. (4.99 kg) of crushed grain with 10 qt. (9.5 L) of 160°F (71°C) water. Let rest at 140°F (60°C) for 15 min. Remove 6 qts. (5.7 L) of thick mash and place into a separate kettle, adding 3 qts. (2.8 L) of 150°F (66°C) water. While stirring constantly, heat this decoction mash 15 min., until the temperature reaches 162°F (72°C). Let rest at 162°F (72°C) for 10 min. Bring the decoction mash to a boil and boil 10 min.

Return the decoction mash to the main mash. This should give the main mash a temperature of 152°F (67°C). Let the mash rest for 75 min. Place 2¼ oz. (64 g) of Czech Saaz hop pellets in a hop bag and place in the bottom of the brew kettle. Sparge the mash until 7¼ gal. (27.4 L) of runnings are collected in the brew kettle. Bring the wort to a boil. Boil 40 min. Add ⅔ oz. (19 g) of Czech Saaz hops to a grain bag and add to the brew kettle. Boil 30 min., then add rehydrated Irish moss. Boil 15 min. Turn off heat, remove the hop bags, and chill the wort to 55°F (13°C). Transfer the wort to a primary fermenter, aerate well, and pitch a ⅔-gal. (2½-L) yeast starter. Ferment at 45°F (7°C) for 1 month. Then ferment for 3 days at 60°F (16°C). Prime with corn sugar and bottle. Condition for 2 weeks at 65°F (18°C), then lager the bottled beer for 2 months at 35°F (2°C).

— Al Korzonas, Palos Hills, Illinois, Chicago Beer Society
Brewers of South Suburbia (BOSS), Urban Knaves of Grain

Velvet Divorce Pilsner

YIELD:	5 GAL. (18.9 L)
TOTAL BOILING TIME:	90 MIN.
STARTING GRAVITY:	1.050–1.055
PRIMARY FERMENT:	2 WEEKS
SECONDARY FERMENT:	4 WEEKS
LAGERING:	2 MONTHS

    Wyeast #2278 Czech Pilsner yeast
10 lb. (4.54 kg) DeWolf-Cosyns pilsner malt
 1 lb. (454 g) DeWolf-Cosyns Munich malt
 8 oz. (227 g) DeWolf-Cosyns cara-Vienne malt
1¼ oz. (35 g) Saaz hops, 4.1% alpha, in boil 60 min.
 1 tsp. (5 ml) Irish moss
1¾ oz. (50 g) Saaz hops, 4.1% alpha, in boil 15 min.
1¼ oz. (35 g) Saaz hops, steep

Several days before brewing, begin growing up yeast starter.
    Crush grains and add to 3¾ gal. (14.2 L) of 142°F (61°C) water. Mash at 131°F (55°C) for a 30-min. protein rest. Heat mash to 152°F (67°C) for a 60-min. starch conversion. Raise temperature to 170°F

(77°C) for a 10-min. mash-out. Sparge with 170°F (77°C) water and collect 6 ½ gal. (24.6 L) of wort in brew kettle. Boil 30 min. before adding 1¼ oz. (35 g) of Saaz hops. Boil 30 min., then add Irish moss. Boil 15 min., then add 1¾ oz. (50 g) of Saaz hops. Boil 15 min., remove from heat, and add the remaining 1¼ oz. (35 g) of Saaz. Chill to below 50°F (10°C) and transfer to fermenter. Pitch yeast starter and ferment 2 weeks at 48°F (9°C). Transfer to secondary for 4 weeks at 38°F (3°C). Lager at 33°F (1°C) for at least 2 months. Keg or bottle.

— *David Brockington, Seattle, Washington*
Seattle Secret Skinny Brewers Society

Snow-Pack Pilsner

YIELD:	5 GAL. (18.9 L)
TOTAL BOILING TIME:	105 MIN.
STARTING GRAVITY:	1.045
ENDING GRAVITY:	1.012
PRIMARY FERMENT:	1 WEEK
SECONDARY FERMENT:	1 WEEK
LAGERING:	6 WEEKS

7 lb. (3.18 kg) DeWolf-Cosyns pilsner malt
1 lb. (454 g) DeWolf-Cosyns malted wheat
1 lb. (454 g) Briess flaked maize
⅓ oz. (9 g) Mt. Hood hops, 4.8% alpha, first wort hopped
1 oz. (28 g) Mt. Hood hops, 4.8% alpha, in boil 60 min.
1 oz. (28 g) Mt. Hood hops, 4.8% alpha, in boil 18 min.
⅔ oz. (19 g) Mt. Hood hops, 4.8% alpha, in boil 8 min.
  Wyeast #2042 Danish Lager yeast, 1-qt. (946-ml) starter
¾ c. (206 ml) corn sugar, for priming

Crush grains and add to 2½ gal. (9.4 L) of water and heat to 122°F (50°C). Let rest for 30 min. Heat mash to 140°F (60°C) and let rest for 30 min. Heat to 158°F (70°C) and let rest for 30 min. Mash-out at 170°F (77°C) for 10 min. Sparge mash with 168°F (76°C) water, collecting wort in brew kettle. Collect 7 gal. (26.5 L) of wort. Add ⅓ oz. Mt. Hood. Boil 45 min. before adding 1 oz. (28 g) of Mt. Hood hops. Boil 42 min., then add 1 oz. (28 g) of Mt. Hood. Boil 10 min., then add ⅔ oz. (19 g) of Mt. Hood.

Boil 8 min., then turn off heat. Chill wort, transfer to fermenter, and pitch yeast starter. Ferment 1 week at 50°F (10°C), then rack to secondary for 1 week at 40°F (4°C). Pack snow around carboy and lager for 6 weeks. Prior to bottling, allow fermenter to rest at 50°F (10°C) for 1 week. Prime with corn sugar and bottle.

— *Michael Mendenhall, Salt Lake City, Utah*

BAVARIAN LIGHT LAGER: HELLES

Munich Helles

YIELD:	5 GAL. (18.9 L)
TOTAL BOILING TIME:	60 MIN.
STARTING GRAVITY:	1.053
ENDING GRAVITY:	1.013
PRIMARY FERMENT:	1 WEEK
SECONDARY FERMENT:	2 WEEKS

Wyeast #2206 Bavarian Lager yeast
½ tsp. (2.5 ml) calcium chloride
1½ lb. (680 g) German pilsner malt
1 lb. (454 g) German Munich malt
½ lb. (227 g) German light crystal malt
4 lb. (1.81 kg) Old Bavarian Munich Blend extract
2 lb. (907 g) light malt extract
¾ oz. (21 g) Northern Brewer hops, in boil 55 min.
1½ oz. (43 g) Hallertauer Hersbrucker hops, in boil 15 min.
½ oz. (14 g) Hallertauer Hersbrucker hops, steep
1 package Bru-Vigor yeast food
¾ c. (206 ml) corn sugar, for priming

Prepare yeast starter prior to brewing day.

Add crushed grains and calcium chloride to 1 gal. (3.8 L) of 160°F (71°C) water and steep for 30 min. Sparge grains with 1 gal. (3.8 L) or more of 168°F (76°C) water into brew kettle. Bring wort to a boil, then turn off heat and add malt extracts. Boil 5 min. before adding Northern

Brewer hops. Boil 40 min., then add 1½ oz. (43 g) of Hallertauer Hersbrucker hops. Boil 15 min., then add the last ½ oz. (14 g) of Hallertauer Hersbrucker hops and turn off heat. Steep a few minutes, then chill the wort, transfer to fermenter, and top off to 5 gal. (18.9 L) with cold water. Pitch yeast along with Bru-Vigor yeast food. Ferment 1 week at 45° – 55°F (7° – 13°C). Rack to secondary for 2 weeks at 45° – 55°F (7° – 13°C). Prime with corn sugar and bottle.

— DeFalco's Home Wine & Beer Supplies, Houston, Texas

DORTMUNDER

Dortmunder Export

YIELD:	5 GAL. (18.9 L)
TOTAL BOILING TIME:	60 MIN.
STARTING GRAVITY:	1.054
ENDING GRAVITY:	1.013
PRIMARY FERMENT:	1 WEEK
SECONDARY FERMENT:	2 WEEKS

    Wyeast #2206 Bavarian Lager yeast
2½ lb. (1.13 kg) German pilsner malt
 ½ lb. (227 g) German light crystal malt
 4 lb. (1.81 kg) light malt extract
 2 lb. (907 g) Old Bavarian Munich Blend extract
 1 oz. (28 g) Northern Brewer hops, in boil 60 min.
 1 oz. (28 g) Hallertauer Hersbrucker hops, in boil 15 min.
 1 oz. (28 g) Hallertauer Hersbrucker hops, steep
 1 package Bru-Vigor yeast food
¾ c. (206 ml) corn sugar, for priming

Prepare yeast starter prior to brewing day.

    Crush grains and add to 1 gal. (3.8 L) of 160°F (71°C) water and steep for 30 min. Sparge the grains with 1 gal. (3.8 L) or more of 168°F (76°C) water into brew kettle. Bring wort to a boil, then turn off heat and add malt extracts. Boil 5 min. before adding Northern Brewer hops. Boil 40 min., then add 1 oz. (28 g) of Hallertauer Hersbrucker hops. Boil 15 min., add the last oz. (28 g) of Hallertauer Hersbrucker hops, and turn off heat. Steep a few min., then chill the wort, transfer to fermenter, and top off to 5 gal. (18.9 L) with cold water. Pitch yeast along with Bru-Vigor yeast food. Ferment 1 week at 45° – 55°F (7° – 13°C). Rack to secondary for 2 weeks at 45° – 55°F (7° – 13°C). Prime with corn sugar and bottle.

— *DeFalco's Home Wine & Beer Supplies, Houston, Texas*

Spuyten Duyvel

YIELD:	5 GAL. (18.9 L)
TOTAL BOILING TIME:	90 MIN.
STARTING GRAVITY:	1.049
ENDING GRAVITY:	1.011
PRIMARY FERMENT:	13 DAYS
SECONDARY FERMENT:	30 DAYS

First place in the Dortmunder export category at the 1990 Dixie Cup.

- 7 lb. (3.18 kg) 2-row pale malt
- ½ lb. (227 g) cara-pils malt
- 1½ lb. (680 g) flaked maize
- ¾ oz. (43 g) Hallertauer hops, 3.7% alpha, in boil 40 min.
- ½ oz. (14 g) Hallertauer hops, 3.7% alpha, in boil 25 min.
- ¼ oz. (7 g) Tettnanger hops, 4.8% alpha, in boil 25 min.
- 1 tsp. (1.0 ml) Irish moss
- ½ oz. (14 g) Saaz hops, 6.8% alpha, 15 min. steep
  Wyeast #2206 Bavarian Lager yeast
- ¾ c. (206 ml) corn sugar, for priming

Mash-in grains in 8 qts. (7.6 L) of 125°F (52°C), preboiled water. Hold at 120°F (49°C) for 30 min. Add 4 qts. (3.8 L) of boiling water and the maize. Maintain mash at 150°F (66°C) for 15 min. Heat to 156°F (69°C) and hold for 60 min. Heat to 168°F (76°C) and hold for 5 min. Sparge with 5 gal. (18.9 L) of 168°F (76°C) water that has been adjusted to 5.7 pH. Collect 6 ½ gal. (24.6 L) of wort and transfer to brew kettle. Boil 50 min. Add ¾ oz. (43 g) of Hallertauer hops. Boil 15 min. Add ½ oz. (14 g) of Hallertauer hops and Tettnanger hops. Boil 10 min. Add Irish moss and boil 15 min. Turn off heat and add ½ oz. (14 g) of Saaz hops. Steep 15 min.

Chill the wort, transfer to fermenter, and pitch yeast. Ferment 13 days at 53°F (12°C). Rack to secondary for 30 days at 43°F (6°C). Prime with corn sugar and bottle.

— *Val J. Lipscomb, San Antonio, Texas, Bock'n'Aleians*

Unnamed Dort

YIELD:	10 GAL. (37.9 L)
TOTAL BOILING TIME:	60 MIN.
STARTING GRAVITY:	1.052
ENDING GRAVITY:	1.010
PRIMARY FERMENT:	7 DAYS
SECONDARY FERMENT:	14 DAYS
LAGERING:	90 DAYS

This classic Dortmunder-style beer is a very well balanced, clean, complex beer with a malty taste and a nice hoppy bitterness.

   20 lb. (9.07 kg) Durst pilsner malt
    1 lb. (454 g) Durst Munich malt
    1 oz. (28 g) Liberty hops, 2.7% alpha, in boil 45 min.
    1 oz. (28 g) Hallertauer hops, 3.2% alpha, in boil 45 min.
1½ oz. (43 g) Mt. Hood hops, 5.4% alpha, in boil 45 min.
1½ oz. (43 g) American Saaz hops, 4.8% alpha, in boil 45 min.
  ½ oz. (14 g) Liberty hops, 2.7% alpha, in boil 15 min.
  ½ oz. (14 g) Hallertauer hops, 3.2% alpha, in boil 15 min.
  ½ oz. (14 g) Mt. Hood hops, 5.4% alpha, in boil 15 min.
  ½ oz. (14 g) American Saaz hops, 4.8% alpha, in boil 15 min.
    1 oz. (28 g) Liberty hops, 2.7% alpha, steep
    1 oz. (28 g) Hallertauer hops, 3.2% alpha, steep
    1 oz. (28 g) Mt. Hood hops, 5.4% alpha, steep
    1 oz. (28 g) American Saaz hops, 4.8% alpha, steep
      Wyeast #2042 Danish Lager yeast, 2-qt. (1.9-L) starter
1½ c. (413 ml) corn sugar, for priming

Crush grains and add to 7 gal. (26.5 L) of hard water. Heat to 122°F (50°C) for 20 min. Heat to 153°F (67°C) for 60 min. Heat to 157°F (69°C) for 20 min. Mash-out at 169°F (76°C) for 5 min. Sparge with 169°F (76°C) water adjusted to pH 5.3. Collect 12 gal. (45.4 L) of wort in brew kettle. Boil 15 min. Add 1 oz. (28 g) each of Liberty and Hallertauer hops and 1½ oz. (43 g) each of Mt. Hood and Saaz hops. Boil 30 min., then add ½ oz. (14 g) each of Liberty, Hallertauer, Mt. Hood, and Saaz hops. Boil 15 min. and turn off heat. Add 1 oz. (28 g) each of Liberty, Hallertauer, Mt. Hood, and Saaz hops and allow to steep for a couple of min. Chill the wort, transfer to fermenter, and pitch yeast. Ferment 7 days at 50°F (10°C). Rack to secondary for 11 days at 48°F (9°C). Allow fermenter to warm to 57°F (14°C) and continue fermenting 3 more days. Lager 90 days at 32°F (0°C). Prime with the corn sugar and bottle.

— *"Beer" Rich Mansfield, San Jose, California*
Washoe Zephyr Zymurgists

Special Dortmunder #2

YIELD: .... 5 GAL. (18.9 L)
TOTAL BOILING TIME: .... 90 MIN.
STARTING GRAVITY: 1.060
PRIMARY FERMENT: .... 3 WEEKS
LAGERING: .... 4 MONTHS OR MORE

Wyeast #2308 Munich Lager yeast
6 lb. (2.72 kg) DeWolf-Cosyns pilsner malt
6 lb. (2.72 kg) DeWolf-Cosyns Munich malt
1 oz. (28 g) German Hersbrucker hops, 3.0% alpha, in boil 60 min.
½ oz. (14 g) U.S. Tettnanger hops, 6.2% alpha, in boil 60 min.
1 tsp. (4.9 ml) Irish moss
½ oz. (14 g) German Hersbrucker hops, 3.0% alpha, in boil 15 min.
½ oz. (14 g) Czech Saaz hops, in boil 15 min.
½ oz. (14 g) Liberty hops, steep
½ oz. (14 g) Czech Saaz, steep

Several days before brewing, start the Wyeast, growing it up to ½-gal. (1.9-L) pitching volume.

On brew day, balance your water supply to emulate the Munich water profile. Crush grains and add to 4 gal. (15.1 L) of 142°F (61°C) water. Mash at 131°F (55°C) for a 30-min. protein rest. Heat mash to 152°F (67°C) for 45 min. Heat mash to 170°F (77°C) for a 10-min. mashout. Sparge with 170°F (77°C) water and collect 6 ½ gal. (15.1 L). Boil 30 min., then add 1 oz. (28 g) of Hersbrucker hops and ½ oz. (14 g) of Tettnanger hops. Boil 30 min., then add Irish moss. Boil 15 min., then add ½ oz. (14 g) each of Hersbrucker and Saaz hops. Boil 15 min., remove from heat, and add ½ oz. (14 g) each of Liberty and Saaz hops. Chill wort, transfer to fermenter, and pitch yeast starter. Ferment 3 weeks at 44°F (7°C). Increase temperature to 55°F (13°C) for 2 days as a diacetyl rest. Reduce temperature and lager 4 months or more. Keg or bottle.

— *David Brockington, Seattle, Washington*
Seattle Secret Skinny Brewers Society

VIENNA: MÄRZEN, OKTOBERFEST

Amber Cerveza

YIELD: .... 5 GAL. (18.9 L)
TOTAL BOILING TIME: .... 60 MIN.
STARTING GRAVITY: 1.049
ENDING GRAVITY: 1.012
PRIMARY FERMENT: .... 1 WEEK
SECONDARY FERMENT: .... 2 WEEKS

   Wyeast #2206 Bavarian Lager yeast
  1 lb. (454 g) rice syrup solids
1½ lb. (680 g) domestic 2-row malt
  ½ lb. (227 g) Belgian cara-Vienne malt
  ¼ lb. (113 g) Belgian cara-pils malt
  3 lb. (1.36 kg) amber malt extract
  2 lb. (907 g) light malt extract
  ½ oz. (14 g) Perle hop pellets, in boil 55 min.
  ½ oz. (14 g) Hersbrucker hops, in boil 15 min.
  ½ oz. (14 g) Hersbrucker hops, steep
  1 package Bru-Vigor yeast food
  ¾ c. (206 ml) corn sugar, for priming

Prepare yeast starter prior to brewing day.

Crush grains and add to 1 gal. (3.8 L) of 160°F (71°C) water and let steep for 30 min. Sparge grains with 1 gal. (3.8 L) or more of 168°F (76°C) water. Bring wort to a boil, then turn off heat and add malt extracts. Boil 5 min. before adding ½ oz. (14 g) of Perle hop pellets. Boil 40 min., then add ½ oz. (14 g) of Hersbrucker hops. Boil 15 min., add the last ½ oz. (14 g) of Hersbrucker. Turn off heat. Steep a few min., then chill the wort, transfer to fermenter, and top off to 5 gal. (18.9 L) with cold water. Pitch yeast along with Bru-Vigor yeast food. Ferment 1 week at 45° – 55°F (7° – 13°C). Rack to secondary for 2 weeks at 45° – 55°F (7° – 13°C). Prime with the corn sugar and bottle.

— *DeFalco's Home Wine & Beer Supplies, Houston, Texas*

Octoberfest

YIELD:	5 GAL. (18.9 L)
TOTAL BOILING TIME:	60 MIN.
STARTING GRAVITY:	1.058
ENDING GRAVITY:	1.014
PRIMARY FERMENT:	1 WEEK
SECONDARY FERMENT:	2 WEEKS

    Wyeast #2206 Bavarian Lager yeast
½ tsp. (2.5 ml) calcium chloride
1 lb. (454 g) German pilsner malt
1 lb. (454 g) German Munich malt
¾ lb. (340 g) German medium crystal malt
5 lb. (2.27 kg) Old Bavarian Munich Blend extract
2 lb. (907 g) amber malt extract
⅔ oz. (19 g) Northern Brewer hops, in boil 55 min.
1 oz. (28 g) Hallertauer Hersbrucker hops, in boil 15 min.
½ oz. (14 g) Hallertauer Hersbrucker hops, steep
1 package Bru-Vigor yeast food
¾ c. (206 ml) corn sugar, for priming

Prepare yeast starter prior to brewing day.

Crush grains and add with calcium chloride to 1 gal. (3.8 L) of 160°F (71°C) water and let steep 30 min. Sparge grains with 1 gal. (3.8 L) or more of 168°F (76°C) water. Bring wort to a boil, then turn off heat and add malt extracts. Boil 5 min. before adding Northern Brewer hops. Boil 40 min., then add 1 oz. (28 g) of Hallertauer Hersbrucker hops. Boil 15 min., then add the last ½ oz. (14 g) Hallertauer Hersbrucker hops and turn off heat. Steep a few min., then chill the wort, transfer to fermenter, and top off to 5 gal. (18.9 L) with cold water. Pitch yeast along with Bru-Vigor yeast food. Ferment 1 week at 45° – 55°F (7° – 13°C). Rack to secondary for at least 2 weeks at 45° – 55°F (7° – 13°C). Prime with corn sugar and bottle.

— DeFalco's Home Wine & Beer Supplies, Houston, Texas

Noname Vienna

YIELD:	5 GAL. (18.9 L)
TOTAL BOILING TIME:	90 MIN.
STARTING GRAVITY:	1.055
PRIMARY FERMENT:	3 WEEKS
LAGERING:	4 MONTHS

     Wyeast #2206 Bavarian Lager yeast
  7 lb. (3.18 kg) DeWolf-Cosyns pilsner malt
2½ lb. (1.13 kg) DeWolf-Cosyns cara-Vienne malt,
     25° Lovibond
  2 lb. (907 g) DeWolf-Cosyns Munich malt
  2 oz. (57 g) Ultra hops, 3.8% alpha, in boil 60 min.
  1 tsp. (4.9 ml) Irish moss
 ½ oz. (14 g) Ultra hops, 3.8% alpha, in boil 15 min.
 ½ oz. (14 g) Saaz hops, 4.1% alpha, in boil 15 min.
 ½ oz. (14 g) Ultra hops, steep
 ¼ oz. (7 g) Saaz hops, steep
 ¾ c. (206 ml) corn sugar, for priming

Several days before brewing, begin growing up yeast culture.
     Crush grains and add to 3¾ gal. (14.2 L) of 142°F (61°C) water. Mash at 131°F (55°C) for 30 min. Raise temperature to 154°F (68°C) and rest for 60 min. Sparge with 170°F (77°C) water and collect 6 ½ gal. (24.6 L) of wort in brew kettle. Boil wort for 30 min. before adding 2 oz.

(57 g) of Ultra hops. Boil 30 min., then add Irish moss. Boil 15 min., then add ½ oz. (14 g) each of Ultra and Saaz hops. Boil 15 min. Remove from heat and add ½ oz. (14 g) each of Ultra and Saaz hops. Chill the wort to 44°F (7°C) and pitch yeast. Ferment 3 weeks at 44°F (7°C). Increase temperature to 55°F (13°C) for 2 days as a diacetyl rest. Reduce temperature and lager for 4 months or more. Keg or bottle as usual.

— David Brockington, Seattle, Washington
Seattle Secret Skinny Brewers Society

Work-A-Day Brew

YIELD: .... 5 GAL. (18.9 L)
TOTAL BOILING TIME: .... 60 MIN.
STARTING GRAVITY: 1.055
ENDING GRAVITY: .... 1.010 TO 1.008
PRIMARY FERMENT: .... 7 DAYS
SECONDARY FERMENT: .... 21 DAYS

Third place in the national TRASH VI competition in March 1996.

BrewTek CL-680 East European Lager yeast, 22-oz. starter
 8 lb. (3.63 kg) Briess 2-row malt
 1 lb. (454 g) special roast malt
 1 lb. (454 g) cara-Munich malt
 8 oz. (227 g) Victory malt
 8 oz. (227 g) crystal malt
1½ oz. (43 g) Saaz hops, 4.5% alpha, in boil 60 min.
 ½ oz. (14 g) Saaz hops, 4.5% alpha, in boil 60 min.
 ½ tsp. (2.5 ml) Irish moss
 ¾ c. (206 ml) corn sugar, for priming

Prior to mash day, make a 22-oz. (650-ml) yeast starter.

Mash at 150°F for 1 hour, or until starch conversion is complete. Crush grains and add to 4 gal. (15.1 L) of 168°F (76°C) water. Sparge with 5 gal. (18.9 L) of 170°F (77°C) water. Bring to a boil and add 1½ oz. (43 g) of Saaz hops. Boil 45 min., then add Irish moss. Boil 10 min. and add ½ oz. (14 g) of Saaz hops. Boil 5 min. and turn off heat. Chill the wort, transfer to a fermenter, and pitch yeast starter. Ferment 7 days at 65°F (18°C). Transfer to secondary and ferment at 45°F (7°C) for 21 days. Prime with corn sugar and bottle.

— Bill Campbell, North East, Pennsylvania
Brewing Excellence in the Erie Region (BEER)

Zivio

YIELD:	5 GAL. (18.9 L)
TOTAL BOILING TIME:	60 MIN.
STARTING GRAVITY:	1.040
ENDING GRAVITY:	1.016
PRIMARY FERMENT:	2 DAYS
SECONDARY FERMENT:	22 DAYS

Third place in the 1995 Spirit of Free Beer competition.

¼ tsp. (1.2 ml) gypsum
5 lb. (2.27 kg) Munich malt
4 lb. (15.1 kg) pilsner malt
1 lb. (454 g) pale malt, toasted
1 lb. (454 g) cara-pils malt
1 lb. (454 g) caramel malt
1 lb. (454 g) chocolate malt
1 oz. (28 g) Northern Brewer hops, 9.0% alpha, in boil 60 min.
1 oz. (28 g) Hallertauer hops, 3.3% alpha, in boil 60 min.
1 oz. (28 g) Hallertauer hops, in boil 3 min.
   Wyeast #2206 Bavarian Lager yeast
¾ c. (206 ml) corn sugar, for priming

Treat 4 ½ gal. (17 L) of water with gypsum. Mash grains at 156°F (69°C) for 120 min. Mash-out at 168°F (76°C) for 10 min. Sparge. Collect 6 gal. (22.7 L) of wort. Bring wort to a boil and add 1 oz. (28 g) each of Northern Brewer hops and Hallertauer hops. Boil 57 min., then add ½ oz. (14 g) of Hallertauer. Boil 3 min. and turn off heat. Chill the wort, transfer to fermenter, and pitch yeast. Ferment for 2 days at 67°F (19°C), then drop temperature to 47°F (8°C) for 19 days. Rack to a secondary for 22 days at 40°F (4°C). Prime with corn sugar and bottle.

— Ed Cosgrove, Woodbridge, Virginia
Brewers Association of Northern Virginia (BANOVA)

Springtime in Vienna

YIELD: .... 5 GAL. (18.9 L)
TOTAL BOILING TIME: .... 70 MIN.
STARTING GRAVITY: 1.050
ENDING GRAVITY: 1.011
PRIMARY FERMENT: .... 6 DAYS
SECONDARY FERMENT: .... 14 DAYS
LAGERING: .... 5 WEEKS

Wyeast #2206 Bavarian Lager yeast
8 lb. (3.63 kg) German Vienna malt
1 lb. (454 g) Belgian Munich malt
¾ lb. (340 g) Belgian cara-Vienne malt
¼ lb. (113 g) Belgian cara-pils malt
1 oz. (28 g) Perle hops, 7.4% alpha, in boil 60 min.
1 oz. (28 g) Hallertauer hops, 2.0% alpha, in boil 15 min.

Several days before brewing, make a 1 qt. (946 ml) starter.

Add grains to 12 qt. (11.4 L) 110°F (43°C) water. Temperature should settle out to 105°F (41°C). Hold for 20 min. (acid rest). Heat mash to 122°F (50°C) and hold for 20 min. (protein rest). Add 1⅓ qts. (1.3 L) of boiling water and heat mash until it reaches 150°F (66°C). Hold for 10 min. Heat mash to 158°F (70°C) and hold for 25 min., or until starch conversion is complete. Mash-out at 170°F (77°C) for 5 min. Sparge with 5 gal. (18.9 L) of 170°F (77°C) water and collect 6 ½ gal. (24.6 L) of wort in brew kettle. Boil 10 min., then add Perle hops. Boil 45 min., then add Hallertauer hops. Boil 15 min. and turn off heat. Chill the wort, rack to fermenter, aerate well, and pitch yeast starter. Ferment 6 days at 54°F (12°C). Rack to a carboy and ferment 14 days at 47°F (8°C). Rack to another carboy and lager at 34°F (1°C) for 5 weeks. Keg and carbonate to 2.8 volumes of CO_2.

— *Chris Kaufman, Minneapolis, Minnesota*

Irish Red Lager

YIELD: .... 5 GAL. (18.9 L)
TOTAL BOILING TIME: .... 60 MIN.
PRIMARY FERMENT: .... 7 DAYS
SECONDARY FERMENT: .... 7 DAYS
LAGERING: .... 2 WEEKS

  7 lb. (3.18 kg) 2-row pale malt
  2 lb. (907 g) Munich malt
1¼ lb. (567 g) crystal malt, 40° Lovibond
  1 oz. (28 g) Hallertauer hops, 4.7% alpha, in boil 60 min.
  1 oz. (28 g) Hallertauer hops, 4.7% alpha, in boil 30 min.
  ½ oz. (14 g) Cascade hops, 3.0% alpha, in boil 10 min.
     Wyeast #2308 Munich Lager yeast, 1-pint (473-ml) starter
  ¾ c. (206 ml) corn sugar, for priming

Mash grains in 15½ qts. (14.7 L) of water at 154°F (68°C) for 1 hour. Sparge with 3½ gal. (13.2 L) for 170°F (77°C) water. Bring wort to a boil and add 1 oz. (28 g) of Hallertauer hops. Boil 30 min., then add 1 oz. (28 g) of Hallertauer hops. Boil 20 min., then add Cascade hops. Boil 10 min., then turn off heat. Chill the wort, transfer to fermenter, and pitch yeast. Ferment at 55°F (13°C) for 7 days. Rack to secondary at 45°F (7°C) for 7 days. Rack to another fermenter and lager for 2 weeks at 37°F (3°C). Prime with corn sugar and bottle.

— *Tom Sallese, Baltimore, Maryland, Cross Street Irregulars*

Basenji Oktoberfest Ale

YIELD: .... 2.5 GAL. (9.4 L)
TOTAL BOILING TIME: .... 90 MIN.
STARTING GRAVITY: 1.050
ENDING GRAVITY: 1.007
PRIMARY FERMENT: .... 2 WEEKS
LAGERING: .... 4 WEEKS

3 ¾ lb. (1.7 kg) Durst Munich malt
2 ¼ lb. (1.02 kg) DeWolf-Cosyns Belgian pilsner malt
  8 oz. (227 g) DeWolf-Cosyns cara-Vienne malt
  6 oz. (170 g) DeWolf-Cosyns aromatic malt
  1 oz. (28 g) Hallertauer Hersbrucker hop pellets, 2.0% alpha, in boil 60 min.
  1 tsp. (4.9 ml) Irish moss
    Wyeast #1007 German Ale yeast
  1 tsp. (4.9 ml) bentonite/polyclar

Mash grains in 4½ qts. (4.3 L) of preboiled water to reach temperature of 120°F (49°C). Rest 15 min. Raise temperature to 135°F (57°C); rest 20 min. Raise temperature to 150°F (66°C); rest 45 min. Raise temperature to 170°F (77°C) for a 10-min. mash-out. Sparge to collect 3 ½ gal. (13.2 L). Boil 30 min., then add hops and continue boiling for 1 more hour. In the last 15 min. of the boil, add the Irish moss. Force-chill the wort to 50°F (10°C) and pitch yeast. Ferment at 50°F (10°C) for 2 weeks, lower temperature to 38°F (3°C), and lager for 4 weeks. When ready to keg, add bentonite or polyclar according to the package directions. Keg and force carbonate.

— *Mike Swan, Dallas, Texas*
North Texas Homebrewers Association

More HOMEBREW FAVORITES

9

European Dark Lagers

While bocks may spring to mind for some as the quintessential *European dark lager*, others think first of the dark lagers of Munich. These two styles represent the bulk of the European dark lagers, but the Netherlands and Scandinavia produce their own versions of dark lagers, and in Germany, there are lagers, such as schwarzbier, that are neither bocks nor Munich dunkels.

Dark lagers have many faces and flavors. The bocks are sweet and smooth, with a soft character. The Munich darks are drier, with a soft maltiness from the Munich malts. Schwarzbier is characterized by a rich chocolatey flavor, reminiscent of a porter or stout. Dark lagers are generally normal-gravity beers, with the exception of the bock family, which starts strong at 16° Plato (1.064) and runs up to 28° Plato (1.120) — stronger even than many barleywines!

Munich is the capital of Bavaria, and the dark lagers produced in the region — called Munich Dunkels — are world classics.

Munich Dunkels are normal-gravity beers (original gravity about 1.045 to 1.055). The flavor is predominantly malty, but the maltiness is a nutty, toasty flavor derived from Munich malts. Other malts, such as caramel and black malts, may be used in moderation.

KEY TO RECIPE LOGOS

 EXTRACT RECIPES   PARTIAL MASH RECIPES   ALL-GRAIN RECIPES

Dark lagers from other Bavarian cities — Kulmbach, for example — may be more full bodied and maltier, with starting gravities as high as 1.062. Hopping rates are fairly low in this style, with about 16 to 30 IBUs, and use noble hops, such as Hallertauer. Yeasts used in this style will be European or specifically Bavarian lager strains, such as Wyeast #2206 Bavarian Lager and Yeast Lab L33 Munich Lager.

Schwarzbier. *Schwarz* is the German word for "black," and the adjective does justice to the style. Schwarzbier is in some ways the lager counterpart of stout. It is a robust, very black beer, opaque, with a round, rich chocolate character to it. The style was probably originally an ale, brewed in the area of Köstritz, but with the advent of lager brewing in Germany in the mid-19th century, the style began being brewed at cooler lager temperatures. Although the style is German, several black lagers are made by Japanese breweries.

Schwarzbier derives its color from roasted malts. Homebrew recipes often use a mix of roast barley, chocolate malt, and black patent to achieve the black color and the rich, roasty flavor. Take care not to go overboard on grains like black patent, which can impart a burnt, charcoal-like flavor when used in excess. The bulk of the grain bill will be pilsner malt. This is a normal-gravity beer, or about 1.045 to 1.055. Hops should be moderate in a schwarzbier — about 20 to 35 IBUs. Noble types, such as Hallertauer, Spalt, Tettnang, and Saaz, should balance, but not dominate, the flavor.

Bock beer is thought to have originated in the 14th or 15th century around the area of Einbeck, Germany, where it was probably produced as a strong wheat ale. Today, bock beers are all-malt beers with a distinctive smooth, sweet malt flavor. In Germany, bock must have a starting gravity of at least 16° Plato (about 1.064). Most brewers have no trouble meeting such a requirement. There are several substyles of bock, including a strong bock, called *doppelbock*, that in Germany is required to be at least 18° Plato (1.072). When brewed with a combination of wheat and barley malts, you have a *weizenbock*, or wheat bock (see Chapter 11). A lighter-colored bock called a *maibock*, or a *helles bock*, and a highly concentrated, highly alcoholic doppelbock called *eisbock* are made in Germany.

The standard bock beer is clean, smooth, and malty. It should be full bodied, often with some apparent alcohol, although this should not be overbearing. The grain bill should be light Munich malt with color derived from dark Munich malt. Caramel malt may also be used. Darker roasted malts, such as chocolate and black malts, should not be used in a bock. The beers are usually brewed using a double-decoction mash schedule. Hops should be subdued at about 20 to 30 IBUs, and used almost entirely in bittering. The aroma should be clean malt, without hop, or any yeast by-products. The hops should, however, be evident in the balance and finish. Lager yeasts, such as Wyeast #2206 Bavarian Lager, #2308 Munich Lager, and #2124 Bohemian Lager are reasonable choices. The Yeast Culture Kit Company also has several suitable yeasts, including its L02 Bavarian Lager, L05 Munich Lager, and L09 German Lager.

A helles bock will be smooth and malty like a standard bock, but is much paler. There should be no hops in the aroma, but hops are expected to make their presence known in the balance and finish. As with all bocks, there should be no traces of esters or diacetyl.

Doppelbock is, in some ways, the lager counterpart of a barleywine or strong ale. Made to gravities of 1.072 to 1.100, it is a very dense, strong, highly alcoholic brew. Doppelbocks are full-bodied beers that range in color from tawny amber to dark brown. The style is said to originate with monks of the order of St. Francis of Paula, who called their beer Salvator. Bittering is at the rate of 23 to 40 IBUs (usually from Hallertauer hops) and the color from 18 to 35 SRM. The grain bill is pale Munich and dark Munich malts with some dextrin malt. When brewing higher-gravity beers, keep in mind that longer lagering periods are needed than are used when brewing lighter-bodied styles. Six-to-nine-month lagering periods are common for doppelbocks.

In competition, judges will look for a very smooth malty character, with some soft toffee-like notes, but nothing that would be mistaken for diacetyl. The beers should be exceptionally clean, with no yeast by-products. Aroma hops should not be used in bocks; bocks with a strong hop character will be considered out of style.

BAVARIAN DARK LAGERS

Black Bavarian

YIELD: .... 5 GAL. (18.9 L)
TOTAL BOILING TIME: .... 60 MIN.
PRIMARY FERMENT: .... 9 DAYS
SECONDARY FERMENT: .... 4 WEEKS

6.6 lb. (3 kg) Northwestern amber malt extract
  1 lb. (454 g) crystal malt, 80° Lovibond
½ lb. (227 g) chocolate malt
½ lb. (227 g) roasted barley
  1 oz. (28 g) Galena hops, 10.6% alpha, in boil 60 min.
  1 oz. (28 g) Galena hops, 10.6% alpha, in boil 15 min.
  1 tsp. (4.9 ml) Irish moss
  1 oz. (28 g) Tettnanger hops, 4.8% alpha, in boil 2 min.
    Wyeast #2308 Munich Lager yeast
¾ c. (206 ml) corn sugar, for priming

Add grains to 2 gal. (7.6 L) water and heat to 170°F (77° C). Strain out grains and add malt extract. Bring to a boil and add 1 oz. (28 g) of Galena hops. Boil 45 min. Add 1 oz. (28 g) of Galena hops and Irish moss. Boil 13 min. Add Tettnanger hops and boil 2 min. Turn off heat, cover, and rest 20 min. Chill the wort and transfer to a primary fermenter. Pitch yeast and aerate well. Move fermenter to a refrigerator set at 54°F (12° C) and ferment for 9 days. Rack to a secondary and ferment 4 weeks at 45°F (7° C). Prime with corn sugar and bottle.

— *Robert Clapper, Grand Rapids, Michigan, Prime Time Brewers*

┌─Dunkel Fest─

YIELD:	5 GAL. (18.9 L)
TOTAL BOILING TIME:	60 MIN.
STARTING GRAVITY:	1.052
ENDING GRAVITY:	1.018
PRIMARY FERMENT:	14 DAYS
SECONDARY FERMENT:	9 DAYS

*Third place in the Bavarian dark lager category at the 1996
Crescent City Competition in New Orleans.*

      Wyeast #2112 California Lager yeast
6 lb. (2.72 kg) Maris Munich malt extract
1½ lb. (681 g) Maries Munich dry malt extract
½ lb. (227 g) German caramel malt, 50° Lovibond
¼ lb. (113 g) cara-pils malt
¼ lb. (113 g) cara-Munich malt
⅛ lb. (57 g) chocolate malt
1½ oz. (43 g) Hallertauer Mittelfrüh, 4.7% alpha, in boil 60 min.
½ oz. (14 g) Hallertauer Mittelfrüh, 2.8 alpha, in boil 30 min.
½ oz. (14 g) Hallertauer Mittelfrüh, 2.8 alpha, in boil 5 min.
¾ c. (206 ml) corn sugar, for priming

Prior to brew day, make a 2 c. (551 ml) yeast starter.
      Heat 1½ gal. (5.7 L) of water to 160°F (71° C). Add crushed caramel malt in a grain bag and steep 30 min. Remove grain bag and bring to a boil. Add malt extracts and 1½ oz. (43 g) of Hallertauer Mittelfrüh hops. Boil 30 min., then add ½ oz. (14 g) of Hallertauer Mittelfrüh hops. Boil 25 min., then add ½ oz. (14 g) of Hallertauer Mittelfrüh. Boil 5 min. and turn off heat. Chill the wort, transfer to fermenter, and top off to 5 gal. (18.9 L) with cold water. Pitch yeast and keep at 68°F (20° C) until fermentation begins. Drop temperature to 52°F (11° C) and ferment for 2 weeks. Rack to secondary for 9 days at 56°F (13° C). Prime with corn sugar and bottle.

                                      — Mike Murat, Kenner, Louisiana

Bavarian Black-Out

YIELD: .... 5 GAL. (18.9 L)
TOTAL BOILING TIME: .... 75 MIN.
STARTING GRAVITY: 1.054
PRIMARY FERMENT: .... 3 DAYS
SECONDARY FERMENT: .... 3 MONTHS

Second place as a Munich Dunkel in Commander SAAZ's Homebrew Competition.

    5 lb. (2.27 kg) pale malt
    2 lb. (907 g) Munich malt
    2 lb. (907 g) Vienna malt
  12 oz. (340 g) dextrin malt
    8 oz. (227 g) crystal malt
    4 oz. (113 g) Belgian chocolate malt
    2 oz. (57 g) black patent malt
  ⅓ c. (79 ml) molasses
  1¾ oz. (50 g) Hallertauer hops, 3.9% alpha, in boil 35 min.
  ¼ oz. (7 g) Hallertauer hops, 3.9% alpha, in boil 2 min.
       Wyeast #2112 California Lager yeast
  ¾ c. (206 ml) corn sugar, for priming

Toast 2 lb. (907 g) pale malt in a 350°F (177° C) oven for 10 min. Crush remaining 3 lb. (1.36 kg) pale malt with all other grains and add to 11 qt. (10.4 L) of 168°F (76° C) water. Temperature should stabilize out to 156°F (69° C). Mash until starch conversion is complete. Sparge with 170°F (77° C) water and collect 6½ – 7 gal. (24.6 – 26.5 L). Boil 40 min. Add 1¾ oz. (50 g) of Hallertauer hops and molasses. Boil 33 min., then add ¼ oz. (7 g) Hallertauer hops. Boil 2 min. and turn off heat. Chill the wort, transfer to fermenter, and pitch yeast. When fermentation reaches its peak, rack to a carboy and place in a refrigerator. Start secondary fermentation at 50°F (10° C). Gradually drop the temperature to 36°F (2° C) and continue fermenting for 3 months. Prime with corn sugar and bottle.

— *Matt Zaccheo, Phillipsburg, New Jersey*

SCHWARZBIERS

Schwarzbier Over Here
YIELD: .... 5 GAL. (18.9 L)
TOTAL BOILING TIME: .... 60 MIN.
STARTING GRAVITY: 1.038
ENDING GRAVITY: 1.010
PRIMARY FERMENT: .... 1 WEEK
SECONDARY FERMENT: .... 3 WEEKS

This beer has the color of a stout, yet a fairly light lager flavor, with a little zing from the chocolate malt.

½ lb. (227 g) crystal malt, 44° Lovibond
¼ lb. (113 g) chocolate malt
2 oz. (57 g) black patent malt
3.3 lb. (1.5 kg) Cooper's dark malt extract
1.4 lb. (635 g) Alexander's Kicker dark malt extract
¾ oz. (21 g) Tettnanger hop pellets, 4.8% alpha, in boil 60 min.
¾ oz. (21 g) Tettnanger hop pellets, 4.8% alpha, in boil 25 min.
¼ oz. (7 g) Tettnanger hop pellets, 4.8% alpha, in boil 5 min.
¼ oz. (7 g) Hallertauer hop pellets, 3.2% alpha, in boil 5 min.
Wyeast #2206 Bavarian Lager yeast
¾ c. (206 ml) corn sugar, for priming

Steep crushed grains in 2 gal. (7.6 L) of 150°F (66° C) water for 20 min. Strain out grains and add 3 gal. (11.4 L) of water and malt extracts. Bring to a boil and add ¾ oz. (21 g) of Tettnanger hops. Boil 35 min., then add ¾ oz. (21 g) Tettnanger hops. Boil 20 min., then add ¼ oz. (7 g) each of Tettnanger hops and Hallertauer hops. Boil a final 5 min. and turn off heat. Chill the wort, transfer to primary fermenter and pitch yeast. Let ferment for 1 week at 50°F (10° C). Rack to a secondary fermenter and continue fermenting for 3 weeks at 40°F (4° C). Prime with corn sugar and bottle.

— *Bill Pemberton, Charlottesville, Virginia, Back Door Brewers*

Schwarzbier #1

YIELD: .... 5 GAL. (18.9 L)
TOTAL BOILING TIME: .... 90 MIN.
STARTING GRAVITY: 1.060
ENDING GRAVITY: 1.025
PRIMARY FERMENT: .... 14 DAYS
LAGERING: .... 8 WEEKS

Several blue ribbons, one best of show, and a ribbon in the AHA National Homebrew Competition.

  9 lb. (4.09 kg) DeWolf-Cosyns pilsner malt
  1 lb. (454 g) DeWolf-Cosyns aromatic malt
  1 lb. (454 g) DeWolf-Cosyns Munich malt
  ½ lb. (227 g) DeWolf-Cosyns cara-Vienne malt
  ½ lb. (227 g) chocolate malt
  ¼ lb. (113 g) roasted barley
  ¼ lb. (113 g) black patent malt
  1 oz. (28 g) Perle hops, 7.5% alpha, in boil 60 min.
  1 oz. (28 g) crystal hops, 4.2% alpha, in boil 10 min.
  1 oz. (28 g) crystal hops, steep lager yeast
  ¾ c. (206 ml) corn sugar, for priming

Crush grains and add to 4½ gal. (17 L) of 165°F (74° C) water. Mash at 154°F (68° C) for 60 min., then raise temperature to 168°F (76° C) for a 10-min. mash-out. Sparge with 170°F (77° C) water and collect 7 gal. (26.5 L) of wort. Boil 30 min. before adding the Perle hops. Boil 50 min., then add 1 oz. (28 g) of crystal hops. Boil 10 min., then turn off heat. Add last oz. of crystal hops and let steep a few min. Chill the wort, transfer to fermenter, and pitch yeast. Ferment at 48°F (9° C) for 14 days. Prime with corn sugar and bottle. Let rest 7 days, then lager at 33°F (1° C) for 8 weeks.

— *Delano Dugarm, Arlington, Virginia*
Brewers United for Real Potables (BURP)

Schwarzbier #2

YIELD: .... 15 GAL. (56.8 L)
TOTAL BOILING TIME: .... 60 MIN.
STARTING GRAVITY: 1.050
ENDING GRAVITY: 1.012
PRIMARY FERMENT: .... 7 DAYS
SECONDARY FERMENT: .... 14 DAYS
LAGERING: .... 60 DAYS

First place at the 1995 Nevada State Fair.

   18 lb. (8.16 kg) DeWolf-Cosyns Belgian pilsner malt
   10 lb. (4.54 kg) Durst German Munich malt
   1½ lb. (340 g) DeWolf-Cosyns Belgian chocolate malt
   ½ lb. (227 g) DeWolf-Cosyns Belgian black patent malt
 0.42 oz. (12 g) calcium carbonate
 0.02 oz. (½ g) calcium chloride
    8 oz. (227 g) Czech Saaz hops, 3.3% alpha, in boil 60 min.
    2 oz. (57 g) Czech Saaz hops, in boil 30 min.
    3 oz. (85 g) Czech Saaz hops, in boil 15 min.
       Wyeast #2308 Munich Lager yeast
   2¼ c. (619 ml) corn sugar, for priming

Crush grains and mash in 10 gal. (37.9 L) of distilled water treated with calcium carbonate and calcium chloride. Heat mash to 122°F (50° C) and hold for 30 min. Heat mash to 152°F (67° C) and hold for 90 min. Mashout at 169°F (76° C) for 10 min. Sparge with 169°F (76° C) water. Collect 16 gal. (60.6 L) of wort. Bring wort to a boil and add 8 oz. (227 g) of Czech Saaz hops. Boil 30 min., then add 2 oz. (57 g) of Czech Saaz hops. Boil 15 min. Then add 3 oz. (85 g) of Czech Saaz hops. Boil 15 min. Turn off heat. Chill wort, transfer to fermenter, and pitch yeast. Ferment 7 days at 50°F (10° C). Rack to secondary for 11 days at 48°F (6° C). Allow fermenter to warm up to 57°F (14° C) and ferment for 3 more days. Lager 60 days at 32°F (0° C). Prime with corn sugar and bottle.

— *"Beer" Rich Mansfield, San Jose, California*
Washoe Zephyr Zymurgists

Schwarzbier #3

YIELD: .... 5½ GAL. (20.8 L)
TOTAL BOILING TIME: .... 120 MIN.
STARTING GRAVITY: 1.069
PRIMARY FERMENT: .... 7 DAYS
SECONDARY FERMENT: .... 3 WEEKS

   6 lb. (2.72 kg) Briess 2-row malt
   4 lb. (1.81 kg) Belgian Munich malt
   4 lb. (1.81 kg) cara-Vienne malt
  11 oz. (312 g) Belgian special-B malt
   ½ oz. (14 g) Cluster hops, 7.2% alpha, in boil 60 min.
   ½ oz. (14 g) Cascade hops, 4.6% alpha, in boil 30 min.
   ½ oz. (14 g) Willamette hops, 4.0% alpha, in boil 15 min.
      Wyeast #2308 Munich Lager yeast
   ¾ c. (206 ml) corn sugar, for priming

Add grains to 3 ½ gal. (13.2 L) of 170°F (77° C) water and mash for 30
min., or until starch conversion is complete. Sparge with 7 gal. (26.5 L)
of 170°F (77° C) water. Boil 60 min., then add Cluster hops. Boil 30 min.,
then add Cascade hops. Boil 15 min., then add Willamette hops. Boil 15
min. and turn off heat. Chill wort, transfer to fermenter, and pitch yeast.
Ferment 7 days, then rack to secondary fermenter for 3 weeks at under
45°F (7° C). Prime with corn sugar and bottle.

— Neil Flatter, Terre Haute, Indiana
Wabash Valley Vintners' and Homebrewers' Club

BOCKS: MAIBOCK, DOPPELBOCK

Aaahh Bock

YIELD: .... 6 GAL. (22.7 L)
TOTAL BOILING TIME: .... 60 MIN.
STARTING GRAVITY: 1.058
ENDING GRAVITY: 1.012
PRIMARY FERMENT: .... 12 DAYS

The malt flavor and aroma really shine through on this dark and heady brew. The chocolate malt adds just the right amount of roasted flavor, too. The full-bodied taste lasts all the way to the last lip-smacking drop. It's not as hearty as a doppelbock, but then again, it's a pretty strong beer.

  ¼ lb. (113 g) chocolate malt
  ¼ lb. (113 g) crystal malt, 40° Lovibond
3 ¾ lb. (1.7 kg) Black Rock Reserve Bock extract
  3 lb. (1.36 kg) Muntons dark dried malt extract
  1 lb. (454 g) corn sugar
1½ oz. (43 g) Hallertauer whole hops, 4.2% alpha, in boil 60 min.
  ½ oz. (14 g) Tettnanger hop pellets, 4.5% alpha, in boil 15 min.
0.42 oz. (12 g) dry lager yeast
  ¾ c. (206 ml) corn sugar, for priming
  1 tbsp. (14.8 ml) beverage settler, for priming

Crush grains, and steep in 1 gal.(3.8 L) of 170°F (77°C) water for 15 min. Strain out grains. Add malt extracts, corn sugar, and the Hallertauer hops and boil 45 min. Add Tettnanger and boil 15 min. Pour wort into fermenter containing cold water. Top off to 6 gal. (22.7 L) and pitch yeast when wort is below 80°F (27° C). Ferment 12 days below 50°F (10° C). Prime with corn sugar and beverage settler and bottle.

— *Marc Battreall, Plantation Key, Florida*

"Coupla Bockers" Bock

YIELD: .... 5 GAL. (18.9 L)
TOTAL BOILING TIME: .... 60 MIN.
STARTING GRAVITY: 1.050
ENDING GRAVITY: 1.018
PRIMARY FERMENT: .... 5 DAYS
SECONDARY FERMENT: .... 4 WEEKS

- 1 lb. (454 g) Munich malt
- 1 lb. (454 g) light crystal malt
- 1 lb. (454 g) dark crystal malt
- 2 oz. (57 g) chocolate malt
- 6.6 lb. (3 kg) Ireks light malt extract
- 1 lb. (454 g) Briess light dry malt extract
- 2 oz. (57 g) Tettnanger hops plug, 4.5% alpha, in boil 60 min.
- ½ oz. (14 g) Tettnanger hops plug, 4.5% alpha, in boil 10 min.
  Wyeast #2124 Bohemian Lager yeast
- ¾ c. (206 ml) corn sugar, for priming

Crush grains and add to 3 qt. (2.8 L) of 170°F (77°C) water. Steep about 20 min. Strain out grains and add to 2½ gal. (9.4 L) of water. Bring to a boil and add malt extracts and 2 oz. (57 g) of Tettnanger hops plug. Boil 50 min., then add ½ oz. (14 g) of Tettnanger hops plug. Boil 10 min., then turn off heat. Chill wort, transfer to fermenter, and top off to 5 gal. (18.9 L) with cold water. Pitch yeast and ferment 5 days at 55°F (13° C). Rack to secondary for 4 weeks at 40°F (4° C). Prime with corn sugar and bottle.

— *Jon Maxy and Ruth Andrews, Torrance, California*
Strand Homebrewers

German Bock

YIELD: .... 5 GAL. (18.9 L)
TOTAL BOILING TIME: .... 60 MIN.
STARTING GRAVITY: 1.066
ENDING GRAVITY: 1.016
PRIMARY FERMENT: .... 1 WEEK
SECONDARY FERMENT: .... 2 WEEKS

Wyeast #2206 Bavarian Lager yeast
½ tsp. (2.5 ml) calcium chloride
1 lb. (454 g) German pilsner malt
1 lb. (454 g) German Munich malt
1 lb. (454 g) German medium crystal malt
6 lb. (2.72 kg) Old Bavarian Munich Blend extract
2 lb. (907 g) amber malt extract
¾ oz. (21 g) Northern Brewer hops, in boil 55 min.
1 oz. (28 g) Hallertauer Hersbrucker hops, in boil 15 min.
½ oz. (14 g) Hallertauer Hersbrucker hops, steep
1 package Bru-Vigor yeast food
⅝ c. (172 ml) corn sugar, for priming

Prepare yeast starter prior to brewing day.

Crush grains and add with calcium chloride to 1 gal. (3.8 L) of 160°F (71° C) water and steep 30 min. Sparge grains with 1 gal. (3.8 L) or more of 168°F (76° C) water. Bring wort to a boil, then turn off heat and add malt extracts. Boil 5 min. before adding the Northern Brewer hops. Boil 40 min., then add 1 oz. (28 g) of Hallertauer Hersbrucker hops. Boil 15 min., add the last ½ oz. (14 g) of Hallertauer Hersbrucker hops, and turn off heat. Steep a few min., then chill the wort, transfer to fermenter, and top off to 5 gal. (18.9 L) with cold water. Pitch yeast along with Bru-Vigor yeast food. Ferment 1 week at 45° – 55°F (7° – 13° C). Rack to secondary fermenter for 2 weeks at 45° – 55°F (7° – 13° C). Prime with corn sugar and bottle.

— *DeFalco's Home Wine & Beer Supplies, Houston, Texas*

Hallerbock

YIELD: .... 10 GAL. (37.9 L)
TOTAL BOILING TIME: .... 60 MIN.
STARTING GRAVITY: 1.067
ENDING GRAVITY: 1.015
PRIMARY FERMENT: .... 20 DAYS
SECONDARY FERMENT: .... 14 DAYS

24 lb. (10.89 kg) Durst Munich malt

4 lb. (1.81 kg) Durst pilsner malt

2 lb. (907 g) Durst dark caramel malt

½ lb. (227 g) Belgian cara-Vienne malt

3 oz. (85 g) chocolate malt

2½ oz. (71 g) Spalter Select hops, 4.7% alpha, in boil 60 min.

0.35 oz. (10 g) Irish moss

1 oz. (28 g) Spalter Select hops, 4.7% alpha, in boil 15 min.
BrewTek CL-650 Old Bavarian Lager yeast

1⅓ c. corn sugar, for priming

Crush grains and add to 8 gal. (30.3 L) of 165°F (74° C) water. Mash temperature should settle to 152°F (67° C). Mash 90 min. Mash-out at 170°F (77° C) for 10 min. Sparge with 10 gal. (37.9 L) of 170°F (77° C) water. Collect 13½ gal. (51.1 L) of wort. Heat to a boil and add 2½ oz. (71 g) of Spalter Select hops. Boil 40 min., then add Irish moss. Boil 5 min., then add 1 oz. (28 g) of Spalter Select hops. Boil 15 min., then turn off heat. Chill the wort, transfer to fermenter, and pitch yeast starter. Ferment 20 days at 50°F (10° C), then rack to secondary fermenter for 14 days. Prime and bottle.

— *Steven and Paula Stacy, and Richard Hall, Rolla, Missouri*
Missouri Association of Serious Homebrewers (MASH)

Bock and a Half

YIELD: .... 5 GAL. (18.9 L)
TOTAL BOILING TIME: .... 60 MIN.
STARTING GRAVITY: 1.070
ENDING GRAVITY: 1.050
PRIMARY FERMENT: .... 2 WEEKS
LAGER: .... 2 MONTHS

4¼ lb. (1.93 kg) Belgian Munich malt
4 lb. (1.81 kg) Belgian pilsner malt
1 lb. (454 g) crystal malt, 60° Lovibond
1 lb. (454 g) Belgian aromatic malt
3 lb. (1.36 kg) malt extract
2 oz. (57 g) Ultra hops, 3.0% alpha, in boil 60 min.
½ oz. (14 g) Ultra hops, 3.0% alpha, in boil 15 min.
   Wyeast #2112 California Lager yeast
¾ c. (206 ml) corn sugar, for priming

Mash grains in 3 ½ gal. (13.2 L) of water at 152°F (67° C) for 90 min. Mash-out at 170°F (77° C) for 10 min. Sparge with 170°F (77° C) water and collect 6 – 6½ gal. (22.7 – 24.6 L) of wort. Add malt extract to wort and bring to a boil. Add 2 oz. (57 g) of Ultra hops and boil 45 min. Add last ½ oz. (14 g) of Ultra hops and boil 15 min. Turn off heat. Chill wort and transfer to fermenter. Pitch yeast. Ferment 2 weeks at 46°F (8° C). Rack to secondary fermenter and lager for 2 months below 40°F (4° C). Prime with corn sugar and bottle.

— *Steven Zabarnick, Dayton, Ohio*
Dayton Regional Amateur Fermentation Technologists (DRAFT)

Maybock

YIELD: .... 5 GAL. (18.9 L)
TOTAL BOILING TIME: .... 60 MIN.
STARTING GRAVITY: 1.066
ENDING GRAVITY: 1.016
PRIMARY FERMENT: .... 1 WEEK
SECONDARY FERMENT: .... 2 WEEKS

   Wyeast #2308 Munich Lager yeast
1 lb. (454 g) German pilsner malt
1 lb. (454 g) Munich malt
1 lb. (454 g) light crystal malt
½ tsp. (2.5 ml) calcium chloride
4 lb. (1.81 kg) Old Bavarian Munich Blend extract
4 lb. (1.81 kg) light malt extract
1 oz. (28 g) Northern Brewer hops, in boil 55 min.
1½ oz. (43 g) Hallertauer Hersbrucker hops, in boil 15 min.
½ oz. (14 g) Hallertauer Hersbrucker hops, steep
1 package Bru-Vigor yeast food
⅝ c. (172 ml) corn sugar, for priming

Prepare yeast starter prior to brewing day.
   Add crushed grains and calcium chloride to 1 gal. (3.8 L) of 160°F (71° C) water and steep for 30 min. Sparge grains with 1 gal. (3.8 L) or more of 168°F (76° C) water. Bring wort to a boil, then turn off heat and add malt extracts. Boil 5 min. before adding the Northern Brewer hops. Boil 40 min., then add 1½ oz. (43 g) of Hallertauer Hersbrucker hops. Boil 15 min., add the last ½ oz. (14 g) of Hallertauer Hersbrucker hops, and turn off heat. Steep a few min., then chill the wort, transfer to fermenter, and top off to 5 gal. (18.9 L) with cold water. Pitch yeast along with Bru-Vigor yeast food. Ferment 1 week at 45° – 55°F (7° – 13° C). Rack to secondary fermenter for 2 weeks at 45° – 55°F (7° – 13° C). Prime with corn sugar and bottle.

— *DeFalco's Home Wine & Beer Supplies, Houston, Texas*

The Liberator

YIELD: .... 15 GAL. (56.8 L)
TOTAL BOILING TIME: .... 60 MIN.
STARTING GRAVITY: 1.069
ENDING GRAVITY: 1.014
PRIMARY FERMENT: .... 7 DAYS
SECONDARY FERMENT: .... 14 DAYS
LAGERING: .... 90 DAYS

Best of show at the 1994 Nevada State Fair, first places in the 1994
California State Fair and the 1994 Sonoma County Harvest Fair.

  25 lb. (11.34 kg) Durst pilsner malt
    5 lb. (2.27 kg) DeWolf-Cosyns pilsner malt
    5 lb. (2.27 kg) Durst Vienna malt
    2 lb. (454 g) DeWolf-Cosyns Munich malt
    2 oz. (57 g) Hersbrucker hops, 3.3% alpha, in boil 60 min.
    1 oz. (28 g) Perle hops, 7.0% alpha, in boil 60 min.
    2 oz. (57 g) Hersbrucker hops, 3.3% alpha, in boil 30 min.
    1 oz. (28 g) Hersbrucker hops, 3.3% alpha, in boil 15 min.
  ½ oz. (14 g) Saaz hops, 3.1% alpha, in boil 15 min.
       Wyeast #2007 Pilsen Lager yeast, ½-gal. (1.9-L) starter
  2 ¼ c. (619 ml) corn sugar, for priming

Crush grains and add to 12 gal. (45.4 L) of water. Heat to 122°F (50° C)
and adjust to pH 5.3. Hold at 122°F (50° C) for 20 min. Heat mash to
152°F (67° C) and rest 90 min. Mash-out at 169°F (76° C) 10 min. Sparge
with 169°F (76° C) water adjusted to pH 5.3 with lactic acid. Collect 16
gal. (60.6 L) of wort. Bring wort to a boil and add 2 oz. (53 g) of
Hersbrucker and 1 oz. (28 g) of Perle. Boil 30 min., then add 2 oz. (53 g)
of Hersbrucker. Boil 15 min., then add 1 oz. (28 g) of Hersbrucker and
½ oz. (14 g) of Saaz. Boil 15 min. and turn off heat. Chill wort, transfer
to fermenter, and pitch yeast. Ferment 7 days at 49°F (9° C). Rack to
secondary fermenter for 14 days at 49°F (9° C), slowly dropping to 40°F
(4° C). Allow to warm up to 55°F (13° C) and continue fermenting for 3
days. Rack to a stainless-steel fermenter and lager for 90 days at 32°F
(0° C). Prime with corn sugar and bottle.

— *"Beer" Rich Mansfield, San Jose, California*
Washoe Zephyr Zymurgists

Lemon Beagle Maibock

YIELD: .... 5 GAL. (18.9 L)
TOTAL BOILING TIME: .... 60 MIN.
STARTING GRAVITY: 1.067
ENDING GRAVITY: 1.022
PRIMARY FERMENT: .... 7 DAYS
SECONDARY FERMENT: .... 30 DAYS

First place in the dark lager category at the 1993 Oregon Homebrew Competition and Festival.

6½ lb. (2.95 kg) lager malt
  3 lb. (1.36 kg) Munich malt
  2 lb. (907 g) lager malt, toasted
  1 lb. (454 g) crystal malt, 10° Lovibond
  1 lb. (454 g) crystal malt, 20° Lovibond
  1 oz. (28 g) Mt. Hood hops, 4.3% alpha, in boil 60 min.
  1 oz. (28 g) Saaz hops, 4.3% alpha, in boil 60 min.
  ½ oz. (14 g) Hallertauer hops, 3.7% alpha, in boil 12 min.
  ⅓ oz. (9 g) Tettnanger hops, 4.2% alpha, in boil 3–4 min.
     Wyeast #2206 Bavarian Lager yeast
0.37 oz. (10.5 g) Tettnanger hops, dry hop
  ⅝ c. (172 ml) corn sugar, for priming

Mash-in grains in 14 qt. (13.2 L) of water and stabilize temperature at 155°F (68°C). Mash for 60 min. Sparge grains with 6 gal. (946 ml) of water at 170°F (77°C). Bring wort to a boil and add Mt. Hood hops and Saaz hops. Boil 48 min. Add Hallertauer. Boil 7 or 8 min., then add ⅓ oz. (9 g) Tettnanger. Boil 3 or 4 min., then turn off heat. Chill the wort, transfer to fermenter, and pitch yeast. Ferment at 52°F (11°C). When primary fermentation is complete, rack to a secondary fermenter, dry hop with 0.37 oz. (10½ g) of Tettnanger hops, and lager for at least 30 days at 35°F (2°C). Prime with corn sugar and bottle.

— *Douglas Faynor, Homebrew Heaven, Salem, Oregon*
Capitol Brewers of Salem

Demonick Maibock

YIELD: .... 5¾ GAL. (21.8 L)
TOTAL BOILING TIME: .... 90 MIN.
STARTING GRAVITY: 1.058
ENDING GRAVITY: 1.017
PRIMARY FERMENT: .... 15 DAYS
SECONDARY FERMENT: .... 13 DAYS
LAGERING: .... 6 WEEKS

Wyeast #2206 Bavarian Lager yeast
8 lb. (3.63 kg) DeWolf-Cosyns 2-row Pilsen malt
3 lb. (1.36 kg) DeWolf-Cosyns Munich malt
1 lb. (454 g) DeWolf-Cosyns crystal malt, 10° Lovibond
1 oz. (28 g) Mt. Hood hops, 5.0% alpha, in boil 60 min.
1 oz. (28 g) Tettnanger hops, 3.4% alpha, in boil 60 min.
0.11 oz. (3 g) Irish moss
1 oz. (28 g) Mt. Hood hops, 5.0% alpha, in boil 15 min.
1 oz. (28 g) Tettnanger hops, 3.4% alpha, in boil 15 min.
¾ c. (206 ml) corn sugar, for priming

Start yeast a couple days before brewing.

Heat 4 gal. (15.1 L) of water to 164°F (73° C) and add crushed grains. Mash at 153°F (67° C) for 80 min., then add 2 gal. (7.6 L) of boiling water to mash-out at 170°F (77° C). Let stand for 10 min. Sparge with 180°F (82° C) water and collect 9 gal. (34.1 L) of wort. Boil 30 min., then add 1 oz. (28 g) each of Mt. Hood and Tettnanger hops. Boil 30 min., then add Irish moss. Boil 15 min., then add 1 oz. (28 g) each of Mt. Hood and Tettnanger hops. Boil 15 min., then turn off heat. Chill wort, transfer to fermenter, and pitch yeast slurry. Ferment 15 days at 46° – 52°F (8° – 11° C). Rack to secondary for 13 days at 46° – 52°F (8° – 11° C). Lager 6 weeks at 34°F (1° C), then prime with the corn sugar and bottle.

— *Domenick Venezia, Seattle, Washington*

Maibock

YIELD: .... 10 GAL. (37.9 L)
TOTAL BOILING TIME: .... 60 MIN.
STARTING GRAVITY: 1.072
ENDING GRAVITY: 1.014
PRIMARY FERMENT: .... 7 DAYS
SECONDARY FERMENT: .... 13 DAYS
LAGERING: .... 90 DAYS

Lovely clear golden color with a big malty aroma.

15	lb. (6.8 kg) Durst pilsner malt
5	lb. (2.27 kg) Durst Vienna malt
5	lb. (2.27 kg) Durst Munich malt
2.47	oz. (70 g) Mt. Hood hops, 5.4% alpha, in boil 60 min.
1.41	oz. (40 g) Liberty hops, 2.7% alpha, in boil 30 min.
1.41	oz. (40 g) Saaz hops, 3.3% alpha, in boil 30 min.
1.06	oz. (30 g) Liberty hops, 2.7% alpha, in boil 15 min.
1.06	oz. (30 g) Saaz hops, 3.3% alpha, in boil 15 min.
	Wyeast #2206 Bavarian Lager yeast, ½-gal. (1.9-L) starter
1½	c. (413 ml) corn sugar, for priming

Crush grains and add to 8 gal. (30.3 L) of water. Heat to 122°F (50°C) and adjust mash to pH 5.3. Let rest at 122°F (50° C) for 20 min. Heat mash to 155°F (68°C) and let rest for 90 min. Mash-out at 165°F (74°C) for 15 min. Sparge with 169°F (76° C) water adjusted to pH 5.3. Collect 12 gal. (45.4 L) of wort. Bring wort to a boil and add 2.47 oz. (70 g) of Mt. Hood hops. Boil 30 min. Add 1.41 oz. (40 g) each of Liberty and Saaz. Boil 15 min. Add 1.06 oz. (40 g) of Liberty and Saaz and boil 15 min. Turn off heat, chill wort, transfer to fermenter, and pitch yeast. Ferment 7 days at 50°F (10°C). Rack to secondary for 10 days at 50°F (10°C), slowly dropping to 40°F (4°C). Warm to 57°F (14°C) for 3 days. Rack and lager 90 days at 32°F (0°C). Prime with corn sugar and bottle.

— *"Beer" Rich Mansfield, San Jose, California*
Washoe Zephyr Zymurgists

Daddy's Doppelbock #4

YIELD: .... 5 GAL. (18.9 L)
TOTAL BOILING TIME: .... 60 MIN.
STARTING GRAVITY: 1.114
ENDING GRAVITY: 1.034
PRIMARY FERMENT: .... 10 DAYS
SECONDARY FERMENT: .... 20 DAYS

½ lb. (227 g) pale malt, toasted
½ lb. (227 g) crystal malt
½ lb. (227 g) chocolate malt
7 lb. (3.18 kg) amber dry malt extract
6 lb. (2.72 kg) dark dry malt extract
2 oz. (57 g) Tettnanger hop pellets, 4.4% alpha, in boil 60 min.
¼ tsp. (1.2 ml) Irish moss
1 oz. (28 g) Tettnanger hop pellets, 4.4% alpha, in boil 10 min.
   Kent European lager yeast
1 qt. (946 ml) reserved wort, for priming

Toast pale malt in a 350°F (177°C) oven for 10 min. Steep crystal, chocolate, and toasted malt in 2 gal. (7.6 L) of 170°F (77°C) water for 5 min. Strain liquid into the brew kettle with amber and dark dry malt extracts. Bring to a boil and add 2 oz. (57 g) of Tettnanger hop pellets. Boil 45 min., then add the Irish moss. Boil 5 min. and add 1 oz. (28 g) of Tettnanger hop pellets. Boil 10 min. Chill the wort and transfer to fermenter. Top off to 5 gal. (18.9 L). Remove 1 qt. (946 ml) of wort and save in a sanitized container in the refrigerator. Pitch yeast. Ferment 10 days. Rack to secondary for another 20 days. Prime with the reserved wort and bottle.

— *Kirk K. DeRusha, Dover, New Hampshire*

Sami-Close

YIELD: .... 5 GAL. (18.9 L)
TOTAL BOILING TIME: .... 45 MIN.
STARTING GRAVITY: 1.120
PRIMARY FERMENT: .... 3 WEEKS
SECONDARY FERMENT: .... 2 WEEKS
LAGERING: .... 2 MONTHS

This beer tastes similar to Samuel Adams Triple Bock. It has done very well in AHA competitions.

    2 lb. (907 g) 6-row German pale malt
    1 lb. (454 g) Munich malt
   ¾ lb. (340 g) chocolate malt
 13.2 lb. (6 kg) Ireks light malt extract
   ½ oz. (14 g) Tettnanger hop pellets, 6.0% alpha, in boil 45 min.
 1½ oz. (43 g) Hallertauer whole hops, 4.7% alpha, in boil 45 min.
   1 oz. (28 g) Northern Brewer hops, 3.9% alpha, in boil 15 min.
   1 oz. (28 g) Hallertauer hops plug, 2.9% alpha, steep
   1 tsp. (4.9 ml) yeast nutrient
      Wyeast #2206 Bavarian Lager yeast
   1 package Red Star dry champagne yeast
   ¾ c. (206 ml) corn sugar, for priming

Crush grains and add to 5 qt. (4.7 L) of 163°F (73°C) water. Mash until starch conversion is complete. Sparge with 5 gal. (18.9 L) of 170°F (77°C) water. Bring wort to a boil and add the malt extract, ½ oz. (14 g) of Tettnanger hop pellets, and 1½ oz. (43 g) Hallertauer whole hops. Boil 45 min., then add Northern Brewer hops and yeast nutrient. Boil 15 min. and turn off heat. Add 1 oz. (28 g) of Hallertauer and steep a few min. Chill the wort, transfer to fermenter, and pitch yeast. Ferment 1 week at 48°F (9°C), then add champagne yeast. Ferment 1 week at 48°F (9°C), then raise temperature to 60°F (16°C) for an additional week. Rack to secondary for 2 weeks at 34° – 38°F (1° – 3°C). Prime with corn sugar, bottle, and condition 3 weeks at 60°F (16°C). Move all bottles to the refrigerator and lager for at least 2 months at 34° – 38°F (1° – 3°C).

— Bill Rust, St. Louis, Missouri
Brew Cru Homebrewers Club

A merican lagers are derived from the pale golden pilsners of Bohemia, although the relation might be hard to see at a side by side tasting. American lagers deviated from their European counterparts in the late 19th century as American brewers made use of the more plentiful — and cheaper — 6-row barley. This barley has high protein levels and more husk material. These properties are not very desirable in an all-malt beer, but can be used to good advantage when mashed with other grains — especially corn.

The flavor of American lagers is very light. Extremely low hopping rates are often used. The high adjunct content contributes fermentables, but little flavor, so the malt component of this beer is also very low. The beers are extremely pale in color and highly carbonated. They are known as light, refreshing beers for frequent drinking. Some common variations include dark American lager and cream ale. Some homebrewers brew these beers to their pre-prohibition character, using fewer adjuncts than modern versions.

American light lagers are often brewed using American 6-row barley malt, which has high diastatic power and the ability to convert starches from non-malt adjunct grains. Corn is the adjunct grain

KEY TO RECIPE LOGOS

 EXTRACT RECIPES

 PARTIAL MASH RECIPES

 ALL-GRAIN RECIPES

of choice, although some homebrewers have experimented with rice in an effort to emulate one popular mass-market brand. Adjuncts lighten the body and flavor while providing additional sugars to bring the alcohol up to normal levels. For this purpose, several homebrewers use honey as an adjunct. This method seems to work especially well for homebrewers using malt extracts.

When brewing an all-grain version of this beer, the base will be U.S. 6-row malt with 25 to 40 percent corn or rice. You may need to boil these adjuncts before mashing to gelatinize the starches or use the double-mash system described in Dave Miller's *Homebrewing Guide*. Starting gravities should be slightly lower than normal, from about 1.040 to 1.050. There are several good, clean yeast strains available for use in making American lagers. Try Wyeast #2035 American Lager or Yeast Lab L 34 St. Louis Lager. Hops should be very low. Good hop choices include any German hop or American Hallertau hybrids, such as Mt. Hood.

American Dark Lagers. By adding some caramel syrup to an American light lager, you can make an American dark lager. But this beer will not be much different from its light counterpart, lacking the smoothness or robustness of the European varieties. Homebrewers can also make dark lagers using very small amounts of dark malts.

Pre-Prohibition Lagers. Before Prohibition, American brewers made more robust lagers than they do today. Brewers used the 6-row barley commonly grown in this country, but would temper the mash with 20 percent corn to compensate for the high protein levels in 6-row malt — half the adjunct level of modern American lagers. The result was a more robust, flavorful beer that tended to have a good malty sweetness. These beers were also brewed with more reasonable hopping rates (about 25 to 40 IBUs), giving them a good hop character. The color was a deep golden, with an original gravity of 1.050 to 1.070. Many homebrewers are enthusiastically brewing beers to this profile and the substyle is newly-recognized in the 1997 AHA National Homebrew Competition.

Cream ale is often brewed as a light lager, or a light ale. Some commercial examples are reputed to mix lager and ale to make their cream ale. It may also be brewed like a Kölsch, using an ale yeast and then lagering the beer to create a smoother character. Some brewers also make cream ale by blending ale and lager yeast and fermenting at 55°F (13°C). This is usually a very light-colored, light-bodied beer, similar in many respects to American light lagers, which is why it is included in this chapter. Cream ale looks, smells, tastes, and feels like standard American lagers, but sometimes has a light fruitiness contributed by the ale yeast.

In homebrew competitions, judges look for very light, clean-tasting beers. No haze should be seen and no sediment should be visible. The color should be extremely pale for standard lagers. Some character of cooked corn is sometimes apparent in the flavor and aroma. This is dimethyl sulfide (DMS) and is not a significant problem at low levels, but can keep your beer from winning awards if it becomes excessive.

AMERICAN LIGHT LAGERS

Stinky Dog Lager

YIELD:	5 GAL. (18.9 L)
TOTAL BOILING TIME:	60 MIN.
STARTING GRAVITY:	1.041
ENDING GRAVITY:	1.009
PRIMARY FERMENT:	2 WEEKS
SECONDARY FERMENT:	1 WEEK
LAGERING:	3 WEEKS

5 lb. (2.27 kg) Laaglander light dry malt extract
1 lb. (454 g) light clover honey
1 oz. (28 g) Mt. Hood hops, 4.8% alpha, in boil 60 min.
½ oz. (14 g) Mt. Hood hops, in boil 15 min.
½ oz. (14 g) Mt. Hood hops, finish
    Yeast Lab A07 Canadian Ale yeast
¾ c. (206 ml) corn sugar, for priming

Bring 6 gal. (22.7 L) of water to a boil. Add the extract, honey, and 1 oz. (28 g) of Mt. Hood hops and boil 45 min. Add ½ oz. (14 g) of Mt. Hood hops and boil 15 min. Remove from heat and add another ½ oz. (14 g) of Mt. Hood hops. Force-chill the wort to about 55°F (13°C) and transfer to fermenter. Pitch yeast. Ferment 2 weeks at 55°F (13°C). Rack to secondary for 1 more week. Reduce temperature to 38°F (3°C) and lager 3 weeks. Prime with corn sugar and bottle.

— Keith Hooker, Upper Marlboro, Maryland
Brewers United for Real Potables (BURP)

American Pilsner

YIELD:	5 GAL. (18.9 L)
TOTAL BOILING TIME:	60 MIN.
STARTING GRAVITY:	1.047
ENDING GRAVITY:	1.011
PRIMARY FERMENT:	1 WEEK
SECONDARY FERMENT:	2 WEEKS

    Wyeast #2035 American Lager yeast
1 lb. (454 g) domestic 6-row lager malt
4½ lb. (2.04 kg) light malt extract
1½ lb. (680 g) brewery-grade corn syrup or rice syrup solids
½ oz. (14 g) Cluster hops, in boil 55 min.
½ oz. (14 g) Liberty hops, in boil 15 min.
½ oz. (14 g) Liberty hops, steep
½ tsp. (2.5 ml) calcium chloride
1 package Bru-Vigor yeast food
⅞ c. (241 ml) corn sugar, for priming

Prepare yeast starter prior to brewing day.

    Crush grains and add with calcium chloride to 1 gal. (3.8 L) of 160°F (71°C) water and steep 30 min. Sparge the grains with 1 gal. (3.8 L) or more of 168°F (76°C) water. Bring wort to a boil, then turn off heat and add malt extract and corn syrup or rice syrup solids. Boil 5 min. before adding ½ oz. (14 g) of Cluster hops. Boil 40 min., then add ½ oz. (14 g) of Liberty hops. Boil 15 min., then add the last ½ oz. (14 g) of Liberty hops and turn off heat. Steep a few min., then chill the wort, transfer to fermenter, and top off to 5 gal. (18.9 L) with cold water. Pitch yeast along with Bru-Vigor yeast food. Ferment 1 week at 45° – 55°F (7° – 13°C). Rack to secondary for 2 weeks at 45° – 55°F (7° – 13°C). Prime with corn sugar and bottle.

— *DeFalco's Home Wine & Beer Supplies, Houston, Texas*

Alex's Laborious Lager

YIELD: .... 5 GAL. (18.9 L)
TOTAL BOILING TIME: .... 60 MIN.
STARTING GRAVITY: 1.034
ENDING GRAVITY: 1.008
PRIMARY FERMENT: .... 11 DAYS
SECONDARY FERMENT: .... 6 WEEKS

 2 lb. (907 g) crystal malt, 40° Lovibond
 6 lb. (2.27 kg) light dry malt extract
 2 oz. (57 g) Cascade hops, 4.1% alpha, in boil 60 min.
½ oz. (14 g) coriander seeds
½ oz. (14 g) Cascade hops, 4.1% alpha, in boil 15 min.
½ oz. (14 g) Cascade hops, 4.1% alpha, 2-min. steep
 1 tsp. (4.9 ml) Irish moss
½ oz. (14 g) coriander seeds, added to secondary fermenter
   Wyeast #2035 American Lager yeast
¾ c. (206 ml) corn sugar, for priming

Crush crystal malt and add to 2 ½ gal. (9.4 L) of 170°F (77°C) water. Steep 15 minutes, then strain out grain. Add malt extract and 2 oz. (57 g) of Cascade hops and boil 30 min. Add ½ oz. (14 g) coriander seeds. Boil 15 min., then add ½ oz. (14 g) of Cascade hops. Boil 15 min., then turn off heat. Add final ½ oz. (14 g) of Cascade hops and steep 2 min. Chill the wort, transfer to fermenter, and top off to 5 gal. (18.9 L) with cold water. Pitch yeast and ferment 11 days at 55°F (13°C). Rack to secondary and add ½ oz. (14 g) of coriander seeds. Ferment 6 weeks at 37° – 50°F (3° – 10°C). Prime with corn sugar and bottle.

— *Scott E. Manchuso, Cincinnati, Ohio, AOL FDN Brewers*

Mexican Cerveza

YIELD: .... 5 GAL. (18.9 L)
TOTAL BOILING TIME: .... 60 MIN.
STARTING GRAVITY: 1.047
ENDING GRAVITY: 1.011
PRIMARY FERMENT: .... 1 WEEK
SECONDARY FERMENT: .... 2 WEEKS

Wyeast #2007 Pilsen Lager yeast
1 lb. (454 g) domestic 2-row malt
¼ lb. (113 g) Belgian cara-pils malt
4 lb. (1.81 kg) light malt extract
2 lb. (907 g) brewery-grade corn syrup
⅓ oz. (9 g) Cluster hop pellets, in boil 55 min.
½ oz. (14 g) Hallertauer Hersbrucker hops, in boil 15 min.
½ oz. (14 g) Hallertauer Hersbrucker hops, steep
1 package Bru-Vigor yeast food
⅞ c. (241 ml) corn sugar, for priming

Prepare yeast starter prior to brewing day.

Crush grains and add to 1 gal. (3.8 L) of 160°F (71°C) water and let steep for 30 min. Sparge the grains with 1 gal. (3.8 L) or more of 168°F (76°C) water. Bring wort to a boil, then turn off heat and add malt extract. Boil 5 min. before adding ⅓ oz. (9 g) of Cluster hop pellets. Boil 40 min., then add ½ oz. (14 g) of Hallertauer Hersbrucker hops. Boil 15 min., add the last ½ oz. (14 g) of Hallertauer Hersbrucker hops, and turn off heat. Steep a few min., then chill the wort, transfer to fermenter, and top off to 5 gal. (18.9 L) with cold water. Pitch yeast along with Bru-Vigor yeast food. Ferment 1 week at 45° – 55°F (7° – 13°C). Rack to secondary for 2 weeks at 45° – 55°F (7° – 13°C). Prime with corn sugar and bottle.

— *DeFalco's Home Wine & Beer Supplies, Houston, Texas*

Old 49er Golden Honey Lager

YIELD: .... 6 GAL. (22.7 L)
TOTAL BOILING TIME: .... 60 MIN.
STARTING GRAVITY: 1.052
ENDING GRAVITY: 1.012
PRIMARY FERMENT: .... 2 WEEKS
SECONDARY FERMENT: .... 2 WEEKS

    1 tsp. (4.9 ml) gypsum
    6 lb. (2.27 g) pale ale malt
    1 lb. (454 g) crystal malt, 40° Lovibond
    1 lb. (454 g) crystal malt, 20° Lovibond
    2 lb. (907 g) clover honey
 1½ oz. (43 g) Cascade hops, 6.0% alpha, in boil 60 min.
    1 tsp. (4.9 ml) Irish moss
    1 oz. (28 g) Saaz hops (domestic), 4.0% alpha, in boil 15 min.
    1 oz. (28 g) Saaz hops pellets, dry hopped in secondary
       Wyeast #2042 Danish Lager yeast
    1 c. (275 ml) corn sugar, for priming

Treat 2 gal. (7.6 L) of mash water with gypsum. Add grains and let rest
at 131°F (55°C) for 30 min. Mash at 152°F (67°C) for 2 hours. Mash-out
at 168°F (76°C) for 10 min. Sparge grain with 8 gal. (30.3 L) of 180°F
(82°C) water. Bring wort to a boil and add clover honey and Cascade
hops. Boil 45 min. Add Irish moss and 1 oz. (28 g) of Saaz hops. Boil
15 min. Turn off heat and chill wort. Transfer to fermenter, pitch yeast,
and ferment 2 weeks at 52°F (11°C). Rack to secondary for 2 weeks at
52°F (11°C). Prime with corn sugar and bottle.

— *John Hartline, Marysville, Washington*
North Florida Brewers League

Black Lake Pils

YIELD: .... 5 GAL. (18.9 L)
TOTAL BOILING TIME: .... 60 MIN.
STARTING GRAVITY: 1.046
ENDING GRAVITY: 1.012
PRIMARY FERMENT: .... 2 WEEKS
SECONDARY FERMENT: .... 2 MONTHS

5 lb. (2.27 kg) 2-row pale malt
1 lb. (454 g) cara-pils malt
1 lb. (454 g) light dry malt extract
2 lb. (907 g) clover honey
1 oz. (28 g) Mt. Hood hops, 6.0% alpha, in boil 60 min.
1 oz. (28 g) Saaz hop pellets, 3.2% alpha, in boil 5 min.
1 oz. (28 g) Saaz hop pellets, 3.2% alpha, 10-min. steep
¼ oz. (7 g) Tettnanger hops, dry hopped in secondary
    Wyeast #2007 Pilsen Lager yeast
¾ c. (206 ml) corn sugar, for priming

Add crushed grains to 2 gal. (7.6 L) of water and heat mash to 120°F (49°C). Rest for 20 min. Heat mash to 140°F (60°C) and rest 15 min. Heat mash to 154°F (68°C) and rest until starch conversion is complete, about 60 min. Mash-out at 168°F (76°C) for 10 min. Sparge with 170°F (77°C) water. Collect 6 gal. (22.7 L) of wort in brew kettle. Add dry malt extract and honey. Bring to a boil and add the Mt. Hood hops. Boil 55 min., then add 1 oz. (28 g) of Saaz hop pellets. Boil 5 min. Turn off heat and add 1 oz. (28 g) of Saaz hop pellets and steep 10 min. Chill the wort and let settle for 30 min. Rack wort off trub into a primary fermenter and pitch yeast. Ferment 2 weeks at 60°F (16°C). Rack to secondary for 2 months at 34°F (1°C). Prime with corn sugar and bottle.

— *Rick Bedor, Merrickville, Ontario, Canada, The Boilover Boys*

Maple Leaf Lager

YIELD:	5½ GAL. (20.8 L)
TOTAL BOILING TIME:	10 MIN.
STARTING GRAVITY:	1.034
ENDING GRAVITY:	1.020
PRIMARY FERMENT:	3 DAYS
SECONDARY FERMENT:	18 DAYS

1¾ gal. (6.6 L) maple sap, 1.090 OG
3.3 lb. (1.5 kg) Munton & Fison hopped lager malt extract
½ tsp. (2.5 ml) Irish moss
    Edme dry yeast, 1.27-c. (300-ml) starter
¾ c. (206 ml) corn sugar, for priming

Bring maple sap to a boil. Turn off heat and add malt extract and Irish moss. Boil 10 min., then chill the wort. Transfer to fermenter, pitch yeast starter, and top off to 5½ gal. (20.8 L) with cold water. Ferment 3 days, then rack to a secondary fermenter. Ferment for 18 days in a refrigerator. Prime with corn sugar and bottle.

— Neil Flatter, Terre Haute, Indiana
Wabash Valley Vintners' and Homebrewers' Club

PRE-PROHIBITION-STYLE AMERICAN LAGERS

Prepro Golden Lager

YIELD:	5 GAL. (18.9 L)
TOTAL BOILING TIME:	90 MIN.
STARTING GRAVITY:	1.066
PRIMARY FERMENT:	2 WEEKS
SECONDARY FERMENT:	4 WEEKS
LAGERING:	6 WEEKS

    Wyeast #2007 Pilsen Lager yeast, in a ½-gal. (1.9-L) starter
10 lb. (4.54 kg) Briess 6-row pale malt
 3 lb. (1.36 kg) flaked corn
¼ lb. (113 g) Great Western malted wheat
1½ oz. (43 g) Perle hops, 5.5% alpha, in boil 45 min.

    1 tsp. (4.9 ml) Irish moss
    ¾ oz. (21 g) Liberty hops, in boil 15 min.
    ¾ oz. (21 g) Liberty hops, steep
    1 c. (275 ml) corn sugar, for priming, or force carbonate

Several days before brewing, begin growing up yeast starter.

Crush grain and add with flaked corn to 4½ gal. (17 L) of 133°F (56°C) water. Mash at 122°F (50°C) for a 30-min. protein rest. Heat mash to 158°F (70°C) for a 60-min. starch conversion. Raise temperature to 170°F (77°C) for mash-out. Sparge with 170°F (77°C) water and collect 6½ gal. (24.6 L) of wort in brew kettle. Heat and boil wort for 45 min. before adding 1½ oz. (43 g) of Perle hops. Boil 15 min., then add the Irish moss. Boil 15 min., then add ¾ oz. (21 g) of Liberty hops. Boil 15 min., remove from heat, and add the remaining ¾ oz. (21 g) of Liberty hops. Chill the wort to below 50°F (10°C) and transfer to fermenter. Pitch yeast starter and ferment 2 weeks at 48°F (9°C). Transfer to secondary for another 4 weeks at 48°F (9°C). Lager at 33°F (1°C) for 6 weeks. Keg or bottle.

— *David Brockington, Seattle, Washington*
Seattle Secret Skinny Brewers Society

Barefoot Lager

YIELD:	15 GAL. (56.8 L)
TOTAL BOILING TIME:	90 MIN.
STARTING GRAVITY:	1.056
ENDING GRAVITY:	1.010
PRIMARY FERMENT:	1 WEEK
SECONDARY FERMENT:	3 WEEKS

      lager yeast slurry
    27 lb. (12.25 kg) 6-row malted barley
     4 lb. (1.81 kg) corn grits, cooked
     2 oz. (57 g) Tettnanger hops, 5.5% alpha, in boil 30 min.
     2 oz. (57 g) Cluster hops, in boil 30 min.
     4 oz. (113 g) Saaz hops, in boil 15 min.

Before brewing, start your yeast or obtain a slurry from a brewery.

Mash barley and cooked corn grits in 10 gal. (37.9 L) of water for 30 min. at 130°F (54°C). Increase temperature to 150°F (66°C) for 90 min. of saccharification rest. Raise temperature to 170°F (77°C) for mash-out. Sparge to collect 12½ gal. (47.3 L). Boil 60 min. Add 2 oz. (57 g) of Tettnanger and Cluster hops and boil 15 min. Add 4 oz. (113 g) of Saaz hops. Boil 15 min. and turn off heat. Chill the wort to 60°F (16°C) and pitch lager yeast slurry. Dilute to 15 gal. (18.9 L) and ferment 1 week at 55°F (13°C). Rack to secondary for 3 weeks at 40°F (4°C). Keg or bottle.

— *Tim Artz, Lorton, Virginia*
Brewers United for Real Potables (BURP)

AMERICAN DARK LAGERS

French Silk Chocolate Lager

YIELD: .... 5 GAL. (18.9 L)
TOTAL BOILING TIME: .... 60 MIN.
STARTING GRAVITY: 1.052
ENDING GRAVITY: 1.020
PRIMARY FERMENT: .... 5 DAYS
SECONDARY FERMENT: .... 4 WEEKS

- ½ lb. (227 g) dextrin malt
- ½ lb. (227 g) crystal malt, 90° Lovibond
- ½ lb. (227 g) chocolate malt
- 4¾ lb. (2.15 kg) amber dry malt extract
- 1 lb. (454 g) dark dry malt extract
- 8 oz. (227 g) Baker's unsweetened chocolate
- 1 c. (237 ml) blackstrap molasses
- ⅛ oz. (3.5 g) artificial chocolate flavoring
- 1 oz. (28 g) Bullion hops, 9.2% alpha, in boil 60 min.
- 1 oz. (28 g) Tettnanger hops, 4.5% alpha, in boil 60 min.
- 1 oz. (28 g) Bullion hops, 9.2% alpha, in boil 20 min.
- 1 oz. (28 g) Tettnanger hops, 4.5% alpha, in boil 3 min.
  Wyeast #2035 American Lager yeast
- 1 c. (275 ml) light dry malt extract

AMERICAN DARK LAGERS

213

Crush grains and steep in a grain bag in 2 gal. (7.6 L) of 165°F (74°C) water for 20 min. Remove grains and add malt extracts, Baker's chocolate, molasses, and chocolate flavoring. Heat to boiling and add 1 oz. (28 g) each of Bullion and Tettnanger hops. Boil 40 min., then add 1 oz. (28 g) of Bullion hops. Boil 17 min., then add 1 oz. (28 g) of Tettnanger hops. Boil 3 min. and turn off heat. Chill the wort, transfer to fermenter, and top off to 5 gal. (18.9 L) with cold water. Pitch yeast and ferment 5 days at 60°F (16°C). Rack to secondary for 4 weeks at 40°F (4°C). Prime with light dry malt extract and bottle.

— *Ken Schmidt, Chesterfield, Michigan*
Clinton River Association of Fermenting Trendsetters (CRAFT)

Honey Brown Lager

YIELD: .... 5 GAL. (18.9 L)
TOTAL BOILING TIME: .... 45 MIN.
STARTING GRAVITY: 1.040–1.044
ENDING GRAVITY: 1.010–1.014
PRIMARY FERMENT: .... 7–10 DAYS
SECONDARY FERMENT: .... 3 WEEKS

½ lb. (227 g) carastan malt, 36° Lovibond
¼ c. (69 ml) roasted barley
4 lb. (1.81 kg) Superbrau unhopped amber malt extract
2 lb. (907 g) clover honey
1 oz. (28 g) Cascade hop pellets, 5.2% alpha, in boil 30 min.
1 oz. (28 g) Mt. Hood hop pellets, 3.8% alpha, in boil 5 min.
2 packets Paine's lager yeast
¾ c. (206 ml) corn sugar, for priming

Crush grains and steep in 6 qt. (5.7 L) of 170°F (77°C) water. Strain out grains and add malt extract and honey. Boil 15 min., then add 1 oz. (28 g) of Cascade hop pellets. Boil 25 min., then add 1 oz. (28 g) of Mt. Hood hop pellets. Boil 5 min. and turn off heat. Chill the wort, transfer to a fermenter, and top off to 5 gal. (18.9 L) with cold water. Pitch yeast and ferment 7 – 10 days at 53° – 58°F (12° – 14°C). Rack to secondary for 3 weeks below 50°F (10°C). Prime with corn sugar and bottle.

— *Bill Koch and Paul Dyster, Niagara Falls, New York*
Niagara Homebrewers League

CREAM ALE

In Your Pants

YIELD: .... 10 GAL. (37.9 L)
TOTAL BOILING TIME: .... 60 MIN.
STARTING GRAVITY: 1.052
ENDING GRAVITY: 1.016
PRIMARY FERMENT: .... 1 WEEK
SECONDARY FERMENT: .... 1 WEEK
LAGERING: .... 3 WEEKS

 2 lb. (907 g) flaked maize
 1 lb. (454 g) flaked barley
15 lb. (6.8 kg) 2-row pale malt, crushed
 2 lb. (907 g) crystal malt, 20° Lovibond, crushed
 1 oz. (28 g) chocolate malt, crushed
 ¾ oz. (21 g) Willamette hops, 5.3% alpha, in boil 60 min.
 ¾ oz. (21 g) Cascade hops, 4.4% alpha, in boil 60 min.
 ¼ oz. (7 g) Willamette hops, 5.3% alpha, in boil 30 min.
 ¼ oz. (7 g) Cascade hops, 4.4% alpha, in boil 30 min.
 ¼ oz. (7 g) Willamette hops, 5.3% alpha, steep
 ¼ oz. (7 g) Cascade hops, 4.4% alpha, steep
    Wyeast #1056 American Ale yeast
1½ c. (413 ml) corn sugar, for priming

Add all grains to 5 gal. (18.9 L) of 170°F (77°C) water and mix well. Rest at 155°F (13°C) for 30 min. Heat to 158°F (70°C) and hold until starch conversion is complete. Sparge with 10 gal. (37.9 L) of 180°F (82°C) water and collect 13 gal. (49.2 L) of wort. Bring to a boil and add ¾ oz. (21 g) each of Willamette and Cascade hops. Boil 30 min., then add ¼ oz. (7 g) each of Willamette and Cascade hops. Boil 30 min. and turn off heat. Add last ¼ oz. (7 g) each of Willamette and Cascade hops and steep for a min. or two, then chill the wort. Transfer to a fermenter and pitch yeast. Ferment 1 week at ale temperatures (60° – 65°F [16° – 18°C]), then rack to secondary for another week at ale temperature (60° – 65°F [16° – 18°C]), then lager at below 45°F (7°C) for 3 weeks. Prime with corn sugar and bottle.

— *John Nicholas Varady, Lafayette Hill, Pennsylvania*

More HOMEBREW FAVORITES

11

Wheat Beers

Wheat beers are often regarded as refreshing summertime drinks. Light, somewhat tart, with complex aromas of spiciness, they're a real taste treat. Wheat beers should not be regarded only in this way, however — a hearty Bavarian weizenbock is a strong, substantial beer that might lend itself more to a chilly winter evening by the fireplace than a warm summer day on the deck. While wheat beers may be regarded as a southern German brew, the tart Berliner weisse, the light American wheats, and the spiced Belgian wit beers (described in Chapter 6) all bear witness that wheat brews are international citizens of the beer community, each quite different as the brewing process and ingredients change from substyle to substyle. Wheat beers are also increasingly used by homebrewers and craft brewers as the base for fruit and spiced beers, as is apparent from the large number of raspberry wheat beers appearing on tap at brewpubs and beer bars.

Weizenbier. Wheat beers are often referred to as *weizenbier*, or sometimes as *weissbier*. The term generally denotes the widely known wheat beer style of southern Germany. It is the most popular of the various wheat beer styles, and one of the most emulated

KEY TO RECIPE LOGOS

 EXTRACT RECIPES

 PARTIAL MASH RECIPES

 ALL-GRAIN RECIPES

by today's homebrewing community. A weizen will often be cloudy and have yeast sediment in the bottom of the bottle. In commercial examples, this may be noted on the label as *mit hefe*, or the beer may be labeled *hefe-weizen*. *Hefe* is yeast, and the beers are unfiltered, or may contain additional yeast added at bottling. The added yeast is often a lager or ale strain, so homebrewers who culture yeast from these bottles may not be obtaining a true wheat beer yeast. While many of the German wheat beers do have noticeable yeast and sediment in the bottles, others appeal to mass-market aesthetics and filter their beer to produce a clear wheat beer, labeled *kristall*.

Bavarian Wheats. If you want a southern German weizen that's close to the brews produced by the brewmasters of Bavaria, try using a decoction mash (single or double). If you've been sticking to infusion mashes or step mashes, the decoction mash may seem more complex and time consuming, but it's the traditional way of producing weizen beers. It reduces haze and also the proteins that tend to cause stuck runoff when working with wheat. The grist composition of a southern German-style wheat beer will generally be at least 50 to 70 percent wheat, with pale barley malt making up the remainder. Dark wheat beers can be made using either dark wheat malt (if available) or dark malted barley, in very small amounts, or possibly cara-Munich or cara-Vienne. The color of a weizen, either with or without yeast, should be very pale — generally less than 10 SRM, similar to pale ales. Dunkelweizen is not a black beer, but rather a brownish to deep copper color. You should be able to see through it, with the color range similar to a brown ale.

In a southern German-style weizen beer, use noble hops, such as Hallertauer, but with a light touch, generally included only in the full boil without additions for flavor or aroma. The hops are used for balance, rather than for their flavor or aromatic properties, which would compete with the subtle yeast by-product flavors and aromas — clove, banana, phenols, esters — that are the hallmark of a great wheat beer. Competition guidelines typically specify 8 to 14 IBUs.

Water profiles are less important with wheat beers than they are with lagers. According to Eric Warner in his book *German Wheat*, the water profiles used by southern German brewers range in hardness from 50 ppm to 450 ppm total dissolved solids. Munich water is 265 ppm with 190 ppm calcium. Most water sources in the United States should be acceptable without treatment.

The yeast used in a southern German wheat beer is vitally important — more often than not it is the single most important factor that separates a winning wheat beer from a mere competitor. German wheat strains are complex strains that ferment at ale temperatures. Wyeast produces at least four German wheat strains; other yeast sources, such as the Yeast Culture Kit Company have additional strains. Among the Wyeast offerings, the Bavarian Weizen (#3056) strain is the most widely available, and most popular with homebrewers. This yeast is reputedly a mix of ale yeast *(Saccharomyces cerevisiae)* with some *Saccharomyces delbruickii*. Many homebrewers have also had excellent results with Wyeast's Weihenstephan Weizen (#3068), which produces rich, complex aromas full of clove, vanilla, and banana. The Yeast Culture Kit Company's Bavarian Wheat (A05) — also sold as Yeast Lab (W51) — produces abundant phenols and esters and is also an excellent yeast for southern German wheats. Most German wheat beer brewers will pitch at one temperature and ferment at another, says Eric Warner, but the sum of the two temperatures will equal 30°C. According to Warner, pitching at 12°C (54°F) and fermenting at 18°C (64°F) is a common combination.

A *dunkelweizen* (dark wheat) has a good, malty character with a bit of sweet chocolate flavor, combined with the complexity of a wheat beer and the hallmark spicy clove or banana aroma. A *weizenbock* is a cross between a wheat beer and a bock. It is brewed to bock strength, which in Germany means an original gravity above 1.066. It is, therefore, quite a substantial beer, with a full body and a healthy amount of sweetness.

The procedures used to make a dunkelweizen are the same as for a weizen; however, the grist will include some darker grain — either dark malted wheat or a darker malted barley — for added color. Again, the color is not black, but is rather brownish, so a restrained hand on the colored malt is vital. Hops are also restrained, about an ounce of noble hops (Hallertauer is fine) in 5 gallons. The starting gravity is sometimes slightly higher for a dunkelweizen than for a weizen, but this is by no means usual. The beer should, however, have a good malty character, subdued hopping level, and a bit less of the yeast flavors, not due to changes in process, but due instead to the flavors of the colored malt.

Weizenbocks follow the basic procedures used for other southern German wheats, and the grain bill is typically anywhere from 40 to 60 percent wheat. Malt is the predominant flavor in this beer, although the cloves and banana are still present. Quite a bit of residual sweetness is common. Hops are generally not increased over the amounts used for a standard weizen, in spite of the increased starting gravity. This lets the malt character dominate the flavor profile of the beer.

Shifting areas from southern Germany to Berlin, we find the wheat beer of that city, known as *Berliner weisse*, to be a much lighter-bodied beer, with a tart, acidic bite that is refreshing and light. Berliner weisse, made in that city for 400 years or more, is certainly a venerable citizen among the world's beer styles. The beer is made with a grist of up to 75 percent malted wheat, with pale malted barley rounding out the other 25 percent or so. The gravity is very low — typically 1.028 to 1.032. This is definitely a beer that can be consumed in quantity, even on a hot summer day. The beer is known for having aggressive carbonation and a thick white head that dissipates fairly quickly. In addition to yeast, the beer is fermented with *Lactobacillus delbruickii*, which lends the beer its acidic tartness. Hops should be low in this beer — about 3 to 12 IBUs. Less than an ounce in a 5-gallon (18.9-L) batch would do it.

American Wheats. Jumping continents to America, wheat beers brewed in many of the brewpubs and microbreweries are using less wheat than in Germany. Instead of a complex yeast that imparts phenols, esters, and myriad other subtle aromas and flavors, brewers here favor ale yeasts that produce a less complex beer. In terms of grist, some American wheat brewers use as little as 35 percent wheat; others may use 50 percent. The starting gravity is typically 1.030 to 1.050, so it can range from a light-bodied beer to a normal-gravity beer. Color is usually very pale, although some brewers produce somewhat darker versions. Hopping is light, as it is in German wheat beers. Hops can be of several types, although U.S. hybrids of noble hops, such as Mt. Hood, work well because of their fairly low alpha acid content. The hopping rate of an American wheat should be 5 to 17 IBUs.

In competition, judges look for complexity in the German styles and simplicity in the American style. A weizen should have a rich array of yeast-induced by-products, including phenols and esters. Clove, banana, vanilla, and other spice flavors and aromas are expected in a weizen beer. Sourness or tartness is expected in a Berliner weisse. Cloudiness is appropriate in all wheat beer styles, other than kristall. American wheats should be light and refreshing, with low hops aroma, and without the noticeable phenols and esters that make German weizens such a joy to drink.

WEIZEN: BAVARIAN WHEATS

Breakfast Brew

YIELD: .... 5½ GAL. (20.8 L)
TOTAL BOILING TIME: .... 60 MIN.
STARTING GRAVITY: 1.045
ENDING GRAVITY: 1.010
PRIMARY FERMENT: .... 7–10 DAYS

6.6 lb. (3 kg) John Bull wheat extract
2 lb. (907 g) clover honey
2 c. (551 ml) dry Wheatena hot breakfast cereal
¾ oz. (21 g) Willamette hops, 5.3% alpha, in boil 60 min.
¼ oz. (7 g) Willamette hops, 5.3% alpha, in boil 3 min.
2 packets Muntons ale yeast
3 c. (826 ml) Laaglander dried malt extract, for priming

Add wheat extract and honey to 2 gal. (7.6 L) of 180°F (82°C) water. Steep 15 min. Add ¾ oz. (21 g) of Willamette hops and Wheatena. Boil 42 min., then add ¼ oz. (7 g) of Willamette hops. Boil 3 min., then turn off heat.

Chill the wort, transfer to fermenter, top off to 5½ gal. (20.8 L) with cold water, and pitch yeast. Ferment 7 – 10 days at 60°F (16°C), then prime with dried malt extract, and bottle.

— Robert D. Beyer, Jr., North Catasauqua, Pennsylvania

Brewlab Thursday Nighter

Tangerine Dreams Wheat

YIELD: .... 5 GAL. (18.9 L)
TOTAL BOILING TIME: .... 60 MIN.
PRIMARY FERMENT: .... 7 DAYS
SECONDARY FERMENT: .... 7–14 DAYS

7 lb. (3.18 kg) 60/40 wheat malt extract
½ lb. (227 g) chocolate malt crushed
1 oz. (28 g) Tettnanger hops, in boil 45 min.
½ oz. (14 g) Tettnanger hops, in boil 30 min.
½ oz. (14 g) Tettnanger hops, in boil 15 min.
1 oz. (28 g) Willamette hops, steep
3 tangerine peels, torn into ½-in. (1.3-cm) chunks
1 oz. (28 g) Willamette hops, dry hop in secondary
Wyeast #3068 Weihenstephan Wheat yeast
¾ c. (206 ml) corn sugar, for priming

Add crushed chocolate malt to 2 gal. (7.6 ml) of 180°F (82°C) water, steep for 30 min., then strain out grains. Add malt extract then boil 15 min. before adding 1 oz. (28 g) of Tettnanger hops. Boil 15 min., then add ½ oz. (14 g) of Tettnanger hops. Boil 15 min., then add last ½ oz. (14 g) of Tettnanger hops. Boil 15 min., then turn off heat. Add 1 oz. (28 g) of Willamette hops and tangerine peels and steep 10 – 15 min. Chill the wort, transfer to fermenter, and top off to 5 gal. (18.9 L) with cold water. Pitch yeast and ferment 1 week, or until kraeusen falls. Rack to secondary and dry hop with 1 oz. (28 g) of Williamette hops and continue fermenting for 7–14 days, then prime with corn sugar, and bottle.

— Daniel Fernandez, Costa Mesa, California

Carrie's Pleasure Wheat

YIELD: .... 5 GAL. (18.9 L)
TOTAL BOILING TIME: .... 60 MIN.
STARTING GRAVITY: 1.051
ENDING GRAVITY: 1.016
PRIMARY FERMENT: .... 3 DAYS
SECONDARY FERMENT: .... 16 DAYS

1 lb. (454 g) crystal malt, 10° Lovibond
8 lb. (3.63 kg) 60/40 wheat malt extract
1 oz. (28 g) Saaz hop pellets, in boil 60 min.
½ oz. (14 g) Saaz hop pellets, in boil 30 min.
½ tsp. (2.5 ml) Irish moss
½ oz. (14 g) Saaz hop pellets, steep and end of boil
 Wyeast #3068 Weihenstephan Wheat yeast
¾ c. (206 ml) corn sugar, for priming

Add crystal malt to 2 gal. (7.6 L) of water and heat to 150°F (66°C) water. Steep for 30 min., then strain out grains. Add wheat malt extract, bring to a boil, and add 1 oz. (28 g) of Saaz hop pellets. Boil 30 min., then add ½ oz. (14 g) of Saaz hop pellets. Boil 15 min., then add ½ tsp. (2.5 ml) Irish moss. Boil 15 min., then turn off heat. Add last ½ oz. (14 g) of Saaz hop pellets and steep 5 – 10 min. Chill the wort; strain out hops while transferring to fermenter. Top off to 5 gal. (18.9 L) with cold water and pitch yeast. Ferment 9 days using a blow-off tube. Rack to secondary for 16 days. Prime with corn sugar and bottle.

— *Alex Aaron, Oceanside, California*

Weizen

YIELD:	4½ GAL. (17 L)
TOTAL BOILING TIME:	60 MIN.
STARTING GRAVITY:	1.046
ENDING GRAVITY:	1.007
PRIMARY FERMENT:	3 WEEKS

First place in the wheat beer category at the 1993 Central Illinois Homebrew Competition.

- 5 lb. (2.27 kg) wheat malt
- 3 lb. (136 kg) 2-row malt
- 0.05 oz. (1½ g) gypsum
- ½ oz. (14 g) Hallertauer whole hops, 4.1% alpha, in boil 55 min.
- ¼ oz. (7 g) Hallertauer whole hops, 4.1% alpha, in boil 30 min.
- ½ tsp. (2.5 ml) Irish moss
- Yeast Lab W51 Bavarian Weizen yeast
- Yeast Lab L32 Bavarian Lager yeast
- 1 c. (275 ml) dry malt extract, for priming

Crush grains and add to 2 ⅔ gal. (10.1 L) of 100°F (38°C) water treated with gypsum. Heat mash to 122°F (50°C). Rest 20 min. Remove 40% of the mash and heat to 155°F (65°C). Let rest for 30 min. Boil decocted portion 20 min. Remix decoction with main mash and adjust mash temperature to 154°F (68°C). Hold at 154°F (68°C) for 30 min. Heat mash to 170°F (77°C) for a 10-min. mash-out. Sparge with 5 gal. (18.9 L) of 172°F (78°C) water. Collect 6 – 6½ gal. (22.7 – 24.6 L) of wort. Boil 5 min. before adding ½ oz. (14 g) of Hallertauer hops. Boil 25 min., then add ¼ oz. (7 g) of Hallertauer hops and Irish moss. Boil 30 min., then turn off heat. Chill the wort, transfer to fermenter, and pitch both yeasts. Ferment for 3 weeks, then prime with dry malt extract and bottle.

— *Steven and Paula Stacy, Rolla, Missouri*
Missouri Association of Serious Homebrewers (MASH)

DUNKELWEIZENS

Dark Wheat Beer

YIELD: .... 5 GAL. (18.9 L)
TOTAL BOILING TIME: .... 60 MIN.
STARTING GRAVITY: 1.052
ENDING GRAVITY: 1.013
PRIMARY FERMENT: .... 1 WEEK
SECONDARY FERMENT: .... 1 WEEK

Wyeast #3056 Bavarian Weizen yeast or Wyeast #3068
Weihenstephan Wheat yeast

- 1 lb. (454 g) (454 g) wheat malt
- 1 lb. (454 g) 6-row pale malt
- ½ lb. (227 g) German medium crystal malt
- 5½ lb. (2.49 kg) wheat malt extract
- ½ lb. (227 g) dark malt extract
- ⅔ oz. (19 g) Perle hops, in boil 55 min.
- ½ oz. (14 g) Hallertauer Hersbrucker hops, in boil 15 min.
- ½ oz. (14 g) Hallertauer Hersbrucker hops, steep
- 1 package Bru-Vigor yeast food
- ¾ c. (206 ml) corn sugar, for priming

Prepare yeast starter prior to brewing day.

Crush grains and add to 1 gal. (3.8 L) of 160°F (71°C) water and let steep 30 min. Sparge the grains with 1 gal. (3.8 L) or more of 168°F (76°C) water. Bring wort to a boil, then turn off heat and add malt extracts. Boil 5 min. before adding ⅔ oz. (19 g) of Perle hops. Boil 40 min., then add ½ oz. (14 g) of Hallertauer Hersbrucker hops. Boil 15 min., add last ½ oz. (14 g) of Hallertauer Hersbrucker hops, and turn off heat. Steep a few min., then chill the wort, transfer to fermenter, and top off to 5 gal. (18.9 L) with cold water. Pitch yeast along with Bru-Vigor yeast food. Ferment 1 week. Rack to secondary for 1 week. Prime with corn sugar and bottle.

— *DeFalco's Home Wine & Beer Supplies, Houston, Texas*

Dunkels Weissbier

YIELD: .... 5 GAL. (18.9 L)
TOTAL BOILING TIME: .... 70 MIN.
STARTING GRAVITY: 1.052
ENDING GRAVITY: 1.017
PRIMARY FERMENT: .... 14 DAYS
SECONDARY FERMENT: .... 6 DAYS

A dark beer with a spicy clove-like aroma; it compares well with Franziskaner.

    Wyeast #3068 Weihenstephan Wheat yeast
 ¼ c. (69 ml) pale dry malt extract
 5 lb. (2.27 kg) Briess dark dry wheat malt extract
 1 lb. (454 g) Laaglander dark dry malt extract
 ½ oz. (14 g) Liberty hops, 5.2% alpha, in boil 70 min.
 ¼ oz. (7 g) Liberty hops, 5.2% alpha, in boil 30 min.
 ¼ oz. (7 g) Liberty hops, 5.2% alpha, in boil 15 min.
 ¾ c. (206 ml) corn sugar, for priming

Prepare a yeast starter 24 hours in advance.

Bring 1½ gal. (680 g) of water to a boil and add malt extracts. Add ½ oz. (14 g) of Liberty hops and boil 40 min. Add ¼ oz. (7 g) of Liberty hops and boil 15 min. Add final ¼ oz. (7 g) of Liberty hops and boil 15 min. Turn off heat, chill the wort, and transfer to fermenter. Top off to 5 gal. (18.9 L) with cold water and pitch yeast starter. Ferment 2 weeks at 69°F (21°C). Rack to secondary for 6 days at 65°F (18°C). Prime with corn sugar and bottle.

— *Mike Murat, Kenner, Louisiana*

Humpadingdong
Dunkelweizen

YIELD: .... 5 GAL. (18.9 L)
TOTAL BOILING TIME: .... 60 MIN.
STARTING GRAVITY: 1.048
ENDING GRAVITY: 1.012
PRIMARY FERMENT: .... 4–5 DAYS
SECONDARY FERMENT: .... 10 DAYS

 ⅓ lb. (151 g) chocolate malt
6.6 lb. (3 kg) Northwestern wheat malt extract

1½ oz. (43 g) Mt. Hood hops, 4.8% alpha, in boil 60 min.
   Yeast Lab W51 Bavarian Weizen yeast
¾ c. (206 ml) corn sugar for priming

Soak the chocolate malt in 6 gal. (22.7 L) of 180°F (82°C) water for 5 – 10 min., then strain out the grain and discard. Bring liquid to a boil and add extract and hops. Boil 60 min. Force-chill the wort, transfer to fermenter, and pitch yeast. Ferment 4 – 5 days at 65°F (16°C), then transfer to a secondary fermenter for another 10 days. Prime and bottle.

— Keith Hooker, Upper Marlboro, Maryland
Brewers United for Real Potables (BURP)

WEIZENBOCKS

The Heavyside Layer

YIELD: .... 5 GAL. (18.9 L)
TOTAL BOILING TIME: .... 45 MIN.
STARTING GRAVITY: 1.090–1095
ENDING GRAVITY: 1.015–1.020
PRIMARY FERMENT: .... 10 DAYS
SECONDARY FERMENT: .... 4 WEEKS

Best of show at an AHA competition in Tennessee in 1995.

¼ lb. (113 g) crystal malt, 64° Lovibond
3.3 lb. (1.5 kg) John Bull hopped amber malt extract
3.3 lb. (1.5 kg) John Bull hopped dark malt extract
3.3 lb. (1.5 kg) Muntons wheat extract
½ oz. (14 g) Willamette hops, 5.5% alpha, in boil 45 min.
1 oz. (28 g) Willamette hops, 5.5% alpha, in boil 5 min.
   Wyeast #1084 Irish Ale yeast
¾ c. (206 ml) corn sugar, for priming

Steep crystal malt 30 min. at 100°F (38°C). Strain out grains. Add malt extracts and ½ oz. (14 g) of Willamette hops. Boil 40 min. Add 1 oz. (28 g) Willamette hops. Boil 5 min. Turn off heat; chill wort. Transfer to large fermenter, pitch yeast; aerate well. Ferment 10 days. Rack to secondary 4 weeks. Prime; bottle. Age 3 months.

— Marc Gottfried, St. Ann, Missouri, The St. Louis Brews

Bavarian Bath

YIELD:	9 GAL. (34.1 L)
TOTAL BOILING TIME:	2 HOURS
STARTING GRAVITY:	1.060
ENDING GRAVITY:	1.021
PRIMARY FERMENT:	7 DAYS
SECONDARY FERMENT:	7 DAYS

*First place in the wheat category and third in the best of show
round at the 1996 Spirit of Free Beer competition.*

      Wyeast #3068 Weihenstephan Wheat yeast
15.4 lb. (7 kg) wheat malt
 8.8 lb. (4 kg) dark Munich malt
 6.6 lb. (3 kg) Munich malt
2.82 oz. (80 g) Perle whole hops, 3.5% alpha, in boil 60 min.
0.71 oz. (20 g) Perle whole hops, in boil 10 min.
  2 tbsp. (30 ml) Irish moss
  3 qt. (2.8 L) gyle, for priming

Several days before brewing, begin growing yeast up to 2 qt. (1.9 L).
     Crush grains and add to 10¼ gal. (38.8 L) of 123°F (51°C) water.
Mash at 115°F (46°C) for 15 min. Heat mash to 129°F (54°C) over a 30 min.
period. Remove 40% of the mash for the first decoction. Raise decoction
temperature to 162°F (72°C) for 15 min. Raise decoction to a boil and hold
for 20 min. Add the decoction back to the mash to achieve a temperature of
142°F (61°C). Raise mash to 147°F (64°C). Remove 40% of the mash for the
second decoction. Raise temperature to 162°F (72°C) for 15 min., bring to
boil, and let boil 20 min. Return decoction to mash, yielding a temperature
of 158°F (70°C). Bring mash to 163°F (73°C) for 15 min. Raise temperature
to 170°F (77°C) for a 10-min. mash-out. Sparge with 170°F (77°C) water,
collecting 11 gal. (41.6 L) of wort. Boil 1 hour. Add 2.82 oz. (80 g) of Perle
hops. Boil 50 min. Add 0.71 oz. (20 g) of Perle hops and Irish moss. Boil 10
min. and turn off heat. Chill the wort, then transfer to fermenter. Save
3 qt. (2.8 L) of wort in a sanitized container and refrigerate until bottling.
Pitch yeast. Ferment 7 days, then rack to secondary for 7 days. Prime with
the saved wort (gyle) and bottle.

                        — *Andy Anderson, Bath, England*
                  Brewers United for Real Potables (BURP)

Whitewater Weizenbock

YIELD: .... 5 GAL. (18.9 L)
TOTAL BOILING TIME: .... 90 MIN.
STARTING GRAVITY: 1.076
ENDING GRAVITY: 1.021
PRIMARY FERMENT: .... 8 DAYS
SECONDARY FERMENT: .... 8 DAYS

Second place in BURP's 1994 wheat beer contest and a ribbon in the 1994 Dixie Cup competition.

- 8 lb. (3.6 kg) German dark Munich malt
- 6.6 lb. (3 kg) Ireks wheat malt extract (100% wheat)
- ⅔ oz. (19 g) U.S. Hallertauer whole hops, 5.3% alpha, in boil 15 min.
- 1 tbsp. (15 g) Irish moss
- Wyeast #3068 Weihenstephan Wheat yeast, 1-qt. (1-L) slurry
- 1⅛ c. (310 g) corn sugar, for priming

Crush grains and add to 4 gal. (15 L) of 133°F (56 °C) water. Mash 15 min. at 125°F (52°C) for the protein rest. Remove 40% of the mash, heat it to 160°F (71°C), and rest 25 min. Heat decocted portion to boiling and add back to the main mash, yielding a mash temperature of 142°F (61 °C). Rest 10 min. Take a second 40% decoction and again raise it to 160°F (71°C) for 25 min. and then boil 20 min. Add the decoction back to the mash, yielding a mash temperature of 158°F (70°C). Rest 25 min. Raise mash temperature to 170°F (77°C), sparge, and collect 6 ½ gal. (24.6 L) of wort in brew kettle. Add wheat extract and bring wort to a boil. Boil 75 min., then add ⅔ oz. (19 g) of Hallertauer hops and Irish moss. Boil 15 min., then turn off heat. Chill the wort to 60°F (16°C), transfer to fermenter, and pitch yeast. Ferment 8 days, then rack to secondary for additional 8 days. Prime with corn sugar and bottle.

— *Andy Anderson, Bath, England*
Brewers United for Real Potables (BURP)

AMERICAN WHEATS

Star Thistle Wheat

YIELD: .... 5 GAL. (18.9 L)
TOTAL BOILING TIME: .... 60 MIN.
STARTING GRAVITY: 1.036
ENDING GRAVITY: 1.020
PRIMARY FERMENT: .... 4 DAYS
SECONDARY FERMENT: .... 11 DAYS

Second place in the wheat category in the 1996 Queen of Beers contest.

    4 oz. (113 g) roasted barley
    4 lb. (1.81 kg) pale malt extract
    4 lb. (1.81 kg) Alexander's wheat malt extract
    1 lb. (454 g) Yellow Star Thistle Honey
 1½ oz. (43 g) Fuggles hops, 4.3% alpha, in boil 60 min.
    1 tsp. (4.9 ml) Irish moss
   ½ oz. (14 g) Fuggles hops, 4.3% alpha, in boil 5 min.
       Doric ale yeast
 1¼ c. (340 g) Munton & Fison plain wheat dry extract, for priming
    1 tsp. (4.9 ml) gelatin, for priming
    1 tsp. (4.9 ml) ascorbic acid, for priming
    1 tsp. (4.9 ml) heading agent, for priming

Add grain to 2½ gal. (9.5 L) of water in a brewpot and heat to 160°F (71°C). Let steep for 30 min. Strain out grains and add extracts and honey. Bring to boil and add 1½ oz. (43 g) of Fuggles hops. Boil 45 min., then add Irish moss. Boil 10 min., then add ½ oz. (14 g) Fuggles hops. Boil 5 min. Turn off heat and chill the wort. Transfer wort to primary fermenter and top off to 5 gal. (18.9 L). Pitch yeast and ferment for 4 days. Rack to secondary fermenter and ferment for 11 days. Make a priming solution by first boiling 1¼ c. (340 g) Munton & Fison plain wheat dry extract in 1 pt. (473 ml)of water for 5 min. Remove from heat and add gelatin, ascorbic acid, and heading agent. Prime and bottle.

— *Nora Keller-Seeley, El Dorado Hills, California*
Hangtown Association of Zymurgy Enthusiasts (HAZE)

Mad Bee Wheat

YIELD: .... 5 GAL. (18.9 L)
TOTAL BOILING TIME: .... 60 MIN.
STARTING GRAVITY: 1.060
ENDING GRAVITY: 1.018
PRIMARY FERMENT: .... 7 DAYS
SECONDARY FERMENT: .... 7 DAYS

This beer has a lot of residual sweetness and citric overtones from the Cascade.

4 lb. (1.81 kg) wheat malt extract (60% barley, 40% wheat)
3½ lb. (1.59 kg) light malt extract
1½ lb. (680 g) orange-blossom honey
1½ oz. (43 g) Hallertauer hops, 3.1% alpha, in boil 60 min.
½ oz. (14 g) Cascade hops, 5.5% alpha, in boil 10 min.
½ oz. (14 g) Cascade hops, 5.5% alpha, 10 min. steep
    Wyeast #3068 Weihenstephan Wheat Ale yeast, in 25.4-oz.
    (750-ml) starter
¾ c. (206 ml) corn sugar, for priming

Heat 2 gal. (8 L) of water to 170°F (77°C). Turn off heat and add malt extracts and honey, stirring well. Turn on heat and bring to a boil. Add 1½ oz. (43 g) of Hallertauer hops and boil 50 min. Add ½ oz. (14 g) of Cascade hops and boil 10 min. Turn off heat, add final ½ oz. (14 g) of Cascade hops, and let steep for 10 min. Chill the wort, transfer to fermenter, and top off to 5 gal. (18.9 L) with cold water. Pitch yeast and ferment 2 days at 65°–70°F (18°–21°C), then lower fermentation temperature to 62°–65°F (17°–18°C) for another 5 days. Rack to secondary at 62°–65°F (17°–18°C) for 7 days. Prime with corn sugar and bottle.

— *Woody Weaver, Oakland, California*

Red, Weiss-en, Brew

YIELD: .... 5 GAL. (18.9 L)
TOTAL BOILING TIME: .... 60 MIN.
STARTING GRAVITY: 1.068
ENDING GRAVITY: 1.018
PRIMARY FERMENT: ....9 DAYS AT 65°F (18°C)
SECONDARY FERMENT: .....11 DAYS AT 65°F (18°C)

Reddish gold color with a crisp, bold wheat flavor and a touch of alcohol.

Wyeast #3056 Bavarian Weizen yeast, 3-c. (710-ml) starter
3 lb. (1.36 kg) light dry malt extract
6.6 lb. (3 kg) Ireks 100% wheat extract
½ lb. (227 g) Victory malt
½ lb. (227 g) crystal malt, 20° Lovibond
½ lb. (227 g) wheat malt
1½ oz. (43 g) crystal hops, 3.2% alpha, in boil 60 min.
1 tsp. (4.9 ml) Irish moss
½ oz. (14 g) crystal hops, 3.2% alpha, in boil 5 min.
½ c. (138 ml) corn sugar, for priming
½ c. (138 ml) maple syrup, for priming
2 tbsp. (30 ml) orange-blossom honey, for priming

Make a yeast starter 2–3 days before brewing.
Mash grains at 155°F (68°C) for 60 min. in 2½ gal. (9.4 L) of water. Sparge with 1 gal. (3.8 L) of 170°F (77°C) water. Bring to a boil and add malt extracts and 1½ oz. (43 g) of crystal hops. Boil 45 min., then add Irish moss. Boil 10 min., then add ½ oz. (14 g) of crystal hops. Boil 5 min. Chill to 70°F (21°C), transfer to fermenter, and pitch yeast. Ferment 9 days at 65°F (18°C). Transfer to secondary for 11 days. Prime with corn sugar, maple syrup, and orange-blossom honey, then bottle.

— *Jonathan Sutter, Sarasota, Florida*

Wheat Beer

YIELD: .... 5 GAL. (18.9 L)
TOTAL BOILING TIME: .... 60 MIN.
STARTING GRAVITY: 1.046
ENDING GRAVITY: 1.011
PRIMARY FERMENT: .... 1 WEEK
SECONDARY FERMENT: .... 1 WEEK

1 package Windsor ale yeast, or Wyeast #3056
½ lb. (227 g) wheat malt
½ lb. (227 g) 6-row malt
¼ lb. (113 g) cara-pils malt
6 lb. (2.72 kg) wheat malt extract
½ oz. (14 g) Perle hop pellets, in boil 55 min.
½ oz. (14 g) Hallertauer Hersbrucker hops, in boil 15 min.
½ oz. (14 g) Hallertauer Hersbrucker hops, steep
1 package Bru-Vigor yeast food
¾ c. (206 ml) corn sugar, for priming

Prepare yeast starter a few days prior to brewing day.

Crush grains and add to 1 gal. (3.8 L) of 160°F (71°C) water and steep 30 min. Rinse grains with 1 gal. (3.8 L) or more of 168°F (76°C) water into brew kettle. Bring wort to a boil, then turn off heat and add malt extract. Boil 5 min. before adding ½ oz. (14 g) of Perle hop pellets. Boil 40 min., then add ½ oz. (14 g) of Hallertauer Hersbrucker hops. Boil 15 min., add last ½ oz. (14 g) of hops, and turn off heat. Steep a few min., then chill the wort, transfer to fermenter, and top off to 5 gal. (18.9 L) with cold water. Pitch yeast along with Bru-Vigor yeast food. Ferment 1 week. Rack to a secondary for another week. Prime with corn sugar and bottle.

— *DeFalco's Home Wine & Beer Supplies, Houston, Texas*

Uncle Paddy's
Whiskey Wheat

YIELD: .... 15 GAL. (18.9 L)
TOTAL BOILING TIME: .... 90 MIN.
STARTING GRAVITY: 1.057
ENDING GRAVITY: 1.009
PRIMARY FERMENT: .... 14 DAYS

First place in the Fermental Order of Renaissance Draughtsmen's
December 1995 Holiday Ale competition.

    10 lb. (4.54 kg) Belgian wheat malt
     9 lb. (4.08 kg) Briess pale malt
     1 lb. (454 g) Gambrinus Honey Malt
     1 oz. (28 g) crystal hops, 3.9% alpha, in boil 60 min.
     2 oz. (57 g) crystal hops, 3.9% alpha, in boil 30 min.
     1 tbsp. (14.8 ml) Irish moss
    10 lb. (4.54 kg) clover honey
     1 oz. (28 g) crystal hops, 3.9% alpha, in boil 5 min.
     1 tbsp. (14.8 ml) gelatin
        Wyeast #1056 American Ale yeast, 3-qt. (2.8-L) starter
  1½ c. (355 ml) honey, for priming

Mash grains in 6.6 gal. (25 L) of untreated 140°F (60°C) water. Mash temperature should settle out to 133°F (56°C). Mash at 133°F (56°C) for
30 min. Heat to 152°F (67°C) and hold for 90 min. Mash-out at 170°F
(77°C) for 15 min. Sparge with 170°F (77°C) water and collect 15 gal. (18.9
L) of wort. Boil 30 min. Add 1 oz. (28 g) of crystal hops and boil
30 min. Add 2 oz. (57 g) of crystal hops and boil 15 min. Add Irish moss and
boil 10 min. Add honey and 1 oz. (28 g) of crystal hops. Boil 5 min. Turn off
heat and chill wort. Transfer to three 5-gal. (18.9-L) fermenters. Pitch
yeast and top off with cold water, allowing for headspace. Attach blow-off
tubes and ferment. When kraeusen falls, replace blow-off tubes with air
locks. After 14 days of fermentation, boil gelatin in 3 pt. (1.4 L) of
water for 5 min. Add 1 pt. (473 ml) to each fermenter and allow to stand
for 2 – 3 days. Mix 1½ c. (355 ml) of honey with 3 pt. (1.4 L) of water. Use
1 pt. (473 ml) per fermenter for priming, and bottle.

                                    — Pat Babcock, Canton Township, Michigan
                    The Fermental Order of Renaissance Draughtsmen (FORD)

'R' Squared

YIELD: .... 5 GAL. (18.9 L)
TOTAL BOILING TIME: .... 60 MIN.
STARTING GRAVITY: 1.052
ENDING GRAVITY: 1.011
PRIMARY FERMENT: .... 1 WEEK
SECONDARY FERMENT: .... 1 WEEK

*First place in the wheat beer category at the 1994 Emerald Coast
Brewfest and at the 1995 Trub VII. Full flavored with a hint of hops.*

 3 lb. (1.36 kg) 2-row pale malt
 3 lb. (1.36 kg) wheat malt
 ½ lb. (227 g) aromatic malt
 ½ lb. (227 g) cara-pils malt
2½ lb. (1.13 kg) clover honey
 ½ oz. (14 g) Northern Brewer hops, 7.5% alpha, in boil 60 min.
 ½ oz. (14 g) Fuggles hops, 3.6% alpha, in boil 20 min.
 ½ oz. (14 g) Fuggles hops, 3.6% alpha, in boil 2 min.
    Yeast Lab A07 Canadian Ale
 ¾ c. (206 ml) corn sugar, for priming

Mash-in grains with 1¾ gal. (6.6 L) of 143°F (62°C) water for protein rest
at 130°F (54°C) for 30 min. Add 1 gal. (3.8 L) of boiling water to raise the
mash temperature to 152°F (67°C). Mash at 152°F (67°C) for 60 min., or
until starch conversion is complete. Sparge with 5 gal. (18.9 L) of
167°F (75°C) water. Bring to a boil and add honey and Northern Brewer
hops. Boil 40 min., then add ½ oz. (14 g) of Fuggles hops. Boil 18 min.,
then add last ½ oz. (14 g) of Fuggles hops. Boil 2 min. and turn off heat.
Chill the wort, transfer to fermenter, and pitch yeast. Ferment 1 week at
68°F (20°C), then rack to secondary for 1 week. Prime with corn sugar
and bottle.

Bill Dunning, Langley Air Force Base, Virginia
Hampton Roads Brewing & Tasting Society

More HOMEBREW FAVORITES

12

Fruit Beers

Fruit beer is not a style of beer; rather, it reflects an ingredient added to a beer of another style to materially affect its flavor, aroma, and color. Most commonly, the base beer used for a fruit beer will be a fairly light-bodied, nonassertive style that will combine with the often subtle and elusive fruit flavors. Heavier-bodied or assertively flavored base beers may dominate the fruit flavors to the point where no fruit flavor is detectable. There are exceptions to these rules, and some homebrewers and craft brewers have enjoyed great success with very heavy base beers, a raspberry imperial stout, for example. When using assertively flavored base beers, however, the amount of fruit must be very high, so high that the beer can be extravagantly expensive. Light lagers, pale ales, and wheat beers make good base beers for fruit beers, and all of these have been used from time to time in commercial craft breweries.

Balance is the key to a successful fruit beer. The flavors of the base beer must be perceptible, yet they cannot mask the fruit. Fruit can also add flavor elements that need to be balanced with flavors of beer. For example, fruits generally contain acid, which provides

KEY TO RECIPE LOGOS

 EXTRACT RECIPES   PARTIAL MASH RECIPES   ALL-GRAIN RECIPES

a tart flavor. An artistic brewer is aware of the contribution of acid to the flavor profile of the beer, and balances it, perhaps with a maltier, sweeter base beer for high-acid fruits. Whereas bitterness from hops is often used to balance malt sweetness, the hops can be decreased in fruit beers because the acid will, to some degree, balance the sweetness.

In classic styles, fruit is generally regarded as an ingredient that has no place in brewing. Many purists in the homebrewing and craft-brewing industries view fruit beers as toys for novices, yet one of the great advantages of homebrewing is that experimentation with flavor combinations — like fruit beer — can yield fabulous tastes that no commercial brewery could market. In the commercial brewing arena, it seems that only the Belgians have a history of working with fruit beers prior to today's craft-brewing revolution. Belgian lambic ales have, for many years, been available in versions flavored with raspberries, cherries, and other fruits.

There are four points in the brewing process at which fruit can be added to a beer, and each has its advantages and disadvantages. These points are: in the kettle, in the primary fermenter, in the secondary fermenter, and at bottling.

Two considerations, both important to the brewer, come into conflict when developing fruit beer recipes. On the one hand, sanitation is always a vitally important part of the brewing process, and heat-treating the fruit will help ensure that infections are not spread to the beer. Heat has the added advantage of denaturing numerous enzymes contained in fruit that could render complex sugars fermentable, giving you a gushing bottle of beer. On the other hand, the often delicate and elusive fruit aromas and flavors can be damaged and fruit color changed by heat. Further, heat can set up pectin in the fruit, causing it to gel and thus be difficult to work with. The latter problem can be solved with the judicious use of enzymes, such as pectinase, but no magic solution exists to cure destroyed aroma.

Fruit flavors and aromas can come from a number of sources, including fresh fruit, fruit juices, processed fruit, jams, fruit essences, fruit wine bases, fruit-flavored liqueurs, and even fruit-flavored teas. While purists maintain that fresh fruit gives the cleanest, most natural flavor, it is often difficult to work with. Many homebrew-supply shops sell fruit extracts that are inexpensive and easy to use. Some craft brewers use packaged, processed fruit that comes in plastic bags. Although this is available to the homebrewing community, it's difficult to find.

Technique. Fruit can be added at any of several steps in the brewing process. Currently, most homebrewers favor adding fresh fruit to the secondary fermenter because many of the delicate aromas can be lost in a vigorous primary fermentation, and the alcohol is high enough to inhibit bacteria growth. One of the best ways of handling fresh fruit is the method described by Charlie Papazian in his *New Complete Joy of Homebrewing*. He suggests that at the end of the boil, add the fruit when the wort is between 150 and 180°F (66 and 82°C). Let it steep for 15 minutes or so. This is hot enough to sanitize the fruit and denature enzymes, but not so hot that it should materially affect the flavor. A different solution suggested by Randy Mosher in his *Brewer's Companion* is to soak fruit in vodka, creating what he calls "potions." Mosher also suggests adding liqueurs, which should work well when added just before bottling. Fruit juices work best when added to the secondary fermenter. Artificial fruit flavors work best when they are added at bottling.

The amount of fruit added to a beer depends on the base style, the flavor desired, and the nature of the fruit. A good starting point is 1 lb. (454 g) of fruit per gallon of beer. Subtle fruits, like strawberries, might well require substantially more. Strongly flavored fruits — cranberries, for example — might do well with less.

Fruit beers need a longer secondary fermentation time than do beers of equivalent styles made without fruit. The yeast and enzymes must have time to break down and ferment the fruit to avoid possible overcarbonation and to allow the flavors to meld fully with the beer. A secondary fermentation of up to two months may be needed.

In competition, fruit beers will be judged on how well the fruit flavors express themselves. As always, balance is key. The drink should obviously be a beer, but the fruit should also manifest itself. If the fruit cannot be identified in the beer, it will do poorly in the fruit beer category. Similarly, if its fruit flavor is too assertive, tastes artificial, or tastes like a soft drink instead of a beer, it won't do well.

Judges also look for acid balance in fruit beer categories. If highly acidic fruit is used, some tartness is to be expected. If the judge notices a candylike fruit flavor in a beer made with a fruit that is normally acidic, without tartness, he or she may suspect that the beer is not a natural fruit beer, or may feel that it does not exemplify a beer made with that particular fruit. Fruit beer brewers may consider filtering their beer, as many fruit beers have a haze problem that could keep them from winning.

BLUEBERRY BEERS

Blueberry Wheat

YIELD: .... 5 GAL. (18.9 L)
TOTAL BOILING TIME: .... 60 MIN.
STARTING GRAVITY: 1.049
ENDING GRAVITY: 1.008
PRIMARY FERMENT: .... 1 WEEK
SECONDARY FERMENT: .... 2 WEEKS

This beer has a wonderful pinkish cast and the blueberries combine with the Hallertauer hops to produce a unique fruity/floral flavor and aroma. The hops versus the malt is very well balanced.

    5 lb. (2.27 kg) Belgian wheat malt
    3 lb. (1.36 kg) English pale ale malt
    1 lb. (454 g) Belgian Munich malt
 2½ oz. (71 g) Hallertauer hops, 2.8% alpha, in boil 60 min.
    ½ oz. (14 g) Hallertauer hops, in boil 10 min.
 1½ lb. (680 g) frozen blueberries
       Glenbrew dry ale yeast
 2–3 jars natural blueberry extract
    ¾ c. (206 ml) corn sugar, for priming

Mash grains in 3 gal. (11.4 L) of water at 155°F (68°C) for 40 min., or until starch conversion is completed. Mash-out at 170°F (77°C) for 5 min. Sparge with 170°F (77°C) water and collect 6 gal. (22.7 L) of wort. Bring wort to a boil and add 2 ½ oz. (71 g) of Hallertauer hops. Boil 50 min., then add ½ oz. (14 g) of Hallertauer hops. Boil 10 min. and turn off heat. Allow the temperature to drop to 180°F (82°C), then add the frozen blueberries. Steep 10 min., then chill the wort to 80°F (27°C). Transfer to primary fermenter and pitch yeast. Ferment 1 week. Rack to secondary fermenter and add 2 or 3 jars of blueberry extract to taste. Ferment another 2 weeks and prime with corn sugar, and bottle.

— *Julianne Targan, Hop & Vine, Morristown, New Jersey*

Purple Cow Ale

YIELD: .... 5 GAL. (18.9 L)
TOTAL BOILING TIME: .... 60 MIN.
STARTING GRAVITY: 1.042
ENDING GRAVITY: 1.006
PRIMARY FERMENT: .... 4 DAYS
SECONDARY FERMENT: .... 14 DAYS
TERTIARY FERMENT: .... 4 WEEKS

Purple color, like a burgundy wine, with hops balancing malt sweetness.

        Wyeast #1338 European Ale yeast, in 1-qt. (1-L) starter
7 lb. (3.18 kg) blueberries, cleaned and frozen
4 lb. (1.81 kg) 2-row pale malt
3 lb. (1.36 kg) Munich malt
1 lb. (454 g) cara-Munich malt
   spring water for mashing and sparging
1 oz. (28 g) Hallertauer hops, 3.9% alpha, in boil 60 min.
⅓ oz. (9 g) Tettnanger hops, 3.8% alpha, in boil 20 min.
⅓ oz. (9 g) Tettnanger hops, in boil 15 min.
⅓ oz. (9 g) Tettnanger hops, in boil 10 min.
2 Campden tablets
¾ c. (206 ml) corn sugar, for priming (if bottling)

Make a 1-qt. (1-L) yeast starter prior to brewing. Clean and freeze blueberries.

Add crushed 2-row and Munich malts to 2 ½ gal. (9.4 L) of water at room temperature (reserve 1 lb. (454 g) of cara-Munich for later). Heat mash slowly to 122°F (50°C) and let rest for 1 hour, stirring every 15 min. Heat slowly to 157°F (69°C) and hold for 40 min. Heat slowly to 170°F (77°C) and add cara-Munich malt. Rest 10 min. Sparge with 4½ gal. (17 L) of 170°F (77°C) water. Collect approximately 6 ½ gal. (24.6 L) of wort in brew kettle. Bring wort to a boil and add Hallertauer hops. Boil 40 min., then add ⅓ oz. (9 g) of Tettnanger hops. Boil 5 min., then add ⅓ oz. (9 g) of Tettnanger hops. Boil 5 min., then add the final ⅓ oz. (9 g) of Tettnanger hops. Boil 5 more min., then turn off heat. Chill wort and transfer to a 7-gal. (26.5-L) plastic fermenter. Pitch yeast and ferment at 68°F (20°C). Three days into the ferment, thaw the blueberries and add with 1 qt. (946 ml) of sterile water to a second sanitized 7-gal. (26.5-L) plastic fermenter. Mash the blueberries with a sanitized potato masher and mix in 2 crushed Campden tablets. Cover and let sit 24 hours. Rack beer from the primary fermenter into the fermenter containing the blueberries, mixing gently. Continue fermenting for 14 days at 68°F (20°C), then rack to a glass carboy for 9 days at 68°F (20°C), then drop temperature to 38°F (3°C) and continue fermenting for 3 weeks. Keg or bottle.

— Chris Kaufman, Minneapolis, Minnesota

RASPBERRY BEERS

Ripcord Raspberry Ale

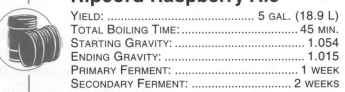

YIELD: .... 5 GAL. (18.9 L)
TOTAL BOILING TIME: .... 45 MIN.
STARTING GRAVITY: 1.054
ENDING GRAVITY: 1.015
PRIMARY FERMENT: .... 1 WEEK
SECONDARY FERMENT: .... 2 WEEKS

    1 lb. (454 g) crystal malt, 60° Lovibond
  3.3 lb. (1.5 kg) Munton & Fison light malt extract
  3.3 lb. (1.5 kg) Munton & Fison amber malt extract
  1¼ lb. (567 g) light clover honey
    1 oz. (28 g) Northern Brewer hops, 7.0% alpha, in boil 45 min.
    1 oz. (28 g) Cascade hops, 4.5% alpha, in boil 20 min.
    1 tsp. (4.9 ml) Irish moss
  1½ oz. (43 g) Fuggles hops, 4.0% alpha, in boil 5 min.
   24 oz. (680 g) frozen raspberries
      Wyeast #1056 American Ale yeast
  ¾ c. (206 ml) corn sugar, for priming

Steep grain in a grain bag for 20 min. in 1 gal. (3.8 L) of 150°F (66°C) water. Remove bag, then add malt extracts and honey. Bring to a boil and add Northern Brewer hops. Boil 25 min., then add Cascade hops. Boil 5 min.; add Irish moss. Boil 10 min.; add 1½ oz. (43 ml) of Fuggles hops. Boil 5 min. and turn off heat. While boiling, make a raspberry tea by adding the frozen berries in a grain bag to 1 qt. (946 ml) of boiled water. Steep 15 – 20 min.; remove bag and squeeze out all liquid. Add raspberry tea to wort, chill the wort and add to 5 gal. of 150°F (66°C) water. Pitch yeast and let ferment 1 week. Rack to secondary fermenter for 2 weeks. Prime with corn sugar and bottle.

— *Jerry Narowski, Derby, Connecticut, Reindeer Homebrewers*

Nutberry Ale

YIELD: .... 5 GAL. (18.9 L)
TOTAL BOILING TIME: .... 60 MIN.
PRIMARY FERMENT: .... 10 DAYS
SECONDARY FERMENT: .... 7 DAYS

Tart taste of raspberry with a sweet nutmeg finish.

6.6 lb. (3 kg) Munton & Fison amber malt extract
  2 oz. (57 g) Hallertauer hops, 2.5% alpha, in boil 60 min.
 ⅓ tsp. (17 ml) ground nutmeg
    Cooper's dry ale yeast
  4 lb. (1.81 kg) frozen raspberries
 ½ c. (138 ml) corn sugar, for priming

Add malt extract syrup to 1½ gal. (5.7 L) of water and bring to a boil. Add hops and boil 40 min. Add nutmeg and boil 20 min. Turn off heat, cool, and transfer to fermenter. Bring up to 5 gal. (18.9 L) with cold water and pitch yeast. Add raspberries when the active fermentation begins. Ferment 10 days, then transfer to secondary for 7 days. Prime and bottle.

— *Mark D. Sullivan, Laurel, Maryland*
Chesapeake Real Ale Brewers (CRAB)

Raspberry Wheat

YIELD: .... 5 GAL. (18.9 L)
TOTAL BOILING TIME: .... 45 MIN.
PRIMARY FERMENT: .... 7 DAYS
SECONDARY FERMENT: .... 2 DAYS

Light and enjoyable with just a touch of raspberry.

3.3 lb. (1.5 kg) Premier wheat malt extract
  2 lb. (907 g) extra light dry malt extract
  1 lb. (454 g) corn sugar
 ½ oz. (14 g) Hallertauer hops, 3.3% alpha, in boil 30 min.
  1 tsp. (4.9 ml) Irish moss
    Wyeast #1056 American Ale yeast
 ½ oz. (14.8 ml) raspberry soda mix, in keg

Add malt extracts and corn sugar to 2 gal. (7.6 L) of water. Bring to a boil and add the Hallertauer hops. Boil 30 min., then add the Irish moss. Boil 15 min. and turn off heat. Chill wort, transfer to fermenter, and top off to 5 gal. (18.9 L) with cold water. Pitch yeast and ferment 7 days. Rack to secondary for 2 days. Keg, add ½ oz. (14.8 ml) raspberry soda mix, and force carbonate.

— Ronald J. Sup, Morrow, Ohio, Bloatarian Brewing League

——Raspberry Cinnamon Wheat—

YIELD: .... 5 GAL. (18.9 L)
TOTAL BOILING TIME: .... 60 MIN.
PRIMARY FERMENT: .... 7 DAYS

- 4 lb. (1.81 kg) fresh (or frozen) whole raspberries, pureed in blender
- 4 lb. (1.81 kg) Munton's plain wheat dry extract
- 3.3 lb. (1.5 kg) Brewferm Raspberry Framboise extract
- 5 4-in. (10.2 cm) cinnamon sticks
- 2 oz. (57 g) Hallertauer hops, 3.2% alpha, in boil 60 min.
- 1 oz. (28 g) Saaz hops, 5.4% alpha, in boil 60 min.
- 1 oz. (28 g) Hallertauer hops, in boil 30 min.
- 1 oz. (28 g) Saaz hops, in boil 30 min.
- 1 tsp. (4.9 ml) Irish moss
- 1 oz. (28 g) Tettnanger hops, 3.4% alpha, in boil 10 min.
- 5 gal. (18.9 L) spring water
  Wyeast #3068 Weihenstephan Wheat yeast
- ¾ c. (206 ml) corn sugar, for priming

Add 3 gal. (11.4 L) of water and pureed raspberries to the primary fermenter. Cover and set aside. Bring 2 gal. (7.6 L) of water and extracts to a boil. Add cinnamon sticks, 2 oz. (57 g) of Hallertauer hops, and 1 oz. (28 g) of Saaz hops. Boil 30 min., then add 1 oz. (28 g) each of Hallertauer and Saaz hops. Boil 15 min., then add Irish moss. Boil 5 min., then add 1 oz. (28 g) of Tettnanger hops. Boil 10 min. and turn off heat. Chill wort, transfer to fermenter, and pitch yeast. Ferment 7 days at 68° – 70°F

(20° – 21°C), then strain through cheesecloth or muslin to remove berry seeds. Prime with corn sugar and bottle.

— Mitchell Rogers, Prospect Heights, Illinois

Malt 'N' Hop Stop Brew Club

Raspberry Spring Ale

YIELD: .... 5 GAL. (18.9 L)
TOTAL BOILING TIME: .... 60 MIN.
PRIMARY FERMENT: .... 7 DAYS
SECONDARY FERMENT: .... 3 WEEKS

½ lb. (227 g) crystal malt, 40° Lovibond
6.6 lb. (3 kg) Northwestern amber malt extract
2 oz. (57 g) Tettnanger hops, 5.0% alpha, in boil 60 min.
1 oz. (28 g) Willamette hops, 4.0% alpha, in boil 15 min.
1 tsp. (4.9 ml) Irish moss
1 oz. (28 g) Willamette hops, in boil 2 min.
1.18 oz. (33.5 g) (1 full box) Bigelow red raspberry herb tea bags
Edme ale yeast
¾ c. (206 ml) corn sugar, for priming

Add crystal malt to 2 gal. (7.6 L) of water and heat to 170°F (77°C). Strain out grains and add malt extract and 2 oz. (57 g) of Tettnanger hops. Boil 45 min. Add 1 oz. (28 g) of Willamette hops and Irish moss. Boil 13 min. Add last oz. of Willamette hops and boil 2 min. Turn off heat and add tea. Steep 20 min. Chill the wort, then strain the wort through the tea bags. Rinse the tea bags with 1 gal. (3.8 L) of water. Top off fermenter to 5 gal. (18.9 L). Pitch yeast when wort is below 75°F (24°C) and aerate well. Ferment 1 week. Rack to secondary for 3 more weeks. Prime with corn sugar and bottle.

— Robert Clapper, Grand Rapids, Michigan, Prime Time Brewers

"The Cat's Ras"

YIELD: .... 5 GAL. (18.9 L)
TOTAL BOILING TIME: .... 30 MIN.
STARTING GRAVITY: 1.042
ENDING GRAVITY: 1.001
PRIMARY FERMENT: .... 4 DAYS
SECONDARY FERMENT: .... 2 – 4 DAYS

Clear, crisp brew with a great raspberry nose and a faintly tart aftertaste. The head is pearly white and creamy.

   4 lb. (1.81 kg) Muntons Connoisseur Range hopped pilsner extract
   8 oz. (227 g) orange-blossom honey
1½ lb. (680 g) corn sugar
   1 oz. (28 g) Hallertauer hop pellets, 2.4% alpha, in boil 30 min.
   2 lb. (907 g) fresh raspberries
  ½ oz. (14 g) Hallertauer hop pellets, 15 min. steep
0.21 oz. (6 g) dry lager yeast
0.18 oz. (5 g) dry ale yeast
  ¾ c. (206 ml) corn sugar, for priming
  1 tbsp. (14.8 ml) beverage settler, for priming

Boil extract, honey, 1½ lb. (680 g) corn sugar, and 1 oz. (28 g) of Hallertauer hop pellets in 1½ gal. (5.7 L) of water for 30 min. Remove from heat; allow the wort to cool to below 180°F (82°C). Add raspberries and ½ oz. (14 g) of Hallertauer hop pellets; steep 15 min. Transfer the wort to primary fermenter (fruit included); pitch yeast when the wort has cooled to below 80°F. When fermentation slows, about 4 days later, rack to secondary, straining out fruit. Ferment in secondary 2 – 4 days. Bottle with corn sugar and beverage settler and bottle. Age at least 10 days.

— *Marc Battreall, Plantation Key, Florida*

┌──Red Raspberry Wheat──

YIELD: .... 5 GAL. (18.9 L)
TOTAL BOILING TIME: .... 30 MIN.
STARTING GRAVITY: 1.045
ENDING GRAVITY: 1.015
PRIMARY FERMENT: .... 4 DAYS
SECONDARY FERMENT: .... 8 DAYS

Ruby red color with the aroma and flavor of fresh raspberry.

- 1 lb. (454 g) light crystal malt
- 6.6 lb. (3 kg) Munton & Fison wheat extract
- ¼ lb. (113 g) clover honey
- ½ oz. (14 g) Fuggles leaf hops, in boil 30 min.
- 1 tsp. (4.9 ml) Irish moss
- ½ oz. (14 g) Fuggles leaf hops, in boil 3 min.
- 2½ lb. (1.13 kg) frozen red raspberries, thawed and crushed
  Edme ale yeast
- ⅔ c. (184 ml) corn sugar, for priming

Crush grain and steep in 1 qt. (946 ml) of water at 155°F (68°C) for 10 min. Strain out grains and add 1 gal. (3.8 L) of cold water, wheat extract, and honey. Bring to a boil and add ½ oz. (14 g) of Fuggles hops and Irish moss. Boil 27 min., then add ½ oz. (14 g) of Fuggles leaf hops. Boil 3 min. and turn off heat. Cool wart to 170°F (77°C) and add crushed raspberries. Steep at 160°F (71°C) for 20 min. Pour into primary fermenter containing 3 gal. (11.4 L) of cold water. Top off to 5 gal. (18.9 L) with cold water. Pitch yeast when wort is below 80°F (27°C). Ferment 4 days. Carefully strain off surface fruit and rack to secondary for 8 days, then prime with corn sugar and bottle.

— *Gloria Franconi, Red Hook, New York, Hudson Valley Homebrewers*

Raspberry Ale

YIELD: .... 5½ GAL. (20.8 L)
TOTAL BOILING TIME: .... 10 MIN.
PRIMARY FERMENT: .... 1 WEEK
SECONDARY FERMENT: .... 1 WEEK

Wyeast #3056 Bavarian Wheat yeast, 1-pt. (300-ml starter)
6.6 lb. (3 kg) Premier wheat extract
1 tsp. (4.9 ml) grape tannin
½ tsp. (2.5 ml) Irish moss
¾ c. (206 ml) corn sugar, for priming
4 oz. (118 ml) raspberry concentrate, for priming
1 tsp. (4.9 ml) ascorbic acid, for priming

Prepare starter from liquid yeast in advance of brew day.

Bring 3 gal. (11.4 L) of water to a boil. Turn off heat and add the wheat extract, grape tannin, and Irish moss. Boil 10 min. Turn off heat, chill the wort, and transfer to fermenter. Pitch yeast and top off to 5½ gal. (20.8 L). Ferment 1 week, then rack to secondary for 1 more week. Prime with ¾ c. (206 ml) corn sugar, raspberry concentrate, ascorbic acid, and 1 pt. (473 ml) of boiled water. Bottle or keg.

— *Neil Flatter, Terre Haute, Indiana*
Wabash Valley Vintners' and Homebrewers' Club

Stras"berry" Ale

YIELD: .... 5 GAL. (18.9 L)
TOTAL BOILING TIME: .... 60 MIN.
STARTING GRAVITY: 1.061
ENDING GRAVITY: 1.013
PRIMARY FERMENT: .... 5 DAYS
SECONDARY FERMENT: .... 9 DAYS

7 lb. (3.18 kg) light dry malt extract
½ oz. (14 g) Saaz hops, 3.9% alpha, in boil 60 min.
½ oz. (14 g) Saaz hops, in boil 2 min.
4½ lb. (2.04 kg) strawberries, crushed
3 lb. (1.36 kg) raspberries, crushed
1 tsp. (4.9 ml) amylase enzyme
1 pack Cordon Brew yeast energizer

Munton & Fison ale yeast
¾ c. (206 ml) corn sugar, for priming

Add malt extract to 5 gal. (18.9 L) of water and bring to boil. Add ½ oz. (14 g) Saaz hops and boil 58 min. Add ½ oz. (14 g) Saaz hops. Boil 2 min. and turn off heat. Add crushed fruit, amylase enzyme, and yeast energizer; cover and steep 20 min. Chill wort and transfer to fermenter. Pitch yeast and ferment 5 days at 70°F (21°C). Rack to secondary, discarding fruit. Ferment 9 days at 70°F (21°C). Prime with corn sugar and bottle.

— *Ed Cosgrove and Rory Schultz, Woodbridge, Virginia*
Brewers Association of Northern Virginia (BANOVA)

Thptzzt!

YIELD: .... 5 GAL. (18.9 L)
TOTAL BOILING TIME: .... 60 MIN.
STARTING GRAVITY: 1.050
ENDING GRAVITY: 1.014
PRIMARY FERMENT: .... 5 DAYS
SECONDARY FERMENT: .... 4 WEEKS

Third place in the specialty beer category at the 16th Annual AugustFest.

  5 lb. (2.27 kg) pilsner malt
  2 lb. (907 g) wheat malt
  ½ lb. (227 g) crystal malt, 80° Lovibond
  ¼ lb. (113 g) flaked wheat
  1 oz. (28 g) Mt. Hood hops, 5.3% alpha, in boil 60 min.
  4 oz. (113 g) HopTech raspberry extract
     Wyeast #3056 Bavarian Weizen yeast
  ¾ c. (206 ml) corn sugar, for priming

Crush grains and add to 10 qt. (9.46 L) of 168°F (76°C) water. Mash 60 min. Sparge with 5 gal. (18.9 L) of 170°F (77°C) water. Bring to a boil and add Mt. Hood hops. Boil 60 min., then turn off heat. Chill wort, transfer to fermenter, add raspberry extract, and pitch yeast. Ferment 5 days at 68°F (20°C). Rack to secondary for 4 weeks at 60°F (16°C). Prime with corn sugar and bottle.

— *Keith Schwols, Ft. Collins, Colorado*

BLACKBERRY BEERS

┌─Whitely's Dark Wheat─

YIELD: .... 5 GAL. (18.9 L)
TOTAL BOILING TIME: .... 30 MIN.
STARTING GRAVITY: 1.038
ENDING GRAVITY: 1.008
PRIMARY FERMENT: .... 5 DAYS
SECONDARY FERMENT: .... 3 WEEKS

Delicious light, dark beer with a blackberry aftertaste.

   4 lb.(1.81 kg) Alexander's wheat extract
1.4 lb.(635 g) Alexander's Kicker dark malt extract
   1 lb. (454 g) amber spray dried malt extract
   1 oz. (28 g) Cluster hops, 7.0% alpha, in boil 30 min.
   1 oz. (28 g) Hallertauer hops, 3.1% alpha, in boil 2 min.
   4 oz. (113 g) blackberry wine flavoring
     Wyeast #3056 Bavarian Weizen yeast
 ¾ c. (206 ml) corn sugar, for priming

Mix malt extracts with 1 gal. (3.8 L) of cold water and add 1 oz. (28 g) of Cluster hops. Boil 28 min., then add 1 oz. (28 g) of Hallertauer hops and blackberry wine flavoring. Boil 2 min., then turn off heat. Chill the wort, transfer to fermenter, and top off to 5 gal. (18.9 L) with cold water. Pitch yeast and ferment 5 days. Rack to secondary for 3 weeks, then prime with corn sugar, and bottle.

— *Carol A. Whitely, Arbor Wine & Beermaking Supplies*
East Islip, New York

Blackberry Porter

YIELD: .... 5 GAL. (18.9 L)
TOTAL BOILING TIME: .... 60 MIN.
STARTING GRAVITY: 1.076
ENDING GRAVITY: 1.024
PRIMARY FERMENT: .... 5 DAYS
SECONDARY FERMENT: .... 15 – 20 DAYS

Third place in the fruit beer category in the 1995 Santa Rosa Brewfest, Fort Walton Beach, Florida.

    3 c. (826 ml) crystal malt, 40° Lovibond
    3 c. (826 ml) Special-B malt
    ½ c. (138 ml) chocolate malt
    2 tbsp. (29.6 ml) gypsum
  6.6 lb. (3 kg) dry malt extract
    1 in. (2.5 cm) brewer's licorice
    8 oz. (227 g) malto-dextrin
    2 oz. (57 g) Liberty hops, 3.5% alpha, in boil 15 min.
    2 packs Munton & Fison ale yeast
    5 lb. (2.27 kg) frozen blackberries, thawed
    ¾ c. (206 ml) corn sugar, for priming

Place grains in a hop sack and add to 2½ gal. (9.4 L) of water treated with gypsum. Heat to 160°F (71°C) for 15 min. Sparge grains and remove. Bring wort to a boil, add dry malt extract, brewer's licorice, and boil 45 min. Add malto-dextrin and Liberty hops. Boil 15 min., then turn off heat. Chill the wort, transfer to fermenter, and top off to 5 gal. (18.9 L) with cold water. Pitch yeast and ferment 5 days. Add the thawed blackberries to a sanitized fermenter and rack the beer on top of the berries. Ferment 15 – 20 days. Rack beer very carefully into a bottling bucket, prime with corn sugar, and bottle.

— Bryan F. Schwab, Panama City, Florida

CRANBERRY BEER

Cranberry Ale

YIELD: .... 5 GAL. (18.9 L)
TOTAL BOILING TIME: .... 60 MIN.
STARTING GRAVITY: 1.060
ENDING GRAVITY: 1.012
PRIMARY FERMENT: .... 7 DAYS
SECONDARY FERMENT: .... 2 WEEKS

Second place in the Spirit of Free Beer competition.

¼ lb. (113 g) wheat malt
½ lb. (227 g) crystal malt, 80° Lovibond
3.3 lb. (1.5 kg) Munton & Fison extra light unhopped malt extract
3.3 lb. (1.5 kg) Northwestern Gold malt extract
⅕ lb. (91 g) thistle honey
1 oz. (28 g) Saaz hops, in boil 60 min.
1 oz. (28 g) Hallertauer hops, steep
24 oz. (680 g) cranberries
Wyeast #1056 American Ale yeast
1 tbsp. (14.8 ml) pectinase enzyme
18 oz. (510 g) cranberries, in secondary
¾ c. (206 ml) corn sugar, for priming

Steep wheat and crystal malt in 1 gal. (3.8 L) of 150°F (66°C) water for 35 min., then strain into boiler containing 4 gal. (15.1 L) water. Add malt extract and honey; boil 1 hour, adding 1 oz. (28 g) of Saaz hops at the beginning of the boil and the Hallertauer hops after removing wort from heat. Cool the wort and reserve about 1 pt. (473 ml). Add 24 oz. (680 g) cranberries and the pt. of removed wort to a blender and whirl briefly. Add cranberry mixture to chilled wort in a primary fermenter. Pitch yeast and ferment 7 days at 65°F (66°C). Rack to secondary, using a strainer on the racking tube; add pectinase enzyme. Add 18 oz. (510 g) of thawed and crushed cranberries. Ferment another 2 weeks, prime with corn sugar and bottle.

— Polly Goldman, Alexandria, Virginia
Brewers United for Real Potables (BURP)

PUMPKIN BEERS

Thanksgiving Pumpkin Ale

YIELD: .... 5 GAL. (18.9 L)
TOTAL BOILING TIME: .... 60 MIN.
STARTING GRAVITY: 1.040
PRIMARY FERMENT: .... 1 WEEK
SECONDARY FERMENT: .... 3 WEEKS

   2 sugar pumpkins, total prepared weight 4–5 lb. (1.81-2.27 kg)
   1 lb. (454 g) chocolate malt, crushed
   1 lb. (454 g) crystal malt, crushed
 6.6 lb. (3 kg) amber malt extract
 2½ oz. (71 g) Northern Brewer hops, in boil 60 min.
   6 sticks cinnamon
   1 tbsp. (14.8 ml) allspice
2 or 3 tsp. (29.6 or 44.4 ml) whole cloves
   1 tbsp. (14.8 ml) nutmeg
   1 tsp. (4.9 ml) Irish moss
   1 oz. (28 g) Willamette hops, in boil 5 min.
     ale yeast
  ¾ c. (206 ml) corn sugar, for priming

Split and clean 2 sugar pumpkins. Bake pumpkins at 350°F (177°C) for 1 hour. In a brew kettle, steep crushed grains in 2 gal. (7.6 ml) of 160°F (71°C) water. Strain out grains. Add malt extracts to brew kettle. Bring to a boil and add Northern Brewer hops, cinnamon, allspice, cloves, and nutmeg. Boil 40 min. Add pumpkin and Irish moss. Boil 15 min., then add Willamette hops. Boil 5 min. Turn off heat and strain wort during transfer to fermenter. Top off wort to 5 gal. (18.9 L). When wort is below 70°F (21°C), pitch yeast and ferment 1 week. Rack to secondary for 3 weeks. Two or 3 additional rackings during this time will improve clarity. Prime with corn sugar and bottle.

                — Lawrence and Elizabeth Vernaglia, Worcester, Massachusetts
                               New College Winemakers' Association

Pumpkin Ale #1

YIELD: .... 5 GAL. (18.9 L)
TOTAL BOILING TIME: .... 90 MIN.
PRIMARY FERMENT: .... 5 DAYS
SECONDARY FERMENT: .... 5 DAYS

Mild and smooth pumpkin flavor. Be sure to use diastatic malt extract!

     1 tsp. (4.9 ml) gypsum
12 ½ lb. (5.67 kg) fresh pumpkin, skinned, and cut into 1-inch
        chunks
   3.3 lb. (1.5 kg) Edme diastatic light malt extract
   3.1 lb. (1.4 kg) Alexander's pale malt extract
  1½ oz. (43 g) Willamette hops, in boil 60 min.
     5 tbsp. (74 ml) pumpkin pie spice
     1 tsp. (4.9 ml) Irish moss powder
        Wyeast #1056 American Ale yeast
   ½ c. (138 ml) corn sugar, for priming

Heat 5 gal. (18.9 L) water to about 160°F (71°C), then add gypsum and malt extracts, and pumpkin. Steep 30 minutes. Boil 15 min., then add hops and spice. Boil 45 min., then add Irish moss. Boil 15 min., then turn off heat. Chill the wort, transfer entire contents of brew kettle to a primary fermenter without straining. Pitch yeast and ferment 5 days. Rack to secondary, straining off and squeezing out the pumpkin. Ferment 5 days, then prime and bottle.

— *Heidi Gibson, Palo Alto, California*

Pumpkin Ale #2

YIELD: .... 5 GAL. (18.9 L)
TOTAL BOILING TIME: .... 90 MIN.
STARTING GRAVITY: 1.037
ENDING GRAVITY: 1.007
PRIMARY FERMENT: .... 7 DAYS
SECONDARY FERMENT: .... 10 DAYS

Orange-amber color with a flavor described as "liquid pumpkin pie."

    9 lb. (4.08 kg) fresh pumpkin
  3.3 lb. (1.5 kg) light malt extract
    2 lb. (907 g) amber dry malt extract
  1.4 lb. (635 g) Alexander's Kicker pale malt
    1 lb. (454 g) light dry malt extract
  ½ lb. (227 g) crystal malt, crushed
    1 oz. (28 g) Perle hops, in boil 90 min.
    1 oz. (28 g) Cascade hops, 6.1% alpha, in boil 90 min.
    1 oz. (28 g) Hallertauer hops, in boil 90 min.
    2 tsp. (9.4 ml) pumpkin pie spice
    1 tsp. (4.9 ml) ground nutmeg
    1 tsp. (4.9 ml) ground cinnamon
  ½ oz. (14 g) Cascade hops, 6.1% alpha, in boil 2 min.
      Wyeast #1214 Belgian Abbey yeast
  ¾ c. (206 ml) corn sugar, for priming

Peel, clean, and cut pumpkin into lengthwise pieces. Place in baking pan with ½ c. (118 ml) water. Cover pumpkin with foil and bake at 375°F (19°C) 30 min. Puree pumpkin in food processor. Add ½ lb. (227 g) crushed crystal malt to 1 gal. (3.8 L) water and steep at 160°F (71°C) for 20 min. Strain into brewpot. Add malt extracts and pumpkin to brew kettle with 4 gal. (15.1 L) water and bring to a boil. Add 1 oz. (28 g) each of Perle, Cascade, and Hallertauer hops. Boil 60 min. Add spices and boil 28 min. Add ½ oz. (14 g) of Cascade hops and boil 2 min. Turn off heat and chill wort. Strain wort while filling fermenter and pitch yeast. Ferment 7 days at 70°F (21°C), then rack to secondary for 10 days at 69°F (21°C). Prime with corn sugar and bottle.

— Ed Cosgrove and Rory Schultz, Woodbridge, Virginia
Brewers Association of Northern Virginia (BANOVA)

SQUASH BEER

Butternut Porter

YIELD: .... 5 GAL. (18.9 L)
TOTAL BOILING TIME: .... 75 MIN.
PRIMARY FERMENT: .... 7 DAYS
SECONDARY FERMENT: .... 10 DAYS

Third place in a Calgary homebrew competition.

    3 lb. (1.36 kg) butternut squash
    3 lb. (1.36 kg) 2-row pale malt, crushed
    1 lb. (454 g) dark caramel malt, crushed
    ½ lb. (227 g) black malt, crushed
 4.4 lb. (2 kg) light malt extract syrup
    1 oz. (28 g) Goldings hops, in boil 60 min.
    ½ oz. (14 g) Fuggles hops, in boil 45 min.
    ½ oz. (14 g) Goldings hops, in boil 30 min.
    ½ oz. (14 g) Goldings hops, in boil 15 min.
      Wyeast #1056 American Ale yeast
 2½ tsp. (12.3 ml) gypsum, if needed
    ¾ c. (206 ml) corn sugar, for priming

Peel and cut squash into pieces. Bake 30 min. at 375°F (191°C). Remove from oven. Put in blender and pulse to a mash consistency. Add 1 gal. (3.8 L) of water to squash mixture and raise temperature to 130°F (54°C). Add crushed grains. This should yield a temperature of about 125°F (52°C). Cover and rest 30 min. Raise temperature to 150°F (66°C) for 90 min. Sparge, collecting 6 ½ gal. (24.6 L) of wort. Bring wort to a boil, add extract syrup, and boil 15 min. Add 1 oz. (28 g) of Goldings hops and boil 15 min. Add Fuggles hops and boil 15 min. Add another ½ oz. (14 g) of Goldings hops and boil 15 min. Add another ½ oz. (14 g) of Goldings and boil 15 min. Remove from heat, force-chill the wort, transfer to fermenter, and pitch yeast. Ferment 1 week at 65°F (16°C). Rack to secondary for 1 – 2 weeks. Prime and bottle.

— *Bill Shirley, Houston, Texas/Washington, D.C., Houston Foam Rangers*
Brewers United for Real Potables (BURP)

APPLE BEER

Granny Ale

YIELD:	5 GAL. (18.9 L)
TOTAL BOILING TIME:	45 MIN.
STARTING GRAVITY:	1.051
ENDING GRAVITY:	1.008
PRIMARY FERMENT:	8 DAYS
SECONDARY FERMENT:	30 DAYS

First place in the specialty category at the 1994 Puddle Dock Homebrew Competition, Portsmouth, New Hampshire.

- 6.6 lb. (3 kg) Munton & Fison light malt extract
- 1 lb. (454 g) corn sugar
- ½ oz. (14 g) Fuggles hops, 4.5% alpha, in boil 45 min.
- 12 lb. (5.44 kg) Granny Smith apples
- ½ oz. (14 g) Fuggles hops, steep 15 min.
- Edme ale yeast
- ¾ c. (206 ml) corn sugar, for priming

Add malt extract, 1 lb. (454 g) of corn sugar, and ½ oz. (14 g) of Fuggles hops to 1½ gal. (5.7 L) of water. Boil 45 min. While wort is boiling, prepare apples by cutting each into 8 – 10 slices. After the 45-min. boil is over, turn off heat and add apple slices and ½ oz. (14 g) of Fuggles hops. Steep 15 min. Pour everything into a sanitized plastic bucket and top off to 5 gal. (18.9 L) with cold water. Pitch yeast when wort is below 80°F (27°C). Ferment 8 days, then skim off apples. Rack beer to secondary for 30 days. Prime with corn sugar and bottle.

— *Steve Rogers, Dover, New Hampshire*

PEACH BEERS

Peach Ale

YIELD: .... 5 GAL. (18.9 L)
TOTAL BOILING TIME: .... 10 MIN.
STARTING GRAVITY: 1.034
PRIMARY FERMENT: .... 3 DAYS
SECONDARY FERMENT: .... 18 DAYS

3 lb. (1.36 kg) cara-pils malt
1 lb. (454 g) lager malt
3.3 lb. (1.5 kg) Munton & Fison hopped lager malt extract
½ tsp. (2.5 ml) Irish moss
Wyeast #2565 Kölsch yeast, 10.1-oz. (300-ml) starter
¾ c. (206 ml) corn sugar, for priming
3 oz. (89 ml) peach concentrate, for priming

Mash the grains in 2 gal. (7.6 L) of water at 158°F (70°C) for 1 hour. Strain out grains and sparge. Bring to a boil. Turn off heat and add malt extract and Irish moss. Boil 10 min. Chill the wort, transfer to a primary fermenter, and pitch yeast. Ferment 1 week, then rack to secondary for 18 days. Prime beer and bottle.

— Neil Flatter, Terre Haute, Indiana
Wabash Valley Vintners' and Homebrewers' Club

Apricot Peach Beer

YIELD: .... 5 GAL. (18.9 L)
TOTAL BOILING TIME: .... 60 MIN.
PRIMARY FERMENT: .... 1 WEEK
SECONDARY FERMENT: .... 1–2 WEEKS

½ lb. (227 g) DeWolf-Cosyns cara-pils malt
3 lb. (1.36 kg) Munton & Fison light dry malt extract
2 lb. (907 g) Northwestern light dry malt extract
1½ lb. (680 g) clover honey
1⅖ oz. (40 g) crystal hops, 3.9% alpha, in boil 60 min.

1 oz. (28 g) Saaz hops, 2.0 % alpha, In boil 60 min.
  Yeast Culture Kit Company's Whitbread ale yeast
2 lb. (907 g) canned peaches
4 oz. (113 g) HopTech apricot flavoring
¾ c. (206 ml) corn sugar, for priming

Steep the cara-pils malt in 2 gal. (2.6 L) of 150°F (66°C) water for 30 min.
Strain out the grain and bring liquid to a boil. Add extracts, honey, and
hops and boil 60 min. Chill the wort to 65°F (16°C), transfer to fermenter,
and pitch yeast. Ferment 1 week. Rack to secondary and add the canned
peaches. Allow to ferment an additional 1 – 2 weeks. Transfer to a
bottling bucket. Add the HopTech apricot flavoring to the beer in the
bottling bucket, prime with corn sugar, and bottle.

— *Delano Dugarm, Arlington, Virginia*
Brewers United for Real Potables (BURP)

PRUNE BEER

Warrior's Stout

YIELD: .... 5 GAL. (18.9 L)
TOTAL BOILING TIME: .... 60 MIN.
STARTING GRAVITY: 1.052
ENDING GRAVITY: 1.018
PRIMARY FERMENT: .... 1 WEEK
SECONDARY FERMENT: .... 1 WEEK

  1 lb. (454 g) crystal malt
½ lb. (227 g) black patent malt
⅓ lb. (151 g) roasted barley
6.6 lb. (3 kg) dark malt extract
1½ oz. (43 g) Northern Brewer hops, 13.2% alpha, in boil 60 min.
  1 oz. (28 g) Tettnanger hops, in boil 2 min.
  2 qt. (1.9 L) prune juice without preservatives
    ale yeast
¾ c. (206 ml) corn sugar, for priming

Crush grains and steep in 2 qt. (1.9 L) water for 30 min. at 150°F (66°C). Strain into boiling kettle and rinse grains with an additional 1 qt. (946 ml) of water. Add malt extract and 1½ oz. (43 g) of Northern Brewer hops. Add water to bring up volume to 2 ½ gal. (9.4 L) and bring to a boil. Boil 58 min., then add 1 oz. (28 g) of Tettnanger hops. Boil 2 min. and turn off heat. Add prune juice and steep 5 min. Chill the wort, transfer to fermenter, and top off to 5 gal. (18.9 L) with cold water. Pitch yeast and ferment 1 week at 60°F (16°C). Rack to secondary for 1 week at 60°F (16°C). Prime with corn sugar and bottle.

— Paul Busman, Troy, New York

CHERRY BEERS

Flanders Brown Ale

YIELD: .... 3 GAL. (11.4 L)
TOTAL BOILING TIME: .... 45 MIN.
STARTING GRAVITY: 1.064
ENDING GRAVITY: 1.018
PRIMARY FERMENT: .... 8 DAYS
SECONDARY FERMENT: .... 10 DAYS

Rich, malty character with a tart cherry flavor.

- 1 lb. (454 g) light crystal malt
- 6.6 lb. (3 kg) Munton & Fison wheat extract
- ¾ oz. (21 g) Cascade hop pellets, in boil 45 min.
- 1 tsp. (4.9 ml) Irish moss
- ½ oz. (14 g) Tettnanger leaf hops, in boil 5 min.
- Munton & Fison ale yeast
- ½ c. (138 ml) corn sugar, for priming
- 4 oz. (118 ml) cherry wine flavoring, for priming

Steep crystal malt in 1 qt. (946 ml) of 155°F (68°C) water for 10 min. Strain out grains and add 1 gal. (3.8 L) of water. Add extract and bring to a boil. Add Cascade hop pellets and boil 15 min. Add Irish moss and boil 25 min. Add Tettnanger hops and boil 5 min. Pour wort into fermenter containing 1½ gal. (5.7 L) of cold water. Top off to 3 gal. (11.4 L). Pitch yeast when wort is below 80°F (27°C). Ferment 8 days. Rack to secondary for 10 days. Prime with corn sugar and cherry flavoring and bottle.

— Gloria Franconi, Red Hook, New York

Hudson Valley Homebrewers

Double Springs Chocolate Cherry Imperial Stout

YIELD:	5 GAL. (18.9 L)
TOTAL BOILING TIME:	90 MIN.
STARTING GRAVITY:	1.084
ENDING GRAVITY:	1.024
PRIMARY FERMENT:	7 DAYS
SECONDARY FERMENT:	14 DAYS

12 lb. (5.44 kg) Dewolf-Cosyns pale malt

3 lb. (1.36 kg) 2-row pale malt

1 lb. (454 g) roast barley

1 lb. (454 g) flaked barley

¾ lb. (340 g) Special-B malt

¼ lb. (113 g) chocolate malt

1 lb. (454 g) Baker's unsweetened chocolate

1 oz. (28 g) Columbus hops, 15.4% alpha acid, in boil 90 min.

1 oz. (28 g) East Kent Goldings hops, 6% alpha acid, in boil 15 min.

Wyeast #1084 Irish Ale yeast

¾ c. (206 ml) corn sugar, for priming

4 oz. (118 ml) Steinbarts cherry extract, for priming

Mash-in grains in 6 gal. (22.7 L) of 168°F (76°C) water. Temperature should settle to 152°F (67°C). Maintain 152°F (67°C) for 90 min. Mash-out at 168°F (76°C) for 15 min. Sparge with 7 gal. (26.5 L) of 170°F (77°C) water. Bring wort to a boil and add chocolate and Columbus hops. Boil 75 min. Add East Kent Goldings hops. Boil 15 min., then turn off heat. Chill the wort, transfer to fermenter, and pitch yeast. Ferment 7 days at 64°F (18°C). Rack to secondary for 14 days. Prime beer with corn sugar and cherry extract and bottle.

— James Earl Tesh, Double Springs Homebrew Supply

Valley Springs, California

LEMON BEER

Summer Lemon Wheat

YIELD: .... 5 GAL. (18.9 L)
TOTAL BOILING TIME: .... 50 MIN.
STARTING GRAVITY: 1.068
ENDING GRAVITY: 1.012
PRIMARY FERMENT: .... 7 DAYS
SECONDARY FERMENT: .... 7 DAYS

Second place at the 1996 Wisconsin State Fair. Good lemon aroma and a sweet aftertaste.

6.6 lb. (3 kg) Northwestern weizen extract
  3 lb. (1.36 kg) light dry malt extract
  2 lb. (907 g) honey
1½ oz. (43 g) Hallertauer hops, in boil 50 min.
  ½ oz. (14 g) Hallertauer hops, steep
  2 oz. (57 g) pure lemon extract
  4 whole lemons
    dry ale yeast
  1 c. (275 ml) corn sugar, for priming

Boil 2 gal. (7.6 L) of water, remove from heat, and add malt extracts, honey, and 1½ oz. (43 g) of Hallertauer hops. Boil 50 min. Remove from heat, add the remaining ½ oz. (14 g) of Hallertauer hops, the lemon extract, and the juice from the 4 lemons. Chill wort to 72°F (22°C), transfer to fermenter, and pitch yeast. Ferment 7 days at 72°F (22°C). Rack to secondary for 7 days. Prime with corn sugar, bottle, and let sit for 4 weeks.

— *Mike Haag, Greenfield, Wisconsin, Mike's Mystery Malts*

ORANGE BEER

Orange and Spice and Everything Nice

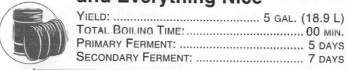

YIELD: .... 5 GAL. (18.9 L)
TOTAL BOILING TIME: .... 00 MIN.
PRIMARY FERMENT: .... 5 DAYS
SECONDARY FERMENT: .... 7 DAYS

This brew is well balanced with a hint of oranges and a subtle aroma of clove.

3.3 lb. (1.5 kg) Munton & Fison light malt extract
  2 lb. (907 g) clover honey
  1 oz. (28 g) Cascade hops, 4.4% alpha, in boil 60 min.
  3 lb. (1.36 kg) navel oranges, quartered
  2 tsp. (9.9 ml) ground cloves
  1 tsp. (4.9 ml) allspice
  ½ oz. (14 ml) Cascade hops, 4.4% alpha, in boil 20 min.
  1 tsp. (4.9 ml) Irish moss
  ½ oz. (14 g) Cascade hops, 4.4% alpha, in boil 5 min.
    Munton & Fison ale yeast
  ¾ c. (206 ml) corn sugar, for priming

Add malt extract and honey to 1½ gal. (5.7 L) of water and bring to a boil. Add 1 oz. (28 g) of Cascade hops. Boil 30 min. and then add the quartered oranges, ground cloves, and allspice. Boil 10 min., then add ½ oz. (14 g) of Cascade hops and Irish moss. Boil 15 min., then add ½ oz. (14 g) of Cascade hops. Boil 5 min. and turn off heat. Cool and transfer to fermenter and pitch rehydrated yeast. After 5 days, rack to secondary for 7 more days. Prime with corn sugar and bottle.

— *Michael Gershenson, Massapequa, New York*

BANANA BEER

Ape Over Ale
YIELD: .... 5½ GAL. (20.8 L)
TOTAL BOILING TIME: .... 10 MIN.
PRIMARY FERMENT: .... 1 WEEK
SECONDARY FERMENT: .... 20 DAYS

2½ lb. (1.13 kg) cara-pils malt
½ lb. (227 g) Belgian pilsner malt
2 lb. (907 g) English pale malt
3.3 lb. (1.5 kg) Munton & Fison hopped lager malt extract
4 oz. (113 kg) banana flakes
½ tsp. (2.5 ml) Irish moss
1 tsp. (4.9 ml) ground nutmeg
Wyeast #2565 Kölsch yeast, 10.1-oz. (300-ml) starter
5 lb. (2.27 kg) fresh banana, sliced, added to secondary
¾ c. (206 ml) corn sugar, for priming

Add grains to 3 gal. (11.4 L) of water. Heat mash slowly to 150°F (66°C) and rest 45 minutes. Sparge and bring wort to a boil. Turn off heat and add malt extract, banana flakes, Irish moss, and nutmeg. Boil 10 min., then chill the wort. Transfer to fermenter, top off to 5½ gal. (20.8 L) with cold water, and pitch yeast. Ferment 1 week, then rack to secondary containing 5 lb. (2.27 kg) of sliced bananas. Make sure your secondary fermenter is large enough to hold a very active fermentation, as the bananas have lots of sugar. Ferment 20 days, then prime with corn sugar and bottle.

— Neil Flatter, Terre Haute, Indiana
Wabash Valley Vintners' and Homebrewers' Club

Herb & Spice Beers

More HOMEBREW FAVORITES

13

L ike fruit beers, spiced beers can be built up from a number of different styles of beer as the underlying base. You might start with a pale ale or a brown ale and add spices to suit your taste. However, it's important to keep in mind the concept of balance, and it's important to let the characteristics of the base beer come through along with the flavors of the spices.

Mulling spice mix. While any spices may be used in beer, there are certain spices and combinations that have worked well for many brewers. The most popular is probably what we call the *mulling spice mix*, or it could also be known as the "Christmas cookie" spice mix. Generally, this includes a blend of cinnamon, nutmeg, cloves, and allspice. The mix can be used in various ways. Add the spices directly to the boil, or make a spice "tea" and add it to the boiled wort. Or you can soak the spices in vodka, creating a "potion" that is then added at bottling time, as described by Randy Mosher in his *Brewer's Companion*.

Ginger beers. Of course, ginger is ever popular for making spiced beer. A restrained hand is the key to success with ginger. A

KEY TO RECIPE LOGOS

 EXTRACT RECIPES

 PARTIAL MASH RECIPES

 ALL-GRAIN RECIPES

number of very heavily gingered flavored beers have done well in competition, though, so your taste should dictate how you spice your own beers.

Herb Beers. There are a number of herbs that can flavor beer. Italian herbs, such as oregano and basil, can be used, as could sage, thyme, marjoram, and any of a wide range of similar herbs. These spices tend to be most effective in a light-bodied beer with low hopping rates.

Pepper Beers. Chili pepper beers are increasingly popular. The heat varies wildly depending on the type and quantity of chili. *Brewers should use discretion* when brewing with hot peppers! Jalapeños are fairly light in terms of heat compared to some of the chili pepper beers that homebrewers have concocted (who would put habenero peppers in beer?). Since there are some outstanding meads flavored with Chinese hot peppers, it's clear that a pepper beer with a barleywine base could work well. The sweetness would, to some extent, help cut the heat of the peppers.

Gruits. One of the most challenging and interesting of all the spice blends are the *gruits*. Before the dawn of hops, medieval brewers blended various herbs and spices into a mixture called gruit that performed much of the function of hops. While most spiced beers are novelties, the gruit beer is an exception. A wide range of wildflowers, herbs, tree bark, and seeds were used. Some common ingredients include rosemary, sweet gale, and yarrow. The ancient Picts from Scotland also brewed ale using heather. It's a taste of archaeology and brewing history in a glass.

In competitions, spiced beers often exhibit fundamental problems that may be attributed to lack of experience. Cloudy beers crop up regularly, as do beers with excessive carbonation. Lack of balance is a common problem with spiced beers. Flavors don't come through as well as a brewer might have expected, perhaps from a poor choice in base style. A clean beer that shows off the spices, but is first and foremost also a good, solid beer will do well. On the other hand, a beer that is one dimensional, either with no sign of the spices, or with abundant spices and no sign of a quality beer lying beneath the surface, will likely fare poorly.

GRUIT

─Ancient Gruit Ale─

YIELD: .... 5 GAL. (18.9 L)
TOTAL BOILING TIME: .... 60 MIN.
STARTING GRAVITY: 1.076
ENDING GRAVITY: 1.018
PRIMARY FERMENT: .... 2 WEEKS
SECONDARY FERMENT: .... 3 WEEKS

This is an example of a beer from the Middle Ages. The flavors mix to prevent one from dominating.

- 1 lb. (454 g) oatmeal (dry weight), boiled
- 1 tsp. (4.9 ml) gypsum
- ½ tsp. (2.5 ml) brewing salts
- 10 lb. (4.54 kg) English pale malt
- 2 ¼ lb. (1.02 kg) Munich malt
- 1¼ lb. (567 g) cara-pils malt
- ¾ lb. (380 g) crystal malt, 40° Lovibond
- ½ lb. (227 g) German smoked malt
- ½ lb. (227 g) special roast domestic malt
- ¼ lb. (113 g) wheat malt
- ¼ lb. (113 g) roast barley
- ¼ lb. (113 g) chocolate malt
- ½ oz. (14 g) Columbus hops, 15% alpha, in boil 60 min.
- 1 tsp. (4.9 ml) Irish moss

Gruit:

- 2 tbsp. (29.6 ml) dandelion root, dried and lightly roasted
- 2 tbsp. (29.6 ml) dandelion leaves
- 15 nasturtiums (leaves and flowers)
- 1 oz. (28 g) ginger
- 3 in. (7.6 cm) fresh rosemary
- 1 6-in. (15.2 cm) cinnamon stick
- 10 pods cardamom, crushed

10 cloves
11 oz. (325 ml) cranberry puree
     Wyeast #1968 London ESB yeast
½ c. (138 ml) corn sugar, for priming

Boil oatmeal in 1 gal. (3.8 L) of water for 15 min. Treat 4 gal. (15.1 L) of water with gypsum and brewing salts and heat water to 170°F (77°C). Add crushed grains plus the boiled oatmeal to the water and let rest for 90 min. at 149° to 155°F (65° – 68°C). Sparge and collect 6 gal. of wort in brew kettle. Bring wort to a boil and add hops. During this time, prepare the gruit by combining all gruit ingredients in a single bowl. After wort has boiled for 55 min., add gruit. Boil 5 min., then turn off heat. Chill the wort, transfer to fermenter, and pitch yeast. Ferment 2 weeks at 70°F (21°C). Rack to secondary for 3 weeks. Prime with corn sugar and bottle.

— *Ted Manahan, Albany, Oregon*
Heart of the Valley Homebrewers

WINTER MULLING SPICES: CINNAMON, ALLSPICE, AND CLOVE BEERS

Liquid Fruitcake

YIELD: .... 5 GAL. (18.9 L)
TOTAL BOILING TIME: .... 60 MIN.
STARTING GRAVITY: 1.080
ENDING GRAVITY: 1.018
PRIMARY FERMENT: .... 10 DAYS
SECONDARY FERMENT: .... 10 DAYS

First place in the specialty beers category at the 1996 "War of Worts" competition.

    3 lb. (1.36 kg) 2-row pale malt
    1 lb. (454 g) crystal malt
    ½ lb. (227 g) wheat malt
    2 oz. (57 g) chocolate malt
  3.3 lb. (1.5 kg) Munton & Fison light malt extract
    3 lb. (1.36 kg) Laaglander light dry malt extract
    2 lb. (907 g) orange-blossom honey
    1 oz. (28 g) Styrian hop pellets, 4.5% alpha, in boil 60 min.
 0.14 oz. (4 g) mace
 0.14 oz. (4 g) nutmeg
    1 2-in. (5.1 cm) cinnamon stick, crumbled
    1 vanilla bean, split
       zest of 5 oranges
    ½ oz. (14 g) Styrian hop pellets, 4.5% alpha, in boil 15 min.
       Wyeast #1056 American Ale yeast
    ¾ c. (206 ml) corn sugar, for priming

Mash grains in 1½ gal. (5.7 L) of water at 152°F (67°C) for 90 min.
Mash-out at 170°F (77°C) for 10 min. Sparge with 2 – 3 gal. (7.6 – 11.4
L) of 170°F (77°C) water. Add all malt extracts and honey and add
water until the total volume in the brew kettle is 6½ – 7 gal. (24.6 – 26.5 L).
Bring to a boil and add 1 oz. (28 g) of Styrian hop pellets. Boil 30 min.,
then add all spices and orange zest. Boil 15 min., then add ½ oz.
(14 g) of Styrian hop pellets. Boil a final 15 min. and turn off heat. Chill
the wort, transfer to fermenter, and pitch yeast. Ferment 10 days and
then rack to secondary for 10 days. Prime with corn sugar and bottle.

— *Alan L. Folsom, Jr., Warrington, Pennsylvania, Keystone Hops*

Xmas Herbal

YIELD: .... 5 GAL. (18.9 L)
TOTAL BOILING TIME: .... 60 MIN.
STARTING GRAVITY: 1.050
PRIMARY FERMENT: .... 3 DAYS
SECONDARY FERMENT: .... 12 DAYS

½ lb. (227 g) crystal malt
½ c. (138 ml) black patent malt
3 oz. (85 g) roasted barley
3 lb. (1.36 kg) extra-light dry malt extract
3 lb. (1.36 kg) amber dry malt extract
1 lb. (454 g) clover honey
1⅜ oz. (39 g) Northern Brewer hops, 7.4% alpha, in boil 60 min.
1½ oz. (43 g) grated gingerroot
1 cinnamon stick
4 tsp. (19.7 ml) grated orange peel
1 tsp. (4.9 ml) ground nutmeg
1 vanilla bean, split in half
½ oz. (14 g) Saaz hops, 3.9% alpha, in boil 2 min.
Wyeast # 1098 British Ale yeast
2 tsp. (9.9 ml) ground nutmeg, added to secondary
1 cinnamon stick, added to secondary
¾ c. (206 ml) corn sugar, for priming

Add grains to 1 gal. (3.8 L) of water and steep 10 min. at 160°F (71°C). Add malt extracts and honey to 3 gal. (11.4 L) of water and bring to a boil. Strain grains and sparge with 1 gal. (3.8 L) of water into boiling wort. Add Northern Brewer hops and boil 50 min. Add ginger, 1 cinnamon stick, orange peel, 1 tsp. (4.9 ml) ground nutmeg, and ½ vanilla bean and boil 8 min. Add ½ oz. (14 g) of Saaz hops and boil 2 min., then turn off heat. Chill the wort, transfer to fermenter, and pitch yeast. Racking to secondary 3 days later. Bring 1 qt. (946 ml) of water to a boil and add 2 tsp. (9.9 ml) of ground nutmeg, 1 cinnamon stick, and ½ vanilla bean and let steep for 3 min. Pour this spice mixture into the secondary fermenter. Continue fermenting 12 days at 70°F (21°C), then prime with corn sugar and bottle.

— *Matt Zaccheo, Phillipsburg, New Jersey*

Christmas Spice '95

YIELD: .... 5 GAL. (18.9 L)
TOTAL BOILING TIME: .... 45 MIN.
STARTING GRAVITY: 1.065
ENDING GRAVITY: 1.012
PRIMARY FERMENT: .... 14 DAYS

6 lb. (2.72 kg) Mahogany Coast English ale malt extract
3 lb. (1.36 kg) amber dry malt extract
1 oz. (28 g) Cascade hops, 4.6% alpha, in boil 45 min.
1 tsp. (4.9 ml) ground allspice
1 tsp. (4.9 ml) ground cinnamon
1 tsp. (4.9 ml) vanilla extract
¼ tsp. (1.2 ml) nutmeg
1 lb. (454 g) clover honey
½ c. (138 ml) brown sugar
  Danstar Nottingham dry yeast
½ oz. (14 g) Goldings hops, 5.8% alpha, dry hopped
⅔ c. (184 ml) corn sugar, for priming

Add malt extracts to 2 gal. (7.6 L) of water and bring to a boil. Add 1 oz. (28 g) of Cascade hops and boil 45 min. In a separate pot, add all spices, honey, and brown sugar to 1 gal. (3.8 L) water and simmer 10 min. Add spice mix to wort 5 min. before the end of the 45-min. boil. When boil is done, turn off heat and chill the wort. Transfer wort to a primary fermenter, bring up to 5 gal. (18.9 L), and pitch yeast. Ferment 7 days, then rack to secondary and add ½ oz. (14 g) of Goldings hops. Continue fermenting 7 days, then prime with corn sugar and bottle.

— *Jim White, Southgate, Michigan*
Down River Brewers Guild

Cinnamon Wheat Ale

YIELD: .... 5 GAL. (18.9 L)
TOTAL BOILING TIME: .... 45 MIN.
PRIMARY FERMENT: .... 7 DAYS
SECONDARY FERMENT: .... 7 DAYS

¾ lb. (340 g) 2-row pale English malt
½ lb. (227 g) crystal malt
6.6 lb. (3 kg) Munton & Fison wheat extract
2½ oz. (71 g) Willamette hops, in boil 45 min.
6 2-inch-long (5.1-cm) cinnamon sticks
1 tsp. (4.9 ml) Irish moss
½ oz. (14 g) Cascade hops
¼ oz. (7 g) Cooper's ale yeast
¾ c. (206 ml) corn sugar, for priming

Toast the pale malt for 10 min. in a 400°F (204°C) oven. Steep grains in
1½ gal. (5.7 L) of hot water. After steeping 20 minutes, strain out grains.
Add malt extract and Willamette hops. Boil 15 min. Add cinnamon sticks
and Irish moss and boil 25 min. Add Cascade hops and boil 5 min.
Remove from heat, cool, and transfer to fermenter. Bring up the volume to 5 gal. (18.9 L) with cold water and pitch yeast when the wort is
below 75°F (24°C). Ferment 7 days, then rack to secondary for 7 days.
Prime with corn sugar and bottle. Age 3 weeks.

— *Peter Cammann, Waitsfield, Vermont*

Cock's Holiday Ale '95

YIELD: .... 5 GAL. (18.9 L)
TOTAL BOILING TIME: .... 60 MIN.
STARTING GRAVITY: 1.075
PRIMARY FERMENT: .... 1 WEEK
SECONDARY FERMENT: .... 2 WEEKS

1 lb. (454 g) crystal malt, 40° Lovibond
2 oz. (57 g) roasted barley
6 lb. (2.72 kg) light malt extract
2 lb. (907 g) light dry malt extract
1 lb. (454 g) honey
2 oz. (57 g) malto-dextrin powder
1 oz. (28 g) cinnamon stick
1¼ oz. (35 g) Northern Brewer hops, 7.0% alpha, in boil 60 min.
½ oz. (14 g) East Kent Goldings hops, 5.1% alpha, in boil 60 min.
¾ oz. (21 g) East Kent Goldings hops, in boil 15 min.
¼ oz. (7 g) Northern Brewer hops, in boil 15 min.
½ oz. (14 g) ground nutmeg
½ oz. (14 g) Hallertauer hops, 4.7% alpha, in boil 5 min.
ale yeast
¾ oz. (21 g) East Kent Goldings hops, dry hop
¾ c. (206 g) corn sugar, for priming

Crack and steep crystal malt and roasted barley at 155° – 170°F
(68° – 77°C) for 45 min. in ½ gal. (1.9 L) of water. Strain out grain and add
2 gal. (7.6 L) of water, malt extracts, honey, and malto-dextrin powder.
Bring to a boil and add 1¼ oz. (35 g) of Northern Brewer hops and ½ oz.
(14 g) of East Kent Goldings hops. Boil 45 min., then add ¾ oz. (35 g) East
Kent Goldings hops and ¼ oz. (7 g) of Northern Brewer. Boil 10 min., then
add nutmeg and ½ oz. (14 g) of Hallertauer hops. Boil 5 min. and turn off
heat. Chill the wort, transfer to a primary fermenter, and pitch yeast.
Ferment 1 week, then rack to secondary and dry hop with ¾ oz. (21 g)
of East Kent Goldings hops. Ferment another 2 weeks, then prime with
corn sugar and bottle.

— *Steve Karr, Kirkland, Washington*

Spiced Elderberry Wheat Beer

YIELD:	5 GAL. (18.9 L)
TOTAL BOILING TIME:	2 HOURS
PRIMARY FERMENT:	4–5 DAYS
SECONDARY FERMENT:	1 WEEK

3 lb. (1.36 kg) Muntons wheat dried malt extract
3 lb. (1.36 kg) Dutch amber dried malt extract
2 oz. (57 g) crystal hops, in boil 120 min.
1 oz. (28 g) crystal hops, in boil 5 min.
4 oz. (113 g) dried elderberries
1 packet J. Crow Mulled Cider Spice
  Edme ale yeast
¾ c. (206 ml) corn sugar, for priming.

Add malt extracts to 6 qt. (5.7 L) of boiling water. Add 2 oz. (57 g) of crystal hops. Boil 115 min. Add 1 oz. (28 g) of crystal hops elderberries and spice packet and boil 5 min. Turn off heat, chill the wort, transfer to fermenter, and top off to 5 gal. (18.9 L) with cold water. Pitch yeast and ferment 4 - 5 days. Rack to secondary for 1 week, then prime with corn sugar and bottle. Age 1 month.

— Paul and Becky Dyster, Niagara Falls, New York
Niagara Homebrewers League

Santa's Bun Warmer

YIELD:	15 GAL. (56.8 L)
TOTAL BOILING TIME:	90 MIN.
STARTING GRAVITY:	1.065
ENDING GRAVITY:	1.015
PRIMARY FERMENT:	8 DAYS
SECONDARY FERMENT:	10 DAYS

24 lb. (10.89 kg) 2-row pale malt
 6 lb. (2.72 kg) Munich malt
 3 lb. (1.36 kg) crystal malt, 90° Lovibond
 3 lb. (1.36 kg) wheat malt
1½ lb. (680 g) cara-pils malt
 ¾ lb. (340 g) chocolate malt

¾ lb. (340 g) black patent malt
3 lb. (1.36 kg) orange-blossom honey
1½ c. (355 ml) molasses
4½ oz. (128 g) Nugget hops, in boil 90 min.
1½ oz. (128 g) fresh grated ginger, in boil 90 min.
3 oz. (85 g) Willamette hops, in boil 10 min.
3 tsp. (14.8 ml) cardamom, ground
9 cinnamon sticks, crushed
1½ oz. (43 g) fresh grated ginger, in boil 15 min.
   zest of 12 Valencia oranges
2 tsp. (10 ml) nutmeg
   Wyeast #1028 London Ale yeast
   Wyeast #1098 British Ale yeast
   Wyeast #3056 Bavarian Weizen yeast

Crush all grains, keeping the dark grains separate. Add all grains except dark grain to 12 gal. (45.4 L) of water. Heat mash to 104°F (40°C) and hold for 15 min. Heat mash to 140°F (60°C) and rest for 45 min. Heat mash to 158°F (70°C), add dark grains, and hold for 30 min. Mash-out at 170°F (77°C) for 20 min. Sparge with 170°F (77°C) water, collecting 17 gal. (64.4 L) of wort in brew kettle. Bring wort to a boil and add Nugget hops and 1½ oz. (43 g) of ginger. Boil 80 min., then add 3 oz. (85 g) of Willamette hops, honey, molasses, orange zest, and all remaining spices. Boil 10 min. and turn off heat. Chill the wort, transfer to three different fermenters, and pitch 1 yeast strain per fermenter. Ferment 8 days at 68°F (20°C). Rack to secondary fermenters for 10 days at 68°F (20°C). Keg.

— *Rich Byrnes, Pat Babcock, and Mike Preston, Warren, Michigan*
Fermental Order of Renaissance Draughtsmen (FORD)

GINGER BEERS

Jamaican Ginger Beer

YIELD: .... 5 GAL. (18.9 L)
TOTAL BOILING TIME: .... 60 MIN.
STARTING GRAVITY: 1.044
ENDING GRAVITY: 1.015
PRIMARY FERMENT: .... 1 WEEK
SECONDARY FERMENT: .... 2 WEEKS

8 oz. (227 g)	crystal malt, 20° Lovibond
5 lb. (2.27 kg)	light dry malt extract
2 oz. (57 g)	malto-dextrin powder
½ oz. (14 g)	Chinook hops, 13.2% alpha, in boil 60 min.
6 oz. (170 g)	fresh gingerroot, peeled and thinly sliced
½ oz. (14 g)	Willamette hops, in boil 3 min.
	lager yeast
1 oz. (28 g)	lemongrass, in secondary
¾ oz. (21 g)	orange peel, grated, in secondary
8–10	whole cloves, in secondary
10–15	whole allspice, in secondary
1 c. (237 ml)	lime juice, in secondary
¾ c. (206 ml)	corn sugar, for priming

Steep crushed crystal malt for 30 min. in 1 gal. (3.8 L) of water at 150° – 160°F (66° – 71°C). Strain and sparge grains. Add 1 gal. (3.8 L) of water, malt extract, and malto-dextrin powder. Bring to a boil and add ½ oz. (14 g) of Chinook hops. Boil 45 min., then add sliced ginger. Boil 12 min., then add ½ oz. (14 g) of Willamette hops. Boil 3 more min., then turn off heat. Chill and transfer to fermenter, topping off to 5 gal. (18.9 L) with cold water, and pitch yeast. Ferment 1 week, then rack to a secondary fermenter and add lemongrass, grated orange peel, cloves, allspice, and lime juice. Ferment 2 weeks, then prime with corn sugar and bottle. You may also add additional cloves and allspice at bottling time.

— *Douglas Faynor, Homebrew Heaven, Salem, Oregon*
Capitol Brewers of Salem

Ginger Bear

YIELD: .... 5 GAL. (18.9 L)
TOTAL BOILING TIME: .... 90 MIN.
STARTING GRAVITY: 1.041
ENDING GRAVITY: 1.009
PRIMARY FERMENT: .... 7 DAYS
SECONDARY FERMENT: .... 20 DAYS

Ginger is apparent but not assertive.

   1 lb. (454 g) crystal malt, 10° Lovibond
  ½ lb. (227 g) chocolate malt
 6.6 lb. (3 kg) Munton & Fison plain malt extract
  ¾ lb. (340 g) American ginger, hand grated
1½ oz. (43 g) Cascade hop pellets, in boil 45 min.
   1 tbsp. (14.8 ml) Irish moss
  ½ oz. (14 g) Kent Goldings hops plug, in boil 10 min.
  ½ oz. (14 g) Cascade hops plug, in boil 5 min.
       Wyeast #1098 British Ale yeast
  ¾ c. (206 ml) corn sugar, for priming

Crush grains and add to 8 c. (946 ml) of water. Steep at 150° – 170°F (66° – 77°C) for 20 min. Strain out grains and add to 2 gal. (1.9 L) of water. Add malt extract and ginger. Boil 45 min. Add 1½ oz. (43 g) of Cascade hop pellets and boil 30 min. Add Irish moss and boil 5 min. Add Kent Goldings hops plug and boil 5 min. Add ½ oz. (14 g) of Cascade hops plug and boil 5 min. Turn off heat, chill the wort, transfer to fermenter, top off to 5 gal. (18.9 L) with cold water, and pitch yeast. Ferment 7 days, then rack to secondary for 20 days. Prime with corn sugar and bottle.

— *Justin Gyi and Robert Petersen, Dunstable, Massachusetts*

BIA Brewing Club

Gingerroot Honey Lager

YIELD: .... 5 GAL. (18.9 L)
TOTAL BOILING TIME: .... 60 MIN.
STARTING GRAVITY: 1.060
ENDING GRAVITY: 1.029
PRIMARY FERMENT: .... 5 DAYS
SECONDARY FERMENT: .... 5 DAYS

 4 oz. (113 g) fresh gingerroot
6.6 lb. (3 kg) Munton & Fison plain malt extract syrup
2 ½ lb. (1.13 kg) clover honey
 ½ oz. (14 g) Northern Brewers hops plug, 7.5% alpha,
    in boil 60 min.
 ¼ tsp. (1.2 ml) Irish moss
 ½ oz. (14 g) Cascade hops plug, 6.4% alpha, in boil 5 min.
 2 packs of Superior lager yeast
 ¾ c. (206 ml) honey, for priming.

In a large pot, bring 2 gal. (7.6 L) of water to a boil. Chop gingerroot into small pieces. When water boils, add malt extract, honey, gingerroot, Northern Brewer hops plug, and Irish moss. Boil 55 min., then add Cascade hops plug. Boil 5 min. and turn off heat. Strain hops while pouring wort into the primary fermenter. Sparge hops. Add cold water to fermenter to make 5 gal. (18.9 L) of wort. Pitch yeast when wort is 60°F (16°C). Ferment 5 days. Rack to secondary for 5 more days. Prime with corn sugar and bottle.

— *Scott Walsh, Lee, New Hampshire*

HERB BEERS

Kiwi Mint Ale

YIELD: .... 5 GAL. (18.9 L)
TOTAL BOILING TIME: .... 60 MIN.
STARTING GRAVITY: 1.060
ENDING GRAVITY: 1.010
PRIMARY FERMENT: .... 7 DAYS
SECONDARY FERMENT: .... 2 WEEKS

Second place in the Spirit of Free Beer competition.

      1 c. (275 ml) steel-cut oats
      1 c. (275 ml) malted wheat
     ½ lb. (227 g) crystal malt, 40° Lovibond
   3.3 lb. (1.5 kg) Telford's unhopped amber malt extract
      3 lb. (1.36 kg) extra-light dry malt extract
      1 oz. (28 g) Cascade hops, 5.1% alpha, in boil 45 min.
    15 kiwifruits
   1½ c. (413 ml) loosely packed fresh mint leaves and stems
         Wyeast #1056 American Ale yeast
     ¾ c. (206 ml) corn sugar, for priming

Steep oats, wheat malt, and crystal malt in 1 gal. (3.8 L) of 150°F (66°C) water for 35 min. Strain into boiler containing 1 gal. (3.8 L) of water. Add malt extracts and bring to boil. Boil 60 min., adding hops for last 45 min. Turn off heat. Scoop fruit from the kiwifruits and place in the bottom of a pan. Add mint. Pour a few cups of the just-boiled wort over the top of the kiwifruit and mint and let sit while you chill the rest of the wort. Add chilled wort to the primary fermenter and strain liquid off kiwifruit and mint into fermenter. Pitch yeast and ferment at 65°F (18°C) for 7 days. If desired, rack to secondary for another 2 weeks. Prime with corn sugar and bottle.

— Polly Goldman, Alexandria, Virginia
Brewers United for Real Potables (BURP)

Raspberry Tea Beer

YIELD: .... 2½ GAL. (9.4 L)
TOTAL BOILING TIME: .... 15 MIN.
STARTING GRAVITY: 1.052
ENDING GRAVITY: 1.015
PRIMARY FERMENT: .... 12 DAYS

The raspberry tea also had a small amount of cloves, contributing to the great flavor!

3 lb. (1.36 kg) Hollander extra-light dry malt extract
½ oz. (14 g) B.C. Kent Goldings hops, 5.8% alpha, in boil 15 min.
8 bags raspberry tea, 15-min. steep
  Danstar Windsor dry ale yeast
⅜ c. (103 ml) corn sugar, for priming

Add malt extract to 2 ½ gal. (9.4 L) of water in a kettle. Bring to a boil and add B.C. Kent Goldings hops. Boil 15 min. Turn off heat and add tea bags. Steep for 15 min. Remove tea bags, chill the wort, and transfer to the fermenter. Pitch yeast and ferment 12 days. Prime with corn sugar and bottle. Age at least 1 month.

— *Jim White, Southgate, Michigan*
Down River Brewers Guild

PEPPER BEERS

Jalapeño Pepper Ale

YIELD: .... 5 GAL. (18.9 L)
TOTAL BOILING TIME: .... 45 MIN.
PRIMARY FERMENT: .... 7 DAYS
SECONDARY FERMENT: .... 7 DAYS WITH PEPPERS

First place at the "Some Like It Hot" Hot & Spicy Cooking Contest at Sam Rupert's Restaurant, Warren, Vermont.

- ½ lb. (227 g) medium crystal malt
- 4 lb. (1.81 kg) Alexander's light
- 1½ lb. (680 g) extra-light dry malt extract
- 1½ oz. (43 g) Cascade hops, in boil 45 min.
- ½ tsp. (2.5 ml) Irish moss
- ½ oz. (14 g) Fuggles hops, in boil 5 min.
  jalapeño peppers, your choice of heat level:
    - 2 lb. (907 g) for hot
    - 3 lb. (1.36 kg) for extra hot
    - 4 lb. (1.81 kg) for "Scorched Earth & Mouth" (this version took first place)
- ¼ oz. (7 g) Cooper's ale yeast
- 1 c. (275 ml) corn sugar, for priming

Steep crystal malt in 1½ gal. (5.7 L) of 150°F (66°C) water. Strain out grain. Add malt extracts and Cascade hops. Boil 30 min. Add Irish moss and boil 10 min. Add Fuggles hops and boil 5 min. Turn off heat, cool, and strain wort into fermenter containing 3 ½ gal. (13.2 L) of cold water. Pitch yeast when the wort is below 75°F (24°C). Ferment 1 week at 65°F (18°C). After the first week of fermentation, remove the seeds and stems from the jalapeños. Place the peppers into a steamer and cook 10 min. Add steamed peppers to a sanitized carboy and rack the ale into it. Ferment 1 more week. Prime with corn sugar and bottle. Age 6 – 8 weeks.

— *Peter Cammann, Waitsfield, Vermont*

Hallelujah Jalapeño Beer

YIELD: .... 15 GAL. (56.8 L)
TOTAL BOILING TIME: .... 90 MIN.
STARTING GRAVITY: 1.054
ENDING GRAVITY: 1.009
PRIMARY FERMENT: .... 7 DAYS
SECONDARY FERMENT: .... 11 DAYS
LAGERING: .... 90 DAYS

*First place in the 1993 AHA National Competition and one of the
last three beers in the best-of-show round.*

      36 lb. (16.3 kg) Ireks pilsner malt
    1½ lb. (680 g) flaked wheat
          distilled water
  0.04 oz. (1 g) calcium carbonate
  0.04 oz. (1 g) magnesium sulfate
  0.02 oz. (½ g) calcium chloride
      18 jalapeño peppers, roasted, with most seeds removed
        6 oz. (170 g) Czech Saaz hops, 3.3% alpha, in boil 60 min.
    1.1 oz. (31 g) Czech Saaz hops, in boil 10 min.
          Wyeast #2124 Bohemian Lager yeast
    2 ¼ c. (619 ml) corn sugar, for priming

Crush grains and add to 12 gal. (45.4 L) of distilled water treated with
calcium carbonate, magnesium sulfate, and calcium chloride, if
needed. Heat to 122°F (50°C) and rest 30 min. Heat to 138°F (59°C)
and rest 30 min. Heat to 150°F (66°C) and rest 60 min. Heat to 155°F
(68°C) and rest 40 min. Heat to 169°F (76°C) and rest 1 min. Sparge
with 169°F (76°C) water adjusted to pH 5.3 with lactic acid. Collect 17
gal. (64.4 L) of wort. Boil 30 min. (During the boil, roast jalapeños at
350°F (177°C) for 10 min., cool, and remove seeds.) Add 6 oz. (170 g) of
Saaz hops and boil 50 min. Add 1.1 oz. (31 g) of Saaz hops and boil 10
min. Turn off heat and add jalapeño peppers. Steep for 15 min. Chill
the wort to 60°F (16°C), transfer to fermenter, and pitch yeast.
Ferment 7 days at 50°F (10°C), then rack to secondary for 11 days at
50°F (10°C). Allow fermenter to warm up to 57°F (14°C) and continue

fermenting for 3 days. Rack to another fermenter and lager at 32°F (0°C) for 90 days. Prime with corn sugar and bottle.

— "Beer" Rich Mansfield, San Jose, California

Washoe Zephyr Zymurgists

Jalapeño Blast

YIELD:	5 GAL. (18.9 L)
TOTAL BOILING TIME:	60 MIN.
STARTING GRAVITY:	1.042
ENDING GRAVITY:	1.017
PRIMARY FERMENT:	4 DAYS
SECONDARY FERMENT:	9 DAYS

Third place for Herb & Spice in the specialty division category in the 1996 Queen of Beers contest.

       4 lb. (1.81 kg) Alexander's pale malt extract
       2 lb. (907 g) extra-pale malt rice extract
       2 tsp. (9.9 ml) gypsum
       1 oz. (28 g) Cascade hops, 5.1% alpha, in boil 45 min.
       4 oz. (113 g) jalapeño peppers, diced (with seeds)
       1 tsp. (4.9 ml) Irish moss
       ½ oz. (14 g) Tettnanger hops, 4.6% alpha, in boil 2 min.
    0.41 oz. (11.5 g) Edme ale yeast
       ¾ c. (206 ml) corn sugar, for priming
       1 tsp. (4.9 ml) gelatin, for priming
       1 tsp. (4.9 ml) ascorbic acid, for priming
       1 tsp. (4.9 ml) heading agent, for priming

Bring 2 ½ gal. (9.4 L) of water to a boil. Remove from heat and add extracts and gypsum. Boil 15 min. Add Cascade hops. Boil 30 min., then add Irish moss and diced jalapeños. Boil 13 min., then add Tettnanger hops. Boil 2 more min. Turn off heat and chill the wort. Transfer to fermenter and top off to 5 gal. (18.9 L) with cold water. Pitch yeast and ferment 4 days. Rack to secondary for 9 days. Prime, add gelatin, ascorbic acid, and heading agent and bottle.

— Nora Keller-Seeley, El Dorado Hills, California

Hangtown Association of Zymurgy Enthusiasts (HAZE)

Perplex Pepper Poise Potion

YIELD: .... 5 GAL. (18.9 L)
TOTAL BOILING TIME: .... 60 MIN.
STARTING GRAVITY: 1.056
ENDING GRAVITY: 1.020
PRIMARY FERMENT: .... 1 WEEK
SECONDARY FERMENT: .... 2 WEEKS

Nice pepper aroma and finish.

- 1 lb. (454 g) crystal malt, 120° Lovibond, crushed
- 8 lb. (227 g) amber malt extract
- 1 oz. (28 g) Mt. Hood hop pellets, 5.1% alpha, in boil 60 min.
- 7 banana peppers, halved, with seeds removed
- 6 jalapeño peppers, halved, with seeds removed
- 9 serrano peppers, halved, with seeds removed
- 1 tsp. (4.9 ml) Irish moss
- 1 oz. (28 g) Willamette hop pellets, 4.3% alpha, in boil 15 min.
  Wyeast #1056 American Ale yeast
- ¾ c. (206 ml) clover honey, for priming

Heat 2 gal. (7.6 L) of charcoal-filtered water to 150°F (66°C) and add crushed crystal malt in a grain bag. Steep 30 min., then remove and discard grain. Bring to a boil and add the malt extract and Mt. Hood hop pellets. Also add 5 banana peppers, 3 jalapeño peppers, and 5 serrano peppers. Boil 45 min., then add 1 tsp. (4.9 ml) Irish moss and 1 oz. (28 g) of Willamette hop pellets. Boil 15 min., then turn off heat. Chill the wort and transfer to fermenter, straining out peppers. Microwave remaining peppers on high for 1 min. to sanitize, then add to fermenter. Pitch yeast and ferment until fermentation is complete (1 – 2 weeks). Transfer to bottling bucket, leaving peppers behind, prime with clover honey boiled in ½ c. (118 ml) water, and bottle.

— *Jim Case, Arlington, Texas*
The Knights of the Brown Bottle

Hace Calor

YIELD: .... 5 GAL. (18.9 L)
TOTAL BOILING TIME: .... 60 MIN.
STARTING GRAVITY: 1.025
ENDING GRAVITY: 1.007
PRIMARY FERMENT: .... 1 WEEK
SECONDARY FERMENT: .... 2 WEEKS

Jalapeño bite, but not overpowering.

    4 lb. (1.81 kg) Alexander's pale malt extract
    1 lb. (454 g) brewer's rice syrup
    4 oz. (113 g) malto-dextrin
    1 tbsp. (14.8 ml) water crystals (if needed)
    1 oz. (28 g) Hallertauer hops, 4.8% alpha, in boil 60 min.
    ½ oz. (14 g) Saaz hops, 3.1% alpha, in boil 60 min.
    ½ oz. (14 g) Willamette hops, 4.2% alpha, in boil 2 min.
    4 large jalapeño peppers, sliced
       Edme ale yeast
    2 oz. (57 g) mesquite wood chips, in secondary
    5 large jalapeño peppers, sliced, in secondary
    ¾ c. (206 ml) corn sugar, for priming

Add malt extract, rice syrup, malto-dextrin, and water crystals to 2½ gal.
of water and bring to a boil. Add 1 oz. (28 g) of Hallertauer hops and
½ oz. (14 g) of Saaz hops. Boil 58 min. Add ½ oz. (14 g) of Willamette hops
and boil 2 min., then turn off heat. Add 4 sliced jalapeño peppers and
steep 20 min. Chill the wort, transfer to fermenter, and pitch yeast.
Ferment 1 week at 70°F (21°C). Prior to racking, bake mesquite wood
chips at 350°F (117°C) for 10 min. to sanitize, then rack beer into a
secondary fermenter, adding the wood chips and 5 sliced jalapeño
peppers. Ferment 2 weeks, then prime with corn sugar and bottle.

— *Ed Cosgrove and Rory Schultz, Woodbridge, Virginia*
Brewers Association of Northern Virginia (BANOVA)

More HOMEBREW FAVORITES

14

Hybrid Styles

T**he beers in this chapter are a mix** of unrelated styles that do not fit neatly into the chapters used in this book. They are, nonetheless, important styles in their own right. We begin with the California Common — or steam beer — style, discuss the rauchbier — or smoked beer — style, then other specialty beers.

California common is the name used today for the steam beer style exemplified by Anchor Steam, the only representative left of a style for which the West Coast was once known. As the only remaining example, Anchor has trademarked the term "Steam beer." The name "steam" was used because of the high carbonation levels of the beer. Another theory about the origin of the term is that it derives from the steam-powered equipment used in early mechanized breweries. California common is an all-malt beer, typically made with U.S. 2-row pale malt and caramel malt for color. It has a moderate hop level at about 30 to 35 IBUs. While Anchor uses Northern Brewer hops for its Steam beer, Roger Bergen, in his article on steam beer in *Brewing Techniques* magazine (Jan/Feb 1994), suggests that Cluster may also be an authentic hop for the style. Steam beer is made using a lager yeast brewed at warm temperatures. Some good choices

KEY TO RECIPE LOGOS

 EXTRACT RECIPES

 PARTIAL MASH RECIPES

 ALL-GRAIN RECIPES

We'd love your thoughts...

Your reactions, criticisms, things you did or didn't like about this Storey Book. Please use space below (or write a letter if you'd prefer — even send photos!) telling how you've made use of the information . . . how you've put it to work . . . the more details the better! Thanks in advance for your help in building our library of good Storey Books.

Pamela B. Art

Publisher

Book Title: _____

Purchased From: _____

Comments: _____

_____

_____

_____

_____

_____

_____

Your Name: _____

Address: _____

☐ Please check here if you'd like our latest Storey's *Books for Country Living* Catalog.

☐ You have my permission to quote from my comments, and use these quotations in ads, brochures, mail, and other promotions used to market your books.

Signed _____ Date _____

email=Feedback@Storey.Com PRINTED IN USA 12/96

From: _____

BUSINESS REPLY MAIL

FIRST-CLASS MAIL   PERMIT NO 2   POWNAL, VT

POSTAGE WILL BE PAID BY ADDRESSEE

STOREY'S BOOKS FOR COUNTRY LIVING
STOREY COMMUNICATIONS INC
RR 1   BOX 105
POWNAL VT 05261-9988

of yeast are Wyeast's Bohemian Lager (#2124) and Munich Lager (#2308).

Like it or not, fair or unfair, in this style competition judges will compare your beer to Anchor Steam. If it looks like Anchor, smells like Anchor, and tastes like Anchor, you've got a winner.

German *rauchbier* — which means literally "smoke beer" — is a traditional smoked beer style, made along the lines of a Vienna lager but with malt smoked over beechwood fires. The beer has a fairly malty, sweet flavor with a smoky phenolic aroma and after-taste. This smoky character varies from subtle to assertive from beer to beer. These are normal-gravity beers — about 1.048 to 1.060 — with fairly low hopping rates of about 20 to 30 IBUs. Hops are generally added only in the boil.

Smoked malt is available to homebrewers and the beechwood-smoked German malt is best for this style. It is possible to smoke malt at home using hardwood chips soaked in water. Some extract brewers make smoked beers using liquid smoke, which is found in the spice section at supermarkets. Brands without vinegar are generally preferred.

Although German beechwood-smoked malt is the first choice for making a smoked beer, it is not the only smoked malt. A peat-smoked malt from Scotland is also available. While Scottish beers are not made with smoked malt (this smoked Scottish malt is really intended for use in whisky distilling), some homebrewers and craft brews, such as the widely available Samuel Adams Scottish Ale, use it with good results. Be aware that it is harsher and more phenolic than German-smoked malt.

Other specialty styles of beer can also be made with smoked grains. There is historical evidence pointing to smoked wheat beers, but these styles are not generally available commercially, and homebrewers don't seem to make them. Other styles, notably porter, have been made with smoked malts with great success.

Brewers have always been inventors at heart, and there is no limit to the possible variations on beer recipes that could consti-tute good specialty beers. Experiments with alternative grains and other starch-containing foods are always popular. Wild rice and maple sap can provide satisfying brews.

Although we do not provide recipes for them here, there are also styles of beer that were once commercially brewed, but that are now lost but for references in historical literature; these could make great specialty beers for today's innovative homebrewers. For example, there was once a sour mash beer brewed in Kentucky in which the mash was done in a way similar to that used by whiskey distillers. In *Michael Jackson's Beer Companion*, Jackson describes a smoked wheat beer called "Grodzisk" that was once brewed in Poland. A homebrewer experimenting with home-smoking their own grains could likely produce a good smoked wheat beer that would truly stand out from the crowd at any homebrew meeting or competition! Steve Snyder's "Graetzer" recipe on page 29 is a good example of how a homebrewer could make a smoked wheat beer.

CALIFORNIA COMMONS

California Common #1

YIELD: .... 5 GAL. (18.9 L)
TOTAL BOILING TIME: .... 60 MIN.
PRIMARY FERMENT: .... 1 WEEK
SECONDARY FERMENT: .... 1 WEEK

- 1 lb. (454 g) crystal malt, 50°–60° Lovibond
- 7 lb. (3.18 kg) Alexander's pale malt extract
- 2 oz. (57 g) Northern Brewer hops, 7.0% alpha, in boil 60 min.
- 1 tbsp. (14.8 ml) Irish moss
- 1 oz. (28 g) Northern Brewer hops, 7.0% alpha, in boil 5 min.
  Wyeast #2112 California Lager yeast
- ¾ c. (206 ml) corn sugar, for priming

Add grain to 2 ½ gal. (9.4 L) of water and heat to 180°F (82°C). Strain out grain and add malt extract. Bring to a boil and add 2 oz. (57 g) of Northern Brewer hops and Irish moss. Boil 55 min., then add 1 oz. (28 g) of Northern Brewer hops. Boil 5 min., then turn off heat. Chill the wort, transfer to fermenter, and bring up to 5 gal. (18.9 L) with cold water. Pitch yeast when temperature is below 80°F (27°C). When fermentation is complete, prime with the corn sugar and bottle.

— *Mark Garetz, Pleasanton, California, HopTech*

California Common #2

```
YIELD: ............................................. 5 GAL. (18.9 L)
TOTAL BOILING TIME: ................................... 60 MIN.
STARTING GRAVITY: ........................................ 1.049
ENDING GRAVITY: .......................................... 1.012
PRIMARY FERMENT: .................................... 1 WEEK
SECONDARY FERMENT: ............................... 1 WEEK
```

Wyeast #2112 California Lager yeast
1½ lb. (680 g) 2-row pale malt, crushed
½ lb. (227 g) cara-pils malt, crushed
½ lb. (227 g) British medium crystal malt, crushed
1 package Burton water salts
6 lb. (2.72 kg) light malt extract
1½ oz. (43 g) Northern Brewer hops, in boil 55 min.
½ oz. (14 g) of Northern Brewer hops, in boil 15 min.
1 oz. (28 g) Cascade hops, steep
1 package Bru-Vigor yeast food
¾ c. (206 ml) corn sugar, for priming

Prepare yeast starter prior to brewing day.

Add crushed grains and water salts to 1 gal. (3.8 L) of 160°F (71°C) water and steep 30 min. Sparge grains with 1 gal. (3.8 L) or more of 168°F (76°C) water into brew kettle. Bring wort to a boil, then turn off heat and add malt extract. Boil 5 min. before adding 1½ oz. (43 g) of Northern Brewer hops. Boil 40 min., then add ½ oz. (14 g) of Northern Brewer hops. Boil 15 min., add last ½ oz. (14 g) of the Cascade hops, and turn off heat. Steep a few min., then chill the wort, transfer to fermenter, and top off to 5 gal. (18.9 L) with cold water. Pitch yeast along with Bru-Vigor yeast food. Ferment for 1 week. Rack to secondary for 1 week. Prime with corn sugar and bottle.

— *DeFalco's Home Wine & Beer Supplies, Houston, Texas*

Onward through the
Fog Steam Beer

YIELD: .... 5 GAL. (18.9 L)
TOTAL BOILING TIME: .... 60 MIN.
STARTING GRAVITY: 1.054
ENDING GRAVITY: 1.011
PRIMARY FERMENT: .... 6 DAYS
SECONDARY FERMENT: .... 8 DAYS

*The color of this beer matches Anchor Steam. The hop flavor
dominates, with a hint of Fuggles in the aroma.*

    Wyeast #2122 California Lager yeast
2 lb. (907 g) 2-row pale malt
1 lb. (454 g) crystal malt, 30° Lovibond
6 lb. (2.72 kg) Briess pale malt extract
1 lb. (454 g) Briess amber malt extract
1¾ oz. (50 g) Northern Brewer hops, 7.1% alpha, in boil 60 min.
¾ oz. (21 g) Northern Brewer hops, in boil 2 min.
1 oz. (28 g) Fuggles hops, 2.6% alpha, dry hop
1¼ c. (344 ml) amber dry malt extract, for priming

Make a yeast starter 1–3 days in advance.

    Mash grains in 2.2 gal. (8.3 L) of water at 158°F (70°C) for
40 min. Strain out grains and sparge with 170°F (77°C) water. Add
malt extracts and bring to a boil. Add 1¾ oz. (50 g) of Northern
Brewer hops. Boil 58 min., then add ¾ oz. (21 g) of Northern Brewer.
Boil 2 min., then turn off heat. Chill the wort, then strain out hops
while transferring to fermenter. Pitch yeast and add Fuggles hops.
Ferment 6 days at 61°F (16°C). Rack to secondary for 8 days. Prime
and bottle. Age 1 month.

— *Joseph Crowe, Round Rock, Texas*

SMOKED BEERS

Rauch Märzen

YIELD:	15 GAL. (56.8 L)
TOTAL BOILING TIME:	90 MIN.
STARTING GRAVITY:	1.057
ENDING GRAVITY:	1.014
PRIMARY FERMENT:	7 DAYS
SECONDARY FERMENT:	14 DAYS
LAGERING:	90 DAYS

Big malty palate with a clean, dry smoke flavor. Similar to Aecht Schlenkerla Rauch Bier. First place at Nevada State Fair.

- 25 lb. (11.34 kg) German rauch malt
- 5 lb. (2.27 kg) DeWolf-Cosyns Belgian pilsner malt
- 2 lb. (907 g) Durst Munich malt
- 1 lb. (454 g) DeWolf-Cosyns Belgian aromatic malt
- 1.6 oz. (45 g) Nugget hops, 15.6% alpha, in boil 60 min.
- 2.1 oz. (60 g) Hallertauer hops, 3.2% alpha, in boil 45 min.
- 1.1 oz. (31 g) Hallertauer hops, in boil 15 min.
- Wyeast #2308 Munich Lager yeast, ½-gal. (1.9-L) starter
- 2¼ c. (619 ml) corn sugar, for priming

Crush grains and add to 11 gal. (41.6 L) of water. Mash at 122°F (50°C) for 30 min. Heat to 152°F (67°C) for 90 min. Mash-out at 169°F (76°C) for 15 min. Sparge with 169°F (76°C) water adjusted to pH 5.3. Collect 17 gal. (64.4 L) of wort in brew kettle. Boil 30 min. before adding 1.6 oz. (45 g) of Nugget hops. Boil 15 min., then add 2.1 oz. (60 g) of Hallertauer hops. Boil 30 min., then add 1.1 oz. (31 g) of Hallertauer hops. Boil 15 min. and turn off heat. Chill wort, transfer to fermenter, and pitch yeast. Ferment 7 days at 50°F (10°C). Rack to secondary fermenter for 14 days at 48°F (9°C). Rack and lager for 90 days at 32°F (0°C). Prime with corn sugar and bottle.

— "Beer" Rich Mansfield, San Jose, California
Washoe Zephyr Zymurgists

Dragon's Belch

YIELD: .... 5 GAL. (18.9 L)
TOTAL BOILING TIME: .... 90 MIN.
STARTING GRAVITY: 1.050
ENDING GRAVITY: 1.016
PRIMARY FERMENT: .... 3 WEEKS
SECONDARY FERMENT: .... 4 WEEKS

Second place in the specialty beer category at the 7th Annual Dredhop and Regale competition, a second place in the "other" category at the 4th Annual Rocky Mountain Homebrew Shootout, a second place in the specialty beer category at the 16th Annual AugustFest, and a silver certificate at the 1995 AHA National Competition.

6 lb. (2.72 kg) rauch malt
1 lb. (454 g) aromatic Munich malt
1 lb. (454 g) German pilsner malt
6 oz. (170 g) Belgian special-B malt
2 oz. (57 g) chocolate malt
1 oz. (28 g) Styrian Goldings hops, 5.2% alpha, in boil 60 min.
1 tsp. (4.9 ml) Irish moss
    Wyeast #2308 Munich Lager yeast
¾ c. (206 ml) corn sugar, for priming

Crush grains and add to 3 gal. (11.4 L) of water. Heat to 128°F (53°C) and rest 30 min. Remove a portion of the mash and heat it to boiling. Return decoction portion to the mash to raise mash temperature to 150°F (66°C). Rest at 150°F (66°C) until starch conversion is complete. Sparge with 168°F (76°C) water and collect 6 ½ gal. (24.6 L) of wort. Boil 30 min. before adding Styrian Goldings hops. Boil 45 min., then add Irish moss. Boil 15 min., then turn off heat. Chill the wort, transfer to fermenter, and pitch yeast. Ferment 3 weeks at 52°F (11°C). Rack to secondary for 4 weeks at 38°F (3°C). Prime with corn sugar and bottle.

— *Keith Schwols, Ft. Collins, Colorado*

Graetzer

YIELD:	5 GAL. (18.9 L)
TOTAL BOILING TIME:	70 MIN.
STARTING GRAVITY:	1.056
ENDING GRAVITY:	1.014
PRIMARY FERMENT:	1 WEEK

4 lb. (1.81 kg) wheat malt, smoked
6 lb. (2.72 kg) 2-row lager malt
½ lb. (227 g) crystal malt, 40° Lovibond
⅘ oz. (23 g) Cascade hops, 4.4% alpha, in boil 60 min.
⅘ oz. (23 g) Cascade hops, in boil 20 min.
1½ oz. (43 g) Hallertauer hops, 4.6% alpha, in boil 2 min.
    ale yeast

Smoke the wheat malt for about 45 min. with oak chips in a barbecue grill. Crush grains and add to 3½ gal. (13.2 L) of 132°F (56°C) water. Rest at 122°F (50°C) for 30 min. Heat mash to 155°F (68°C) and hold for 1 hour. Heat mash to 160°F (71°C) and hold for 10 min. Sparge with 170°F (77°C) water and collect 6 ½ gal. (24.6 L) of wort in brew kettle. Boil 10 min. before adding ⅘ oz. (23 g) of Cascade hops. Boil 40 min., then add ⅘ oz. (23 g) of Cascade hops. Boil 18 min., then add 1½ oz. (43 g) of Hallertauer. Boil 2 min. and turn off heat. Chill the wort, transfer to fermenter, and pitch yeast. Ferment 1 week, then keg. Age 1 month.

— *Steve Snyder, Seattle, Washington*

SPECIALTY BEERS

Wild Rice Blonde Ale

YIELD: .... 5 GAL. (18.9 L)
TOTAL BOILING TIME: .... 42 MIN.
PRIMARY FERMENT: .... 7 DAYS
SECONDARY FERMENT: .... 7 DAYS

Second place in the light ale category at the 1996 Boston Homebrew Competition.

   ½ lb. (227 g) wild rice
6 ¾ lb. (3.06 kg) Alexander's Sun Country pale malt extract
1½ oz. (43 g) Goldings hops, in boil 40 min.
   ½ tsp. (2.5 ml) Irish moss
   ½ oz. (14 g) Willamette hops, in boil 2 min.
   ¼ oz. (7 g) Cooper's ale yeast
   1 c. (275 ml) corn sugar, for priming

In a large pot, add 1½ gal. (5.7 L) water and wild rice. Heat to 150°F (66°C) for 40 min. Strain the rice from the water and add malt extract and Goldings. Boil 15 min. Add Irish moss and boil 25 min. Add Willamette hops and boil 2 min. Turn off heat, cool, and strain wort into fermenter containing 3½ gal. (13.2 L) of cold water. Ferment 7 days. Rack to secondary for 7 days. Prime with corn sugar and bottle. Age 4 weeks.

— Peter Cammann, Waitsfield, Vermont

Maple Sap Ale

YIELD: .... 5 GAL. (18.9 L)
TOTAL BOILING TIME: .... 42 MIN.
PRIMARY FERMENT: .... 7 DAYS
SECONDARY FERMENT: .... 7 DAYS

½ lb. (227 g) pale malt

½ lb. (227 g) medium crystal malt

5 gal. (18.9 L) fresh maple sap

6 ¾ lb. (3.06 kg) Alexander's light malt extract

1½ oz. (43 g) Goldings hops, in boil 42 min.

½ oz. (14 g) Cascade hops, in boil 42 min.

½ tsp. (2.5 ml) Irish moss

½ oz. (14 g) Willamette hops, in boil 2 min.

¼ oz. (7 g) Cooper's ale yeast

1 c. (275 ml) corn sugar, for priming

Toast the pale malt for 10 min. in a 400°F (204°C) oven. Add the grain and 1½ gal. (5.7 L) of maple sap in a large pot and turn heat on high. Just before the boil begins, strain out the grains. Add malt extract, Goldings, and Cascade hops. Boil 15 min. Add Irish moss and boil 25 min. Add Willamette hops and boil 2 min. Turn off heat, cool wort, and strain into a carboy containing the remaining 3 ½ gal. (13.2 L) of maple sap. Pitch yeast when wort is below 75°F (24°C) and ferment 1 week. Rack to secondary for 1 week. Prime with corn sugar and bottle. Age 4–6 weeks.

— *Peter Cammann, Waitsfield, Vermont*

More HOMEBREW FAVORITES

15

Meads

Mead is not beer. It's not made like beer, it doesn't look or smell like beer, and it certainly doesn't taste like beer. Instead of the familiar ingredients — water, barley malt, hops, and yeast — we're now working with just honey, water, and yeast. These three simple ingredients can produce myriad flavors and characters. Adding fruit, spice, or other ingredients can change the character in yet more wonderful ways.

Mead is an ancient drink, having been made and enjoyed for thousands of years. One of the oldest works of literature in the English language is the poem *Beowulf* — written over 1,200 years ago. Mead is mentioned in this poem, and the drink continues to evoke images of fierce kings and warriors.

Although more akin to wine than beer, it is with homebrewers that mead finds itself most at home. Most homebrewers occasionally brew meads, and mead is a long-recognized style in the American Homebrewers Association National Homebrew Competition, as well as in most large regional homebrew competitions.

Honey is the major contributor to the flavor profile and its source of fermentable sugars. To balance the sweetness of the honey, you may want to add an acid, such as citric or malic. Many mead makers prefer adding the acid after fermentation to avoid changing the pH of the *must* and, consequently, the activity of the yeast. "Must" is what a mead maker calls the unfermented mead — it's the equivalent of the word "wort" to a beer brewer. Honey can be purchased in virtually any supermarket, yet many mead makers seek out purer, less processed, specialty honeys that can be used to impart their distinctive flavors to the mead. Honey purchased at the grocery store is likely to be a light clover honey. It will produce a very light, delicate mead. Darker honeys, such as wildflower, and those with identifiable flavors, such as tupelo and orange blossom, create meads with quite different flavors, colors, and aromas. Each of these meads can be appreciated for its own merits, and a serious mead maker will experiment with small batches of a variety of different honeys to gauge their character.

Traditional mead is made with only honey, water, and yeast, but mead also includes separate subcategories. These substyles are spiced mead, called *metheglin;* fruit mead, called *melomel;* mead made by replacing the water with apple juice, called *cyser;* mead made by replacing the water with grape juice, called *pyment;* and mead made with a blend of honey and barley malt, called *braggot* or *bracket.*

Water is the major ingredient in mead, just as it is in beer, but mead makers worry far less about water differences — and for good reason. In beer, many of the ions present in brewing water affect the mash characteristics; there is no mash in mead making, so this issue becomes irrelevant. Any drinkable water will produce good mead. You may want to add yeast nutrients to make up for the nutritional shortcomings of honey.

Yeast is a popular topic of discussion among mead makers. Several years ago, many homebrewers made creditable meads using fairly low gravities and standard ale yeasts. Most mead makers, however, brew to fairly high gravities and use an alcohol-tolerant wine yeast. Yeast selection can be an important part of achieving either a dry or a sweet character. Most wine yeasts may produce a drier-tasting mead. If you prefer a sweeter character to your mead, try one of the sweet mead yeasts on the market, such as Wycast #3184 or Yeast Culture Kit Company's W12 (Yeast Lab M62). Of the two, the Wyeast is less attenuative and should give a sweeter flavor. No matter which yeast you use, however, adding a yeast nutrient is always recommended with meads, and pitching large starters is a good practice.

Metheglin (spiced mead) can accommodate a wide variety of spices. While quite a few mead makers use traditional Christmas cookie or wassail-type spices, such as cinnamon, nutmeg, allspice, and clove, real dividends can be realized by trying less ubiquitous spices and combinations. Italian herbs — basil and oregano — can make very good meads. Mint meads are a natural. Tea works as an interesting spice, and some herbal teas lend fruity flavors to the mead as well. Spicy chili pepper meads can be sublime. Experiment, tweak recipes, and don't forget that mead makers often blend their batches to achieve balance.

Fruit meads, or melomels, also represent a smorgasbord of flavors. Berries always work well, as do soft fruits like plums, peaches, and apricots. Remember that fruit naturally contains acid, so it will take less added acid to balance a fruit mead than it would a traditional mead or a metheglin. Fruit can be added in any of several forms, as we discussed in the fruit beer chapter on page 234. Fresh fruit is, of course, usually preferred — especially by purists — but fruit juices, frozen fruit, extracts, liqueurs, and canned or packaged fruits are all possibilities.

Cysers and pyments are interesting mead styles in that the liquid is not water, but cider in the case of cyser, or grape juice in the case of pyment. Naturally, these drinks have a considerable amount of their flavor contributed by the underlying fruit of the juice. Brewers making pyment experiment with different types of grape juices, and the wine kits sold at homebrew shops make an excellent base.

Braggots, a cross between beer and mead, are included in this chapter, although few brewers make them. Braggots get at least half their fermentable sugars from honey, but include malt — often malt extract — as an important source of sugar. They have a complex taste, blending the toasty flavors of malt with the more subtle flavors of honey. Let's hope that more brewers will venture into this realm and try their hand at making a drink with history, one that they'll never get to taste if they stick to commercial brews.

In a competition, a good mead judge will look for a clean, strong honey flavor and aroma. This is called *honey expression* and is what separates mead from other drinks. If you can't tell your mead from a Chablis, then it probably won't do well in competition. The other critical component of a mead is balance. A judge wants some complexity in the mead, not just a one-dimensional sweetness, nor a one-dimensional dryness or astringency. The sweetness of the honey is balanced by adding acid: citric, malic, tartaric, or a blend. Remember, acid can come from fruit in a melomel. Sweetness can also be balanced by other flavors. The heat of a Szechuan pepper, for example, can perfectly balance a mead.

Some competitions include a separate category, for purists, called "show mead." In this competition category, no additives or ingredients that contribute undetectable flavors are allowed — just honey, water, and yeast.

TRADITIONAL MEAD

Unconscious Blond Mead

YIELD:	5 GAL. (18.9 L)
TOTAL BOILING TIME:	10-MIN STEEP
STARTING GRAVITY:	1.100
ENDING GRAVITY:	1.005
PRIMARY FERMENT:	7 DAYS
SECONDARY FERMENT:	21 DAYS
TERTIARY FERMENT:	18 MONTHS

First place and runner-up to best of show at the 1994 Nevada State Fair, first place at the 1994 California State Fair, and first place at the Sonoma County Harvest Fair in 1994.

     tartaric acid
15 lb. (6.8 kg) Nevada honey
 2 tsp. (9.9 ml) Super Ferment yeast nutrient
     Lalvin EC-1118 yeast

Preboil 5 gal. (18.9 L) of water and decant to remove precipitate. Adjust the total acidity with tartaric acid, by titration. Add honey and Super Ferment to the preboiled water, heat to 140°F (60°C), and steep 10 min. Chill, transfer to fermenter, and pitch yeast. Ferment 7 days at 68°F (20°C). Rack to secondary for 21 days at 65°F (16°C). Rack to another fermenter and continue fermenting for 18 months, then bottle without priming sugar.

— *"Beer" Rich Mansfield, San Jose, California*
Washoe Zephyr Zymurgists

METHEGLIN: SPICED MEADS

Harrods Mead

YIELD:	5 GAL. (18.9 L)
TOTAL BOILING TIME:	A FEW MIN.
STARTING GRAVITY:	1.090
ENDING GRAVITY:	1.015
PRIMARY FERMENT:	14 DAYS
SECONDARY FERMENT:	6 WEEKS

    1   whole package Harrods Tea, containing hibiscus, apples, rose
        hips, elderberry, orange peel, and marigold
   12   lb. (5.44 kg) honey
    ½   lb. (227 g) cane sugar
    3   tsp. (14.8 ml) acid blend
   1¼   tsp. (6.2 ml) Yeastex-61 (yeast nutrient)
    1   tsp. (4.9 ml) gypsum
    2   packages Lalvin KIV-1116 yeast

Bring 3 gal. (11.4 L) of water to a boil and add entire package of tea. Let stand for 20 min. Pour liquid through a strainer and into brewpot. Add honey, cane sugar, acid blend, yeast nutrient, and gypsum and turn on heat. Skim off foam as it forms. When boil begins, turn off heat, chill, and transfer to a primary fermenter. Top off to 5 gal. (18.9 L) with cold water and pitch yeast. Ferment 14 days, then rack to a secondary fermenter for 6 weeks before bottling.

— Bill Campbell, North East, Pennsylvania
Brewing Excellence in the Erie Region (BEER)

Go For Grenedaness

YIELD:	5 GAL. (18.9 L)
TOTAL BOILING TIME:	20 MIN.
STARTING GRAVITY:	1.090
ENDING GRAVITY:	1.030
PRIMARY FERMENT:	3 WEEKS
SECONDARY FERMENT:	9 WEEKS

Second place in the specialty brew category at the 1996 Cheyenne Quick Draw Competition.

2½ tsp. (12.4 ml) acid blend
4 tbsp. (59.4 ml) nutmeg
1 tbsp. (15 ml) mace
1 tbsp. (15 ml) yeast nutrient
10 lb. (4.54 kg) Rice's unfiltered honey
3 lb. (1.36 kg) Colorado unfiltered honey
1 tsp. (5 ml) Irish moss
Wyeast (#3184) Sweet Mead yeast

Add acid blend, spices, and yeast nutrient to 4 gal. (15.1 L) of water. Boil 5 min. Add honey and Irish moss. Boil 15 min., then turn off heat. Chill, transfer to a primary fermenter, and pitch yeast. Ferment 3 weeks at 66°F (19°C). Rack to secondary for 9 weeks at 66°F (19°C). Bottle without priming sugar.

— Keith Schwols, Ft. Collins, Colorado

Hot to Trot

YIELD:	4 GAL. (15.1 L)
TOTAL BOILING TIME:	. 10-MIN. BOIL, 15-MIN. STEEP
STARTING GRAVITY:	1.120
ENDING GRAVITY:	1.035
PRIMARY FERMENT:	3 WEEKS
SECONDARY FERMENT:	SEVERAL MONTHS

Second place mead at the 7th Annual Dreadhop and Regale Competition and third place at the 1996 AMA National Mead Ambrosia Competition.

  1 tbsp. (14.8 ml) acid blend
  5 tbsp. (74.3 ml) cinnamon powder
  1 stick cinnamon, freshly ground
  1 tbsp. (14.8 ml) dried red pepper flakes (like at a pizza parlor)
  ⅛ tsp. (0.6 ml) red food coloring
1½ tbsp. (22.3 ml) yeast nutrient
15 lb. (6.8 kg) Colorado honey
  2 packages Montrochet dry yeast

Bring 3 gal. (11.4 L) of water, acid blend, spices, food coloring, and yeast nutrient to a boil and let boil 10 min. Remove from heat and add honey. Steep 15 min., then chill. Transfer to fermenter and pitch yeast. Ferment 3 weeks at 68°F (20°C), then rack to secondary for several months. Bottle without priming sugar.

— *Keith Schwols, Ft. Collins, Colorado*

Keep Your Wits about You

YIELD:	5 GAL. (18.9 L)
TOTAL BOILING TIME:	STEEPED, BUT NOT BOILED
STARTING GRAVITY:	1.100
ENDING GRAVITY:	1.035
PRIMARY FERMENT:	3 WEEKS
SECONDARY FERMENT:	6 WEEKS
ADDITIONAL FERMENTATION:	SEVERAL MONTHS

First place as a traditional mead in the 1996 AMA National Mead Ambrosia Competition.

  5 lb. (2.27 kg) Colorado Western Slope honey
  3 qt. (2.8 L) North Dakota Farmer's honey
  2 tbsp. (29.6 ml) orange peel
  2 tbsp. (29.6 ml) coriander
  2 tbsp. (29.6 ml) Irish moss
  1 tbsp. (14.8 ml) yeast nutrient
1¼ tsp. (6.2 ml) tartaric acid
1¼ tsp. (6.2 ml) malic acid
 ½ tsp. (2.5 ml) citric acid
     Wyeast (#3184) Sweet Mead yeast

Bring 4¾ gal. (18 L) water to a boil. Turn off heat and add all ingredients except yeast. Bring almost to a boil. Remove from heat and chill. Transfer to fermenter and pitch yeast. Ferment 3 weeks at 68°F (20°C). Rack to secondary for 6 weeks at 68°F (20°C). Rack to a third fermenter for several months, then bottle without priming sugar.

— *Keith Schwols, Ft. Collins, Colorado*

MELOMEL: FRUIT MEADS

Mel O' Mel

YIELD: .... 5 GAL. (18.9 L)
TOTAL BOILING TIME: .... 10 MIN.
STARTING GRAVITY: 1.180
PRIMARY FERMENT: .... 17 DAYS
SECONDARY FERMENT: .... 6 MONTHS

   4 tsp. (19.7 ml) yeast nutrient
   1 tsp. (4.9 ml) acid blend
 17 lb. (7.71 kg) honey
 20 kiwis, crushed
   3 lb. (kg) strawberries, crushed
   2 mangoes, crushed
0.35 oz. (10 g) Champagne yeast
   1 pack Edme ale yeast

Heat 4 gal. (15.1 L) of water with 4 tsp. (20 ml) of yeast nutrient and 1 tsp. (4.9 ml) acid blend. Add honey and boil 10 min. Turn off heat and add fruit. Cover and steep 20 min. Chill, transfer all to fermenter, and pitch yeast. After 10 days, remove fruit by straining through sieve or cheesecloth. Ferment for another 7 days, then rack to another fermenter for 6 months before bottling.

— *Ed Cosgrove, Woodbridge, Virginia*
Brewers Association of Northern Virginia (BANOVA)

Blueberry Ambrosia

YIELD: .... 4½ GAL. (17 L)
TOTAL BOILING TIME: .... 20-MIN. STEEP
STARTING GRAVITY: 1.120
ENDING GRAVITY: 1.020
PRIMARY FERMENT: .... 30 DAYS
SECONDARY FERMENT: .... 30 DAYS

Sweet melomel with a beautiful burgundy color and an unmistakable blueberry flavor.

       5 tsp. (24.7 ml) yeast nutrient
       1 tsp. (4.9 ml) acid blend
      15 lb. (6.8 kg) clover honey
      12 lb. (5.44 kg) fresh blueberries, cleaned and crushed
       2 packs Red Star Champagne yeast

Add yeast nutrient and acid blend to 4 gal. (15.1 L) of water and begin heating. Add honey and crushed blueberries. Bring to 180°F (82°C) and hold for 20 min., skimming foam as it forms. Turn off heat, chill, and pour into a large fermenter. Pitch yeast and ferment 30 days at 65°F (18°C). Strain mead through cheesecloth, squeezing out and discarding blueberry skins and seeds. Ferment 30 days at 65°F (18°C), then bottle. Age 6 months.

— *Karl Lutzen, Rolla, Missouri*
Missouri Association of Serious Homebrewers (MASH)

Blue By You

YIELD: .... 11 GAL. (3.8 L)
TOTAL BOILING TIME: .... 20-MIN. BOIL,
STARTING GRAVITY: 1.094
ENDING GRAVITY: 0.998
PRIMARY FERMENT: .... 30 DAYS
SECONDARY FERMENT: .... 60 DAYS

- 4 tbsp. (59.4 ml) yeast nutrient
- 5 tsp. (24.7 ml) acid blend
- 3 gal. (36 lb.) wildflower honey
- 28 lb. (12.70 kg) fresh blueberries, crushed
- 1½ tsp. (7.4 ml) pectic enzyme
  - Lalvin K1V-1116 Montpelier wine yeast
- ½ c. (138 ml) corn sugar, for priming

Add yeast nutrient and acid blend to 6 gal. (22.7 L) of water and begin heating. Add honey, rinsing honey containers with a total of 3 additional gal. (11.4 L) of water, and add to brewpot. Boil 20 min., skimming foam as it forms. Turn off heat and add crushed blueberries. Steep 20 min., chill, and pour into a large fermenter. Pitch yeast, add pectic enzyme, and ferment 30 days at 65°F (18°C). Strain through cheesecloth, squeeze out and discard blueberry skins and seeds. Ferment 60 days at 65°F (18°C). Bottle with or without priming. Age at least 6 months.

— *Karl Lutzen, Rolla, Missouri*
Missouri Association of Serious Homebrewers (MASH)

Hawaiian Punch

YIELD: .... 5 GAL. (18.9 L)
TOTAL BOILING TIME: .... 20-MIN. STEEP
STARTING GRAVITY: .... 1.080 (WITHOUT FRUIT)
ENDING GRAVITY: 1.010
PRIMARY FERMENT: .... 3 WEEKS
SECONDARY FERMENT: .... 3 WEEKS
ADDITIONAL FERMENTATION: .... SEVERAL MONTHS

Second place in the mead category at the 1995 Unfermentable Homebrew Shoot-out.

10 lb. (4.54 kg) North Dakota Farmer's honey
10 lb. (4.54 kg) cherries, pitted and frozen
 4 lb. (1.81 kg) green plums, pitted and frozen
 1 tsp. (4.9 ml) malic acid
 ½ tsp. (2.5 ml) citric acid
   Wyeast (#3184) Sweet Mead yeast

Add honey, fruit, and acids to 4½ gal. (17 L) of water and pasteurize for 20 min. at 165°F (74°C). Chill, transfer to a plastic bucket or other wide-mouth fermenter, and pitch yeast. Ferment 3 weeks, then rack off the fruit pulp into a glass secondary fermenter. Ferment 3 weeks, then rack to another fermenter for several months. Bottle without priming sugar.

— *Keith Schwols, Ft. Collins, Colorado*

Summer's Lease II
Apricot Melomel

YIELD: .... 2¾ GAL. (10.4 L)
TOTAL STEEPING TIME: .... 90 MIN.
STARTING GRAVITY: 1.127
ENDING GRAVITY: 1.023
PRIMARY FERMENT: .... 30 WEEKS
SECONDARY FERMENT: .... 5 WEEKS

Gold medal at the 1995 New Mexico State Fair. Excellent acid balance with good apricot and heavy character.

9 lb. (4.08 kg) (approximately 1 gal. [3.8 L] apricot juice)
5½ lb. (2.49 kg) Questa honey
½ lb. (227 g) Sourwood honey
⅒ lb. (45 g) Star Thistle honey
2 packets Lalvin K1V-1116 Montpelier wine yeast
1½ lb. (680 g) clover honey
½ tsp. (2.5 ml) ascorbic acid
1 oz. (28 g) calcium carbonate
2 tbsp. (29.6 ml) sodium benzoate

Add apricot juice and all honey except for clover honey to 1 gal. (3.8 L) of water. Heat to 150°F (66°C) and hold for 90 min. Chill, transfer to fermenter, and pitch yeast. Ferment at 65° – 75°F (18° – 24°C) for 30 weeks. Rack to secondary for 5 weeks, then add 1 oz. (28 g) of calcium carbonate, and to kill the yeast add 2 tbsp. (30 g) of sodium benzoate. Also steep 1½ lb. (680 g) of clover honey added to 1 pt. of water at 160°F (71°C) for 20 min., then add this to the fermenter. Let it sit at least 24 hours to settle out, then bottle.

— *Michael Hall, Los Alamos, New Mexico*
Los Alamos Atom Mashers

CYSER

Simple Cyser

YIELD: .... 1 GAL. (3.8 L)
TOTAL STEEPING TIME: .... 5 MIN.
PRIMARY FERMENT: .... 6 WEEKS
SECONDARY FERMENT: .... SEVERAL WEEKS

Simple cyser with a taste close to white wine.

1 gal. (3.8 L) apple juice (organic)
2 lb. (907 g) clover honey
0.18-oz. (5-g) package Cote des Blanks yeast
3 cloves
2 sticks cinnamon

Remove enough juice from the jug to allow for the addition of honey (it helps to run the honey jar under warm water to thin it). Place juice, in jug, in warm water. Increase temperature to 150°F (66°C). Pour honey into jug, using a funnel if necessary. Hold the temperature at 150°F (66°C) for about 5 min. Cool jug to below 80°F (27°C). Add yeast nutrient and yeast. Ferment at room temperature. Fermentation should slow after 3 weeks. After 6 weeks, rack to a second jug into which you have placed the cloves and cinnamon. Continue to rack every few weeks, whenever a layer of sediment appears in the bottle, until the cyser clears, then bottle.

— *Bill Shirley, Houston, Texas/Washington, D.C., Houston Foam Rangers*
Brewers United for Real Potables (BURP)

BRAGGOTS

Smoke Your Nose

YIELD: .... 1 GAL. (3.8 L)
TOTAL BOILING TIME: .... 15-MIN. BOIL, 15-MIN. STEEP
STARTING GRAVITY: 1.150
ENDING GRAVITY: 1.040
PRIMARY FERMENT: .... 4 WEEKS
SECONDARY FERMENT: .... 8 WEEKS
ADDITIONAL FERMENTATION: .... 1 YEAR

First place in the Stranger Than Life category at the 1996 AMA National Mead Ambrosia Competition.

   2 lb. (907 g) smoked malt
1½ qt. (1.42 L) North Dakota Farmer's honey
 ⅛ tsp. (0.6 g) malic acid
 ⅛ tsp. (0.6 g) tartaric acid
 ⅛ tsp. (0.6 g) citric acid
     Wyeast #3632 Dry Mead yeast

The smoked malt is a combination: peat-smoked, beechwood-smoked, and homemade applewood-smoked pale malt. Mash the crushed grains in 2 ⅔ qt. (2.52 L) water at 155°F (68°C), until starch conversion is complete. Sparge with 170°F (77°C) water until 1 gal. (3.8 L) of liquid is collected. Boil 15 min. Turn off heat and add honey and acid blends. Steep 15 min., then chill, transfer to a primary fermenter, and pitch yeast. Ferment 4 weeks at 68°F (20°C), then rack to secondary for 8 weeks at 68°F (20°C). Rack to another fermenter for about 1 year. Bottle without priming sugar.

— *Keith Schwols, Ft. Collins, Colorado*

Hairy-Chested Wheat Mead

YIELD: .... 6 GAL. (22.7 L)
TOTAL BOILING TIME: .... 45 MIN.
STARTING GRAVITY: 1.061
ENDING GRAVITY: 1.010
PRIMARY FERMENT: .... 18 DAYS

4 lb. (1.81 kg) pale malt extract

2.2 lb. (1 kg) Morgan Master Blend Australian wheat malt extract

¾ oz. (43 g) Kent Goldings hops, in boil 45 min.

5 lb. (2.27 kg) clover honey

¼ oz. (7 g) Kent Goldings hops, in boil 3 min.

2 packets Nottingham yeast

⅞ c. (241 ml) corn sugar, for priming

Add malt extracts to 2 gal. (7.6 L) of water in brew kettle. Bring to a boil and add ¾ oz. (43 g) of Kent Goldings hops. During the boil, heat the honey in a microwave oven to 180°F (82°C). Hold for 20 min. Do not boil the honey. After boiling the wort for 42 min., add ¼ oz. (7 g) of Kent Goldings hops. Boil 3 min., then turn off heat. Allow wort to cool for 10 – 15 min., then add honey. Chill the wort, transfer to a primary fermenter, and top off to 6 gal. (22.7 L) with cold water. Pitch yeast and ferment 18 days at 70°F (21°C). Prime with the corn sugar and bottle.

— *Robert D. Beyer, Jr., N. Catasauqua, Pennsylvania*
Brewlab Thursday Nighter

Bibliography

Bergen, Roger. "American Wheat Beers." *Brewing Techniques* vol. 1, no. 1 (May/June 1993): 14.

———. "A Stout Companion." *Brewing Techniques* vol. 1, no. 4 (Nov/Dec 1993): 18.

———. "California Steamin'." *Brewing Techniques* vol. 2, no. 1 (Jan/Feb 1994): 20.

Brockington, David. "West Coast Amber Ale." *Brewing Techniques* (Nov/Dec 1995): 36.

Busch, Jim. "Cask Conditioning Ales at Home." *Brewing Techniques* (Nov/Dec 1995): 30.

———. "Stepping Up to Lager Brewing — Part I: An Overview of the Brewing Process." *Brewing Techniques* vol. 4, no. 3 (May/June 1996): 24.

———. "Stepping Up to Lager Brewing — Part II: Chemistry of Cold Storage." *Brewing Techniques* vol. 4, no. 4 (July/Aug 1996): 24.

Dawson, Tim. *Beer Style Guidelines*. 1995.

———. "Smoky Beer — Brewing with Smoked Malts." *Brewing Techniques* vol. 4, no. 3 (May/June 1996): 44.

deClerck, Jean. *A Textbook of Brewing*. London: Chapman and Hall, 1957.

Eckhardt, Fred. *The Essentials of Beer Style*. Portland, OR: Fred Eckhardt Associates, 1989.

Fix, George. *Vienna*. Boulder, CO: Brewers Publications, 1994.

Foster, Terry. "Perfect Your Porter." *zymurgy* vol. 19, no. 2 (Summer 1996): 54.

———. *Porter*. Boulder, CO: Brewers Publications, 1992.

———. *Pale Ale*. Boulder, CO: Brewers Publications, 1990.

Frane, Jeff. "Brew Traditional European Pilsner." *Brew Your Own* vol. 2, no. 9 (Sept 1996): 19.

Hall, Michael. "A Treatise on Judging Mead." 1996.

Hardy, Norm. "Altbier." *Brewing Techniques* vol. 3, no. 1 (Jan/Feb 1995): 36.

Harrison, John. "Capturing the Flavour of Beers Gone By." *Brewers' Guardian* (Nov 1995): 48.

———. *An Introduction to Old British Beers and How to Make Them*. London: Durden Park Beer Circle, 1976, 1991.

Jackson, Michael. *Michael Jackson's Beer Companion*. Philadelphia: Running Press, 1993.

———. *The Great Beers of Belgium*. Antwerp: CODA, 1991.

Jolda, Deb. "The Yeast Directory — The Compleat Guide to Commercially Available Yeast Strains." *The 1996 Brewer's Market Directory*. Eugene, OR: New Wine Press, 1996.

La Pensée, Clive. *The Historical Companion to House-Brewing*. Beverly, England: Montag Publications, 1990.

Lewis, Michael. *Stout*. Boulder, CO: Brewers Publications, 1996.

McConnell, Daniel and Ken Schramm. "Mead Success: Ingredients, Processes, and Techniques." *zymurgy* vol. 18, no. 1 (Spring 1995): 32.

Miller, Dave. *Dave Miller's Homebrewing Guide*. Pownal, VT: Storey Publishing, 1995.

———. *Continental Pilsner*. Boulder, CO: Brewers Publications, 1990.

Mosher, Randy. *The Brewers Companion*. Seattle, WA: Alephanalia Press, 1994.

Papazian, Charlie. *The New Complete Joy of Homebrewing*. New York: Avon Books, 1991.

———. *The Home Brewer's Companion*. New York: Avon Books, 1994.

Price, Susanne. "Stimulate Your Senses with Mead." *zymurgy* vol. 15, no. 3 (Fall 1992): 32.

Protz, Roger. *The Ultimate Encyclopedia of Beer*. London: Carlton Books, 1995.

Rhodes, Christine (ed.). *The Encyclopedia of Beer*. New York: Henry Holt Publishers, 1995.

Slosberg, Pete. "The Road to an American Brown Ale." *Brewing Techniques* vol. 3, no. 3 (May/June 1995): 32.

Stevens, Mark and Karl Lutzen. *Cat's Meow*, 1991–1997.

Thomas, Keith. "A Peak into Porter's Past." *zymurgy* vol. 19, no. 2 (Summer 1996): 47.

Thomlinson, Thom. "India Pale Ale Part I: IPA and Empire — Necessity and Enterprise Give Birth to a Style." *Brewing Techniques* (Mar/Apr 1994): 20.

———. "India Pale Ale Part II: The Sun Never Sets." *Brewing Techniques* (May/June 1994): 20.

Warner, Eric. *German Wheat*. Boulder, CO: Brewers Publications, 1992.

Index

A

Aaahh Bock, 190
Aaron's Abbey Ale, 123–24
Adelaide sparkling ale, 46
Alex's Laborious Lager, 206
Alki Point Sunset Kölschbier, 137–38
Alleycat Stock Ale, 32
Al's Rye Ale, 157
Alt beers
 described, 130–31
 recipes, 140–44
Alt Enough to Drink, 141–42
Amber Cerveza, 172–73
American Brown Ale, 61
American brown ales
 described, 48
 recipes, 58–61
American "CRAB" Ale, 31
American lagers
 cream ale, 203–4, 214
 dark, 203, 212–13
 described, 202–4
 light, 202–10
 Pre-Prohibition-style, 203, 210–12
 recipes, 204–14
American Mild, 51
American Pale Ale, 35
American pale ales
 described, 18
 recipes, 30–41
American Pilsner, 205–6
American wheat beers
 described, 218–19
 recipes, 228–33
Ancient Gruit Ale, 265–66
Ape Over Ale, 262
Apple beer, 255
Apricot Peach Beer, 256–57
A2 Sparkling Ale, 46
Auld Rabbie Burns, 149

B

Banana beer, 262
Barefoot Lager, 211–12
Barleywine, 151

Barleywine recipes, 151, 154
Basenji Oktoberfest Ale, 179
Basic Pale Ale, 26
Bavarian Bath, 226
Bavarian Black-Out, 185
Bavarian dark lagers, 183–85
Bavarian light lagers. *See* Munich
 Helles
Bavarian wheat beers. *See* Weizenbier
Beagle Boys Brown Ale, 55
Beaver Brown Ale, 58
Belgian Ale #1, 109
Belgian Ale #2, 111
Belgian ales
 described, 106–9
 lambics, 108, 128–29
 oud bruin, 108, 115
 pale, 107, 109–12
 recipes, 109–29
 strong, 107, 113–14
 Trappist, 107–8, 116–24
 wit beers, 108–9, 124–27
Belgian Nectar, 121
Belgian Spice, 110
Belgian Strong Ale, 114
Belgian Tripel, 122
Belgian Triple, 119
Best Brown This Side o' the Pecos, 60
Big Chief Amber Ale, 37–38
Big Murphy Special Red, 19
Bill's Pils, 162–63
Black Bavarian, 183
Blackberry beers, 248–49
Blackberry Porter, 249
Black Currant Lambic, 128
Black Honey Porter, 81
Black Lake Pils, 209
Black Whisker Bitter, 20–21
Blueberry Ambrosia, 302
Blueberry beers, 237–39
Blueberry Wheat, 237–38
Blue By You, 303
Bock and a Half, 194
Bocks
 described, 181–82

doppel-, 182, 191, 200
helles, 182
mai-, 195, 197–99
recipes, 190–201
Bodacious Bellhop, 75
Braggots
described, 296–97
recipes, 306–7
Brain Wipe Tripel, 112
Breakfast Brew, 219–20
Brewing process, 13
extract brewing, 11
fermentation, 12
mashing, 11–12
Brown Ale, 56–57
Brown ale(s)
American, 48, 58–61
described, 47–49
English, 48, 54–58
mild, 49–53
recipes, 49–62
specialty, 62
Brown and robust porters, 66–78
Buck's Brutal Barleywine, 154
Buffalo-Buttocks Brown Ale, 57–58
Butternut Porter, 254

C

Cafe Mocha Porter, 84
California Common #1, 286–87
California Common #2, 287
California commons (steam beers)
described, 284–85
recipes, 286–88
Canadian Ale, 39–40
Carpe Diem, 88–89
Carrie's Pleasure Wheat, 221
"Cat's Ras, The," 244
Cherry beers, 258–59
Chocoberry Stout, 105
Chocolate Stout, 97
Christmas Spice '95, 269
Cinnamon Wheat Ale, 270
Cock's Holiday Ale '95, 271
Cocoa & Cream Porter, 79–80
Cole Porter, 68
Columbian Gold IPA, 45
Competitions, styles and, 13–14
"Coupla Bockers" Bock, 191
Craig's Pale Ale (CPA), 33
Cranberry Ale, 250
Crankcase Stout, 95

Cream ale
described, 203–4
recipe, 214
Cream Kölsch, 136–37
Cysers
described, 296
recipe, 305–6
Czecherboard Pilsner, 164–65
Czech Pilsner, 163–64

D

Daddy's Doppelbock #4, 200
Dark Ale, 56
Dark lagers, American
described, 203
recipes, 212–13
Dark lagers, European
Bavarian, 183–85
bocks, 181–82, 190–201
described, 180–82
Munich dunkels, 180–81
recipes, 183–201
schwarzbiers, 181, 186–89
Dark Wheat Beer, 223
Delano's Entire Butt, 77
Democratic Sunrise Pale Ale, 41
Demonick Alt, 140–41
Demonick Maibock, 198
Divine Wind Oud Bruin, 115
Dog Day Dark, 71
Domestic Bliss Mild, 52
Dortmunder Export, 168–69
Dortmunder lagers
described, 159
recipes, 168–72
Double Springs Chocolate Cherry
Imperial Stout, 259
Dragon's Belch, 290
Dunkel Fest, 184
Dunkels Weissbier, 224
Dunkelweizens
described, 217–18
recipes, 223–25
Dusseldorf-Style Alt—The Alternative,
144

E

Ed's Red, 21–22
English brown ales
described, 48
recipes, 54–58
English Mild, 53

English pale ales
    described, 17–18
    recipes, 19–30
English Porter, 78
English sweet stouts, described, 86–87
Eugenehead Oatmeal Stout, 100
Extract brewing, described, 11

F

Fermentation, described, 12
Fire Island Scotch Ale, 146
Flanders Brown Ale, 258–59
Foreign stouts
    described, 87
    recipes, 95–99
Framboise Wit Ale, 127
French Silk Chocolate Lager, 212–13
Fruit beers
    apple, 255
    banana, 262
    blackberry, 248–49
    blueberry, 237–39
    cherry, 258–59
    cranberry, 250
    described, 234–37
    lemon, 260
    orange, 261
    peach, 256–57
    prune, 257–58
    pumpkin, 251–53
    raspberry, 240–47
    recipes, 237–62
    squash, 254
Fruit meads. *See* Melomels

G

German ales
    alt beers, 130–31, 140–44
    described, 130–32
    Kölsch beers, 131–32, 135–40
    recipes, 135–44
German Bock, 192
Ginger Bear, 275
Ginger beers
    described, 263–64
    recipes, 274–76
Gingerroot Honey Lager, 276
Go For Grenedaness, 299
Graetzer, 291
Granny Ale, 255
Gruits
    described, 264
    recipes, 265–66

H

Hace Calor, 283
Hairy-Chested Wheat Mead, 307
Hallelujah Jalapeño Beer, 280–81
Hallerbock, 193
Halloween Mile, 49
Hammer of the Dogs Imperial Stout,
    102
Harrods Mead, 298–99
Hawaiian Punch, 304
Heavyside Layer, The, 225
Helles (Bavarian light lager), 167–68
Herb beers
    described, 264
    recipes, 277–78
Holiday Ale, 22
Holistic Porter II, 76
Honey Brown Lager, 213
Honey Porter, 83
Hoppy Hoppy, Joy Joy, 29–30
Hoppy Pale Ale, 30–31
Hops, described, 8–10
Hot to Trot, 300
Humpadingdong Dunkelweizen, 224–25

I

Imhoff Triple Bock, 152
Imperial Stout, 103
India pale ales, 42–45
Indy Racing Ale, 20
Ingredients, styles and, 5
    hops, 8–10
    malt, 6–8
    water, 10
    yeast, 10–11
In Your Pants, 214
Irish Ambush, 92
Irish dry stouts, classic, 88–92
Irish Oreo Stout, 94
Irish Porter, 67
Irish Red Lager, 178

J

Jalapeño Blast, 281
Jalapeño Pepper Ale, 279
Jamaican Ginger Beer, 274
Judy's Light Irish Stout, 89

K

Keep Your Wits about You, 300–301
Kick in the Abbey, A, 117
Kitchen Sink, 104
Kiwi Mint Ale, 277

Kölsch, 138–39
Kölsch beers
    described, 131–32
    recipes, 135–40
Kölsch Call III, 135–36
Kölsch '96, 139–40
Kris Krumple, 113

L

Lagers. *See* American lagers; Dark lagers,
    European; Light lagers, European
Lambics
    described, 108
    recipes, 128–29
Lemon Beagle Maibock, 197
Lemon beer, 260
Liberator, The, 196
Light Dubbel, 120
Light lagers, American
    described, 202–3
    recipes, 204–10
Light lagers, European
    described, 158–62
    Dortmunder lagers, 159, 168–72
    Munich Helles (Bavarian light), 159,
        167–68
    Oktoberfest lagers, 173–74, 179
    pilsners, 158–59, 162–68
    recipes, 162–79
    Vienna lagers, 159–60, 172–79
Lights Out Oatmeal Stout, 101
Lights Out Stout, 98
Liquid Fruitcake, 266–67
Load King, 38–39
Lucky Day Stout, 90

M

Mad Bee Wheat, 229
Maibock, 199
Malt, described, 6–8
Maple Leaf Lager, 210
Maple Sap Ale, 293
Mashing, described, 11–12
Maybock, 195
Meads
    braggots, 296–97, 306–7
    cysers, 296, 305–6
    described, 294–97
    fruit (melomels), 296, 301–5
    recipes, 297–307
    spiced (metheglins), 296, 298–301
    traditional, 297–98
Mel O'Mel, 301–2

Melomels (fruit meads)
    described, 296
    recipes, 301–5
Metheglins (spiced meads)
    described, 296
    recipes, 298–301
Mexican Cerveza, 207
Mild ales, 49–53
Miner Alt, 143
Mission Mountain Mocha Porter, 82
Mitch's Best Bitter, 23
Mulling spices
    described, 263
    recipes, 266–73
Munich dunkels, 180–81
Munich Helles (Bavarian light lagers)
    described, 159
    recipe, 167–68

N

Nekkid Druids Nut Brown Ale, 54
1995 Surreal Cap, 155
No Name Stout, 96
Noname Vienna, 174–75
Northwest Stout, 99
Nothook ESB, 28–29
Nutberry Ale, 241

O

Oatmeal stouts
    described, 87
    recipes, 100–101
O'Brien Pale Ale, 25
O'Cosgraigh Strong Ale, 156
Octoberfest, 173–74
Oktoberfest lagers, 173–74, 179
Old Ale, 153–54
Old Familiar, 28
Old 49er Golden Honey Lager, 208
Onward through the Fog Steam Beer, 288
Orange and Spice and Everything Nice, 261
Oud bruin
    described, 108
    recipe, 115
Overnight Stout Lite, 91

P

Pale ales
    Adelaide sparkling ale, 46
    American, 18, 30–41
    Belgian, 107, 109–12
    described, 15–18, 107
    English, 17–30

Pale ales *(continued)*
  India, 42–45
  recipes, 19–46, 109–12
Palmer's Perfect Porter, 69
Parachute Pale Ale, 40
Peach Ale, 256
Peach beers, 256–57
Pegleg Porter, 66–67
Pepper beers
  described, 264
  recipes, 279–83
Perplex Pepper Poise Potion, 282
Phil's Sippin' Abbey Bier, 116
Pilsners
  described, 158–59
  recipes, 162–68
Porters
  described, 63–66
  recipes, 66–84
  robust and brown, 66–78
  specialty, 79–84
Prepro Golden Lager, 210–11
Pre-Prohibition-style lagers
  described, 203
  recipe, 210–11
Prune beer, 257–58
Pumpkin Ale #1, 252
Pumpkin Ale #2, 253
Pumpkin beers, 251–53
Purple Cow Ale, 238–39

R

Raspberry Ale, 246
Raspberry beers, 240–47
Raspberry Cinnamon Wheat, 242–43
Raspberry Spring Ale, 243
Raspberry Tea Beer, 278
Raspberry Wheat, 241–42
Rauch Märzen, 289
Red Raspberry Wheat, 245
Red, Weiss-en, Brew, 230
Revenge!, 150
Ripcord Raspberry Ale, 240
Robb Roy's Scotch Ale, 145
Robust and brown porters, 66–78
'R' Squared, 233
Russian Imperial stouts
  described, 87
  recipes, 102–3

S

Sami-Close, 201
Sandy Porter, 73
Santa's Bun Warmer, 272–73

Schwarzbier #1, 187
Schwarzbier #2, 188
Schwarzbier #3, 189
Schwarzbier Over Here, 186
Schwarzbiers
  described, 181
  recipes, 186–89
Scotch Ale, 147
Scottish ales
  described, 132–33
  recipes, 145–49
Sierra Nevada Porter Clone, 70
Simple Cyser, 305–6
Sinner's Ale, 36
Sister Star of the Sun, 43
Skipjack IPA, 42
Smilin' Red, 34
Smoked beers
  described, 285–86
  recipes, 289–91
Smoke Your Nose, 306–7
Snowflake Strong Scottish Ale, 148
Snow-Pack Pilsner, 166–67
Sourpuss, 129
Special-B Porter, 72
Special Dortmunder #2, 171–72
Special Session, 50
Specialty ales
  described, 134–35
  recipes, 62, 157, 292–93
Specialty brown ale, 62
Specialty porters, 79–84
Specialty stouts, 104–5
Spice beers
  described, 263–64
  ginger beers, 263–64, 274–76
  gruits, 264–66
  herb beers, 264, 277–78
  mulling spices, 263, 266–73
  pepper beers, 264, 279–83
  recipes, 265–83
Spiced Elderberry Wheat Brew, 272
Spiced meads. *See* Metheglins
Springtime in Vienna, 177
Spuyten Duyvel, 169–70
Squash beer, 254
Star Thistle Wheat, 228
Steam beers. *See* California commons
Stinky Dog Lager, 204–5
Stouts
  described, 85–88
  English sweet, 86–87
  foreign, 95–99

Irish dry, classic, 88–92
oatmeal, 100–101
recipes, 88–105
Russian Imperial, 102–3
specialty, 104–5
sweet, 92–94
Stras"berry" Ale, 246–47
Strong ales
barleywines, 151, 154
Belgian, 107, 113–14
described, 107, 133–34
recipes, 113–14, 150–56
specialty, 157
Styles
competitions and, 13–14
defined, 3–4
ingredients and, 5–10
names for, 5
origins of, 4–5
Summer Lemon Wheat, 260
Summer's Lease II Apricot Melomel, 304–5
Sweet Chocolate Stout, 93–94
Sweet Stout, 92–93
Sweet stouts, 92–94

T
Tall, Dark & Strong, 152–53
Tangerine Dreams Wheat, 220
Texas/Belgian White Bier, 124
Thanksgiving Pumpkin Ale, 251
Thptzzt!, 247
Three Roys Agree Ale, 90–97
Trappist ales
described, 107–8
recipes (dubbel and tripel), 116–24
Trappist-style Ale, 118
Trolleyman ESB, 24
Tume Olu, 74
"Two P's in the Pot" Honey Nut Brown
Ale, 62
Tyrant Ale, 59

U
Uncle Paddy's Whiskey Wheat, 232
Unconscious Blond Mead, 297–98
Unnamed Dort, 170–71

V
Velvet Divorce Pilsner, 165–66
Vermont Porter, 80
Vienna lagers
described, 159–60
recipes, 172–79

W
Wales Ales Ya, 27
Warrior's Stout, 257–58
Water, described, 10
Weizen, 222
Weizenbier (Bavarian wheat)
described, 215–18
dunkelweizens, 217–18, 223–25
recipes, 219–27
weizenbocks, 218, 225–27
Weizenbocks
described, 218
recipes, 225–27
Wheat Beer, 231
Wheat beers
American, 218–19, 228–33
described, 215–19
dunkelweizens, 217–18, 223–25
recipes, 219–33
weizenbier (Bavarian), 215–27
weizenbocks, 218, 225–27
Whitely's Dark Wheat, 248
Whitewater Weizenbock, 227
Wild Rice Blonde Ale, 292
Wit beers
described, 108–9
recipes, 124–27
Wits End, 126
Work-A-Day Brew, 175–76

X
Xmas Herbal, 208

Y
Yeast, described, 10–11
Yellow Aster IPA, 44

Z
Zivio, 176
Zoso White, 125

Other Storey Titles
You Will Enjoy

Brew Ware: How to Find, Adapt & Build Homebrewing Equipment, by Karl F. Lutzen & Mark Stevens. Using this handbook, readers can create a home brewery that is safe and makes brewing easier. Project plans include tools and accessories for ingredient processing and storage, chilling and aerating wort, fermenting, measuring, bottling, kegging, and mashing. 304 pages. Paperback. Order #0-88266-926-5.

Dave Miller's Homebrewing Guide: Everything You Need to Know to Make Great-Tasting Beer, by Dave Miller. Miller provides brewers with his two decades of know-how to ensure that they make great-tasting beer or ale every time. Explains equipment of the 1990s, recipe formulation, and troubleshooting. Includes 33 recipes. 296 pages. Paperback. Order #0-88266-905-2.

Great Beer from Kits, by Joe Fisher & Dennis Fisher. Knowing hundreds of people each day decide to make beer from kits, and knowing some of the pitfalls inherent in the "how-to brochures" that accompany such kits, the authors have anticipated the questions and concerns these novices often have. 176 pages. Paperback. Order #0-88266-911-7.

Homebrew Favorites: A Coast-to-Coast Collection of More Than 240 Beer and Ale Recipes, by Karl F. Lutzen & Mark Stevens. Over the Internet, the authors collected recipes from the homebrewing community across North America. All recipes are introduced with tips and comments from the original brewer and many recipes are award winners. 256 pages. Paperback. Order #0-88266-613-4.

Secret Life of Beer: Legends, Lore & Little-Known Facts, by Alan D. Eames. A collection of masterfully combined beeraphernalia . . . historical, and sometimes hysterical, facts, short stories, and illustrations from a world-traveled cultural anthropologist who happens to love everything about beer. Eames explores beer's contribution to the Decline and Fall of the Roman Empire, beer miracles transforming sots to saints, plus beer poetry, beer legends, and of course, beer songs. 176 pages. Paperback. Order #0-88266-807-2.

A Taste for Beer, by Stephen Beaumont. An extensive, comprehensive, yet very browsable "appreciation" reference. From discerning the flavor of a lager versus a stout to matching the best cheese or cigar, Beaumont's friendly style takes the beer enthusiast along for an interesting, useful, and fun exploration of beer enjoyment. 256 pages. Paperback. Order #0-88266-907-9.

These books and other Storey books are available at your bookstore, farm store, garden center, or directly from Storey Publishing, Schoolhouse Road, Pownal, Vermont 05261, or by calling 1-800-441-5700. www.storey.com